CW00926761

INTRODUCTION

Although the origins of the destroyer date back to the introduction of the spar torpedo in the early nineteenth century, it was not until the appearance of the Whitehead torpedo that the ship type became a weapon system to be reckoned with. Allied with the steam engine, it began to make its appearance as a small, fast, expendable craft, generally known as a 'torpedo boat', in the late nineteenth century. Because it was cheap and quickly built, the weaker nations immediately saw in it a means of obtaining a powerful coast defence fleet, capable of challenging the super-powers of the day, without the necessity of constructing a large and expensive navy: Germany, Italy, Austria-Hungary and France began to lay down large numbers of torpedo boats with which to challenge the supremacy of the battleship. However, in the natural progression of things, weapon always produces counter-weapon, in this case the 'torpedo boat destroyer', and although the latter got off to an inauspicious start in the Royal Navy with its original 'torpedo boat catchers', the trend was clearly towards a larger ship - one carrying more

guns to defeat the torpedo boat yet retaining the original torpedo armament.

During the early years of the twentieth century both types of vessel were in evidence in the major fleets, but by 1910 Great Britain had abandoned development of the torpedo boat and concentrated exclusively on destroyers (TBDs); the United States, too, soon dropped the small torpedo boat. It could be argued that in the early years this was merely a rationalization of name, but with the passage of time there appeared in European navies two distinct types: one was the destroyer designed for fleet duties, whilst the other may be described as a fast escort vessel carrying a light gun battery but also a heavy torpedo armament.

In Germany, the destroyer developed from the 'divisional boats' *D1-10*, which were designed to act as leaders for torpedo boat flotillas; the first of these, *D1*, was of 249 tonnes and carried two 5cm guns and three torpedo tubes. Completed between 1886 and 1896, these vessels had, by the outbreak of the First World War, been relegated to second-line duties, although *D8* did get caught up in the

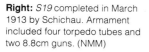

Right: *S19* completed in March 1913 by Schichau. Armament included four torpedo tubes and two 8.8cm guns. (NMM)

action off Heligoland in August 1914. They were followed at the turn of the century by the first of the larger torpedo boats, which were effectively the first of Germany's destroyers, although this term was not generally used by the Germans until the 1930s. Between 1900 and 1911 Germany built ninety-seven torpedo boats which were, according to practice, numbered and not named. These were *S90–107, G108–113, S114–131, G132–137, S138–149, V150–175, S176–179, V180–191* and *G192–197*. In the same period, Britain completed some 104 vessels of this type and France even larger numbers, whilst Imperial Russia and Italy each built up this arm of its fleet.

All the German ships displaced between 400 and 800 tonnes and were twin-funnelled, and the first sixty-one carried an armament of three 5cm or 5.2cm guns and three single 45cm torpedo tubes. Two of the tubes were placed in a well, forward of the bridge, which set the latter further back and, it was claimed, improved seaworthiness by allowing the seas to break before reaching the superstructure. This feature, which could hardly have been acclaimed by the torpedo crews, was discontinued after *V161,* although it did reappear in some war-built classes. The German propensity for the torpedo as a weapon is evident even at this early stage, for contemporary British boats were gun- rather than torpedo-armed, most carrying three or four 12pdrs and only two torpedo tubes. French designs, in contrast, showed six guns and four torpedo tubes and, on paper, appeared to get the best combination of offensive power and speed.

The early German ships were built by three major shipbuilders: Schichau at Elbing, Krupp at Germaniawerft

in Kiel and the Vulkan yard in Stettin. Each of these yards built ships with their own identifying letters – 'S', 'G' and 'V' respectively; later Blohm und Voss at Hamburg (B) and Howaldt at Kiel (H) also built destroyers. The *G174* class of 1910 introduced a heavier calibre torpedo, 50cm, and raised the number of tubes to four, two of which were in a twin mounting, an arrangement not introduced into British destroyers until three years later ('L' class). Propulsion was generally by reciprocating engines, with odd vessels shipping experimental turbines, up to and including the *V150* class of 1907-8.

The years immediately preceding the First World War did not see any great advances in design, and by this time the typical German ship had stabilized around a 700/900-tonne boat, turbine-driven, carrying three 8.8cm guns and with the torpedo armament increased to six tubes. The 10.5cm gun, introduced in the *S13* class of 1912, was not fitted as standard to other classes before the war. During hostilities, the displacement of war-built classes rose to about 1,200 tonnes, with certain ships building for foreign navies (but seized by the Germans) reaching 1,700/1,800 tonnes, and by the surrender the German destroyer had evolved into a 1,200-ton ship, carrying three 10.5cm guns and six 50cm torpedo tubes at a speed of 37 knots. Its British counterpart had caught up in terms of torpedoes and had also begun to ship the 4.7in (12cm) gun, whilst across the Atlantic the latest US vessels were being equipped with twelve torpedo tubes and four 4in (10.2cm) guns. In 1918 there appeared the first of a newer and larger German design which displaced 2,400 tonnes and carried four 15cm guns and four torpedoes at 37 knots. These

Above: *V67*, an AG Vulkan boat completed in 1915, showing the torpedo tubes before the bridge. (NMM)

ships, *S113* and *V116*, were not particularly successful and were still under development at the war's end, a number of their sister-ships remaining incomplete in November 1918. At the other end of the scale, the true torpedo boat was perpetuated in the *A1–A92* classes, the first of which displaced only 137 tonnes but the *A92* class having risen to 392 tons. Armament was generally two 8.8cm guns and one torpedo tube, although earlier units carried only 5cm guns. Like their descendants, these torpedo boats were to be extensively employed in the English Channel.

Between 1900 and the Armistice Germany completed 225 destroyers, of which 67 became war losses, 50 were scuttled at Scapa Flow, 82 were distributed amongst the Allies or, more generally, scrapped, and 16 were retained by Germany post-war. The remainder were discarded by 1929 and most likely cannibalized for spares. Large numbers of destroyers remained uncompleted at the Armistice, since by 1916 surface ship construction had been slowed in favour of submarine building, as was in fact to be the case during the Second World War.

After 1919 Admirals Behnke and Zenker strove to regenerate the German Navy and laid the foundations for their successor, Admiral Raeder, to build upon. Raeder, the person most usually associated by non-Germans with the revival of the German Navy, was Chief of the Admiralty when work began on designing a new breed of destroyers. Termed 'Destroyer Type 34', these were to be well in excess of treaty limitations and were designed to be more than a match for contemporary Russian, Polish and French vessels. They were a development of the 1932 destroyer design which had itself been based upon *S113* and *V116*.

However, the latter, ceded post-war to France and Italy respectively, did not live up to expectations, being top-heavy, unsteady and slow – rather significant deficiencies in the light of similar failings in their Second World War successors.

The *S113* type carried 15cm guns, a large jump in calibre compared to the standard 10.5cm destroyer weapons. The handling of such large projectiles on a lively gun platform, especially one whose seaworthiness was suspect, must have been almost impossible, and the fact that exactly the same problems were encountered in the Type 1936A destroyers when the 15cm gun was reintroduced suggests that German constructors had not had the chance properly to evaluate the action performance of the *S113* type. It is possible, too, that the German Navy preferred weight of shell to rate of gunfire. *S113* and *V116* also introduced a heavier torpedo calibre, 59.9cm, which was not featured by any other destroyer and not reintroduced when the rebuilding of the fleet commenced. Despite the drawbacks experienced by the Kaisermarine with these ships, it is reported that they performed very well under the French and Italian flags in the less demanding environment of the Mediterranean.

Under Article 181 of the Versailles peace terms, the permitted strength of the German Navy was almost derisory, being restricted to a few ancient predreadnoughts, a few equally old light cruisers and a handful of pre-1914 torpedo boats and destroyers. the destroyers comprised *T175*, *T185*, *T190* and *T196* (656/810 tonnes), *V1–3*, *V5* and *V6* (569/697 tonnes), *G7*, *G8*, *G10* and *G11* (573/719 tonnes) and *S18*, *S19* and *S23* (568/695 tonnes); in addition, sixteen torpedo boats were allowed. Of this total, only twelve of each category were allowed in commision at any one time, a force which would in any case have been difficult to maintain. given the age of the vessels and the shortage of manpower.

A number of these old boats were still extant at the time of the Second World War, when they continued to give sterling service, mainly in second line roles but also occasionally on operational duties. so it was with *G7*, *G8*, *G10* and *G11*, now re-named *T107*, *T108*, *T110* and *T111*, which in August 1939 formed the Torpedo School Training flotilla. These were survivors of the once 24-strong *V1* class built 1911-13, eleven of which had been lost during the First World War. The outbreak of a new war saw them employed on patrol and escort duties in the Baltic and the entrance to that sea, whilst the Kriegsmarine endeavoured to prevent British, French and Polish merchant ships from escaping. all, however, were under refit at Flensburg for the first quarter of 1940, after which the flotilla was again assigned to operational tasks, this time, 'Weserübung', the invasion of Norway. Operating from Kiel, the four boats were diverted to protect *Schleswig-Holstein* when the old pre-dreadnought ran aground on the Vengeance bank. Following this, all four were used on convoy escort and trooping duties between Alborg, Fredikshaven, Larvik and Oslo from the beginning of April 1940 until the beginning of July, when they returned to the Eastern Baltic and duties with the U-boat flotillas. Whilst engaged on convoy duties, there were several brushes with British submarines, for these were at this time still active, even in the Kattegat. One such incident occurred on 10 April, when a convoy was attacked by HMS/M *Triton* off Marstrand. The merchantmen *Friedenau* and *Wigbert* were torpedoed and sunk, as well as the former whaler *VP507*. Despite the expenditure of all the flotilla's depth-charges, *Triton* escaped undamaged. Other tasks included the escorting back to Germany of captured Norweigan warships, such as the torpedo boat *Tiger* (ex-*Tor*) and the submarines *B4* and *A2*. Back with the submarine training flotillas, their careers were mundane but pressure of events in the Eastern Baltic 1944/5 led to their use for evacuation duties, *T108* being so used as late as May 1945, *T110* was finally scuttled at the Flenderwerk yard on 5 May, whilst *T111* had earlier been sunk by air attack at Kiel on 3 April 1945. *T108* was eventually allocated to Great Britain but *T107* became the Soviet *Poraschajuschtschi* and had a further career under the hammer and sickle.

By the middle to late 1920s it had become imperative that some units of the Fleet, particularly the aged predreadnoughts, old cruisers and worn-out torpedo boats, be replaced. New construction had in fact cautiously begun in 1921 with the laying down of the cruiser *Emden*, which, however, was little more than a First World War design; similarly, the replacements for the torpedo boats were essentially 1914–18 designs. Under the terms of the peace treaty, replacements could be put in hand, but there were strict limits on the tonnage of individual ships in each category – destroyers, for example, were not to exceed 600 tons. Nevertheless, a start was made with the six units of the 'Raubvogel' class, of which the first, *Möwe*, was launched on 24 March 1926. In practice, it proved impossible to design an effective fighting unit on the tonnage allowed, and these vessels actually displaced 924 tons (standard). They were armed with three 10.5cm guns and six 53.3cm torpedo tubes and were capable of 33 knots. Compared to contemporary destroyers of the British *Amazon*, Dutch *Evertson* and French *Bourrasque* classes, they hardly merited classification as destroyers and they were in fact referred to as 'Torpedoboote Type 23'. Most of this class and the similar 'Raubtier' class (933/1,320 tons standard, 3x10.5cm, 6x53.3cm torpedo tubes, 33 knots) which followed gave good service in the English Channel during the Second World War. Two boats of this latter class mounted the single 12.7cm guns which were eventually adopted for the first of the true destroyers, the Type 34 class.

In appearance, the new Type 34 class betrayed its origins by the similarity in funnel build and torpedo tube layout to *S113* and *V116*. The forecastle deck, too, in common with the 'Raubtier' and 'Raubvogel' classes, had a distinctly First World War appearance, with its complete absence of sheer and the retention of a vestigial turtle-back. The ships were massively built, with tall, heavily cowled, slab-sided funnels suggesting a serious topweight problem. Indeed, it is easy to understand the complaints concerning their seaworthiness when one looks at some of the photographs taken of the earlier units: there may not be much of a sea, but the ships have a distinct bows-down appearance and their lack of sheer is only too evident.

At the time of the keel-laying of the first units in October 1934, the Type 34s were, in theory, far superior to the 'G' class destroyers then being laid down for the Royal Navy: compared to their very pedestrian British contemporaries, they possessed a heavier main armament, both in calibre and numbers, and a much better anti-aircraft capability, and they were almost twice the tonnage. Their appearance, together with that of the *Fubuki* type in Japan, eventually forced the British Admiralty to discontinue the standard destroyers of the 'A' to 'I' classes and build instead the famous 'Tribals'.

Of the other possible adversaries of the new German Fleet, only the French 'contre-torpilleurs' appeared to outclass the Type 34 design. In particular, the new 2,930-tonne *Mogador* class, with its eight 13.8cm guns and 39 knots, was a powerful design, whilst the smaller *L'Audacieux* class of six ships and the eighteen older units of the 2,400-tonne type would also have made well-matched enemies. The Soviet *Leningrad* class too, compared in size and armament, but only two of these vessels were in any possible theatre of German operations. Of the remaining European navies only the Royal Netherlands Navy was of any size, but the bulk of its forces were deployed in the East Indies and thus presented little challenge. Any comparison of the German designs with those of the other three major sea powers of the time, the United States, Japan and Italy, is largely academic: in the 1930s Germany was hardly contemplating hostilities with the USA; Japan was on the other side of the world; and Italy was politically sympathetic. Hence it was undoubtedly the size, composition and technical aspects of the French and Polish Fleets which bore most heavily on the German designers during the period in question.

Having completed twenty-two destroyers to the Type 34 and 36 designs, the Kriegsmarine then began the design of larger destroyers armed with 15cm guns, the intention being to offset Britain's and France's numerical superiority in this class of vessel by the individual superiority of each German ship.* In retrospect, this was almost certainly a mistake, especially in view of the known shortcomings of the Type 34s and 36s – the policy of squeezing a quart into a pint pot has always been questionable, and so it proved in this case. The merits of the larger gun were never demonstrated, and although nominally having the firepower of light cruisers these larger destroyers frequently came off worse in their later encounters with British light cruisers. A total of fifteen ships armed with the 15cm gun were put into service before the gun calibre was reduced to 12.7cm once more, but by the time this belated decision had been made, the war, and in particular the naval war, had been lost to Germany, with the result that only three ships of this type actually entered service, and then not until 1943–4. Two further ships were never completed, nor were thirteen others of later designs. In parallel with this very modest destroyer programme, a number of torpedo boat designs were put into production, resulting in a total of 36 completed units.

Consequent upon the victorious campaigns by the German Army during 1940 and 1941, the Kriegsmarine captured large numbers of enemy warships, many of which were commissioned into German service. The vast majority were small patrol craft, trawlers and escort vessels, but one or two larger vessels were also taken, including a number of destroyers, two of which would be commissioned as such into the Kriegsmarine. The first to be captured was the 1,864-tonne Dutch destroyer *Gerard Callenburgh* building at Rotterdam. She had been launched on 12 October 1939 and scuttled 15 May 1940 by the Dutch, but after being raised by the Germans on 17 July, she was put in hand for completion for the Kriegsmarine. This work was undertaken under the supervision of Blohm und Voss, but such difficulties were experienced that it was not until 11 October 1942 that she commissioned, as *ZH1*, in Rotterdam's Schiehaven for service with the 5th Flotilla before sailing for Hamburg on the 25th. Between this time and October 1943 the destroyer spent much time in dockyard hands, as Blohm und Voss attempted to get her unfamiliar machinery and guns operational, and on work-up training. Not until 31 October was she fit to deploy operationally and her subsequent short career is described elsewhere in this book.

The other ship was the ex-Greek destroyer *Vasilevs Georgios I*, built to the British 'H' class design by Yarrow. She was commissioned into the Greek Navy on 15 February 1939 but was hit by German dive-bombers on 12 April 1941. The bombs damaged her stern compartments and port shaft, and she was put into floating dock at Salamis for repair. However, the German Army overran Greece before repairs were complete, and both destroyer and dock were sunk either by the Greeks themselves or by the Luftwaffe just prior to Greece's capitulation. The

Below: Krupp's Germania yard in Kiel. *Erich Giese* (82) is almost complete and *Erich Koellner* is in the floating dock. Also seen is the old light cruiser *Arkona* and in the background the hull of aircraft carrier 'B' can be seen taking shape. The date is probably the beginning of 1939. (NMM)

1941
Hr Ms. Torpedoboot jager
"Gerard Callenburgh"
R.D.M.

Above: A sketch by Mhr van der Weele showing the former Dutch destroyer *Gerard Callenburgh*, being completed for the Kriegsmarine after salvage. (C.v.d. Weele)

Left: *ZG3*, the ex-Greek, British built destroyer which served in the Kriegsmarine in the Mediterranean. (W. Z. Bilddienst)

captured wreck was subsequently raised and repaired under the supervision of technicians from the Germaniawerft company, and the ship was commissioned into the Kriegsmarine on 21 March 1942 as *ZG3* It was a stroke of good luck for the Germans that this particular ship, unlike *ZH1*, had been designed for German 12.7cm guns (the same 12.7cm SK C/34 weapons used by German destroyers), which considerably simplified ammunition supply.

Apart from *ZG3*, the Kriegsmarine's destroyers served from the North Cape to Cape Finisterre during the years of hostilities; twenty-five were war losses, leaving only fifteen survivors in 1945, one or two of which lasted into the mid-1950s and early 1960s in the hands of France and Russia.

Of the wartime casualties, fifteen were sunk by surface action, five by air attack and four by mines, whilst one was scuttled. The torpedo boats, which operated as a separate arm of the Fleet until the end of April 1942, suffered rather heavier losses, owing to their closer involvement in areas such as the confined waters of the English Channel for most of the war. One ship was lost prior to the outbreak of war, and during the conflict thirteen were lost to air attack, nine were mined, seven were lost in surface action, one was torpedoed by a submarine and one other lost by collision, whilst two further boats were scuttled and one wrecked.

*Hitler informed Admiral Raeder on 27 May 1938 that Britain and France must be considered future enemies.

1. THE PRE-WAR DESTROYERS

During the 1920s Germany's strategic situation was not greatly altered from her position in 1914, with the major exception of the loss of all her overseas colonies. Such losses of territory as occurred in Germany itself, i.e., as a result of the occupation of the Rhineland, Danzig, Memel and Upper Silesia, were either of a temporary nature or of no great strategic consequence. The 'traditional' enemy, France, remained to the west, whilst the creation of the Baltic States and an independent Poland had combined to push the frontiers of Russia far to the east. As far as the Navy was concerned, therefore, by the early 1930s France and Poland were considered the likely main opponents in any future hostilities. At this early stage Russia, involved in tearing herself apart internally and with as yet little interest outside her borders, was presumed to be of little consequence; in any event, her armed forces were in no state to wage a serious war. As for Britain, the traumas of the Great War were far too recent for it to be conceivable that Germany would ever again challenge her. Thus the strategic horizons of the Naval Staff were generally bounded at this period by the limits of the North and Baltic Seas, although, with the experiences of the earlier war digested, the bluewater employment of cruisers, disguised merchantmen and submarines also affected policy. During the period in question, therefore, the strategic requirements impinging upon destroyer design were based upon an operational area encompassing France and Poland, for which a radius of action of no more than 1,000 nautical miles would suffice, upon the defence of a short home coastline, and, rather importantly, upon a not over-large shipbuilding industry, which could turn out about 300,000 tonnes of warships, a total tailored to the available annual capacity.

In recognition of the fact that she could not match France in numbers (and Britain still less), Germany opted for a balanced fleet, with a sensible destroyer/capital ship ratio – an 'all-round force', according to Admiral Raeder, rather than one projected against any one enemy. On the question of numerical inferiority, however, Germany's strategic plans almost certainly took account of the strong rivalry between France and Italy, the net consequence of which could be a reduction in the size of the fleet France would be able to deploy against her. In the 1920s, though, the major factor affecting the strategic plans of the Navy was probably finance: Germany was on the road to horrific inflation and the Weimar Republic had far more pressing problems than the strength of the armed forces.

At a tactical level, the German Staff required the destroyers for the usual task of fleet screening; for this, a high speed was required, given the designed speed of the new battleships of the *Scharnhorst* class. This speed was also to be required for fast offensive minelaying, an important task bearing in mind the shallow waters of the southern North Sea and more particularly the Baltic. Again, there was emphasis on speed as the result of inferiority in numbers. As regards armament, the Ordnance Branch required gunpower equal to that of French destroyers, together with a good torpedo outfit, which, allied to high speed, would make a formidable combination. Their limited operational area meant, further, that the ships would not be required to store for long periods at sea, and thus in contrast to other navies the space given over to victualling and engineering stores could be reduced and the saving put to other use; arguably, too, the restricted range implied that they would not have to face the fury of the Atlantic Ocean and that Baltic conditions would be the main factor affecting seaworthiness.

Nevertheless, any design is a compromise involving size, cost and numbers and also speed, offensive power, range and stability. No final design of any nation can hope to achieve the ideal, the best solution being one which meets most of the required criteria with the least penalty. That the German designs suffered in a number of aspects is probably partly associated with the fact that between 1918 and 1933 no design or sea experience was accumulated: when warships were laid down once more, the designers were forced to catch up very quickly with contemporary practice, and even pioneer new techniques, in an attempt to offset numerical inferiority by technical superiority. In addition, there appeared little compromise in German designs, with unfortunate results in service. For example, the ships, on paper, possessed a high speed, a good range and heavy hitting power, but in practice the weight of the armament on the designed dimensions resulted in problems associated with stability and strength, necessitating a high minimum fuel condition, which in turn considerably *reduced* range.

Until 1935, Germany was prevented from building destroyers of greater size than the Types 23 and 24 torpedo boats by the restrictions of the Treaty of Versailles; even after these restrictions lapsed, the signing of the Anglo-German Naval Treaty in 1935 limited the total tonnage for German destroyers to 52,000 tonnes and, moreover, classed cruisers and destroyers in the same category. In qualitative terms, after Versailles, Germany would have the right to build similar ship types as other sea powers, i.e., with a tonnage not exceeding 1,850 and with guns not greater than 13cm in calibre. This was confirmed by the London Treaty of 1930, which also, however, specified that not more than 16 per cent of the category tonnage might be used for 1,850-ton ships; the bulk could not exceed 1,500 tons.*

It would appear that the German Naval Staff had made tentative war plans, and at a very early stage, at least to secure the coast of Europe as far south as the Pyrenees in order to reach the French Atlantic ports and hence the world's oceans. Similarly, the Norwegian coast as far north as the North Cape was a strategic goal, and the size of future light forces was to be based on the North Cape–Pyrenees concept.† To this end, in November 1932 a preliminary target was set for a force of six destroyer or torpedo boat half-flotillas, and in February 1933 planning began on the reserve destroyers (allowed under the Treaty of Versailles) which were to be laid down in 1934.

In the initial planning stages it was assumed that before the construction of these new ships could be completed a new naval treaty might appear, and it would therefore be as well to pitch their tonnage at a level which might be maximized in that treaty. To this end, a starting-point of 1,500 tons was chosen, and within this figure the requirements were to be (a) maximum hull strength, (b) good seaworthiness, (c) high continuous sea speed, (d) high endurance and (e) a gun-biased armament. The objective was to counter the French and Polish destroyers in the 1,378–1,540-ton category but at the same time to use the ships as substitutes for the absent cruisers. The first sketch design produced by the Construction Office had a displacement of only 1,100 tons, but this was rejected by Raeder on the grounds that it was too similar to the Type 24 design, despite the fact that it exceeded the 800-ton limit. Further design work produced a modified 1,100-ton sketch with a speed of 35 knots and one for 1,500 tons with 38 knots; both designs had bunkers for an endurance of 2,200 miles at 19 knots. Opinions soon favoured the 1,500-ton ship with four 12.7cm guns and two triple sets of torpedo tubes, but the endurance was raised to 3,000 miles at 17–19 knots.

Admiral Raeder decided to press ahead with the 1,500-ton type on 9 March 1933, i.e., some 2½ years before Germany was actually to throw off the shackles of Versailles; this design was the first to exceed the limits of that treaty. Seven weeks later he ordered a further increase in displacement to 1,850 tons, the provision of a fifth 12.7cm gun, and the installation of quadruple torpedo tubes in lieu of the envisaged triple banks. The building of the first four 'reserve' destroyers was confirmed on 1 April 1934, the initial vessel to complete in two years and further ships at the rate of one per month, although because of the political climate the building of these destroyers was not declared publicly. As for propulsion, there was no doubt that high-pressure steam turbines were the only choice, the Construction Office stating that 'with today's technology, for torpedo boats and minesweepers, there is no alternative to high-pressure steam systems'. In the course of a conference between the Design Section (KIe) and the Development Office (A IV) in the summer of 1934, it was confirmed that the weight savings gained by the use of modern machinery would be utilized to increase endurance (5,400 miles at 18 knots) and that speeds would exceed 36 knots.

By early 1934 the number of projected destroyers had risen to forty-eight, of which only six could be of 1,850 tons, so the proposal for a smaller ship was resurrected. This was much discussed, but not proceeded with, although it finally led to the Type 35 torpedo boat, as will be recounted later. The end result was that Raeder decided in March 1935 that the 'large destroyer would remain the Type 34, which would be constructed in some numbers', declaring that 'the Type 34 complies with the requirements that we in our situation demand of a destroyer' and that 'the usable destroyer tonnage will therefore be absorbed by Type 34 ships'.

Construction of this type then continued, but meanwhile some questions were being asked as to weaknesses in the design. Two points were specifically raised: endurance and structural strength. In some quarters of the Fleet it was believed that endurance should be increased; on the question of strength, criticisms were levelled concerning the design lines and framing in the bows, the lack of sheer being noted in particular. After some discussion it was decided to alter the design of the bows from the fifth ship onwards, in order to improve the seakeeping properties. It is noteworthy, however, that this criticism continued to be made against the Type 36A ships.

CLASSIC LINES

The Type 34 destroyers were heavily armed, but, with the exception of their machinery, not particularly innovative in design terms. The first four units were designated 'Type 34' and the next twelve 'Type 34A', these sixteen ships being known outside Germany as the *Maass* class and the

---

*From the 1930s, long tons were used in treaty definitions; 'standard' displacements for pre-war designs are in long tons.

†It is obvious, therefore, that whilst the plans of the radical Admiral Wegener were eschewed in public, his points struck home in the minds of the Naval Staff: they had no intention of being bottled up in the North Sea as in 1914–18.

next six, Type 36, as the *Roeder* class. In Germany, however, and in all German records, these destroyers were always referred to as 'Type 34', 'Type 34A' or 'Type 36'.

The Type 34 (*Z1–4*) design displaced 2,232 tons standard, with a full load figure of 3,156 tons, on a length of 114m between perpendiculars. The next four ships (*Z5–8*), part of the Type 34A group, were slightly reduced in displacement (2,171 tons standard) but retained the same dimensions; *Z9–13* displaced 2,270 tons standard and *Z14–16* 2,239 tons, on a marginally increased length of 116m, mainly as the result of an altered bow form. *Z1–4* were completed with a straight stem and a rounded edge to the forecastle deck, but later units were built with some sheer to the forecastle and without the rounded profile on the sheer strake; all units had a raked, transom stern.

Of classic lines, the Type 34 and 34A ships were heavily built, with a large bridge structure and massive forward funnel crowned with a distinctive clinker screen; the after funnel was smaller, also carried a clinker screen, and formed a part of the bulky after superstructure. Prominent features at the base of both funnels were the large louvred boiler-room fan trunkings. Nos. 1 and 2 guns were disposed on the forecastle and shelter decks, No. 2 being superfiring and each mounting having an arc of fire from Red 145° to Green 145°.

Immediately aft of No. 2 gun was situated the bridge structure. This incorporated a rounded front to the upper bridge in the first five units but was altered to square form during refits in 1938, and later units were originally so completed. It would appear that all ships of the class were intended to have the rounded bridge, since the builder's drawings for *Z14–16* still show the bridge in its original form. The new configuration produced a more spacious wheelhouse and better control deck facilities. Contained within the bridge structure were the wheelhouse, radio and coding offices, a cabin fitted with sleeping accommodation, a large but sparsely fitted chart room and an ammunition handling room. The term 'wheelhouse' is rather a misnomer, since the all-electric steering was by means of a horizontal, athwartships bar, which was pressed down at one end or the other to give port or starboard helm. Engine room telegraphs and revolution indicators were combined into one instrument, assisting engine manoeuvring. Five large, square windows, some with circular clear-view screens, were fitted in the front of the wheelhouse, over which armoured steel shutters could be lowered when in action. The ship was normally conned at this level.

At the forward end of the control deck, or upper bridge, was mounted the director pedestal. In comparison with many contemporary destroyers, this was most inconspicuous and consisted merely of the stabilized binocular master sight mounted on a plinth about 1m square and without any weather protection at all. In action it was manned by a crew of three consisting of the layer on the righthand side, the trainer to port and the gun control officer behind. Firing was by means of the layer blowing down a tube which he gripped in his mouth, thus operating a diaphragm and closing the firing circuits, leaving both hands free to keep the director sights on the target. There was, in addition, a secondary firing mechanism in the form of a lever on the elevation handwheel. Aft of the director stood the 4m optical stereoscopic rangefinder in an open, thin steel tub. It was stabilized for roll along line of sight only, and was served by a crew of three (layer, trainer and range-taker). Director sights for the torpedo armament and searchlights were fitted in the bridge wings.

The after superstructure supported a second 4m rangefinder, the main searchlight and twin 3.7cm anti-aircraft mountings, as well as the secondary steering position. Light alloy was extensively employed for the superstructure in order to reduce topweight. Two motor boats were shipped either side of the forward funnel on the forecastle deck, handled by heavy derricks stepped against the after edge of the signal deck. A cutter was slung from radial davits on the starboard side of the midships structure, the starboard twin 3.7cm gun platform being slightly forward of the port one in order to accommodate the boat. Finally, a small dinghy was secured on its side against the port screen of the same structure. During the ships' war service, large numbers of the typical German square liferafts, as well as a few of the Carley float type, were carried and secured wherever space could be found. They were usually located on the tops and sides of the 12.7cm gun shields, on the bridge wing stanchions, on the after rangefinder platform and on the torpedo tubes.

The quadruple banks of torpedo tubes, shipped on the raised machinery space casings forward and aft of the midships structure, were remote power operated or could be trained under local power or local hand control. Firing arcs were normally restricted to Red/Green 30°–150° for speeds up to 28 knots and 45°–135° for speeds above 28 knots owing to the effect of the water on the torpedo on entering. Three 12.7cm single mountings, Nos. 3, 4 and 5 guns, formed the after group of the main armament. No. 3 gun, mounted at the forward end of the after shelter deck, had somewhat restricted arcs of fire of 30°–150° Green and Red, whilst No. 4 gun superfired over No. 5, both having arcs of fire to about 60° ahead of the beam. Between the two shelter-deck guns, a small deckhouse (which housed the cook's and stewards' mess) supported the light anti-aircraft platform, upon which were mounted two single 2cm guns. Both forward and after shelter decks normally had canvas dodgers lashed to the guard rails, which from a distance gave the impression of being light screen plating. On the quarterdeck, abaft No. 5 gun, was a large winch and right on the transom two lattice davits or cranes.

The hull was of welded construction, transverse framed, and fabricated from the standard German construction steel St52, a 0.20 per cent carbon steel with an ultimate tensile stress (UTS) of 52–61kg/mm² (about 33 to 39 tons per square inch); British destroyer construction was at this time utilizing the well-known 'D' steel which had a slightly higher strength of 37–42tsi. Frame spacing was generally 1.5m but towards the bows it was reduced to 1m and in the forepeak to 0.5m, whilst abaft No. 5 gun spacing was again reduced to 0.5m. Six longitudinals were worked in on either side of the forecastle, and on the main deck they were spaced at 0.4m intervals. All decks were steel plated, those on exposed decks having a raised pattern welded upon them for grip. Non-slip paint or compound was not used, but the welded pattern was not fully effective, especially in rough northern waters.

The hull itself was divided into fifteen separate, watertight compartments, numbered I to XV, all compartments and hull stations being numbered from the stern, as was German practice. The largest and most important spaces were the machinery compartments, which included IV to X and consisted of three boiler rooms and two engine rooms, as well as auxiliary machinery spaces. Each boiler room contained two high-pressure boilers, the uptakes from the foremost two rooms (Nos. 2 and 3) being served by the forward funnel. Separating No. 1 boiler room from the other two was a smaller compartment (VIII) containing the auxiliary boiler room, master stabilizer compartment, diesel generator room ('E. Werke 3') and transformer room. The after funnel served No. 1 boiler room. Despite their twin funnels, these ships did not have their machinery arranged on the unit principle, but the provision of two separate engine rooms considerably reduced the possibility of the loss of all motive power through a single hit.

The two turbine rooms – which also contained a turbogenerator each ('E. Werke 1' and 'E. Werke 2') – were separated by another, smaller, watertight compartment (V) which contained No. 6 magazine space, auxiliary machinery and gyro transformer room, as well as the stabilizer bunker space. The starboard turbine occupied the forward engine room (No. 2), thus making the starboard shaft longer than the port. The machinery spaces accounted for approximately 48 per cent of the ship's length and within this area a double bottom was worked in. Inside the double bottom space were oil fuel bunkers, lubricating oil tanks and cellular tanks for boiler feedwater, the remainder of the fuel oil being accommodated in tanks between the ship's side and the machinery spaces. Bunker capacity totalled about 752 tonnes, giving a designed range of 4,400 miles at 19 knots. However, sea experience soon showed stability problems, which necessitated maintaining a minimum fuel level of 30 per cent, a rather high figure which considerably reduced the vessel's useful range. This lack of range was one of the reasons for the withdrawal from northern waters of Type 34/34As towards the end of 1943. The stowage of a proportion of the fuel in wing tanks in the machinery spaces was common to all German

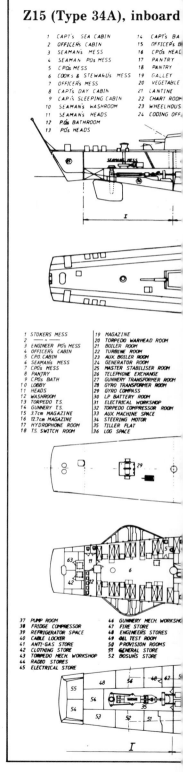

Z15 (Type 34A), inboard

1 CAPT's SEA CABIN
2 OFFICER'S CABIN
3 SEAMAN'S MESS
4 SEAMAN PO's MESS
5 CPO's MESS
6 COOK's & STEWARD's MESS
7 OFFICER's MESS
8 CAPT's DAY CABIN
9 CAPT's SLEEPING CABIN
10 SEAMAN's WASHROOM
11 SEAMAN's HEADS
12 PO's BATHROOM
13 PO's HEADS
14 CAPT's BA
15 OFFICER's B
16 CPO's HEAL
17 PANTRY
18 PANTRY
19 GALLEY
20 VEGETABLE
21 CANTINE
22 CHART ROOM
23 WHEELHOUS
24 CODING OFF.

1 STOKERS MESS
2 ———
3 ENGINEER PO's MESS
4 OFFICER's CABIN
5 CPO CABIN
6 SEAMAN's MESS
7 CPO's MESS
8 PANTRY
9 CPO's BATH
10 LOBBY
11 HEADS
12 WASHROOM
13 TORPEDO T.S.
14 GUNNERY T.S.
15 3.7cm MAGAZINE
16 12.7cm MAGAZINE
17 HYDROPHONE ROOM
18 T.S. SWITCH ROOM
19 MAGAZINE
20 TORPEDO WARHEAD ROOM
21 BOILER ROOM
22 TURBINE ROOM
23 AUX. BOILER ROOM
24 GENERATOR ROOM
25 MASTER STABILISER ROOM
26 TELEPHONE EXCHANGE
27 GUNNERY TRANSFORMER ROOM
28 GYRO TRANSFORMER ROOM
29 GYRO COMPASS
30 LP BATTERY ROOM
31 ELECTRICAL WORKSHOP
32 TORPEDO COMPRESSOR ROOM
33 AUX MACHINE SPACE
34 STEERING MOTOR
35 TILLER FLAT
36 LOG SPACE

37 PUMP ROOM
38 FRIDGE COMPRESSOR
39 REFRIGERATOR SPACE
40 CABLE LOCKER
41 ANTI-GAS STORE
42 CLOTHING STORE
43 TORPEDO MECH. WORKSHOP
44 RADIO STORES
45 ELECTRICAL STORE
46 GUNNERY MECH. WORKSHO
47 FIRE STORE
48 ENGINEER'S STORES
49 OIL TEST ROOM
50 PROVISION STORE
51 GENERAL STORE
52 BOSUN'S STORE

and deck plans

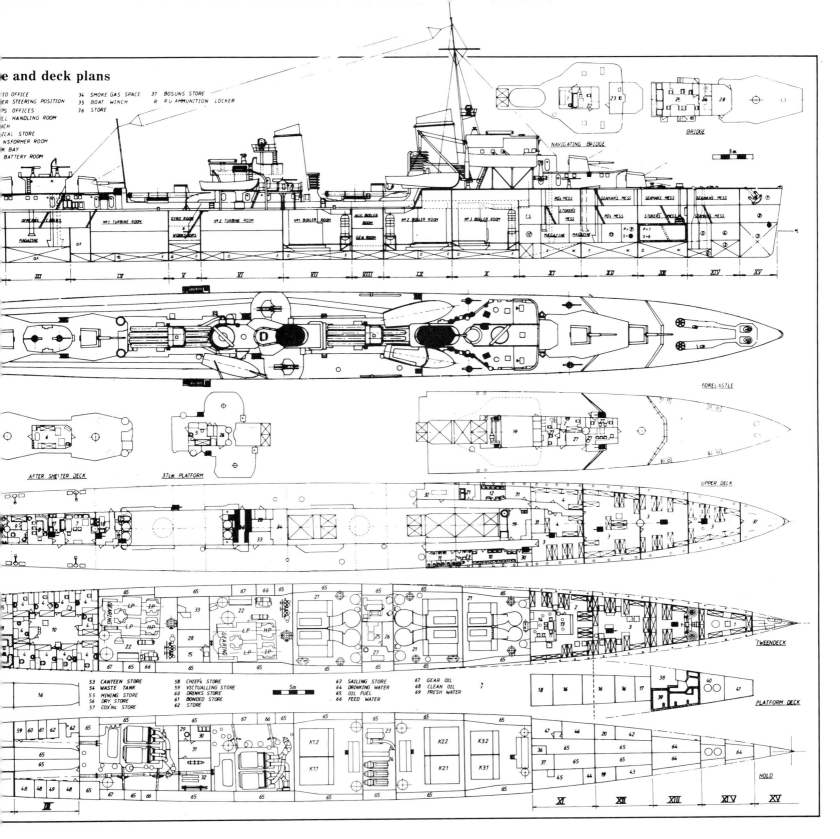

BRIDGE

NAVIGATING BRIDGE

5m.

FORECASTLE

AFTER SHELTER DECK   37cm PLATFORM

UPPER DECK

'TWEENDECK

5m

PLATFORM DECK

HOLD

destroyers and was later to be criticized by Royal Navy personnel on inspection tours after the war; wing or 'peace' tanks had been discontinued in British designs.

An interesting feature of the hull design was the 'Staukeil'. This was a wedge-shaped appendage under the hull, directly abaft the propellers and rudder, which produced a hollow reverse curve in the keel line, the apparent object being to deflect the propeller wash in a downward direction and thereby produce an upward moment of force under the stern, so that at high speeds the ship, instead of squatting down by the stern, would take up a more level attitude. It was found in practice, however, that in any swell, the effect of this lifting of the stern was to make the bows burrow into the sea, throwing spray over the bridge, rendering it impossible to work No. 1 gun and making it hazardous to walk on the upper deck. This effect was accentuated by the heavy concentration of weight forward (guns and bridge) and by the absence of sheer in the deck line. Another and more serious drawback to the idea was that by its very nature it imposed a continuous sagging stress on the hull whenever the ship was under way, even in calm weather, owing to the counteractive effects of the buoyancy in the forward section of the hull. It was soon found necessary to weld stiffening plates on to the hull in the midships area; nevertheless, cracking problems continued, and as a result the Staukeil was first reduced in

size and finally eliminated altogether. Active stabilizers, gyro-controlled, were fitted initially, but these were soon removed and bilge keels added; this seems to suggest an experience similar to that in the Royal Navy's 'Hunt' class escort destroyers, many of which had stabilizers fitted for a time. Spray was, however, a problem, and *Thiele* carried a special strake extending from just aft of the anchors and curving down to main deck level as far as No. 1 gun. This was removed prior to the outbreak of war but, interestingly, *Lody* received a similar spray strake during her 1944-5 refit, except that in this case it did not curve up towards the anchors.

The ship's complement numbered ten officers and 315 men, with an additional four officers and nineteen ratings when a vessel served as flotilla leader. The bulk of the ship's company was accommodated forward, on the upper and 'tween decks, and berthed mainly in double-tiered bunks, although a small proportion lived aft on a mess deck under No. 5 gun. Unusually, most of the bunks were arranged athwartships. The senior rates were accommodated just forward of the after seamen's mess on the 'tween deck, in six cabins and with separate mess and pantry facilities. Further forward still, ten cabins were provided for the offficers. The captain's accommodation, which consisted of day and sleeping cabins together with bath, heads and pantry, took up two-thirds of the after

Below: *Erich Steinbrinck*, a typical pre-war view of the Type 34A ships (W. Z. Bilddienst)

deckhouse and extended its full width. The remainder of this deckhouse was given over mainly to the wardroom. All crew spaces and cabins were fitted with electric radiators, no steam heating being used.

As designed, these ships were fitted with a tall pole foremast, having two yards crossed starfish fashion, above which was a crow's nest. Lower down, at the height of the funnel cap, a larger, canvas-surrounded platform supported the forward searchlight. The short mainmast was stepped, surprisingly, on the blast screen at the forward end of the after shelter deck, immediately in front of No. 3 gun, where its stays must have affected the arcs of fire. W/T aerials were slung between the masts.

In appearance, there were no major variations among any of the sixteen Type 34/34A ships, but there were certain detail differences as completed. There were several arrangements involving the steam pipes on the two funnels for example, some ships having thin, some thick, and others combinations of thin and thick pipes. Those ships constructed by Germaniawerft had the centre bridge window slightly raised in comparison with the other four, while the four Deschimag vessels had a different profile to the plating at the break of the forecastle. In these ships, instead of following a smooth arc which blended with the main deck, the curve was of a smaller radius and at its after end cut square to the deck. This feature became somewhat

hidden when heavy degaussing cables were fitted externally along the sheer strakes during the war.

The outbreak of war did not result in any major changes in appearance, and even camouflage was not adopted until 1940, after the Norwegian campaign; all the units lost at Narvik retained in essence their peacetime finish, although at Trondheim *Riedel* was carrying three-colour patchwork camouflage, a most unusual scheme and one not, as far as is known, applied to any other destroyer. When camouflage was generally adopted, it was usually designed around 'blocky' or 'barred' patterns, often with darker bows and sterns to give a shortening effect. Two-colour schemes were normally used, dark grey on light grey, and false bow and stern waves were often employed. Much research was carried out by the Kriegsmarine into the best methods of camouflage, but it is noteworthy that sea-going personnel questioned the effectiveness of many schemes. In July 1943, for example, Kapitän zur See Max-Eckhart Wolff (Captain D5), whilst his ships were still wearing the dark-barred schemes, considered that an overall light grey was better for destroyers since the presence of dark areas rendered ships of this size more conspicuous. Most, if not all, German destroyers were without camouflage by 1944.

The first four ships were ordered in April 1934 from Deutscher Werke in Kiel and were built in dry dock. The remainder of the class were built by three other major

shipbuilders – Deschimag at Bremen (*Jacobi*, *Riedel*, *Schoemann* and *Heinemann*), Germaniawerft at Kiel (*Zenker*, *Lody*, *von Arnim*, *Giese* and *Koellner*) and Blohm und Voss at Hamburg (*Ihn*, *Steinbrinck* and *Eckoldt*). Subsequently, however, all destroyers, with the exception of *Z37–39*, were built by the Deschimag concern.

The latter half of the 1930s was an era of rearmament, and the shipyards were working to capacity. Germaniawerft A.G. had in hand, besides the destroyers, the heavy cruiser *Prinz Eugen*, advance work on the second aircraft carrier, the escort vessels *F1–6* and twenty-five U-boats (*U7–12, 17–24, 33–36* and *45–55*). Deschimag had design and preparation work on Battleship 'J', the heavy cruiser *Seydlitz* and sixteen U-boats (*U25–82* and *37–44*). Deutsche Werke A.G. were building *Graf Zeppelin*, *Gneisenau* and *Blücher*, as well as ten U-boats (*U1–6* and *13–16*), whilst Blohm und Voss were busy with *Bismarck*, Battleship 'H' and *Hipper*, as well as escorts *F7* and *F8*. This congestion in the yards resulted in extended building times for some of the Type 34/34A destroyers, particularly those ordered late in 1934 from Germaniawerft; these ships took from 40 to 46 months to complete, whereas the first eight took 24–29 months and the Blohm und Voss vessels 33–36 months. Material failures and the late delivery of machinery were other factors in the delayed completion dates, and it may also be relevant, in the case of the Germania boats, that some U-boat officers were unhappy at the standard of boats constructed by that company, whilst it is possible that additional delays were caused by technical and labour difficulties within the yard itself. Be that as it may, the first ship commissioned in early January 1937 but the last, *Erich Koellner*, did not enter service until six days before the outbreak of war. Indeed, inadequate shipbuilding capacity was one of the major factors affecting the realization of the grandiose 'Z' plan.

UNTRIED STEAM PLANT

The most controversial aspect of the Type 34 and subsequent designs was undoubtedly marine engineering and, in particular, the steam plant. The ships were powered by two steam turbines, developing 70,000shp, driving twin screws and supplied from a steam plant of six high-pressure boilers paired in three boiler rooms. Whereas the previous 'Raubtier' and 'Raubvogel' classes of torpedo boats used steam pressures of the order of $18.5kg/cm^2$ (260psi) and contemporary British destroyer figures were about $21kg/cm^2$ (300psi), the new destroyers were to use pressures of $70kg/cm^2$ (1,028psi) and later vessels $110kg/cm^2$ (1,616psi).*

In the late 1920s Blohm und Voss had obtained a licence to build high-pressure steam boilers of the Benson pattern from England. One of these boilers was installed in a freighter, *Uckermark*, built for the HAPAG line. Other

shipbuilders obtained licences for different high-pressure boiler systems: Deutscher Werke, for instance, manufactured the La Mont type. Wagner was the other major system used, whilst Velox were briefly tried before being discarded. The Kriegsmarine was particularly concerned with the reduction of space, i.e., compartment size, in the interests of damage control and, working on the assumption that the higher the pressures used the smaller would be the space occupied, naturally became interested in the new HP systems. Surprisingly, the Kriegsmarine was not initially greatly involved in systems design and was largely in the hands of the shipbuilders in this respect, contenting itself only with the pipework layouts and the selection of competing units. Neither it nor the shipbuilders engaged in research to any degree, relying mainly upon work carried out by university professors as a basis for design improvements, although the facilities for full-scale testing at the yards were lavish.

A land-based testing programme designed to prove the high-pressure concept was terminated in the summer of 1934, and tests continued instead aboard the escort vessel/yacht *Grille*, which commissioned on 19 May 1935 with four Benson $80kg/cm^2$ boilers. Further sea experience was gained by the use of the new fast escort vessels *F1–10*, all of which shipped the La Mont $70kg/cm^2$ boiler except *F7* and *F8* which were fitted with Benson $110kg/cm^2$ outfits. This class of ship was used not only for machinery proving purposes but also for hull design trials, since the underwater form was similar to that of the new destroyers. The Wagner boilers first went to sea aboard the gunnery training ship *Brummer* in 1936.

Unfortunately, in view of the premature termination of the land-based trials, all these ships with the new boiler systems were completed far too late for much operational experience to have been accumulated before the new destroyers were well advanced on the slipways. In fact, some were already afloat, so that had the system been a complete failure it would have been difficult to install an alternative. More importantly, the failure to build a destroyer-type trials vessel delayed the establishment of operation routines for this type of boiler applicable to destroyer service. The result was the entry into service of sixteen ships aboard which the engine room staffs were still tackling the teething troubles – hence their chronic serviceability records. It has already been mentioned that the Velox system was not pursued, and of the three other systems only the Wagner and Benson types were to be installed in destroyers. Eventually, all destroyers were designed for Wagner boilers, which were adopted owing to the more serious production difficulties of the other two types. The first eight Type 34 destroyers shipped the Wagner boiler, while the second eight, *Z9–16*, adopted the Benson type.

The Wagner boiler had an operating pressure of $70kg/cm^2$ at a temperature of 460°F. Air pre-heating was employed, but no economizers were fitted. The air pre-

---

*Contemporary French designs employed pressures of $27kg/cm^2$ but some US ships reached $46kg/cm^2$.

heaters were horizontal, pear-shaped, welded tubes through which the air passed and around which the hot furnace gases flowed. Trouble with corrosion finally led to the adoption of the vertical, circular-tube type, which, although less efficient, had a longer life. The Wagner system employed natural circulation, and considerable trouble with tube failure was experienced until unheated downcomers were fitted; tube renewals were difficult owing to the tortuous curves of tube nests. The superheaters were of the 'U'-bend type, fitting into headers at each end of the boiler, in the middle of the main nest of tubes. The tubes extended less than half the length of the boiler, with a gap at the middle. An inability completely to drain the superheater led eventually to corrosion problems, whilst the tube supports gave rise to further problems in that the 'Sicromal 10' alloy used for plates and angles proved brittle in service, necessitating the later fitting of water-cooled tube supports.

The Benson boiler was designed for steam pressures of 110kg/cm² and required considerable modification before it operated satisfactorily. A vertical steam drum was introduced to stabilize the evaporation end point, which was otherwise subject to violent fluctuations, and rapid changes in output led to considerable priming. Water from this drum was recirculated by introducing it into the second stage of the main feed pump, a practice which led to difficulties with that unit. Later a separate circulating pump had to be fitted. Superheater corrosion and tube failures, due to poor circulation in the nests, were also experienced. Special nozzles were fitted for even circulation in parallel nests of tubes, but these were apt to become blocked and further tube failures resulted. These boilers were fitted with air pre-heaters and Benson economizers and had an operating temperature of 510°F.

The Kriegsmarine considered that automatic control of combustion was obligatory for all boilers, using a minimum number of wide-range burners and operating under Askania hydraulic control. This was a complicated system involving jet pipes, servos, bellows and cams to regulate the fuel quantity, primary air pressure and secondary air pressure. Various interlocks were fitted to prevent accidents, and Saake burners, usually two per boiler, were

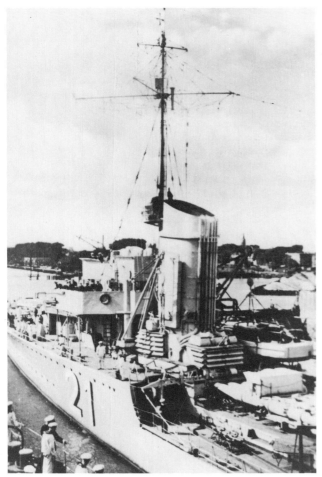

Below: *Paul Jacobi*, showing midships details, including torpedo trolley and loading davit. The prominent boiler room fan intakes are also evident. (W. Z. Bilddienst)

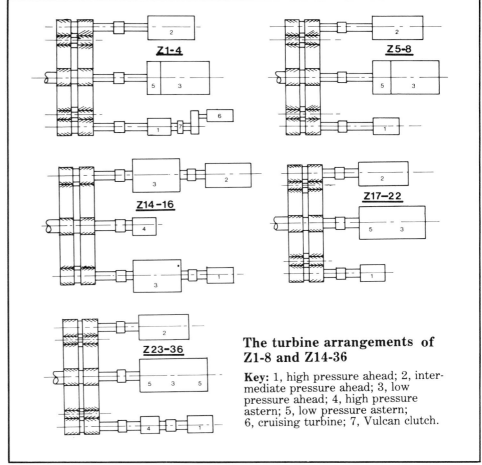

The turbine arrangements of Z1-8 and Z14-36

Key: 1, high pressure ahead; 2, intermediate pressure ahead; 3, low pressure ahead; 4, high pressure astern; 5, low pressure astern; 6, cruising turbine; 7, Vulcan clutch.

fitted in conjunction with this system. The Saake Burner was a spinning cup design, driven by an air turbine, air being supplied by a primary air blower, itself driven by a steam turbine which also drove the fuel pump. The air joined the oil fuel inside the spinning cup. This burner gave carbon dioxide readings of about 13 per cent at full power, falling to 5 or 7 per cent at low power. Despite its complicated nature, engine room personnel exhibited complete confidence in the system, but it would appear that, unless a high excess air setting was maintained, smoke was inevitable during increases of speed, and in cases of failure of the automatic system, boiler control whilst manoeuvring was very difficult.

All boiler feedwater was chemically treated, but salt deposits in the superheater region were a recurring problem, especially in the Benson system where internal tube cleaning was only possible by chemical means. De-aerator feedwater tanks were fitted but worked at atmospheric pressure. However, it seems likely that, in view of the corrosion problems, too high an oxygen content was permitted, since a major cause of boiler corrosion is oxygen or carbon dioxide dissolved in the feedwater; furthermore, it was only in the final boiler designs that economizers or superheaters could be vented or drained. The situation was probably aggravated by the strategic position of the Kriegsmarine, which necessitated the ships spending a great deal of time in harbour. The routine adopted was to light up a boiler every two to three days, raise the water to boiling point at low pressure, then shut down. It is possible that the boilers were topped up with aerated water. The main point of corrosion was in the tubes connecting the top of the steam drum to the collector pipe, which ran parallel to and above it.

In the final analysis, it is obvious that the theoretical merits of the high-pressure system did not prove themselves in practice, with the result that the Kriegsmarine never knew when a heavy cruiser or destroyer might suddenly become unserviceable. It is probable that had the system been given a more prolonged sea trial aboard an experimental destroyer, things might have been different, but war broke out shortly after these destroyers were completed, eliminating the possibility of a leisurely solution to their problems – it is possible that the latter were not evident until the demands of war service were imposed.

It was hoped that the high pressures would lead to high efficiency, but in fact the relative efficiencies of the Benson and Wagner types were 77 and 78 per cent respectively; the Royal Navy's proven Admiralty three-drum boiler achieved 76 per cent, and the German boilers were generally 2–3 per cent lower in efficiency than contemporary American designs. From the point of view of damage control, the desire for a reduction in weight and space was not fully realized either. Both the Type 34 and the Royal Navy's 'G' class destroyers carried their steam plant in three boiler rooms, and in terms of compartment size there was little to choose between them except that the former carried two boilers per room and the latter only one. This made for extremely cramped conditions and was frequently remarked upon by both RN and US Navy officers in the course of post-war inspections. The use of six boilers certainly meant a lower percentage of power loss should one boiler be put out of action, but in the absence of any longitudinal subdivision of the boiler rooms the breaching of one inevitably resulted in the loss of 30 per cent of the powerplant – exactly the same as would be the case with a British 'G' class destroyer. The high-pressure steam system, which was intended to confer several design and operational advantages, proved to be the Achilles' heel of these ships and severely restricted their activities throughout the war years; *Steinbrinck*'s machinery record is enlightening in this respect.

The rigours of wartime service, with long periods in steam, frequent high-speed operations and reduced maintenance, took their inevitable toll on the useful lifespans of the warships of all nations, and whilst many of the vessels scrapped at the end of hostilities were surplus to requirements, many more relatively new ships were simply worn out. It is hardly surprising, therefore, that such a new and untried steam plant caused trouble under active service conditions. The fragility quickly became apparent, with the result that a commission of inquiry had been set up before the end of 1939 to examine the problems.

The main turbines for the first series of sixteen vessels were supplied in equal numbers by Deschimag and Blohm und Voss, *Z1–8* being equipped with the former type and the remainder with the Blohm und Voss design. The layout of the first four ships included a separate cruising turbine, driving, through gearing and a Vulkan hydraulic coupling, on to the HP turbine pinion. However, land trials of the first ship units steamed from a marine high-pressure boiler and witnessed by representatives from OKM (Oberkommando der Marine, or Naval High Command) had shown that the drag in the Vulkan coupling, even when disconnected, was far too high. Other problems were also experienced, particularly in connection with the auxiliary turbine governors. Finally, OKM ordered that the cruising turbines be removed and sets be delivered to the ships without the cruising unit. *Z5–8* were not therefore fitted with cruising turbines.

The general design of the turbines was massive, partly because of the use of three separate cylinders for the HP, IP (intermediate-pressure) and LP stages. This necessitated the use of idler pinions on the HP and IP turbines in order to allow sufficient space to mount the bulky LP and condenser unit centrally, driving on to the top of the main wheel. The astern turbine consisted of a single, two-row Curtis wheel on the after end of the LP rotor. Guaranteed astern power was 7,500hp per shaft, with a design maximum of 9,500hp. All gearing was of the single-reduction, double-helical type.

Ships fitted with the Blohm und Voss turbine had a radically different arrangement of turbine cylinders. In these destroyers, the HP ahead turbine was mounted axially with an LP turbine and drove on to the main wheel without an idler pinion. Similarly, on the other side of the main wheel diameter, the IP rotor was coaxial with a second LP turbine, whilst the HP astern turbine was mounted so as to drive on to the top of the main wheel through a separate pinion. No cruising turbine was fitted, and, without it, the low load performance was very poor and led to rotor blade problems. In the event, however, the Deschimag design of turbine was preferred and was used, in modified form, in all subsequent destroyers. With a power-to-weight ratio of 13.8kg/hp and developing 35,000hp per set, the machinery gave a designed top speed of 38 knots (38.25 in *Z1–4*).

Continuing problems with turbines in the Benson ships led to a decision in January 1941 by the OKM, to order new HP turbines from Germania. These were to be delivered at the rate of one pair per month from April 1943. In the meantime, the Curtis wheel would be removed, reducing the power by 3,000hp per unit.

The ships' main electrical power supply was provided by two turbogenerators each of 200kW at 220v AC, one in each turbine room. Harbour service and supply when the boilers were shut down were provided by three diesel generators in a separate compartment, comprising one 30kW and two 60kW sets (*Z9–16* had three 50kW diesel sets), giving a total generating capacity of 550kW. This was far in excess of the capacity of the contemporary British 'Tribal' class, which could produce only 190kW – and DC at that – suggesting that a much higher proportion of the ships' equipment was power-assisted than was the case in British ships. Certainly, their Lordships were most reluctant to power anything which could be turned by 'Jack' with a handle, and not until the 'Weapon' class of 1944 did generating capacity of RN ships exceed this figure.

A MORE PLEASING APPEARANCE

After the construction of the Type 34 ships had been put in hand, work commenced on an improved design, six units based on which were provided for in the 1935 programme. The failings of the Type 34/34A may have been suspected by the design staffs before any sea experience had been obtained, since the new class, Type 36, incorporated a number of measures which improved seaworthiness. It is possible that the design was altered during construction but there seems to be no actual evidence for this. The Type 36 incorporated a slight increase in length, more beam and a reworked hull section in way of the propellers in order to increase the deadwood astern, in an effort to improve the ships' turning characteristics. Topweight was reduced by cutting down the funnels, reducing the size of the clinker screens and altering the bridge structure slightly, whilst a little more sheer was worked into the forecastle, and the last three units, *Galster*, *Heidkamp* and *Schmitt*, were given clipper bows.

There were certain detail differences among the various ships, mainly associated with the positioning of the searchlights. The three destroyers with clipper bows all had a searchlight platform on the foremast, half-way up to the crosstrees, although of these three only *Galster* had a second light at the base of the mast as well. *Roeder*, *Künne* and *Lüdemann* all had the mast light just above the forward funnel, and all had the second light at bridge level. The last two ships to be completed, *Heidkamp* and *Schmitt*, had noticeably thicker foremasts. In comparison with the previous class, the only other appearance differences were the remodelling of the 3.7cm gun deck, the resiting in symmetrical fashion of the gun mountings abreast the funnel, and the reduction in size of the after deckhouse, to which the mainmast was transferred. In plan view Nos. 2, 3 and 4 gun decks were widened to a near circular form around the mountings to give their crews more working space. Finally, the size of the propeller guards was very much reduced as compared with the Type 34. All in all, this class presented a very much more pleasing appearance, and although the fortunes of war did not favour the design, the sole survivor after 1940, *Galster*, seems to have enjoyed a good reputation.

The machinery plant was similar to the preceding class, but it is possible either that some technical improvements were made or, more likely, that operating routines were refined, since *Galster* had a good serviceability record. All six units were fitted with the Wagner boiler (70kg/cm²) and

---

UNSERVICEABILITY RECORD OF ERICH STEINBRINCK
(commissioned 31.5.38)

Cause:	Dates:	Days:
Water in fuel oil	12.12.39–18.12.39	5
Collison damage	23.12.39– 1. 1.40	8
Refit (Blohm und Voss)	27. 1.40– 5. 5.40	96
Trials, training and work-up	6. 5.40–26. 5.40	20
Machinery failure	8. 6.40–10. 6.40	2
Repairs (Blohm und Voss)	23. 6.40–14. 8.40	52
Trials and work-up	14. 8.40–29. 8.40	14
Turbine damage	5. 9.40–17. 9.40	12
Overhaul (Blohm und Voss), trials, further machinery damage	26.10.40–29. 3.41	150
Machinery breakdown	25. 5.41	10?
Collision damage and refit (Blohm und Voss)	25. 8.41–22. 3.42	
Training and trials	23. 3.42–12. 5.42	360
Machinery damage (new turbine fitted)	12. 5.42– 5. 8.42	
Grounded	3. 9.42	
Repairs (Deschimag, Bremen)	27. 9.42– 1.43	90
Work-up	6. 1.43–10. 1.43	
Further machinery damage	10. 1.43	10
Shaft repairs	30. 1.43	
Rams *Hans Lody*	21.11.43	
Rammed by steamer	26.11.43	
Repairs	2.12.43–17. 1.44	50
Refit (Blohm und Voss)	27. 4.44– 4.45	360
Laid up (fuel shortage)	4.45– 5.45	

their electrical generating capacity was further increased to 600kW by the installation of bigger diesel generators (two at 80kW and one at 40kW); the turbogenerators remained the same. Bunkerage was increased slightly, giving the ships a marginally greater range.

The class also introduced a new arrangement of the turbines, incorporating a combined cruising and HP turbine stage into which the steam was introduced by means of a horseshoe-shaped nozzle box in the middle of the casing; three nozzles were for cruising and a further two for high-power requirements. This combined cylinder drove through idler pinions, as did the IP turbine, whilst atop the main wheel was the combined astern/LP pinion. Once again, all gearing was single-reduction; the OKM never wholeheartedly accepted double-reduction gearing, the only known example of such being aboard *Gneisenau*. Power-to-weight ratio was improved to about 12.3kg/hp, and these turbines, with a consumption rate of 0.33kg/hp, were considered by Deschimag engineers to be the best sets made. Later designs for *Z23–36*, modified at the insistence of OKM, were less economical.

The armament was generally similar to that of the earlier class both in numbers and disposition, with the exception that the reduction in size of the after deckhouse on the after shelter deck displaced the two single 2cm guns, which were re-sited on the enlarged and revised 3.7cm gun platform, a layout retained in subsequent war-built classes. Hull construction was strengthened, thus eliminating the necessity of in-service modifications. All six units were ordered from the Deschimag yard on 6 January 1936, the leading pair, *Roeder* and *Lüdemann*, being laid down on 9 September that year; construction time averaged 22 months, *Galster* and *Heidkamp* completing in only 18. The final ship, *Schmitt*, was not completed until some three weeks after the outbreak of war.

Galster, under refit in Wilhelmshaven between February and May 1940, missed the Norway campaign and hence escaped the fate of her sister-ships, all of which were lost in that operation. She emerged from the refit with a foremast thickened up to the level of the searchlight, long tripod legs

extending up to the crosstrees (where a crow's nest was fitted), and an external degaussing cable around the forecastle and main deck sheer strakes. She appears to have lost her eagle emblem from the front of the bridge at this time and had still not re-shipped it by the summer of 1941. When the new 2cm 'Vierling' became available it was installed on the after deckhouse in a similar manner to the Type 34 ships, displacing the mainmast to the forward end of No. 3 gun's blast shield. In the course of a subsequent refit, the after end of the bridge structure was built up and widened for the installation of radar equipment, the radar aerial being fitted on the roof of this cabin.

Galster retained her full 12.7cm outfit throughout her career, but by 1944 her flak armament had been considerably augmented, in addition to the Vierling, by several 3.7cm and 2cm guns: two single 3.7s were shipped on the midships platform, displacing the 2cm guns (the 3.7cm guns were delivered to Norway by *Ihn* in January 1945). She retained her stabilizer gear until the end of hostilities. Twin 2cm weapons were installed in the bridge wings and the single mountings abreast No. 2 gun were paired; two further single 2cm weapons were fitted on the shelter decks, under the muzzles of Nos. 2 and 4 guns; and, finally, a single 2cm bow-chaser was fitted. *Galster* survived the war, and was taken over by the Soviet Union after the German surrender.

2. THE WAR-BUILT DESTROYERS

In 1934, having completed the Type 34 design, the German Naval Staff gave consideration to the development of a smaller type of destroyer to be used as a torpedo carrier rather than a gun-armed vessel. This proposal was not in fact proceeded with as it was decided that the destroyer tonnage should be reserved for true destroyer types, and a fresh proposal was formulated for the construction of a ship roughly equivalent to the current standard British destroyer, displacing 1,300/1,500 tonnes, armed with four 12.7cm guns and possessing a very high continuous speed (40 knots!). An alternative battery of three 12.7cm and one triaxial 10.5cm flak was suggested, and eight torpedoes in two quadruple banks completed the armament. A range of 5,000-6,000 miles was proposed but nothing came of the idea.

By 1937 the Type 34 destroyers had proved unsuitable in respect of range and seaworthiness for Atlantic employment, and the idea of an ocean destroyer was raised once more. This was now known as the Type 37 design, which was to be not a flotilla leader but an 'Atlantic' destroyer, whose tasks were to be commerce raiding without the support of heavy units, or scouting and torpedo duties when screening larger vessels. Armament was to be sufficient to give a good prospect of success against enemy destroyers, although the ships were not expected to cope with French flotilla leaders; the latter were to be left to the light cruisers or at least two Type 37 ships. After the experiences with the Type 34 destroyers, an increase in gun calibre to 15cm was not sanctioned as it was feared that this would make the ships unsuitable for Atlantic employment: increased gunpower could only be accepted if there were no corresponding reduction in radius or seaworthiness. What was to be avoided was a hybrid cruiser-destroyer type which could properly fullfil neither of these tasks. The initial sketch design proposed a radius of 6,000 miles, with six 12.7cm guns in twin mountings together with a simple but effective fire control system.

By early 1938, however, the design was intended to produce both a commerce destroyer and an ocean escort, with an armament now specifically in excess of that of the French flotilla leaders. Nevertheless, the demands of speed and radius were already suspected of having overtaken the technology of the day, at least until diesels of a lower weight than were currently available became a reality. The armament proposals show that the fears of the previous year – that a hybrid type would emerge – were a real possibility, for there were now four proposals: (a) six 15cm in three twin turrets; (b) eight 12.7cm in four twin mountings; (c) five 15cm in five single mountings; and (d) seven 12.7cm in seven single mountings . The last proposal envisaged the extra two guns sited between the funnels, with limited arcs of fire; and, only one gun's crew and ammunition outfit was to be carried for the pair.

According to the design offices, the light 15cm twin turret was preferable to the twin mounting, which had most of the disadvantages of the turret but none of the advantages. The crucial factor was, as always, weight, three twin 15cm turrets being about 100 tonnes heavier than five single 15cm or seven single 12.7cm guns. It was estimated that the weight of the twin 15cm turret would be between 52,100kg and 56,600kg, depending upon what armour thickness was provided, although with these weights there was in fact little residue for armour, and splinter protection could not be provided for the turret trunks. If one turret were to be omitted, the weight would be only about 10 per cent greater than five single 15cm guns, but the firepower would be less. In view of these problems, and of the fact that there was no such turret yet available and that to await its design would delay the ships' completion, the turret idea was dropped. Other combinations of armament were also discarded on the grounds of weight and availability: three twin 12.7cm turrets were out of the question, as were four twin 12.7cm mountings, the latter on the grounds that power training would be necessary and that the rate of fire would probably be less than the rate provided by equivalent single mountings. Furthermore, weather conditions would undoubtedly affect the electrical systems.

It was finally decided to ship the 15cm gun on the reasoning that its rate of fire was almost the same as that for the 12.7cm under practical conditions and that the effect of any hit was of course much greater. The torpedo armament was to be similar to the Type 34, and all possible means were to be taken to increase the range - in excess of 5,000 miles at 19 knots if possible. Seaworthiness was once again stressed, for the ships were to be employed in all theatres, and special emphasis was laid on the buoyancy of the forward ends following experience with the Type 34. Problems continued to arise in the conflicting requirements of weight, speed, range and offensive power; these could not be solved, however, so on 8 April 1938 Raeder informed the OKM that the building of the Type 37 was to be deferred and, instead, a further eight Type 36 destroyers were to be constructed in slightly modified form as the Type 36A. The main differences were to be the provision of 15cm guns, with the forward pair in a twin turret, and altered machinery for lower revolutions.

ADDED IMPETUS

The eight Type 36A units reverted to the traditional German practice of not naming ships below the size of light cruisers and were therefore numbered *Z23–Z30*.* In view of the intention to install the larger gun, displacement was increased to approximately 3,600 tonnes full load and the hull dimensions to 121.9cm between perpendiculars with a beam of 12m. The basic hull design differed little from that of the previous classes, except that certain alterations were made to the underwater stern form in order to increase the deadwood and thereby improve on the poor turning

*Several were, however, to adopt unofficially the names of destroyers lost earlier in the war, e.g., *Z24 'Georg Thiele'*.

characteristics of the earlier ships; twin rudders were incorporated for the same reasons. Furthermore, like the preceding class, the general hull construction was strengthened in comparison with the Type 34. Outwardly, above water, the hull differed visually only in the substitution of upper deck anchor beds in lieu of the more normal hawsepipes, a feature which was to become standard in German warship design practice. The disposition of the guns, superstructure and torpedo tubes followed the pattern established by the Type 34 except that the provision of a twin turret in No. 1 position eliminated the forward shelter deck, leaving only a small deckhouse (containing a suite of offices) below and forward of the bridge. In the event, the appearance of the turret was severely delayed, which resulted in seven of the eight units completing with a single 15cm gun in an open shield in No. 1 position. That there would be a problem in the delivery of the turrets had been recognized as early as September 1938, when Raeder ordered the completion of *Z23–25* without it to avoid delaying their entry into service.

Internally, the hull was once again divided into fifteen watertight compartments, whose general arrangement was similar to the earlier classes, except that the layout of compartment XII was considerably disturbed to accommodate the trunk and handling arrangements of the twin turret. The machinery spaces accounted for 50 per cent of the length of the vessel, occupying compartments IV to X, in which region a double bottom was

Below: *Z24* as completed and lacking her twin turret. She has radar but no Vierling and the 2cm guns are disposed before the bridge, under No. 3 gun and on the midships platform. (Archiv Gröner)

Type 36A, inboard profile and plan

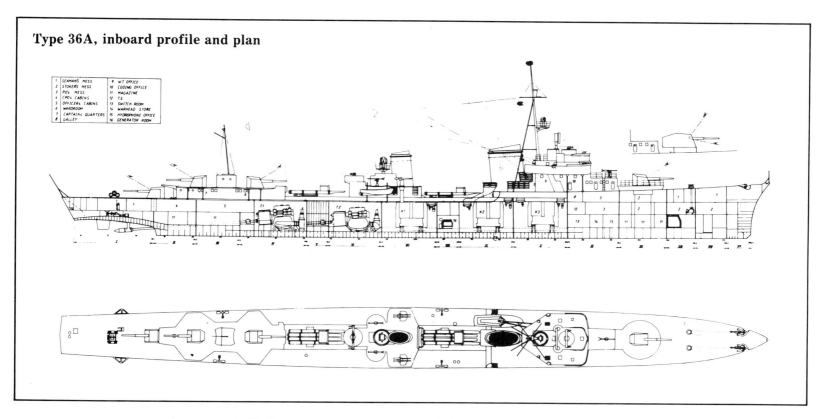

1	SEAMAN'S MESS	9	W.T. OFFICE
2	STOKERS MESS	10	CODING OFFICE
3	PO's MESS	11	MAGAZINE
4	CPO's CABINS	12	T.S.
5	OFFICERS CABINS	13	SWITCH ROOM
6	WARDROOM	14	WARHEAD STORE
7	CAPTAIN'S QUARTERS	15	HYDROPHONE OFFICE
8	GALLEY	16	GENERATOR ROOM

incorporated. Fuel oil stowage was incorporated in the cellular construction of this double bottom space, but a large proportion of the fuel bunkerage continued to be stowed in wing tanks extending the whole length of the machinery spaces. The boiler rooms' oil fuel feed pumps could only take suction from these wing tanks and not from the action double bottom tanks, with the unsatisfactory result that the wing tanks were always full. The bunker capacity was marginally increased compared to the Type 36 design and, with better arrangements, minimum fuel levels were reduced, giving an increase in effective range of some 7–10 per cent in *Z23–27*. One unit, *Z28*, which was modified as a flotilla leader, had a bunkerage of 769 tonnes, giving a range comparable to that of the Type 36, whilst the final two, *Z29* and *Z30*, received a further increase to 825 tonnes, with a consequent increase in range of about 11 per cent in comparison to the Type 36, although the earlier Type 36A ships seem to have been later equipped to stow 825 tonnes also.

The machinery installation comprised six Wagner high-pressure boilers, paired in three boiler rooms. Four were rated at 54,600kg/hr and two at 47,800kg/hr, the latter pair being in the forward boiler room. Two Wagner geared turbines, developing a total of 70,000shp, drove two 3.35m stainless steel propellers, for a designed full speed of 37.5 knots. Synthetic plastic, water-lubricated 'Dytron' material was employed for the shaft bearings instead of the more

usual white metal, which led to severe wear problems in service and also caused vibration. Electrical generating capacity was slightly reduced, to 520kw, current being supplied by a 200kw A.E.G. turbogenerator set installed in No. 1 turbine room and four diesel sets of 80kw each in a separate space on the platform deck. The machinery spaces, extremely congested by Allied standards, were all provided with diagrams showing the locations of major items, and the engine rooms had boards permanently displayed showing pipe layouts into which coloured pegs could be inserted to show the state of the valves. Reference books were issued to engineering personnel which showed similar information. The ventilation arrangements for the engine rooms were particularly good, with fresh air being supplied below the platform deck and hot air being exhausted at deckhead level. *Z38* underwent full-power trials during September 1946 whilst in Royal Navy hands, and the average temperature recorded at the main engine throttles was 86°F (cf. HMS *Marne*'s full power trial in December, when engine room temperature rose to 89°F minimum and 103°F maximum).

The fire and salvage arrangements were also extensive, and there is no doubt that the Kriegsmarine had given rather more thought to damage control than had many other navies at that time. Two electric pumps supplied the fire main, and steam drenching was fitted in boiler, turbine, auxiliary boiler and generator rooms, as well as in the wing oil bunkers; in addition, a permanently fixed gas ring main was installed in all the above compartments, each compartment having its own plant at upper deck level. The plants could be interconnected if necessary. The gas, known as 'CB', was pressure-fed by compressed air and sprayed through fixed valves on to the gas ring main. A main salvage system of unusually large capacity was fitted, comprising three electric pumps, each capable of discharging 300 tonnes/hr; this was in addition to the normal use which could be made of the main circulating suctions, and, furthermore, the auxiliary pumping systems could, via three more pumps, contribute a further 80 tonnes/hr. These comprehensive arrangements were no doubt a factor in the successful salvage of *Z34* after she was torpedoed in the Baltic in 1945, when one turbine room was fully breached. The dire shortage of many raw materials in Germany as a result of the British blockade meant that much of the piping and valving which would normally have been of non-ferrous metal was instead made of steel. This had caused corrosion problems by the end of the war.

Accommodation was provided for a ship's company of eleven officers and approximately 320 men. The officers, the CPOs and about seventy seamen berthed aft, but the majority were accommodated forward, on the upper and 'tween decks. Triple-tier bunks were fitted, but these could

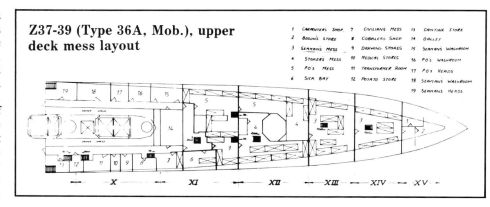

Z37-39 (Type 36A, Mob.), upper deck mess layout

1 Carpenters Shop	7 Civilians Mess	13 Cantine Store	
2 Bosun's Store	8 Cobblers Shop	14 Galley	
3 Seamans Mess	9 Drawing Stores	15 Seamans Washroom	
4 Stokers Mess	10 Medical Stores	16 PO's Washroom	
5 PO's Mess	11 Transformer Room	17 PO's Heads	
6 Sick Bay	12 Potato Store	18 Seamans Washroom	
		19 Seamans Heads	

only cater for half the men, the remainder using hammocks. As has already been mentioned, the turret arrangements severely cramped the mess decks in compartment XII where, on the upper deck, it was subdivided into three small messes for POs and stokers. Each mess deck was fitted with a sink and supplied with hot and cold running water – a luxury in comparison with RN practice. Good washing facilities were also provided, with hot and cold water, plenty of basins, and showers. In the large after mess deck, there were a separate wash place and heads.

Below: *Z24* seen in French waters in 1943, now fitted with the twin turret. Two Vierlinge are now carried as well as extra degaussing cables. (Bundesarchiv)

Aft of No. 1 turbine room, on the 'tween deck, the officers' accommodation consisted of a suite of ten single- and double-berthed cabins, whilst the CPOs were similarly catered for in the next compartment further aft. In the after shelter deck were the captain's accommodation, officers' bathrooms, etc., as well as the officers' mess. This was not a 'wardroom' in the RN sense, for it was only fitted for messing and was rather spartan. With the introduction of the twin turret there was no forward shelter deck as such, but the small deckhouse remaining accommodated the ship's, coxswain's, engineer's and central store offices, and within the bridge structure was the W/T offce, one of the largest spaces in the ship and well equipped with a variety of sets including long-wave, long-wave (short-range), short-wave and ultra-short-wave outfits. Adjacent to the W/T office was the coding office. On the upper bridge, or control platform, a small radar office was fitted at the after end with the forward 3m stereo optical rangefinder before it. In this class, the foremast was stepped sufficiently far aft of the bridge as to allow full rotation of the radar mattress without modification to the mast itself.

Amidships, around the after funnel, the superstructure was enlarged in comparison to the previous classes, and accommodated within it was a secondary navigation position, drying room and store. The spacious flak deck carried the usual two twin 3.7cm SK C/30s symmetrically sided abreast the funnel and, as introduced by the Type 36, two single 2cm C/30 weapons abreast the searchlight. The second rangefinder, now increased to 4m base length and fitted at the after end of the deck, served the after group of 15cm guns. No secondary transmitting station was fitted, however.

The layout of the after shelter deck in respect of the main armament was, with the substitution of 15cm guns for 12.7cm, similar to the earlier vessels. A light flak armament of five 2cm guns was disposed one before the bridge, two amidships, one on the after shelter deck under the barrel of No. 3 gun and one either on the quarterdeck or on the forecastle.

One unit of this class, *Z28*, was modified to act as a flagship for Flag Officer (D) and differed considerably in appearance from her sisters, although utilizing the same building dimensions. In this unit No. 3 gun, at the forward end of the after shelter deck, was deleted in order to enlarge the small ammunition handling room into a suite of offices and cabins extending the full width of the shelter deck and some 12m in length. The displaced 15cm gun was re-sited on an extended deckhouse forward of the bridge, where it superfired on No. 1 gun in a similar manner to the 12.7cm-gunned destroyers; no provision was therefore made to install the twin turret at any later date. Extra 2cm guns were carried forward of No. 2 gun and on the accommodation aft. Completing in August 1941, *Z28* spent most of her active life in Arctic waters before being withdrawn to the Baltic, where she was sunk by air attack on 6 March 1945.

Orders were placed on 23 April 1938, with the Deschimag concern at Bremen, for the first eight Type 36A units, the leading ship, *Z23*, being laid down on 15 November that year. *Z24–26* followed at about six-weekly

Above: *Z34* leaving Kiel in 1942 after fitment of the Vierling forward. (Archiv Gröner)

intervals until April 1939, when the cruiser *Seydlitz* and the torpedo boats *T11* and *T12* left the ways. Construction proceeded apace throughout the year until, two weeks after the first unit of the second phase (*Z28*) was laid down, *Z23* was launched on 15 December 1939. *Z27* had her keel laid at the turn of the year, but the last pair were not laid down until March and April 1940, as *Z24*, *Z25* and *Z26* quickly followed one another down the slips and were towed to the fitting-out berths.

War had by now been declared, giving added impetus to the construction programme for destroyers, so that whereas the first four ships averaged 13 months to launch, the second four averaged only 8¼ months to reach the same stage. *Z23* commissioned at Bremen on 15 September 1940, some 22 months after laying down; *Z24–26* returned similar times, but the second phase was completed in under 18 months, with the exception of *Z28* which was delayed, probably by her design modifications. The overall building times were commendable but would have been extended quite considerably had the decision not been made to commission the ships without the twin turret.

Between her commissioning and December 1940, when the 8th Flotilla was formed, *Z23* had been undergoing the customary round of working-up routines in the Baltic, so the new design's seakeeping abilities were not seriously tested. There may, however, already have been some suspicions as to the likely effect of the heavy armament on

what was not an over-large extension of the Type 36 hull, for during this period work was done on modifying her fore-ends. Icing conditions in the winter Baltic had further hampered the accumulation of any real experience, and it was not until late March, when, in the course of a short deployment to Norway, *Z23*, in company with *Z24*, struck bad weather in the open sea. Two days of rough sea passage through the German Bight to Kristiansand exposed serious deficiencies in the design's seakeeping abilities, particularly in respect of the buoyancy of the forward ends. Bearing in mind the fact that both ships had only the single 15cm gun forward and were thus some 45 tonnes lighter than designed at the bows, their performance called for some detailed investigations. Reports from the COs, Captain (D8), Flag Officer and Admiral Carls all commented unfavourably on the design, and it was feared that the class would never be fully acceptable without a major redesign of the underwater section forward. Modifications do appear to have been attempted, but without conspicuous success.

It was not until 1942 that the first twin turret was ready, when it was allocated to *Z23*, to be installed during a major refit commencing in February. *Z23* remained in dockyard hands until June, when, following a short work-up in the Baltic, she returned once more to the Arctic. Severe weather conditions were not experienced until September, in the course of Operation 'Zarin' out in the Barents Sea.

The destroyer crews' fears were fully justified, for the extra weight of the turret resulted in the bows diving into the seas and water being thrown over the bridges, leaving the turret surrounded by surf and sticking out like a half-tide rock. Clearly, the employment of these ships in open ocean conditions such as pertained in the Arctic and Biscay theatres would pose serious operational problems. Critical reports issued from all quarters of the destroyer force, with Flag Officer (D), Vizeadmiral Bey, being particularly concerned. In his opinion, the design was manifestly unsuited to the twin turret, and he advised that its planned installation in *Z27*, *Z29* and *Z30* should be abandoned; furthermore, *Z33* and *Z38*, then building, should not be commissioned with the turret (*Z24* and *Z25* were already in hand, whilst *Z26* had been lost). As a result of his representations, *Z30* never received a turret and *Z29* was only so fitted in 1945. *Z27* was lost before fitment, but *Z33* and *Z38* were commissioned fully armed with the twin turret. The heavy turret not only affected seakeeping; it was also, at least in the early stages, mechanically unreliable, with the result that there were occasions when a destroyer was devoid of forward gunpower.*

Few in-service modifications of a visible nature were carried out on the Type 36As. Plexiglass weather shields

*A major problem was watertightness: ingress of water caused short circuits, upset control equipment and drenched the crew.

were fitted over the torpedo tube control positions and a Vierling installed on the ammunition lobby aft. Later, to increase the flak firepower in the blind sector across the bows, the single 2cm gun was replaced by a second Vierling; later still, major flak refits were given to three units and modifications made to others (see Chapter 4).

DELAYS AND INDECISION

After the Type 37 had been dropped, another conference on new construction took place on 15 June 1938, at which the Development Office put forward two new proposals. These were:

(a) A design of 3,200 tonnes, four 15cm (2x2) one forward, one aft: one 10.5cm flak; one quadruple bank of tubes on the centre line, two triples one on each beam; 80,000hp combined steam and diesel = 36/37 knots.

(b) 1,550 tonnes with a twin shaft turbine layout armed with four 12.7cm (2x2) one forward, one aft; torpedo outfit as (a); 3,500/4,000nm at 19 knots.

The larger proposal was seen as a good replacement for the Type 37 in the North Sea/North Atlantic, whilst (b) would serve as a good 'work-horse' destroyer for the fleet. The (a) proposal led eventually, after much discussion, argument and indecision, to the Spähkreuzer project, initially as the Type 38A. In October 1938, the

Marinekommandoamt tabulated the military demands of the Type 38B:

Tasks – Fleet tasks including torpedo, scouting and escort duties as well as A/S and screening of fast mine-layers.

Operational Areas – Baltic and North Sea as far as the Shetland/Norway narrows.

Armament
  – four 12.7cm (2x2) in light gun houses, 100rpg
  – two 3.7cm (1x2), 750rpg
  – two 2cm (2x1), 1,000rpg
  – nine 53.5cm (3x3) torpedo tubes
  – four D/C throwers, 2 racks 18d/cs.
Speed at least 36 knots, 3,500nm @ 19 knots.

The building of such a destroyer was felt to be a high priority and the Construction Office reported that it would be possible to order nine in 1939. However, Raeder expressed himself not entirely satisfied with the design in February 1939, criticizing the fact that only four guns were carried. This was not accepted by the other parties who saw the ship as eminently suitable for the close escort of capital ships, being the modern equivalent of the high seas torpedo boat of the First World War and a development of the Type 23/24 torpedo boats. In consequence, the Skl fully supported the design, pointing out that the type 23/24 boats were getting old and the Type 35 torpedo boats were designed for an entirely different role.

By mid February, the Type 38B had risen to a displacement of 1,780/2,353 tonnes with a length of 105m and a torpedo outfit reduced to eight tubes in two quadruple centre-line banks. Perhaps as a result of Raeder's doubts about the design, a new proposal now surfaced for a smaller ship of 1,265/1,670 tonnes, 97m long, armed with four single 12.7cm guns; 35 knots; 2,400 nautical miles at 19 knots.

For the moment however, the Type 38B project went ahead, it being decided in April 1939 to order six units (Z31–Z36) from Seebeckwerft at Bremen, for completion between 1 December 1941 and 31 December 1942, with three more, Z37–Z39, being placed with Stettiner Oderwerke. Admiral Schniewind (Chief of Naval Command) was not in favour of the construction of a new type in a yard unfamiliar with destroyer work and pressed for a change in the allocations, despite the fact that Deschimag had agreed closely to supervise their sister yard. Accordingly, the Navy insisted that Deschimag build the first two at Bremen. In fact, when the first orders were placed, on 28 June 1939, six went to Seebeckwerft as their yard numbers 663–668 and three to Stettiner Oderwerke as their yard numbers 822–824. A month later, Oderwerke received two more, Z40 and Z41, on 21 July 1939.

Raeder remained unconvinced about the Type 38B and, on 8 July, ordered an evaluation of the large torpedo boat project in the 1,265/1,670-tonne 95m long design referred to above. This eventually proved more to his satisfaction

Left: A view of a Type 36a (Mob) ship in camouflage lying at Kiel in 1943. (Real Photos)

and was to reach fruition as the Type 39 *Flottentorpedoboote*. In consequence, and also because of the outbreak of war, the contracts for all Type 38B destroyers were cancelled and they were re-instated as Type 36A boats instead, so that the programme for this variant comprised *Z23* to *Z47*.

However, the outbreak of war immediately caused problems with the supply of materials, with the result that in June 1940 *Z35*, *Z36*, *Z40*, *Z41* and *Z42* were stricken from the programme. In October of that year the programme was once again modified, the suspension of *Z40* being lifted and the ship cleared for completion; at the same time, work was allowed to recommence on *Z33*, *Z34* and *Z39*, using salvage materials, and the cancellation of the main machinery orders for *Z35*, *Z36*, *Z41* and *Z42* was rescinded.

By December 1940 the suspensions on *Z35*, *Z36*, *Z41* and *Z42* for hulls and machinery were fully lifted, although on 17 February the following year *Z40–42* were withdrawn from the destroyer programme and re-ordered as 'Spähkreuzers', *SP1–3*. On the same day, the building contracts for the hulls of *Z43–45* were also placed (their machinery had been ordered in October 1940), as were the contracts for the main machinery for *Z46* and *Z47*, although the hull contracts for the last two were not let until 18 October 1941 and in the event the ships were switched to a new design.

The priorities of the U-boat programme, the calling up of shipyard workmen and a shortage of raw materials soon dislocated the plans of the Skl once more. By April 1942 work was at a standstill on *Z35*, *Z36* and *Z43–47*, all of which had, since December 1941, been modified to the Type 36B design in the light of sea experience with *Z23–26*. *Z40–42* (*SP1–3*) were also suspended, as were *SP4–6*, whose main machinery had been ordered in December 1941 but whose hull orders had not been (and never would be) placed. *Z31–34* and *Z37–39* were now to be completed to a slightly modified design known as Type 36A (Mob), which differed slightly in internal layout and whose external appearance was altered through the provision of a large clinker screen on the forward funnel.

The result of all this indecision was that the Type 36A (Mob) class numbered finally only seven units: *Z31–4* and *Z37–39*. In appearance, the two groups could be distinguished by the lower legs of the tripod mast in the first four ships; internally, the later group had only three diesel generators in the generator room, the fourth being in the after engine room. However, by the time construction got under way in 1940, the demands made upon the dockyards and shipbuilders by the chronic machinery problems of the destroyers in service resulted in serious delays: teams of specialists were continually having to be sent to Norway and France to oversee repairs and examine defects so that the home dockyards were embarrassed by a scarcity of technical staff. Thus the first ship, *Z31*, scheduled for completion in December 1941, was delayed until April the following year; all units suffered, in the case

of *Z38* and *Z39* by as much as thirteen or fourteen months. *Z31*, *Z32* and *Z37* completed before the end of 1942, but only the first of these completed without the twin turret.

The ships saw service in Norway and France (*Z32* and *Z37*) as well as the Baltic in the final stages of the war, and only one (*Z32*) was lost in action, although *Z37* had to be abandoned in France following the Allied invasion. Those of the class to serve in Norway saw little action, and the design had little opportunity to prove itself, but the hull suffered from inadequate dimensions and the class could not be considered any improvement over the Type 36A.

HEAVIER FLAK ARMAMENT

The shortcomings of the 15cm gun designs were by now apparent, a stream of critical reports arriving in from the Fleet. This led to the preparation of a modified design, Type 36B, which dispensed with the 15cm gun and reverted to the well-tried 12.7cm weapon. Even so, the 15cm gun must still have had its proponents, for a variation of this design allowed for the two forward 12.7cm mountings to be replaced by two single 15cm guns, despite the fact that this would have produced a mixed-armament ship still with heavy bow weights; it was not, however, pursued.

Technically, the final design differed little from the Type 36A, with the exception that the boiler temperature was 426°C. The hull dimensions were identical, with the armament disposed in single shields, Nos. 2 and 4 guns superfiring as originally was the case with the pre-war vessels. In appearance, therefore, there was little to distinguish them from the latter. The lighter weight forward, combined with the larger Type 36A hull, would no doubt have improved their seakeeping qualities considerably, but by the time the first ship was commissioned, *Z35* in September 1943, the Kriegsmarine's operational theatres had been severely reduced in size, with the result that none of this class ever left Baltic waters. In consequence, their performance in the exacting environments of the Arctic and the Bay of Biscay were never put to the test.

Commissioning late in the war, these ships completed with a heavier flak armament than did their predecessors: in addition to the Vierling already carried aft, two more were worked in on sponsons at upper bridge level, and the 2cm guns on the midships flak platform were twin mountings, making sixteen barrels in all. The reduction in topweight brought about by the lighter main armament enabled mine capacity to be increased to 76.

Five ships were laid down by Deschimag, but only *Z35*, *Z36* and *Z43* were completed, the last as late as May 1944. *Z44* and *Z45*, although ordered on 17 February 1941, were seriously delayed, and it was not until January 1944 that the former was launched. *Z45* was not launched before the end of the war, but her starboard machinery had undergone shore trials on 16 June 1944. On 4 July, however, the

Type 41, profile and plans

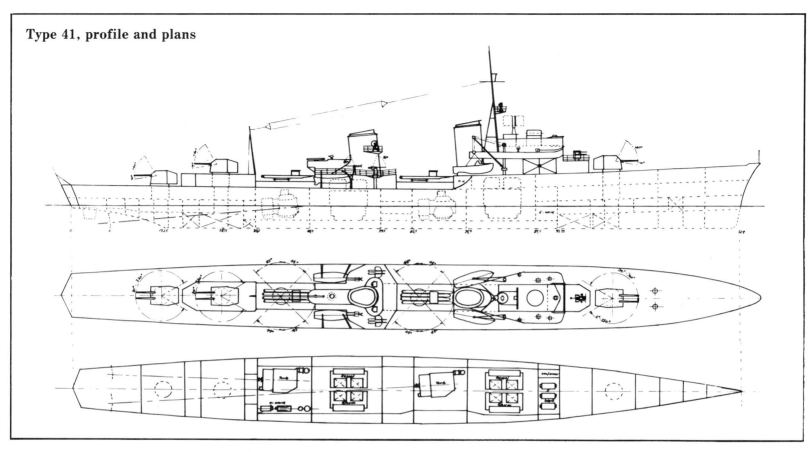

Left: *Z43* off Bornholm in August 1944. This class, Type 36B, reverted to the 12.7cm gun and carried two Vierlinge in the bridge wings. (ourtesy of W. Harnack)

Z46-50 (Type 36C), profile and plans

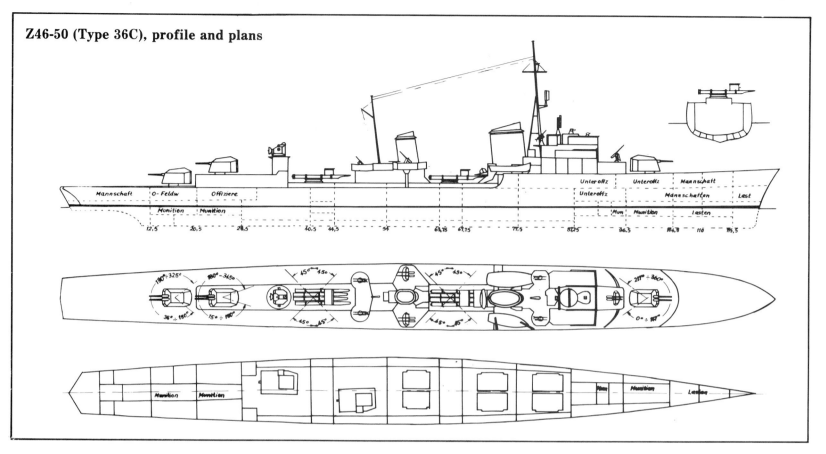

Destroyer Construction Group at Deschimag was forced to inform FdZ that work on both *Z44* and *Z51* was almost at a standstill due to other higher priorities. Three weeks later came the final blow as OKM advised Kreisch that all new destroyer construction was suspended for at least three months. Then, on 29 July 1944, in the course of a heavy air raid on Bremen, *Z44* was hit by bombs and quickly settled on the bottom with only her superstructure above water. Salvage operations were immediately put in hand, but already both she and *Z45* were being cannibalized for spares for *Z39* (which had been damaged a few days earlier) and a completion date could not be fixed. Early in September her stern broke off, and with repair evidently not now a possibility all useful spares and stores were quickly removed from the hull. *Z45* remained incomplete at the end of the war and was scrapped on the slipway. At the time of her sinking, *Z44* was in the final stages of completion, with all machinery installed and may also have had her guns fitted.

As late as 20 February 1945, the salvage of *Z44* was reconsidered despite her having been underwater for more than six months. At this late stage of the war such a proposal was obviously unrealistic and she remained on the bottom.

At the end of 1947 work started on the salvage of the wreck of *Z44*, but progress was limited to the stern section and on 17 March 1948 a contract was awarded to the Hamburg-based Bugsier, Reederie und Bergungs AG by the Weser Port Salvage Authorities for the breaking up of the wreck 'as lies'. The value of the contract was RM 180,000 and was on a basis of 'no success, no pay'. Work began that month and was substantially complete by February 1949.

After fully working-up, all three completed ships served mainly with the 6th Flotilla in the Baltic. *Z35* and *Z36* had relatively short careers, *Z36* having been only ten months in commission when both she and *Z35* were sunk in a German minefield late in 1944. *Z43*, however, was active until a few days before the surrender and was then scuttled after damage. In retrospect, it is probable that had this particular design been utilized instead of the Type 36A, German destroyers, given adequate fuel supplies, would have contributed far more successfully to the Kriegsmarine's war effort than in fact they did.

The Type 36B was the final German destroyer design to reach service. The Design Office, however, continued to finalize sketches for new ships right up to the surrender: some were put into production, but the majority of the later

ones, conceived in the increasingly unreal world of Berlin, could never have been realized given the condition of Germany after 1942. The Type 36 design was further developed as the Type 36C. The basic hull was not greatly altered and the machinery was identical to that of the Type 36A, with boiler temperatures of 400°C. These ships utilized the turbines originally ordered for the Spähkreuzer. The major difference was in the armament, which was to comprise six of the new 12.8cm SK C/41 guns, carried in three LC/41 twin turrets disposed, in common European fashion, one forward and two aft. An enhanced fire control system, radar-controlled for HA/LA use, was fitted aft, but the forward guns on ahead bearings depended on the director sight and rangefinder as in previous classes. The 3.7cm armament was increased to six barrels, all in LM/42 twin mountings, one of which was fitted before the bridge. Further provision was made for four LM/44 2cm twin mountings, although it appears likely that had any of the ships reached service some or all of these would have been replaced by Vierlings or by 3.7cm weapons.

Two ships, *Z46* and *Z47* (originally on order from Deschimag as Type 36Bs), were initially to be built to this design. Production problems associated with the 12.8cm turrets, together with an emphasis on U-boats and other priorities, meant that neither of these vessels were launched, and both were severely damaged by bombing in 1944; construction was abandoned, and the hulls remained on the slips until 1945, when they were blown up by Allied troops.

After the outbreak of war, and following the cancellation of the 'Spähkreuzer' concept, the three vessels (ex-*SP1–3*, ex-*Z40–41*) were redesigned yet again and added to the destroyer programme. The new design, dubbed 'Zerstörer

THE DESTROYER PROGRAMME, 1938–1944	
1938	
8 April	Type 37 design abandoned
23 April	*Z23–30* (Type 36A) ordered
1939	
26 June	*Z31–39* (Type 38A) ordered
19 September	*Z31–40* (Type 36A) ordered; *Z41–47* planned
13 October	*Z41–42* (Type 36A) ordered
1940	
14 June	*Z35–36*, *Z40–42* stricken
5 October	*Z40* reinstated, to be fully completed
	Construction of *Z33–34* and *Z39* to continue, using salvage materials
	Cancellation of main machinery for *Z35–36*, *Z41–42* rescinded
20 December	Hull and machinery suspension on *Z35–36*, *Z41–42* fully lifted
1941	
17 February	*Z40–42* cancelled and re-ordered as 'Spähkreuzer' *SP1–3*
	Z43–45 (Type 36A) ordered
	Z46–47 main turbines ordered on Wumag
16 June	Turbines for *Z48–51* (Type 41) ordered
18 October	Orders placed for *Z46–47* (Type 36A)
1942	
8 April	*Z35–36*, *Z43–45* suspended
5 June	Suspension of *Z35–36*, *Z43–45* rescinded
1944	
14 June	*Z52* and subsequent designs cancelled
November	*Z44–51* suspended

Right: *Z44* from astern, showing *Z45* on the ways above the after deck house. (Archiv Krupp)

Below: Abandoned and forlorn, *Z45* lies rusting on the stocks. (Archiv Bremen)

1941', returned to the destroyer-sized concept, displacing some 2,000 tonnes less than the Spähkreuzer, on dimensions not dissimilar to the Type 36A (Mob) design. Of the Spähkreuzer project, only the machinery arrangement was retained, making the Type 41 unique in that the unit principle was adopted, with boiler rooms and turbine rooms alternating; furthermore, this was to be a four-boiler design. The generating capacity was similar to that of the later Type 36A (Mob) design, but the diesel generator space was moved forward, ahead of the forward boiler room.

Four sub-types of the main design were prepared, 'A' to 'D', all of which adopted the same basic hull dimensions, with 'A' and 'B' at 2,995 tons standard displacement and 'C' and 'D' at 2,805 tons. The designed horsepower was 80,000 ('A' and 'B') or 70,000 ('C' and 'D'), but in general the differences across the four designs were few, being most significant in respect of bunker capacity and hence range: the 'D' sub-type had bunkerage increased by 57 per cent over the 'A' type, with a resultant increase in endurance of some 60 per cent. In appearance, these destroyers would have differed little from their predecessors except that the main armament aft was altered to two LC/38 twin turrets

carrying 12.7cm guns, both commanding the after arcs and with one turret superfiring. The four ships intended to be built to this design were to be designated Z48–51 (turbines were ordered on 16 June 1941), and would probably have been constructed at the Germania yard. It would appear, however, that the design was not favoured by the OKM, who preferred the Type 36C with its obviously superior fire control, new 12.8cm guns and conventional machinery layout. Thus three ships – Z48–50 – were finally allocated to the Type 36C design and ordered from Deschimag (Bremen) on 12 June 1943, but none was laid down. Z51 was redesigned as a prototype for the next class.

DIESEL POWER AND DREAM SHIPS

The next design, Type 42, marked a radical change in destroyer concept for the Kriegsmarine since it was the first of a series to be given diesel propulsion. Diesel power was chosen for its ability to confer longer endurances and also, probably, because diesel fuel was more readily obtainable. The designation covered only one ship, Z51, which was to be used as a test-bed and prototype for the new propulsion system. The hull was similar to, but smaller than, that of

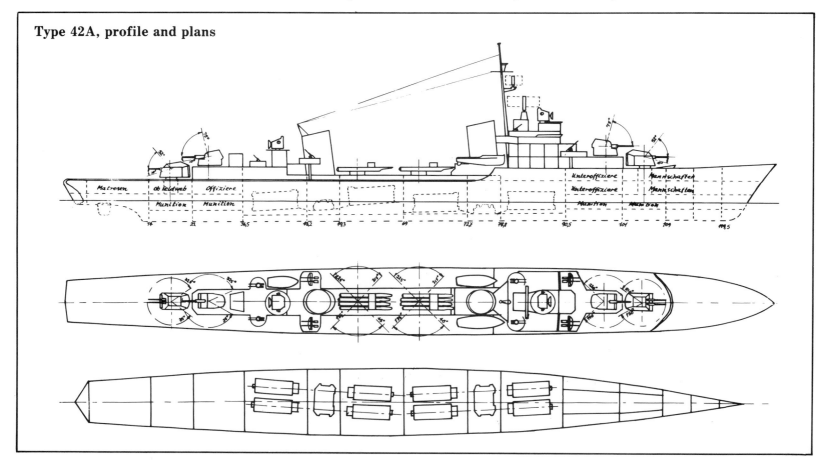

Type 42A, profile and plans

the previous classes, with a displacement of 2,084 tons standard. Originally, the main propulsion was to be six MAN type 12Z32/44, 24-cylinder, two-stroke, 'V'-form diesels, driving three shafts via Vulkan gearing, but in order to complete the ships as quickly as possible it was decided to fit only four diesels (coupled to the centre shaft) and eliminate the wing engines. For similar reasons, the armament was to be a simple outfit only, consisting of the well-tried 12.7cm in four single shields, together with a reduced torpedo armament of six 53.3cm tubes. Z51 was ordered from Deschimag on 25 November 1942 and launched on 2 October 1944; she was sunk during a major air raid on Bremen on 21 March 1945, less than 24 hours after having been moved away from the high-risk fitting-out quay at the Deschimag yard.

Lying abandoned, port side to at the eastern end of the Kohlenhafen alongside the Röchling wharf on the northern side, she was complete only up to the forward and after shelter decks, with no machinery installed and the shaft tunnels welded up watertight, suggesting that her launch had been merely to clear the slip for U-boat construction. During the raid the ship received at least one and possibly two direct hits. One bomb struck in the vicinity of the

bulkhead between compartments X1 and X11, breaking off the fore-ends just abaft No. 2 gun pivot, twisting the severed section and throwing it to port with a pronounced list. In the region of the hit the ship was a tangle of twisted steel work. The rest of the hull lay on even keel but a hit aft had fractured the stern aft of No. 4 gun and the quarterdeck hung down at an angle. Numerous holes, cracks and dents peppered the hull which flooded and settled on the bottom, and a dockside crane fell across the deck above the after motor room.

After the war, on 21 January 1948, the Weser Port Salvage Authorities called for tenders for her breaking up. A number of quotations were received, varying in price from RM 130,000 to RM 200,000 and of four to thirteen months' duration. The contract eventually went to the Deutsches Dampfschiffahrts Hansa, whose final quotation was RM 132,000 and eight months' work, the contract being placed on 17 February 1948.

The Type 42 design was expanded and modified into three sub-types, A, B and C, the first of which, Type 42A, originally proposed a six-diesel, three-shaft arrangement with an armament of four single 12.8cm guns and drew much adverse comment from the various Commands when

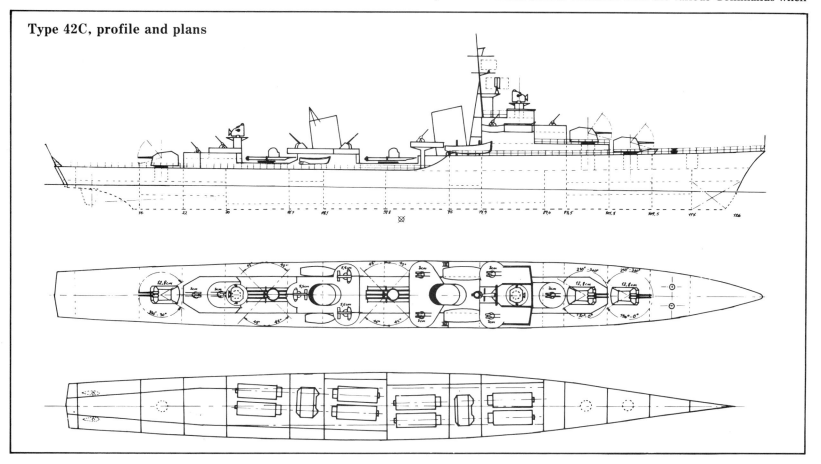

Type 42C, profile and plans

opinions were requested. A new sketch, with one twin turret forward and aft and a single 12.8cm mounting superfiring over each of these, was prepared, but this, too, attracted criticism. By December 1943 the Führer der Zerstörer (FdZ) was demanding the deletion of the single turret forward, in order to keep length down, maintain speed and, presumably, reduce bow weight; further, he requested a minimum elevation of 75° for the single 12.8cm guns. However, at a meeting on 22 January 1944 chaired by Konteradmiral Machens, head of Seekriegsleitung Quartiermeisteramt (Skl QuA) and attended by representatives of all the interested parties, the single and twin layout forward and aft was agreed to by FdZ and Naval Group North when they were informed that the gain in speed for the loss of a gun was only marginal. At this conference details of the new 12.8cm KM/41 gun were given, it being considered the best and most modern quick-firing gun available. It was, however, pointed out that the AA capacity of the design was limited in that none of the main mountings was triaxial (and only the singles biaxial) and, furthermore, that the twin turrets were only capable of 52° elevation (singles 75°). This in turn raised the question of the merits of stabilization for the directors and rangefinders. It was left to the Shipbuilding Commission to work out the figures: if the weight penalty were too great, then stabilization was to be omitted. The problem of flak defence was by now a serious one, and considerable further discussion took place. A decision was taken to replace the LM/44 2cm twin mounts with the new 3cm gun, but in the event of the latter not being available in time the 2cm was to be installed as an interim measure.

Also under development at this time was a new 5.5cm gun for U-boats and other craft, and a proposal to ship this weapon on the Type 42A was discussed at some length. Two main difficulties were apparent. The weight of the new gun, between six and seven tonnes (including directors and sights), meant that four 3.7cm mountings could be replaced by only two 5.5cm, directors being essential in order fully to utilize the greater range offered. The other question concerned the siting of the mountings, there being no obvious place to put them. In the end it was agreed to delete the after single 12.8cm gun and two 2cm twins, to accommodate two 5.5cm, although as it was unlikely that the 5.5cm gun would be ready in time it was planned to ship the 12.8cm on a temporary basis. Another decision taken was the replacing of all the 3.7cm guns by 3cm weapons, to simplify the light flak ammunition supply. All these changes brought forth a request that a new sketch and layout be prepared.

Yet another conference was held on 9 February, at which the question of bow weights and trim was discussed. The Shipbuilding Commission once again attempted to put forward a three-twin-turret design with three 5.5cm guns, a proposal which had been given short shrift at a number of other meetings and was no more successful at this one. Further changes were made, however, including a reversion to the normal torpedo tube disposition, i.e., one set before and abaft the second funnel, and in view of these and earlier modifications the type designation was altered to 42B.

However, over the next few days still further changes were made, and by 14 February the Shipbuilding Commission had won the day with their three-twin-turret design, now designated Type 42C. The layout was completely altered, with two LM/41 twin turrets forward and one aft (controlled by radar equipped directors forward and aft) and the 5.5cm guns now increased to three and regrouped about the after funnel. Hull length was slightly increased, as was displacement, and the main machinery (still eight diesels) moved a little further aft to compensate for the extra turret weight forward. The main propulsion unit was divided into four motor rooms, each with two diesels, each pair of motor rooms being separated by its gearing compartment. The forward unit drove the starboard shaft and the after unit the port. At the same meeting it was confirmed that Z51 would complete with superchargers fitted to her diesels but that Z52 and subsequent vessels would not be so fitted. The reasons for this were four-fold: little experience had as yet been established with these superchargers; setbacks had been experienced in those fitted to U-boats; there would be difficulties in completing them; and, finally, the equipment would unnecessarily complicate the diesel motors.

A class of five ships, Z52–56, was planned, all for construction by Deschimag, but only preliminary assembly work took place, however, and the material was subsequently used elsewhere. This was the last class to receive numbers and also the last on which work was actually started. Nevertheless, design work continued, the next project, Type 43, being once again for a diesel-powered vessel. The diesel concept, whilst it had some distinct advantages, did require a machinery weight some 200 tons in excess of that of the equivalent steam turbine unit developing the same power, and so the Type 43 concentrated on economy of weight in order to redress the balance. Both two- and three-shaft designs were prepared, but the former was preferred for reasons of simplicity. Layout and plans were probably similar to the Type 42C design and the dimensions and tonnage not greatly different, whilst the only major change in the armament was the introduction of quintuple torpedo tubes. This design, like the Type 45, progressed no further than the drawing board, whilst the Type 44 appears to have been merely a modification of the Type 42C, although the latter was still being referred to as such as late as March 1944.

On 1 December 1944, Grossadmiral Dönitz finally rescinded the suspension of new destroyer construction (which had been in force since July) probably as a result of the pressing needs of the eastern front in the Baltic, where the fire power of the fleet was proving useful. Orders were given that work be resumed on Z46 to Z50 as well as on Z51 and Z45 which were well advanced. This was quite

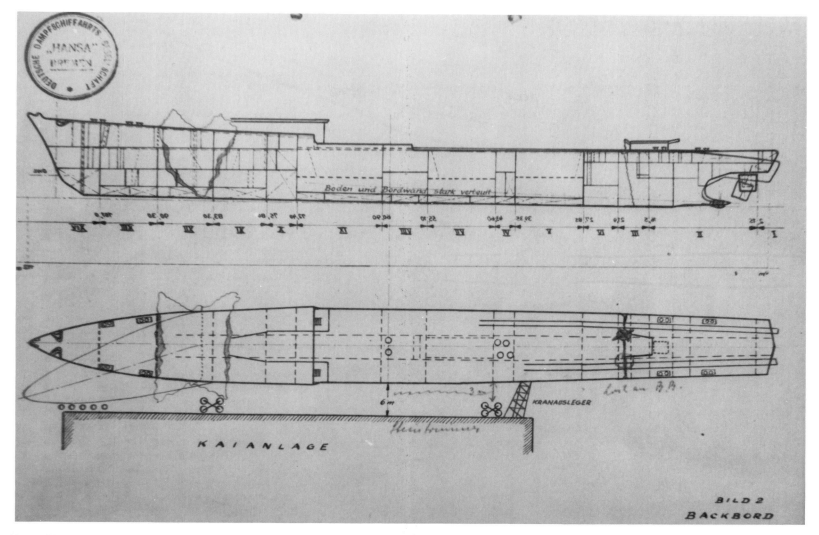

BILD 2
BACKBORD

Above: Diver's sketch of the damaged hull of *Z51* after post-war examination prior to salvage. (Author's Collection)

obviously unrealistic and it is doubtful if any further work was ever done on these ships.

The last design, Type 45, abandoned diesels and reverted to steam turbine propulsion. The machinery was to consist of the well-tried six-boiler, two-shaft geared turbine layout, utilizing Wagner high-pressure boilers and Wagner geared turbines to give a designed horsepower of 80,000 and develop a speed of 40 knots. The hull was similar in dimensions to that of the earlier turbine designs, and standard displacement was 2,657 tonnes. Armament was augmented by the inclusion of an extra twin 12.8cm turret, giving eight guns in all, with four 5.5cm flak and twelve 3cm guns. The usual eight torpedo tubes were shipped, and 100 mines could be carried. For the first time, anti-aircraft rocket launchers were incorporated.

The Type 45 completes the story of German destroyer design and development, for the war was by now lost and no further designs were produced. In fact, there had been little chance of any new projects reaching fruition after late 1942, but this does not appear to have penetrated the corridors of the Skl where designs were initiated for all classes of warship right up to the surrender. Late in 1943, Käpitan zur See (Ing) Heimberg gave a lecture entitled 'Thoughts on the Construction of a High Seas Fleet after the War', in which he outlined the possible future development of German destroyer design. The ships would, he said, act as defence against submarines, light naval forces and aircraft, and particularly against aerial torpedo attack, and might also be used as reconnaissance cruisers. In consequence, they would be at least the same size as existing destroyers but without torpedo tubes and armed with six dual-purpose guns. Maximum speeds would be about 36 knots, i.e., slower than current designs, with a continuous speed of 34 knots. Such ships remained a dream however, and the Kriegsmarine fought the war mainly with the pre-war and Type 36A destroyers.

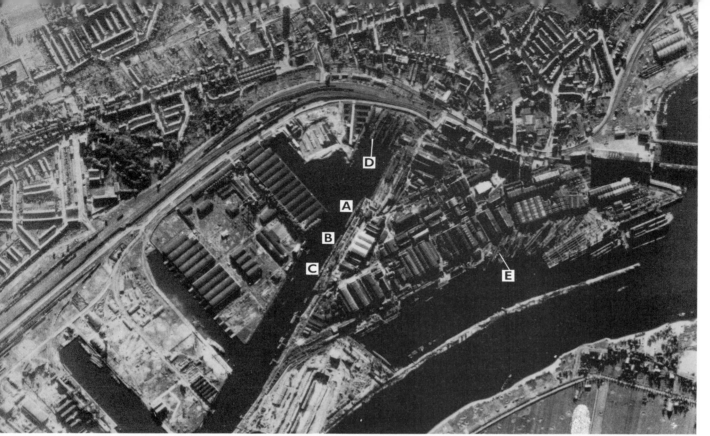

Left: Deschimag shipyard on 28 June 1944, taken from 28,000 feet. At the fitting-out quay are *Z44* (a); *T2* (b); *T7* (c); and on the slip, *Z45* (d). In the yard itself is *Z51* on the slipway (e). (Keele University)

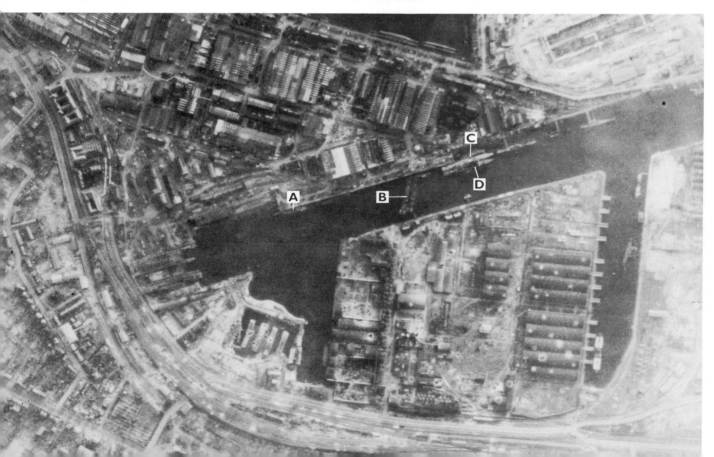

Left: Deschimag shipyard on 7 October 1944. *Z44* lies sunk at (a); two lifting craft are attempting to raise *T7* at (b); *T65* has arrived from Holland (c); and outboard of her is *Z51* (d). (Keele University)

3. TORPEDO BOATS

The torpedo boat featured in the German Navy's order of battle as a specialized warship from the inception of torpedo armament until the end of the Second World War. Its demise in the German Fleet was due solely to the outcome of that conflict and the subsequent dismantling of the Kriegsmarine. By the time a navy was re-established (as the Bundesmarine), the type had become obsolete and does not, therefore, appear today. During the period covered by this volume, the torpedo boat as it existed in the Kriegsmarine was essentially a diminutive of the true fleet destroyer, with the same high speed and similar torpedo armament, but with much reduced gunpower. Its primary tasks were torpedo attack and fast offensive minelaying, but it could also undertake patrol and escort duties. None of the designs to be considered, with the exception of the *Möwe/Wolf* types (and possibly the later Type 40), was primarily intended for fleet duties, nor were the boats often so employed, although in the 1920s and 1930s they were extensively engaged in fleet work with what heavy ships remained to Germany (*Schlesien*, *Schleswig-Holstein* and *Hessen*) after the First World War.* In their black paint, reminiscent of the earlier war, the ships of these two classes were a familiar sight in the North and Baltic Seas during the inter-war period, as the Navy strove to develop new tactics and train a new generation of destroyer officers. They replaced the aged pre-war torpedo boats in this duty, but as soon as sufficient of the new Type 34 destroyers had entered service they reverted to their type role, in which they remained until all were lost.

The torpedo boat arm remained very much a separate entity even after it was taken under the wing of Flag Officer (Destroyers) in 1942. Officers who served in torpedo boats during the war years did not often make the transition from commanding officer of a torpedo boat to captain of a destroyer, although most of the pre-war commanders of torpedo boats graduated to a destroyer command or higher. The torpedo boats were in fact much more actively employed than most of the destroyers (tethered to an inert Fleet), and their crews reached a standard of efficiency which reaped its rewards in several encounters with British forces.

TOO MANY TORPEDOES

The two very similar Type 23 and 24 classes were the first torpedo craft to be constructed in Germany after the First World War and, like the cruiser *Emden*, relied very much on the later designs of that war. The design was, in fact, a slightly modified version of the *H145* class, of which one had joined the Kaiser's fleet just before the Armistice. The Type 23 design, to which six ships were built, displaced about 1,300 tonnes full load and was originally capable of 32–33 knots, the geared turbines developing 23,000shp. All the class were named after birds of prey, names which, with the exception of *Kondor*, were traditional. The armament reflected the boats' ancestry, being disposed in typical First World War fashion with one gun on the forecastle and two aft, all being 1916-pattern 10.5cm Utof (Ubootes–und TorpedobootesFlak) L/45 weapons in single LC/16 mountings. Nos. 1 and 3 guns were fitted with shields, but No. 2 was in an open mounting, possibly to give greater elevation. The torpedo outfit introduced the triple mounting to German torpedo craft but retained the 50cm calibre until the early 1930s when the boats were refitted for the 53.3cm weapon. The armament was completed by a couple of 20mm guns for flak purposes.

The class incorporated a hull with a double bottom, divided into thirteen watertight compartments, and light alloy was used in the superstructure to reduce topweight. The machinery installation showed no advance over First World War designs, being based on a three-boiler steam plant operating at 18.5kg/cm^2, each boiler installed in its own space. The forward boiler was of a smaller size owing to the lines of the ship, whilst an auxiliary machinery space separated No. 1 from No. 2 boiler room. Aft of the boiler rooms were sited the two turbine rooms, the forward one linking to the starboard shaft; the turbines themselves were constructed by Blohm und Voss *(Möwe)*, Vulkan *(Greif* and *Falke)*, Germania *(Seeadler)* and Schichau *(Albatros* and

*That the *Möwe/Wolf* types received the designation 'torpedo boat' was probably due to the restrictions of the Treaty of Versailles, to 1914–18 thinking on the part of the Naval Staff of the Reichsmarine, and to their physical size.

Kondor). The electrical installation consisted of two turbogenerators and one diesel set, developing a total of 75kw. All six ships were built at the Navy Yard at Wilhelmshaven, the first ship, *Möwe*, being launched on 15 July 1926 and commissioning on 1 October the same year. The rest of the class followed in 1927 and 1928, and the last boats, *Falke* and *Kondor*, entered service on 15 July 1928.

While the Type 23s were building, a modified vessel, Type 24, was developed. This closely followed the earlier design, both in visual appearance and in internal layout; the machinery installation, too, differed little, except that one turbodynamo was deleted and replaced by a second diesel set, thereby increasing the generating capacity to 99kW. The hull dimensions were slightly increased, and there was a corresponding rise in displacement to 1,320 tons full load. The main armament, disposed in similar fashion to that of the preceding class, comprised the new 10.5cm SK

C/28 gun in LC/28 mountings, but the weapon was not widely adopted in the German Navy and the consequent shortage of ammunition for it proved an embarrassment to *Jaguar* at the time of the Normandy landings in June 1944.

It was actually proposed to arm this class with 12.7cm guns, to which end a new weapon, the 12.7cm SK C/25, had been developed. Word of the jump in gun calibre for the new vessels reached the ears of the British Ambassador in Berlin who, alarmed at the increase in firepower, pressed the German Government about the matter. British interest was such that Freiherr von Freyberg, the Reichswehrminister for the Navy, finally wrote to the Ambassador in April 1928, informing him that 'technical considerations have shown that it is impracticable to arm the new destroyers with this weapon. The destroyers [sic] will therefore receive 10.5cm guns and the few completed 12.7cm guns will be converted to 10.5cm.' The class once again numbered six units, this time named after wild

Below: Type 24 torpedo boat, *Tiger*, lost just prior to the outbreak of war. (W. Z. Bilddienst)

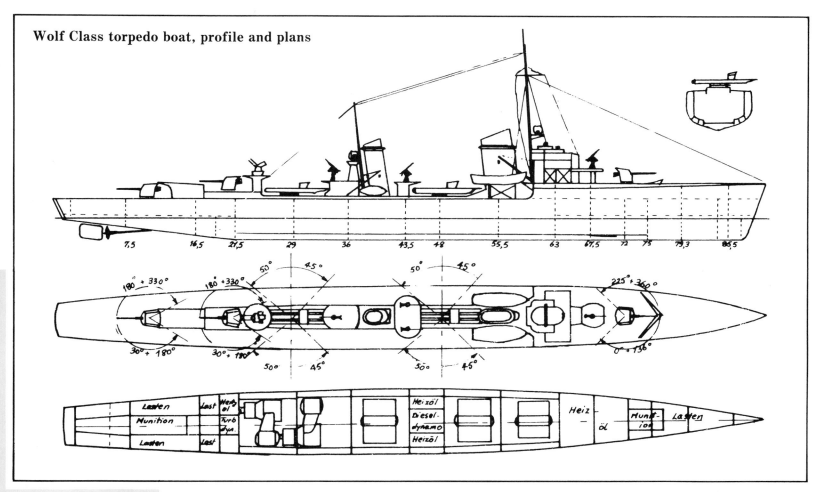

Wolf Class torpedo boat, profile and plans

animals, and was later often referred to as the 'Raubtier' class. All six were again constructed at Wilhelmshaven, and were launched in 1927–8; *Iltis*, the first ship, commissioned on 1 October 1928 and the last, *Jaguar*, on 15 August 1929.

Between the wars the twelve ships formed the 2nd, 3rd and 4th Torpedo Boat Flotillas and gave good service, both in home waters and when they were deployed to waters around Spain during that country's civil war. By the time the Second World War broke out, they were ten to twelve years old and obsolete, although they were robust and, having had all their snags ironed out during peacetime, reliable. In comparison with the next designs to be considered, they had a good all-round armament, despite the fact that they carried too many torpedoes for the role in which they would function. During hostilities they served mainly in the Channel, where they performed well in the cut and thrust of coastal forces warfare, and were actively employed from late 1939 until the last was sunk during the invasion of Europe. The Reichsmarine's planners had no cause to regret their investment.

Some modifications were made after 1939, mainly concerning the armament and the addition of radar. The *Möwe* class ships received a Vierling aft, just forward of No. 2 gun, and three single 2cm guns disposed around the after funnel; two more single guns were fitted in the bridge wings, whilst *Wolf* class ships received a further 2cm gun forward of the bridge. The ships were altered in appearance by the cutting down of the funnels to reduce topweight and by some modifications to the bridge. At the beginning of the war the ships were organized into the 5th and 6th Torpedo Boat Flotillas, but as losses reduced their numbers the 6th Flotilla was disbanded in February 1941 and the survivors allocated to the 5th.

A WASTE OF RESOURCES?

After the last of the *Wolf* class torpedo boats joined the fleet, construction of torpedo craft switched to destroyer-sized vessels and to the much smaller S-boats. Torpedo boat construction as such lapsed for a period of about six years until a new design, the Type 35, was put into

production. This new vessel was much smaller than the Type 34 destroyers then building and, indeed, a little smaller than the previous classes of torpedo boats, and it may have been a development of the 'small torpedo boat' concept exemplified by the 'A' class Flanders boats of the First World War.

The design may have had its genesis in 1934 as a result of a proposal from A IV* that there was a requirement for a small destroyer of less than 1,000 tonnes, armed with two 10.5cm twin flak mountings. This proposal failed to meet with the approval of Raeder on several grounds. First, the gun calibre was inferior to that of all foreign destroyers and, second, the high pedestal necessary for anti-aircraft fire made loading difficult against low-angle targets. Another important objection was that the weight of a 10.5cm twin mounting was some 25 tonnes compared to about 13 tonnes for a single 12.7cm; this would require power training and, for effective HA use, a stabilized director, both of which entailed severe weight penalties. Finally, the complex electrics on such a mounting would be very susceptible to the effects of the weather, causing maintenance problems. Raeder went on to confirm that

*The Development Section.

Germany's likely opponents, Russia, France and Poland, all possessed powerful gun-armed vessels, which was the *raison d'être* of the Type 34 destroyers. Sufficient stress had, therefore, to be placed on gun armament for destroyers to be employed in the Baltic and North Seas, and it was right and proper that this type of ship be continued into 1935. However, there was the possibility of developing a smaller destroyer comparable to the standard British 'A' to 'F' type for ocean employment, discussed in the previous chapter.

The original proposal, for a design of under 1,000 tonnes, was dropped on the grounds that it was nothing more than a fast torpedo carrier, having an inadequate low-angle armament for destroyer duties yet being included in the tonnage allowance for that category by virtue of the fact that it displaced more than 600 tonnes. It was decided, therefore, to develop a true torpedo carrier without a special gun armament. The S-boat was ideal for silent, surprise attacks in coastal waters, but it was not considered suitable for the middle of the North Sea: the new project would therefore combine good sea-going properties with a low silhouette and a good turn of speed for night attacks, to complement the S-boat in more distant theatres – and if such a vessel could be designed without exceeding the 600-

tonne limit it would not consume valuable tonnage which needed to be reserved for true gun-armed destroyers.

In March 1935, the new Construction Office and the Development Office formulated the staff requirements for a 600-ton design:

(a) Highest possible speed, aim for 40kts continuous. 3,000nm @ 20kts.

(b) Good sea-worthiness, high bows, strong hull and frames.

(c) Low silhouette as in S-boats.

(d) Three G7a torpedoes in tubes with simple fire control.

(e) Two single 8.8cm low-angle guns.

(f) If possible, two twin 3.7cm and two MGC/30.

(g) Smoke equipment, depth-charges and bow protection.

To fulfil all these demands on such a small displacement presented an impossible task. The excessive speed requirement necessitated the use of high-pressure steam turbines and the boilers were pressed even harder than those of the Type 34 destroyers, where the output was 2.9 x 10^6K Cal/m^3/hr in contrast with the new design's 3.65 x 10^6K Cal/m^3/hr. This would have serious consequences later. Moreover, the bulk of this machinery crammed into a narrow hull already restricted by wing tanks, made accessibility for maintenance something of a nightmare.

Throughout the year, the requirements were discussed at length, with a suggestion being put forward that the torpedo armament should be doubled by reducing the 3.7cm outfit to one simple single. BdA and BdL were in favour of accepting a reduction in speed to 35/36 knots, to allow the main gun armament to be two 10.5cm but Fleet Command disagreed, stating that for surprise torpedo

attacks, speed was the prime requirement. Other demands included provision for S-Gerät at the expense of the 3.7cm and the motor dinghy. OGG (Otter Geleit Geräte or paravanes) could not be accommodated. Eventually thinking crystallized into the Type 35 torpedo boat, and, in slightly modified form, Type 37, of which a total of twenty-one units were commissioned. The whole concept must, with the benefit of hindsight, be considered a gross waste of resources both in terms of men and materials, for these torpedo boats were rarely employed in their designed role. Wartime experience showed that the S-boat was much more seaworthy than expected and therefore capable of deployment to almost all the anticipated areas of operation of the larger vessel, which itself was never considered the 'expendable' asset it should have been. In consequence, after the loss of *T6* on the first offensive sortie of a torpedo boat in its designed role, there were no further attempts to use it in this manner.

The Type 35 was a handsome, single-funnelled, flush-decked vessel displacing 1,108 tonnes full load on a waterline length of 82.16m. The hull, totalling 310 tonnes and divided into twelve watertight compartments, was gracefully sheered, with a prominent knuckle at the bow. A double bottom extended for 75 per cent of the length, in the cellular construction of which was stowed oil fuel, feedwater and fresh water. As in previous designs, light alloy was employed in the superstructure. Overall, the hull was highly stressed and somewhat weak.

Internally, from aft, the first three compartments on the 'tween deck were given over to accommodation for seamen, CPOs and officers, with stores and magazine spaces on the hold deck below. Immediately forward of frame station 20.5 was the machinery installation, which

Below: *T8* as completed in peacetime colours. (Archiv Gröner)

occupied almost half the ship. As in the contemporary destroyers, the two turbine rooms were adjacent to one another, with the forward room (No. 2) linking to the starboard shaft. Forward of No. 2 turbine room was a smaller compartment, VI, principally the diesel generator space. The two boiler rooms, each housing a pair of boilers, occupied compartments VII and VIII, whilst the forward compartments were once again mainly used for accommodation. On the 'tween deck in compartment IX was situated the torpedo transmitting station, fitted out in a similar manner to that of the destroyers, whilst on the deck below was the gyrocompass room. At upper deck level, the block bridge structure included a roomy W/T office, fitted with two transmitters (40–200m and 500–3,000m) and three receivers (12–20,000m); aft of the W/T office was the galley, whilst to port and starboard were heads and wash places.

The steam plant utilized the same high-pressure concept as did the destroyers. All the ships were fitted with the Wagner 70kg/cm^2, 460°C boiler and suffered in exactly the same way as their larger sisters until the snags could be ironed out. The Wagner geared turbines developed a total of 31,000shp, producing a designed top speed of about 35 knots and a power-to-weight ratio of 11.64kg/hp. The electrical installation consisted of a turbogenerator in each turbine room which, together with two diesel sets, gave a total generating capacity of 224kW at 220V. Normal fuel capacity was 97.8 tonnes, with a maximum of 180.2.

Armament was predominantly the torpedo, six G7a type being carried in two triple banks. The control system was, as usual, comprehensive. On the upper bridge, the main TZA-2 torpedo director, with stabilized optics, was linked to the torpedo transmitting station containing the firing predictor and spread-calculating equipments, and each bank had electrical remote power and a control tub fitted with optical sights. Torpedo transport rails were fitted on the starboard side from the after end of the superstructure to the funnel. In contrast, the gun armament was puny, limited to a single 10.5cm SK C/32 mounting aft, with 50° of elevation. Situated on the quarterdeck, this gun commanded arcs from Red 20° to Green 20° through astern. Only rangefinders were fitted for control purposes, one each on the upper bridge abaft the torpedo director and on the midships deckhouse between the tubes; both were 1.5m base. The remaining gun armament was limited to a single 3.7cm on the after deckhouse, superfiring over the 10.5cm, and two single 2cm C/30 weapons in the bridge wings. As designed, then, these ships were, with the exception of the 2cm guns, completely devoid of forward gunpower.

The other major offensive weapon was the mine, of which 60 EMC type could be carried. For this purpose additional mine rails were embarked, the maximum permissible extra loading being 70 tonnes (excluding the rails), with the proviso that minimum fuel condition not be allowed to fall below 50 per cent. A ship fully loaded with

mines could not use her 10.5cm gun, nor could mining sorties be carried out when sea conditions exceeded State 3.

Twelve Type 35s were constructed, all receiving numbers rather than names: *T1–4*, *T9* and *T10* were ordered from F. Schichau at Elbing in East Prussia, whilst *T5–8*, *T11* and *T12* were ordered from Deschimag's Bremen yard. Contracts were placed in 1935 and 1936, the last three being ordered on 29 June 1936. Construction proceeded slowly owing, no doubt, to the congestion in the yards, and it was not until the close of 1937 that the first vessel went afloat. None of the class was in commission before the outbreak of war, the first to enter service, *T8*, not commissioning until 8 October 1939, under the command of Kapitänleutnant Erdmann.

The Type 37 design was a modification of the earlier torpedo boat, with a slightly shorter and marginally more beamy hull. Internally, arrangements differed only in that the auxiliary machinery space and generator room was eliminated, leaving the forward turbine room adjacent to No. 1 boiler room. The diesel generators were disposed aft, placed immediately abaft No. 1 turbine room and a deck lower than originally – a rather retrograde step from the point of view of damage control since, were the after compartments to flood, all electrical power would be lost if the shock were to stop the turbines. The altered internal arrangements also allowed an increase in bunkerage to 99.7 tonnes normal (199.8 tonnes maximum), giving a consequent increase in radius of action to 1,600 miles at cruising speed. The armament was similar to that of the Type 35, except that 2m base rangefinders were to be fitted, but by the time these ships were completed radar equipment had supplanted the forward pedestal.

Below: *T13* iced up in a severe Baltic winter. Note the large fixed aerials of the Fu Mo 28 radar. (W. Z. Bilddienst)

Torpedo boat (Type 1937), inboard profile and plans

1. BOSUN'S STORE
2. PAINT & TORPEDO STORES
3. SEAMAN'S MESS
4. STORES
5. STORES & WORKSHOPS
6. COOK'S & STEWARD'S MESS
7. SEAMAN'S MESS
8. MAGAZINE & STORES
9. TORPEDO WARHEAD STORE
10. PO'S MESSES
11. TORPEDO T.S.
12. STOKER'S MESS
13. GYRO COMPASS
14. LOG SPACE
15. OFFICERS
16. CPO'S MESS
17. SEAMAN'S MESS
18. WASH-PLACE
19. SIGNAL AMMUNITION
20. WHEELHOUSE
21. CHARTHOUSE
22. MAGAZINE
23. TORPEDO COMPRESSOR

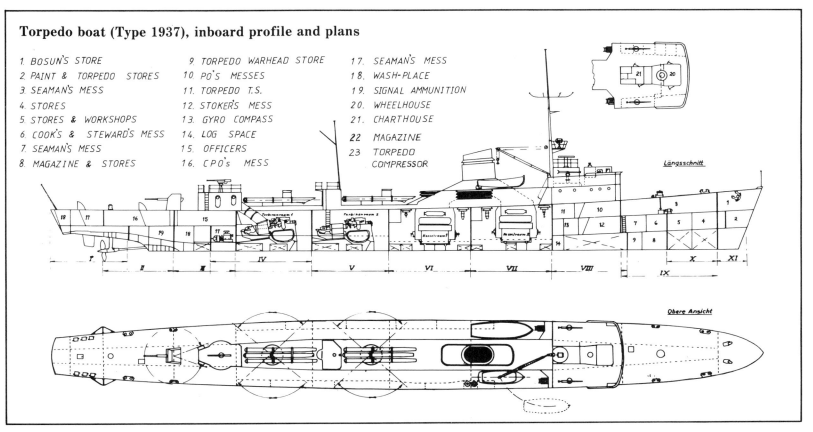

Orders were placed on 18 September 1937 for the first six units (*T13–18*) and on 5 October 1938 for the last three (*T19–21*). All were to be constructed at the Schichau works, which would henceforth be responsible for all torpedo boats with the exception of the Type 40. Once again, work proceeded only slowly, this time because of a shortage of skilled labour brought about by conscription and also because of the chronic problems with the supply of raw materials. *T18–21* were further delayed owing to modifications involving *T13–17* found necessary in the light of sea experience with earlier ships, and not until July 1942 was the last ship, *T21*, commissioned (i.e., after the first ship of the next design).

As these torpedo boats entered service, new flotillas were gradually formed, the 1st and 2nd Flotillas in October 1939 and the 3rd in August 1941, although that month the 1st Flotilla was disbanded and its ships incorporated into the 2nd. However, boiler problems, wetness forward and modifications to the bridge meant that none of the ships saw much active service before June 1940. Subsequent modifications were few, being mainly confined to the addition of radar and the strengthening of the flak outfit.*

*T1 had still not been fitted with radar by February 1945, and was probably never so fitted.

OGG and depth-charge equipment was fitted to the Type 35s at the expense of the 3.7cm gun, which was replaced by a single 2cm in 1939–40 before commissioning in most cases. Later, in 1942, some, including *T4*, *T10* and *T11*, received a 2cm Vierling in lieu of the after tubes and a 2cm single bow-chaser. This was a measure taken for 'Cerberus', the tubes were later replaced. Some units then received a Vierling on the after deck-house, the single being moved to the platform between the tubes, as well as single 2cm guns in the bridge wings. However, because the Type 35 ships were employed mainly on Torpedo School duties from 1943, little more was done until 1944. Not even radar was fitted.

The Type 37 ships were fitted with a 3.7cm bow-chaser and lost the after tubes for a Vierling in 1942 for 'Cerberus'. They also received a fixed aerial pattern radar of limited usefulness. When the tubes were re-shipped, the Vierling was installed on the after deck-house as in the Type 35s. Single 2cm guns were fitted in the bridge wings. The substitution of a Vierling for the tubes brought protests from Skl Quartiermeisteramt, citing the value of torpedoes in the action between units of the 5th Torpedoboat Flotilla and British destroyers on 28/29 March, but Fleet Command rightly pointed out that the boats were more often than not subject to air attacks or by light surface forces such as MTBs. The 3rd Flotilla (Type 37) had the stability reserve to retain both tubes and Vierling but the Type 35s did not. It was to be investigated if lockers for an extra two torpedoes could be accommodated for the forward tubes. Both the Type 35 and Type 37 classes later had twin 2cm guns in the bridge wings, but only the Type 37 ships received a second Vierling.

In total, however, the armament was not greatly increased until the end of 1944. In the autumn of that year, considerable increases in the flak outfits of the destroyers and torpedo boats were proposed and schemes prepared for each class of ship. The intended outfit for Type 35s was to comprise one 3.7cm M/42 twin or 43M single bow-chaser; two 2cm LM/44 twins in the bridge wings; two 2cm LM/44 twins on the charthouse; and one 3.7cm M/43M on all other positions (i.e., on both deckhouses). The Type 37 differed in that a single 3.7cm M/43M was to replace the after bank of torpedo tubes.

This programme, however, never reached completion, and ultimately the most altered units were probably T11, T14, T19 and T20. T19, which was employed in the Skaggerak in 1944–5, landed her bank of torpedo tubes and shipped instead a single 4cm Flak 28 Bofors. Her final flak armament consisted of one 4cm, one 3.7cm and eleven 2cm guns. T20 ended the war with one 3.7cm in the bows and a second amidships, with a Vierling aft and four twin 2cm LM/44 mountings, the latter sited in the bridge wings and abaft the funnel; she was also fitted with twenty-one 8.6cm RAG anti-aircraft rocket launchers. T14 was similarly armed although only three torpedo tubes were retained, whilst T11 had her 4cm Bofors as a bow-chaser, two single 3.7cm (one of which replaced the after tubes) and twelve 2cm in one Vierling and four twins.

The employment of these two classes posed considerable problems for the Naval Staff because they were really only suitable for torpedo attack and the opportunities for that were few. Their gun armament was weak, and although they were deployed into the Channel they could not look after themselves properly in fast-moving coastal forces warfare (for which the older but better-armed *Möwe* and *Wolf* class ships were much more suited). In consequence, they served much of their time in the Baltic on non-operational duties – in fact a good many of them spent long periods decommissioned in reserve. For this to be done in wartime was a clear indication of their limited usefulness. Their only real success was the sinking of the Soviet submarine *S4* by *T3* on 4 January 1945.

FLOTTENTORPEDOBOOTE 39

During September 1939, a series of conferences took place to decide the requirements of a maid-of-all-work design, now that the Type 38B destroyer was not to be proceeded with. Two sketch designs were the subject of discussion, both of similar size to the 'large torpedo boat' referred to in chapter 1, the major differences between the two being the main armament, four (later three) 12.7cm SKC/34 on the one hand or four 10.5cm on the other. The Construction Office pointed out that because of the deck plan and weapons layout, the machinery spaces were larger than required but this would allow the later installation of more powerful machinery. If the engine rooms were reduced, the armament would be correspondingly reduced. A comparison was tabled between the High Seas Fleet *B97* and the new design, to illustrate advances in machinery weights and design. It was pointed out that already increases in armament had reduced speed to 34.8 knots. In general, the interested parties were in favour of the designs, after the cramped machinery spaces of earlier ships no-one objected to this layout and indeed stated that any decrease in gun power was unacceptable. The reduction of speed to 34.8 knots was also accepted but the question of HA or LA main armament did raise concern. The Weapons Office stated that there was no 12.7cm HA mounting available and even if there were, it would not be good for LA use, whilst the Construction Office considered that a 12.7cm outfit for a ship of this size was dubious in any case. If a flak outfit were needed, then the only choice was a 10.5cm weapon. On the other hand, it was felt that this calibre would not allow fulfilment of all the desired tasks – which do not appear to have been fully defined, as the Construction Office requested these to be formulated at a conference on 13 September. By the end of the month these had been laid down:

(a) Main tasks – mine-sweeping, anti-submarine and flak screen for capital ships, Panzerschiffe and cruisers.
(b) Subsidiary tasks – mine-laying, scouting, A/S hunter, convoy escort, picket duty and support of Luftwaffe (*sic*).
(c) Operational area – Baltic and North Sea to Shetland/Norway narrows.
(d) Guns
 – four 10.5cm SKC/32 (4x1)
 – four 3.7cm SKC/30 (2x2)
Torpedoes as Type 37
(e) Machinery
– Two separate units. Good reliability, low pressure steam up to 25kts, robust auxiliaries, 35kts, 2,400 @ 19kts.

The resultant design became the Flottentorpedoboote 39.

MORE GUNS

The Type 39 (*T22–36*) showed a marked increase in size compared to the previous designs and resulted in an altogether more useful warship which gave good service to the Kriegsmarine and later also to the French and Soviet Navies. Visually, the Type 39 was attractive to the eye, its low, flush-decked hull rising with considerable sheer to a curved stem. At the fore-ends, a prominent knuckle gave a good deal of flare, and the overall impression was one of speed.

The hull was 97m long at the waterline (the clipper bow took the overall length to 102.5m) and originally (February 1940) displaced 1,668 tonnes full load. The powerplant was once again the steam turbine, one per shaft supplied from four boilers, each pair in a separate boiler room; here, however, the design differed from other torpedo boats, and indeed from the destroyers, for the 'unit principle' of machinery layout was adopted. This entailed arranging the boiler rooms and turbine rooms alternately (thereby improving damage control) and resulted in a vessel with widely spaced twin funnels. The designed load displacement, with a full complement of mines, was 1,733 tonnes, and for the purposes of calculating hull strength 1,750 tonnes was assumed, with a wave height of L/20 (i.e., one-twentieth of the length). On the 1,415-tonne 'construction displacement' (ship fully equipped with one-third of her fuel, but without reserve feedwater) the maximum designed speed was 34.5 knots at 32,000hp. The power-to-weight ratio was 11.765kg/hp, and oil consumption was calculated as 0.57kg/hp/hr.

By July 1941 some modifications had been made to the design, no doubt in the light of war experience: extra strength had been worked into the hull; the crew had increased from 154 to 166 (it was later increased further); and, most importantly, the maximum oil stowage had been increased from 300 to 393 tonnes. These and other alterations resulted in a full load displacement of 1,776 tonnes, and of 1,841 tonnes with 50 mines. Since the designed horsepower remained the same, the penalty was a quarter of a knot of speed, whilst 4,300hp was now required for the designed 19-knot cruising speed instead of the former 3,940. Radius of action, however, rose to 2,400 nautical miles at 19 knots. The auxiliary machinery consisted of a steam boiler for harbour duties and an electrical installation which included a 160kW turbogenerator set in the forward turbine room and a

Below: *T23* in typical camouflage for the class. There were few distinguishing features between ships of this design, i.e., up to *T29*. (B.f.Z)

separate diesel generator room housing three diesels (two in *T31* and later ships) of 80kW each.

In keeping with its multi-purpose role, the Type 39 design was given a much heavier gun armament than its predecessors. The main armament was four 10.5cm SK C/32 guns in single mountings, disposed one forward, two widely spaced aft and one amidships forward of the after funnel. If there is any criticism of the armament at all, it would concern the midships gun, which commanded only limited arcs to port and starboard. The flak outfit, too, was greatly augmented, four 3.7cm SK C/30 guns in two LC/30 twin mountings being disposed abeam just abaft the after funnel and a Vierling, superfiring over No. 3 gun where it commanded a good sky arc, being fitted.* Fire control was exercised through a 3m base rangefinder and director sight on the bridge linked with a gunnery transmitting station on the platform deck. The lack of a rangefinder aft where three-fourths of the guns were fitted was a weak point.

The torpedo outfit once again consisted of two triple banks of G7a torpedoes controlled by one TZA2 sight in *T22–25* (two in later ships), all with stabilized optics. A separate torpedo TS contained a Zeiss deflection angle calculator, a time switch for ripple salvo firing, and a fully automatic fire control computer. No reserve torpedoes were carried.

The ships were, as usual, fitted for minelaying, although the designed capacity of 60 EMC mines (or an equivalent load of 70 tonnes excluding the rails) could not be carried if sea conditions exceeded State 4 and, in any event, 50 per cent fuel levels had to be maintained for stability purposes. No. 4 gun could not be used whilst the ship was carrying mines. Finally a 'medium' A/S armament, consisting of S-Gerät and four depth-charge throwers, was installed.

In all, the Type 39 torpedo boat was a good design and one to be employed, according to the Naval Staff's recommendation, in areas where air attack was probable; however, it was not to operate against fast surface forces, since it frequently did not make its designed speed, very often being pressed to make 30 knots. As to the Naval Staff's comments about use in areas of likely air attack, although the 10.5cm guns had 70° of elevation they had as yet no real HA control.

Until October 1939 it was planned to build a long series of boats to this design – up to *T60* in fact: *T22-30* were scheduled for construction by Schichau, *T31-48* by Deschimag and *T49-52* by Germaniawerft at Kiel; the builders for *T53-60* had not been decided. The pace of construction was to be such that *T52* was scheduled for completion on 1 April 1942. The outbreak of war wrecked these plans, however, for by 6 October 1939 *T31-60* had been stricken from the programme. *T22-30* were ordered on 10 November, but serious problems arising from labour and material shortages were again experienced, and the

ordering of *T30-36* was delayed until 20 January 1941. By June 1940 the difficulties were such that firm completion dates could only be given for *T22* and *T23*. *T22* did not commission until 28 February 1942, and it was not until eight months later that she reached an operational theatre. Three further units commissioned that year, five more in 1943 and six more in 1944, only six months before the end of hostilities. Some modifications, for example the omission of the knuckle in the bow, were made to the last group, *T31-36*, in order to simplify construction.

Wartime modifications were once again few, for the boats were able to incorporate war experience during their construction. In January/February 1944, units of the 4th Flotilla (*T22*, *T23*, *T24* and *T27*) were fitted with Vierlinge on the bridge sponsons, Naxos (FuMB7) and Wanz G (FuMB8) and a 2m rangefinder in lieu of the searchlight aft. Under the 'Barbara' programme, the flak outfit was to be augmented as follows:

Two LM/44 2cm twin mountings on port and starboard bows
Two 3.7cm M/43 in L/43 single flak mountings in the bridge wings
Two 3.7cm M/42 twin mountings in lieu of after Vierling
Two 3.7cm M/42 twin mountings in lieu of former 3.7cm SK C/30
Two LM/44 2cm twin mountings to port and starboard on the after mine rails

Once again, the situation in Germany at the end of 1944 prevented but a token step towards this outfit: some boats had already received two extra Vierlings in the upper bridge wings, whilst others managed to augment their outfits from local sources. Furthermore, by the beginning of 1945 only *T23*, *T28*, *T33* and *T36* were still afloat. At least one unit, either *T23* or *T28*, received single 4cm or 3.7cm guns in the upper bridge wings and in lieu of the 3.7cm SK C/30 twins abreast the after funnel – four in all – whilst at least one of the other two received further weapons in tubs fitted just forward of the bridge front.

'FLOTTENTORPEDOBOOT 40'

The Type 40 torpedo boat was a rogue from more than one point of view. It was a German design which was to be constructed outside the Reich, and, furthermore, the design itself bore no resemblance to any previous destroyer or torpedo boat of German origin. Its development was prompted by the availability of capacity in foreign shipyards as a result of their occupation by the advancing German armies in 1940.

In Holland, the Rotterdam Droogdok and K. M. de Schelde concerns were constructing three destroyers, *Tjerk Hiddes*, *Gerard Callenburgh* and *Philips van Almonde*, for the Dutch Navy, a fourth, *Isaac Sweers*, having already entered service. The ships still under construction were scuttled by

---

*T22 completed without the Vierling but was retrospectively fitted.

Right: *T28* in 1943. (Archiv Gröner)

Right: *T30* with full mine load. (Archiv Gröner)

Right: *T34* fitted with radar forward and aft. This group, *T30* to *T36*, had no nick in the bow plating. (W. Z. Bilddienst)

the Dutch as their country was overrun by the Germans, although *Gerard Callenburgh* was subsequently raised and completed for the Kriegsmarine as *ZH1* (see Chapter 11). The other two, presumably less advanced (or more thoroughly wrecked), were not proceeded with, but the availability of their turbines led to the Kriegsmarine designing a torpedo boat around them. However, the number of turbines available was only four, plus an unknown (but probably small) quantity of spare sets, altogether only sufficient for three or four ships at most, but the Germans were prepared to place orders for a further eight (later increased to eighteen) sets with the Dutch engineering industry.

The size, visual appearance and armament of the boat itself more closely fitted a destroyer designation than that of a torpedo boat, but, apart from an occasional reference to 'Zerstörer 40' when the design was first mooted, the Kriegsmarine dubbed it 'Flottentorpedoboot 1940'. Externally, the design layout featured a typical destroyer hull, with raised forecastle, a block bridge structure not dissimilar to that of the Type 34 destroyer, and a superimposed armament fore and aft; the hull was in fact only about 4m shorter than the Type 34 destroyer and had the same beam. The full load displacement worked out at 2,632.33 tonnes as of 15 April 1943 (cf. 3,206.5 tonnes for a Type 34 on 7 June 1944), and it was therefore a considerably larger vessel than the Type 39 torpedo boat then under construction at Elbing.

Internally, the layout was unremarkable and the machinery installation, depending as it did on Dutch contractors, did not adopt the high-pressure boiler concept. The three boilers, constructed by Werkspoor, operated at 28kg/cm^2 (380°C) and had a capacity of 70 tonnes/hr. Each occupied a separate boiler room, the uptakes from which were led, by means of conspicuous trunking, to a single large funnel. Abaft the boilers, the two turbine rooms each housed a 24,750hp Parsons geared turbine constructed by Werkspoor with, once again, the forward set powering the starboard shaft. The complete machinery installation weighed 682.53 tonnes (including oil and water), giving a power-to-weight ratio of 13.79kg/hp. Maximum designed speed was 35 knots. One turbogenerator of 160kW built by Stork of Henglo and two Werkspoor 80kW diesel sets made up the electrical installation.

The main armament comprised four 12.7cm SK C/34 guns in single mountings, Nos. 2 and 3 guns being superimposed. Gunnery control included a 3m base rangefinder and director sight on the upper bridge, with a second 4m base rangefinder on the after shelter deck, forward of No. 3 gun. The flak outfit consisted of four 3.7cm SK C/30 in two twin mountings sided abaft the funnel and sixteen 2cm in four Vierlings, two on the upper bridge wings and two amidships between the torpedo tubes. The torpedo armament included eight G7a torpedoes in two quadruple hydraulic power operated sets, each with its own control position. The usual

comprehensive torpedo fire control outfit included director
sights linked to a well-fitted torpedo transmitting station,
but no reserve torpedoes were carried.

Design work proceeded sufficiently quickly for the first
eight units, *T61–68*, to be ordered on 19 November 1940;
orders for four more, *T69–72*, followed on 3 May 1941 and
for a further twelve, *T73–84*, on 27 August 1941. These
last were distributed as follows: Wilton Fijenoord (*T73–75*),
Rotterdam Droogdok (*T76–78*), K. M. de Schelde
(*T79–81*) and Nederlandse Dok (*T82–84*). Despite these
early orders, however, none of the class was destined to see
service. The first six units to complete were to form the 3rd
Destroyer Flotilla, scheduled to form in early 1943.

Construction was delayed and hampered by the Dutch on
the slightest pretext, but it is also probable that the ships
were accorded a low priority since Dutch yards did
complete a large number of fleet minesweepers (60 out of
131 Type 40s) for the Kriegsmarine during the war. By
April 1942, steel and machinery had been assembled or was
in production for the first twelve, but only two had been
laid down and only one of these was completing. The
others were all suspended owing to shortages of brass,
copper and aluminium. Reportedly, eight of the twelve
were laid down by the end of 1942, but by the autumn of
1944 only four were scheduled to complete that year, *T65*
in October, *T61* in November, and *T63* and *T67* in

T37-42 (Type 41) torpedo boats

1 Boatswain's Store
2 Crew Space
3 POs' Mess
4 POs' Mess
5 CPOs' Bathroom
6 CPOs' Mess
7 Officers' Cabin
8 CO's Cabin/Staff Officer
9 CO's Day Cabin/Flotilla
　Commander
10 COs' Sleeping Cabin/
　 Flotilla Commander
11 Officers' Bathroom
12 Wardroom

13 Crew's bathroom
14 Hammock Store
15 Mining Store
16 Pantry
17 Workshop
18 Engineers' Store
19 Drawing Store
20 Auxiliary Boiler Room
21 Torpedo Compressor
　 Room
22 Coding Office
23 Office

24 Paint Locker
25 Cable Locker
26 Hammock Store
27 S Gerat
28 Gunnery TS
29 Fan Room
30 Amplifier Room
31 Gyro Room
32 Torpedo TS
33 Boiler Room
34 Turbine Room

35 Magazine
36 Torpedo Warhead
　 Magazine
37 Transformer Room
38 No 1. Generator Space
39 Refrigerator Machinery
40 Cool Room
41 Provision Room
42 Magazine
43 Torpedo Store
44 Dry Stores

45 Canteen Stores
46 Transformer Room/Store
47 Log Space
48 Engineers' & Electrical
　 Store
49 Electrical Store
50 Officers' Store
51 Ordnance Artificers'
　 Store

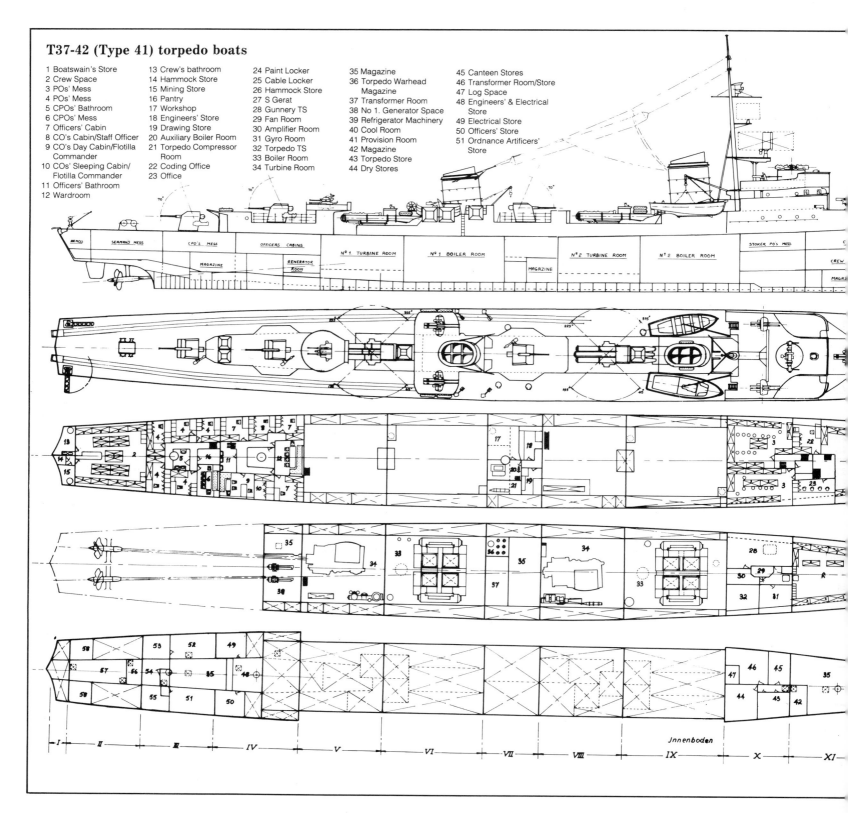

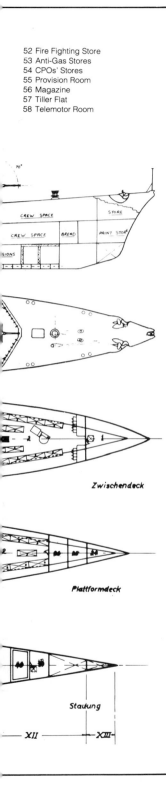

52 Fire Fighting Store
53 Anti-Gas Stores
54 CPOs' Stores
55 Provision Room
56 Magazine
57 Tiller Flat
58 Telemotor Room

Zwischendeck

Plattformdeck

Stauung

December. The remainder were due to complete in 1945 (*T62*, *T64*, *T66* and *T70*) and 1946 (*T68*, *T69*, *T71* and *T72*), *T73-84* not being proceeded with.

In fact, only *T61*, *T63*, *T65* and *T66* are known to have been launched (although *T67* must also have gone afloat if she was to complete by December 1944), but by the time this happened the Allies had landed in France and the position of German forces in Holland was obviously difficult to assess. Accordingly, it was decided to complete the three most advanced units in Germany, and arrangements were made to tow the hulls home. Two, *T63* and *T65*, were successfully brought in, but the third, *T61*, was caught on passage and sunk by Beaufighters of No. 143 Squadron RAF off the West Friesian Islands.★

T63 and *T65* were towed to Elbing for completion by Schichau but, once again, their construction was interrupted, this time by the advancing Soviet Army. On 21 January 1945 a number of incomplete or unserviceable hulls, including those of *T63* and *T65*, were prepared for towing out, and on the following day *T65* was taken via Pillau to Danzig, *T63* following shortly after. Both ships were ordered to be completed at Deschimag (Bremen) and were included in the emergency construction programme, but it was all to no avail, for despite the fact that the pair reached Wesermünde no further work was done. Both were captured on the surrender of Germany and scuttled in the entrance to the Skaggerak, *T63* going down on 31 December 1946, *T65* on 2 July 1946.

UPRATED TURBINES

Mention has already been made of the original intention to continue the Type 39 design into a long series and that the outbreak of war curtailed that ambitious programme. Thus it was not until late 1942 that any further expansion of the torpedo boat programme (in home yards) was put into effect. Design work had naturally continued in the interim, with the result that a modification of the Type 39 design emerged as the Type 41. In effect, this was a slight expansion of the earlier design, having a waterline length of 102m (i.e., an increase of 5m) and a designed full load displacement of 2,190 tonnes. Externally, the design differed little from the *T22* series except that the extra length enabled an additional deckhouse to be worked in between the bridge and No. 1 gun, allowing another 3.7cm SK C/30 twin mounting to be shipped.

The major difference in this design, however, was that the turbines were rated at 40,000hp to give a designed top speed of 34 knots. The Naval Staff were expecting 31 knots in view of the failings of the Type 39, and saw this class as an improvement over the Type 39 design in the same way as the Type 36 destroyer was superior to the Type 34.

★The fate of *T66* remains a mystery. Official Dutch sources give her launch date as 29 July 1944 but no record of her loss, or of her reaching Germany has been found.

Gunnery fire control continued to be entrusted to the 3m base rangefinder forward, together with a director sight on the upper bridge, but there were several differences in the torpedo department as compared with the Type 39, for whilst two TZA-2 directors were fitted, they were not stabilized. It was intended, however, retrospectively to fit a stabilized periscopic sight with a clear-view screen as this became available. The torpedo TS, too, was simplified in that it lacked automatic fire control, although it was intended to fit a semi-automatic outfit later. Finally, the triple torpedo tube banks were hydraulic powered and not electrical.

It was initially intended to build six units to this design, and the turbines were ordered from Schichau in August 1941. The ships themselves were not in fact contracted for until 25 November 1942, as Yard Nos. 1538–1543. In mid-1944 it was expected that the first unit, *T37*, would complete on 30 December 1944 and the last, *T42*, on 17 July 1945, the intervening ships being finished at 4–6 week intervals. By the autumn of the same year, completion had slipped back by 2 or 3 months, with *T37* not now expected to complete until February 1945. East Prussia, where Schichau's works were located, was by now threatened with invasion by the Soviet Army, and all work ceased there on 22 January owing to the failure of power supplies, a shortage of workers and the general situation. *T37*, *T38* and *T39*, the only units approaching completion, were towed out from Elbing at the end of January, whilst *T40*, towed out later, ran aground at Brössen on 12 March. Salvage was put in hand but it is unlikely that she was brought off. Of the other three, *T38* was fitted with only one gearbox and, lacking boilers and turbines, could not be completed, so that only *T37* was finally included in the emergency programme by OKM on 9 March. *T39* was never completed either, and all the boats were scuttled by the Allies in 1946.

On 12 June 1943, some six months after the first series of boats, orders were placed for six more ships, *T43–48*, four more, *T49–51*, following on 11 January 1944; respective yard numbers were 1636–1641 and 1717–1719. This second series differed only in detail from the earlier units, most importantly in the provision of a high-angle fire control director, the Flakleitgerät M/42, for the main armament, which, once again, was to be four single 10.5cm SK C/32 guns (although owing to supply problems an interim outfit of 10.5cm SK C/30 weapons was to be shipped). The heavy flak outfit was altered to include the new 3.7cm Flak M/42, but the number of guns remained the same. None of these ships was very far advanced and in all probability few, if any, had been laid down by the war's end.

CONFLICTING VIEWS

After the Type 41 ships had been put into production, the path of torpedo boat design became rather confused, and it should be noted that none of the subsequent boats ever approached completion. At a conference in Berlin at the end of October 1942, OKM and various staff departments discussed a new design, designated 'Torpedoboot 42'. Surprisingly, no representatives from FdZ Flag Officer (Destroyers) nor from the operational commands of the Fleet were present.

When details did filter through to the destroyer arm, the sketch design was not to the liking of Konteradmiral Bey, for it appeared that the ship was to be of destroyer size, about 2,500 tonnes (i.e., comparable to the Type 34 destroyer), and, furthermore, motor-driven. It had apparently been decided that the high-pressure steam concept would be discontinued and that henceforth all destroyers and torpedo boats were to have diesels installed. The adverse comments of Bey can be summarized as follows:

1. Insufficient speed
2. One gun less than the Type 34 destroyer
3. Two torpedoes fewer than the Type 34 destroyer
4. A radius of action (6,000m) too low for a diesel design

Argument dragged on, and by May 1943 the design was being referred to as 'Flottentorpedoboot 42'; moreover, another design ('Flottentorpedoboot 43') had been introduced, giving parallel lines of development. The latter was referred to as an 'oversized torpedoboat' of 1,600 tonnes. At yet another conference in Berlin, on 1 May 1943, attended this time by representatives from Skl, from FdZ and from Admiral Dönitz, the new designs were further discussed. The outcome of this meeting was inconclusive, for talks were broken off on the grounds that the technical evidence and the demands from the Fleet at sea did not then justify a changeover to diesel propulsion. After this, Flottentorpedoboot 42 and 43 disappear from the records, although the former, in view of its size, may possibly have become the basis for the development of 'Zerstörer 42'.

By the end of 1943 the continuance of the torpedo boat programme had resolved itself into a modification of the Type 41 design, known as the Type 41A. Argument still continued, however, over the precise form of the design, for Flag Officer (Destroyers) set speed, seaworthiness and range as the three most important priorities, whilst Skl was insisting that operational experience had shown that gunpower was the overriding consideration. At a series of meetings in November and December 1943 attempts were made to thrash out the conflicting views. The Skl sketch design, with six 10.5cm KM/44 guns in three twin turrets, involved an increase of 61.7 tonnes, taken up as follows:

Crew 4.4 tonnes
Other 1.2 tonnes
Hull 12 tonnes
Guns 42 tonnes
Auxiliary machinery 2 tonnes

The problem was whether this increase in weight should be compensated by an equivalent reduction in bunkerage or by weight-saving in construction. As it was, the Skl design involved a speed penalty of half a knot.

Bey, however, was working in a different direction. He wanted a ship of about the same displacement as the Type 39 torpedo boat and incorporating the new 'Illies' machinery of 52,000hp which he reported as being 90 per cent complete at Schichau; this increased horsepower was to be achieved with no weight or space penalty. As we have already seen, he placed much importance on speed (preferably 38–39 knots) – a view which would shortly be reinforced by events in the Bay of Biscay. As to armament, a twin turret forward and one aft met his requirements.

TORPEDO BOATS

The conference turned down Konteradmiral Bey's proposals, mainly on the grounds that to switch to the 52,000hp machinery would disrupt the 40,000hp programme, that the availability of men and materials was uncertain, and that there was an inherent risk in the use of untried machinery, and the final decision was that the 42,000hp machinery and three 10.5cm twin turrets would be incorporated. The design was to be put into production, starting with T52.

A year later, in January 1944, discussions were again in progress, but still no orders were imminent. At yet another conference, on the 22nd, things had advanced as far as the preparation of comparative sketches showing both the old 40,000hp outfit and the new 52,000hp 'Illies' machinery, but the destroyer arm's request for the omission of one twin turret in order to gain speed was once again dismissed. Korvettenkapitän Koppenhagen then caused some confusion by announcing that in the course of discussions with the directors of Schichau he had been informed that the shipyard had developed a new design for a small torpedo boat with only four guns, a range as in the Type 39 and a guaranteed speed of 38 knots – suspiciously similar to the demands emanating from Flag Officer (Destroyers) a year previously. Admiral Machens, the chairman, then requested the representatives of Skl and the operational commands to make their precise requirements clear. These were formulated as follows:

1. A maximum speed of 38 knots at 75 per cent full load
2. One twin 10.5cm forward and two singles aft (only if space were a problem was a twin to be shipped aft)
3. Six 3cm twin flak mounts
4. Gunnery control radar forward, with tactical radar aft
5. A gun director forward
6. No mast
7. Four depth-charge throwers
8. Paravane gear

Furthermore, design and construction were to be simplified as much as possible.

On 9 February a follow-up conference was held to continue the discussions. This witnessed the observation

that 36 knots could be achieved on 40,000hp in a small hull, but 38 knots only in a light, weak hull, the dangers of which were obvious; the new 52,000hp machinery could not be installed in the Type 41A. Design work was to continue, to investigate the possibility of installing the 'Illies' equipment in a modified hull of better strength, accepting the sacrifice of ¼–½ knot of speed. Once again, no firm decision had been arrived at, but the Type 41A was superseded very shortly afterwards by the smaller design referred to by Korvettenkapitän Koppenhagen. Flag Officer (Destroyers) appears finally to have got his way!

THE LAST DESIGN

After the long and finally fruitless gestation period of the previous design, a development of it, the Type 44 (T52–57), was put in hand in a relatively short space of time. The new 'Illies' machinery of 52,000hp was to be incorporated, giving these advantages:
1. All auxiliary machinery (simple three-phase motors) electrically driven and therefore independent of steam propulsion
2. Greater efficiency of steam propulsion, particularly at lower speeds (e.g., 19kg/cm at 25 knots)
3. Simplified overhaul of auxiliaries
The ship itself reverted broadly to the dimensions of the Type 39 design, but had a double bottom only between the centre keel and the first longitudinal. No 'Wellgang' was incorporated as the increased power of the engines required larger machinery spaces. Hull stress calculations used the same asumptions as for the Type 35/37 design. Originally, two sketches were prepared, 'A' and 'B', which differed only in that 'A' was 2m longer (and very slightly beamier), and had an extra pair of 3cm guns and ¼-knot less speed. The disposition of the 'A' armament was one twin 10.5cm forward and two singles aft, whilst 'B' incorporated a twin forward and aft.

On a designed full load displacement of 1,821 tonnes, the ship carried four 10.5cm SK C/32 guns, eight 3cm Flak 44 and six torpedoes at 37.25–37.5 knots. The heavy flak outfit was a good step forward, and the 10.5cm guns were also fully high-angle weapons, whilst a flak director was provided on the upper bridge.

At a 28 March 1944 conference involving Skl and representatives of the Fleet and of the construction departments, the final details were decided, with the result that Grossadmiral Dönitz ordered that 'the Type 44 shall be constructed according to the sketch design discussed and all interested parties shall strive for quick completion'. Orders for six units were placed with Schichau on the same day (Yard numbers 3720 to 1725), for completion between 15 September 1946 (T52) and 1 May 1947 (T57). Not surprisingly, at this stage of the war, none of the ships was laid down, and this type remained the last design to be seriously proposed and put into production.

Above: *T63* lying incomplete at Wesermünde in 1945. (National Archives)

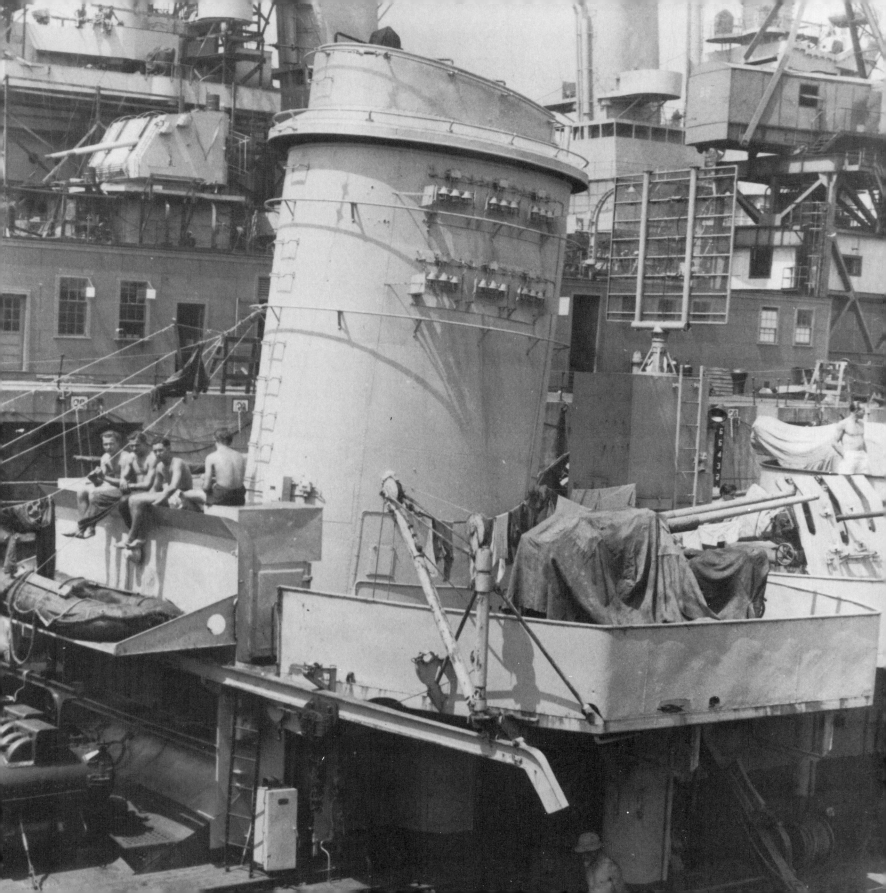

4. ARMAMENT

The Types 34, 34A and 36 destroyers were identically armed and equipped to engage air, surface and sub-surface targets, although their main role was offensive surface action, using the gun and torpedo. German tactical thinking preferred the latter, and with the exception of the battles at Narvik, most destroyer successes were achieved using either the torpedo or the mine. It was the intention of the Kriegsmarine to offset British and French quantity with German quality, and for this reason the armament of the new ships was very carefully planned. Contemporary British destroyers were, without exception, armed with the standard 4.7in (12cm) gun, whilst their French counterparts shipped 13cm (5.1in) guns and the larger 'contre-torpilleurs' a 13.8cm (5.5in) gun.

In the closing years of the First World War, the Kaisermarine had introduced to their destroyers a gun of extremely heavy calibre, the 15cm (5.9in) weapon, but the ships so equipped, *S113* and *V116*, were not considered a success since the weight of their guns made them poor seaboats. It was probably with this experience in mind that the 15cm calibre was not chosen for the new designs; on the other hand, the existing torpedo boat gun, the 10.5cm (4.1in), was far too light. It was decided, therefore, to adopt a new calibre, 12.7cm (5in), which would enable the ships to out-gun British vessels in terms of both size and, since five were to be shipped, numbers, and give them a one-gun advantage over the current 13cm-armed French destroyers.

The new gun was designed in 1930, and production was entrusted to Rheinmetall-Borsig of Düsseldorf. Manufacture went ahead rapidly, so that by 1932 it was possible to send six of these guns to sea for proving trials aboard the Type 24 torpedo boats *Leopard* and *Luchs*. Installed in the same positions as the original three 10.5cm weapons carried by this class, they provided a great deal of valuable data, and a fully developed version was available in 1934 for installation aboard the new destroyers.

The new gun was designated 12.7cm SK C/34 and was actually 128mm in calibre, with a length of 45 calibres. The breech mechanism was of the vertical sliding wedge pattern and the gun fired a 28kg shell using a cased, separately rammed 16kg cordite charge; HE shells were nose-fuzed,

either instantaneous or timed. With a designed muzzle velocity of 830m/sec, a maximum range of 17,400m (11 miles) was obtained.

The gun was carried on a C/34 centre-pivot mounting fitted with an open splinter shield of 8mm Wsh armour plate to protect its crew of ten. Two large sighting ports were cut into the front of the shield for the layer and trainer numbers. Power was provided for laying and training but loading and ramming was done by hand. In theory, the designed rate of fire was 18–20 rounds per minute, but in practice a good crew could achieve only 15–18, although at this rate, with only 120rpg in the magazines, there was only sufficient ammunition for about seven minutes of continuous firing.* Under action conditions, however, the rate of fire probably fell a great deal short of that obtained in practice, especially in the Arctic, where ice, heavy seas and poor visibility often combined to hamper proficiency. Nevertheless, on a number of occasions these destroyers shot off over two-thirds of their outfit in the course of quite short engagements.

The 12.7cm gun was basically a low-angle weapon, having a maximum elevation of only 30°, but it was occasionally used for long-range barrage fire employing specially fuzed shells. Five mountings, each weighing 10,220kg, were shipped in Nos. 1, 2, 3, 4 and 5 positions, 2 and 4 superfiring over 1 and 5 respectively. Four main magazine spaces served the guns, two forward and two aft: Nos. 1 and 2 guns were served by Nos. 1 and 2 magazines, via electric ammunition hoists to the handling rooms below the forward shelter deck and on No. 2 gun deck; Nos. 3 and 4 guns, on the after shelter deck, were both served by No. 3 magazine via hoists into the cook's and stewards' mess on the gun deck; and No. 5 gun was served by No. 4 magazine through a handling room in the lobby at the after end of the after shelter deck. Main and auxiliary hoists were provided in each position. In the magazines, which were not vented, shells and charges were stowed in bins formed

---

*This meagre supply is interesting in the light of British Admiralty estimates that the usual 200rpg supplied for 4.7in (12cm) guns was sufficient for about 35 minutes' action, and even this was increased to 250rpg in later British designs.

by portable wooden planks shipped in vertical steel girders. As a protective measure, all fans were switched off in action and flaps and valves closed, although the offficer of quarters could direct the damage control party to open the ventilation system during long actions if he considered it necessary.

SERIOUS DIFFICULTIES

Following the completion of twenty-two ships to the 12.7cm-gun design, a major (and fateful) decision was made to increase the gun calibre of the succeeding class, Type 36A, to 15cm. Guns of this size had been tried briefly at the close of the First World War, and a new weapon, designated 15cm TBK C/36 (another Rheinmetall-Borsig design), was put into production in the late 1930s,

prototypes being tested at sea by *Heinemann* prior to the outbreak of the Second World War. No trials in heavy weather were carried out, or at high speeds or firing more than two of the five guns at once! Carried initially in single centre-pivot mountings with open shields (LC/36), four of these guns were installed aboard Type 36A destroyers when first commissioned. One mounting forward of the bridge was shipped on a low bandstand, where the twin turret would be installed once production difficulties had been overcome. This gun fired a shell weighing 45kg – twice the weight of the 12.7cm projectile – but was still hand-loaded. The charge was, like that of the 12.7cm, brass-cased and weighed 23.5kg, whilst the end of the cartridge was domed and covered in brass foil to prevent damage during ramming. In its single, shielded form the weapon weighed 16,100kg, i.e., some 6 tonnes more than

Below: A Type 34 ship in a French port, probably Brest in 1940; few changes appear to have been made, except for the depth-charges. (Author's Collection)

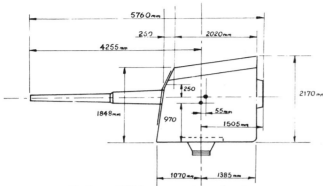

12.7cm C/34 on centre pivot mounting C/34

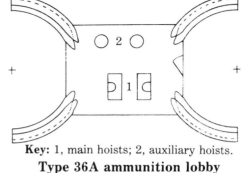

Key: 1, main hoists; 2, auxiliary hoists.

Type 36A ammunition lobby serving Nos. 2 and 3 guns

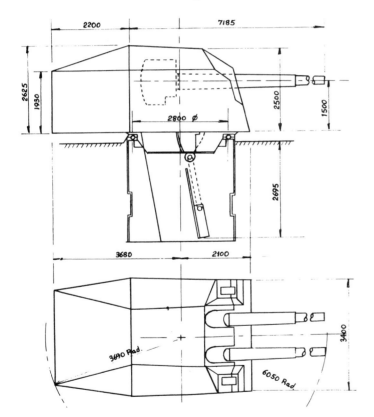

General arrangement and dimensions of a twin 15cm LC/38

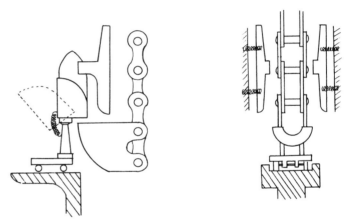

Type 36A ammunition hoists

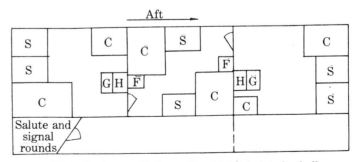

Key: C, charge, F, fuse; G, grid; H, hoist; S, shell.

Type 36A magazine layout

the gun carried by the earlier destroyers, so that when *Z23* first commissioned with the temporary single gun in No. 1 position she was carrying an extra 13 tonnes of topweight arising purely from the increase in calibre, plus an additional 7 tonnes accounted for by the heavier shells and charges, although, admittedly, these were carried much lower down in the ship.

Notwithstanding its problems, the 15cm gun greatly increased the destroyers' hitting power and its range was about 30 per cent greater than that of the 12.7cm weapon. In the single LC/36 mount, it was capable of 30° elevation and 10° depression and was not, therefore, a dual-purpose weapon, although it could be, and was, used for long-range barrage fire. Unfortunately, the larger shell, in the absence of power loading, caused a reduction in the rate of fire and required almost superhuman efforts on the part of the gun crew loading numbers, even under ideal conditions; the effect on the rate of fire under rough sea and Arctic icing conditions can be imagined.

The rate of fire in good conditions cannot in any case have exceeded the speed of the ammunition hoists. Each gun was served by one main and one auxiliary hoist, the main hoists being of the paternoster chain pattern and capable of handling seven or eight separate rounds per minute. Each lifting head could take a shell or a charge, which was placed base first on to a sliding/tilting bucket and then pushed into the hoist, at the same time coming to the vertical position. Here it was picked up by a working head which came up through a slot in the base of the bucket. At the top, the round arrived on a pawl, the nose was pulled out by hand and the projectile or cartridge slid out on to a rubber pad. The hoists delivered into handling lobbies adjacent to each gun, each lobby having double ports or hand-throughs in the port and starboard corners through which the shells and cartridges were pushed out on to semi-circular trays, which extended round the gun as far as Red and Green 90°. The bottom hand-through was for shells and the top for charges, and both had spring-loaded flaps on the outside. In the case of the 15cm twin turret, the revolving structure ended on the second deck above the magazine, so two dredger hoists lifted the ammunition into the gun bay, entering over starwheels to prevent crooked feed. For each single mounting, ten shells and charges were stowed ready for use in the lobby, with the same number in the twin turret. Charges were packed individually in light aluminium alloy cases and stowed in open boxes formed from pressed, galvanized steel sheets.

Despite the pre-war trials, the production 15cm gun installed in the destroyers was beset with numerous problems, some of which were never solved before the end of the war. However, much more serious difficulties arose with the introduction of the twin turret, designed for installation forward of the bridge in No. 1 position and thereby effecting a saving in weight over the provision of two single superfiring 15cm weapons. Unfortunately the reverse proved to be the case. The major drawbacks of this

mounting did not become apparent until early 1942, production problems delaying its appearance considerably and requiring most of the Type 36A ships to commission without it. The turret, designated 'lightweight' C/38, turned out at 60.4 tonnes (almost twice the weight of two single guns) and had a disastrous effect on the already poor seakeeping properties of German destroyers. Serving destroyer officers were most disturbed, and many were quite scathing as to its 'benefits' – in particular over its 'lightweight' designation. In fact it *was* a lightweight turret, for the 15cm twins previously installed in the battlecruisers and battleships were considerably heavier: for example, the 15cm LC/34 twin turrets aboard *Scharnhorst* weighed 120 tonnes, while the same mounting for *Bismarck* weighed between 108 and 116.25 tonnes, depending on trunk height and rangefinder type. The weight-saving was achieved mainly through a great reduction in armour thickness; capital-ship turrets carried armour thicknesses of 100–140mm on the fronts and 60mm on the sides.

The LC/38 turret was a massive, roomy, upper-deck type gunhouse with electric power for training and hydraulic power for elevation. Remote Power Control (RPC) was not fitted. The guns, which were in the same sleeve and thus had no individual elevation facility, incorporated electromagnetic firing and a conventional horizontal sliding wedge breech; hand-ramming was employed but no loading tray was fitted. The turret layer and trainer followed pointers, as in the Royal Navy, and had separate positions for use in quarters firing, for which range and deflection receivers were provided, although there was no fuze-setting clock. Below the turret was the handling room, the shells and charges arriving at the rear (the standing part), then to be transferred by hand to the second hoist in the turret trunk.

Despite the criticisms from the Fleet, the idea of a twin turret made good sense and it was unfortunate that the ships' hulls were not entirely suitable for its installation. It was, for example, a great advantage to have the guns' crews protected from the weather, especially in view of the extreme northerly deployment of most of these destroyers. Furthermore, the twin turret offered greatly increased elevation (65°) as compared to the single mount and thus was much more suitable for use as a dual-purpose weapon; however, its capabilities in this direction were hampered by the absence of any sophisticated high-angle control equipment and its poor rate of fire.

The problems associated with the 15cm gun were such that, after the completion of fifteen vessels armed with this weapon, staff design requirements were changed, with the result that the Type 36B destroyers reverted once more to the 12.7cm SK C/34 gun in the single mounting. This was purely an interim design, however, for the eventual aim was to produce a destroyer with a fully dual-purpose armament. To this end, a new gun, the 12.8cm SK C/41, to be carried in twin Drh LC/41 mountings, was developed, but no destroyer ever commissioned with it.

Above: Gun director on *Z39*.
(USN Historical Center)

THE PRINCIPAL WEAPON

In common with all German warships of the period, and in contrast with many foreign designs, the destroyers received considerable attention in respect of their flak armament. The main outfit consisted of a pair of twin 3.7cm mountings abreast the after funnel and sponsoned out over the upper deck, where they commanded good arcs of fire. The weapon installed on completion was the 3.7cm SK C/30 in the L/30 twin mounting. Of Rheinmetall design, it had a monoblock barrel with a drawn-on breech ring and a vertical sliding block breech mechanism. It was semi-automatic, using fixed ammunition (HE or tracer) in eight-round clips, and had a muzzle velocity of 1,000m/sec, the shell weighing 0.745kg and the complete round 2.1kg. A cyclical rate of fire of 160 rounds per minute was claimed, but the effective rate was only half this. The gun had a vertical range of 6,800m and in its C/30 mounting could be elevated to 85° and depressed 9°. The complete mounting weighed 3,670kg, and 8,000 rounds were carried, stowed in Nos. 7 and 8 magazines. A feature in advance of its time was the gyro-stabilization of the gun and cradle for pitch, roll and corkscrew, but this was not perfect and under action conditions weaknesses revealed themselves. When, in September 1939, *Jacobi* and *Heinemann* were attacked off Heligoland it was found that the gyros were too weak to cope with rolling and sharp turns to allow the guns a good target, and *Jacobi* got off only 28 rounds.

The light armament consisted of six 2cm single mountings, two abreast No. 2 gun, two abreast the derricks and two on the after deckhouse (or, in the case of Types 36, 36A and 36B, on the 3.7cm platform). It is possible that the full outfit was not carried, since most units appear not to have shipped the pair abreast the derricks, although the gun and breech were often removed from the pedestal, making them rather inconspicuous in photographs. The 2cm gun was yet another Rheinmetall product and, designated 2cm C/30, was developed from an earlier Solothurn design, ST-5. On board the destroyers it was carried on L/30 single pedestals which had a conical base and a telescopic centre column which could be raised or lowered by handwheel to alter the firing height, depending upon whether high-level or low-level targets were being engaged. Unlike the Allied Oerlikon, which was free-swinging, the gun was trained and elevated by handwheels. On the right-hand side of the gun a large net, rather like an angler's keepnet, was generally fitted, for catching the spent cartridge cases. This 2cm gun, which was a fully automatic, 65-calibre weapon using fixed ammunition, gave these destroyers, in addition to the 3.7cm guns, quite a respectable high-angle armament for their day. Both Britain and France had light AA weapons, but the 0.5in (12.5mm) machine-guns of the former and 13mm guns of the latter were too light and little more than rifle calibre. The 0.5in weapon was a particularly poor gun while the 1.1in (28mm) gun developed by the Americans was also unsatisfactory. It is true that the Royal Navy had the ubiquitous 2pdr but this, whilst a good barrage weapon, lacked the range and accuracy of the longer-calibre batteries. Only the Dutch, with their 40mm gyro-stabilized, fully tachymetric Hazemeyer guns, appear to have been ahead of the Germans.

The main drawback to the 2cm C/30 gun was its poor rate of fire – 280 (cyclical) or 120 (practical) rounds per minute – due, in part, to an unsatisfactory breech mechanism which often resulted in jamming. The magazine arrangements were not ideal either, since each curved, Bren-gunlike magazine only held 20 rounds and required frequent changing during extended air strikes. Fortunately for the Germans, British air attacks were not particularly successful in the early years of the war, and when they did become more of a menace an improved gun, the 2cm C/38, had come into service.

The gun battery, powerful though it was, did not constitute the destroyers' main armament according to German tactics. The principal weapon was the torpedo, of which eight were carried, shipped in quadruple mountings on the centreline casing above the machinery spaces. This was the first time that German ships had carried quadruple tubes and they were subsequently installed in all the following classes of destroyer as well as, surprisingly, Tirpitz, which received two, probably ex-destroyer banks in 1942. The torpedo carried was the standard 53.3cm (21.7in) G7a compressed-air type. Electric torpedoes of the pattern used by U-boats – G7e – could not be fired because the height of the tubes caused the batteries in the torpedoes to be damaged on entering the water. In any case, it was not important for the surface vessels to carry trackless torpedoes.

The G7 torpedo was, in theory, a superb weapon. It could be set to run at 30, 40 or 45 knots, with ranges of 15,000, 5,000 or 4,000m respectively. Its running depth could be set in 1-metre steps down to 52m(!) and, furthermore, its pattern could, with the weapon still in its tube, be gyro-angled to run up to 90° left or right in 1° steps at the last minute before firing. With its 430kg TNT warhead and the provision of both contact and magnetic pistols, the G7 should have been a formidable missile, but all was not well with the German torpedo testing system and, unknown to the Kriegsmarine at the start of the war, there were serious defects in the magnetic pistol, the depth-control system and the contact pistol, which needed a broad angle of striking. Moreover, little thought had been given to the problem of 'shelf life' and on-board maintenance: all the torpedoes officially tested were always brand-new. Changes in the earth's magnetic field with varying latitude had not been fully realized, and the pistols were extremely unreliable in northern waters, where, by coincidence, most of the destroyers spent their operational lives, whilst the faults in the depth-keeping system often caused torpedoes to run far deeper than they had been set. The net result of these defects was a stream of angry and often abusive reports, from both U-boats and destroyers, which culminated in an enquiry in 1940 which had serious repercussions and caused a notorious scandal within the Kriegsmarine. The defects were subsequently rectified, but not before many valuable prizes had been lost, and it is arguable that the outcome of the Narvik battles might have been reversed had good torpedoes been available.

All German destroyers were designed to carry reload torpedoes, the number of which is usually given as eight. In fact, only four reloads were provided for, except in the Type 42 (none of which was completed). The reload torpedoes were stowed in covered compartments alongside the tubes themselves, in the raised half-deck on which the tubes were mounted, where there was room for the stowage of only one torpedo to port and starboard of each bank. It is noticeable that the width of this half-deck was considerably greater in the Type 42C in order to allow the stowage of the extra four torpedoes. The weapons could be withdrawn for servicing using loading beams fitted to the break of the forecastle and the midships deck; they could also be placed on trolleys which were provided for the purpose and ran on the mine rails (this is probably the reason why the port rails were carried up to the break of the forecastle whilst the starboard set terminated at the after funnel). In action, reloading proved difficult under battle conditions and in any sort of a sea, since the reload system was not purpose-designed as was that employed by the Japanese. There were a few occasions when destroyers did attempt reloading, such as the actions in the Bay of Biscay in 1943 and 1944, when both Z23 and Z32 managed partially to reload, but both ships were seriously hampered by the weather conditions. Z27, in her final action, attempted to reload her torpedoes but was unable to do so. Quite apart from the physical problems, the weight of an extra four torpedoes, some twelve tonnes, cannot have improved the destroyers' already suspect seakeeping properties.

Minelaying was a very important task in the Kriegsmarine, much as it is in the Soviet Navy today. Most ships from cruisers downwards could undertake the task, and the destroyers were no exception, carrying both contact and influence weapons. The designed capacities were 77 for the Types 34 and 34A, 73 for the Type 36 and 74 for the Types 36A and 36B. By 1944, however, the pre-war designs were restricted to 42 mines owing to hull bending problems. The mine rails themselves were removable and not always carried.

The anti-submarine capability was limited, there being, as designed, four depth-charge throwers sided abreast the after superstructure and two racks on the port and starboard quarters. Up to 1939 only eighteen depth-charges (Type WBF or WBG), were carried, six of these in the racks; on surrender in 1945, Z33 was carrying thirty lightweight depth-charges with four throwers.

SOPHISTICATED FIRE CONTROL

Gunnery control was exercised by means of the two optical rangefinders and the 'Artillerierechenstelle' (equivalent to British transmitting station). The fire control computer installed in the TS was basically the Type C34/Z. The low-

angle table carried dials for own-ship, enemy and wind, as well as gyro rings; other dials showed corrections for dip, convergence and drift, which were worked out in the TS instead of at the guns. There was a separate panel for range and bearing plots: the range plot used the mean of both rangefinders to produce a range curve, while the bearing plot was produced by the change of bearing of the director (corrected for yaw), the rate across being measured in the same manner. There were no high-angle fire control arrangements other than a simple range drum which gave the fuze setting for any range or angle of sight. In practice, only barrage fire was used. The light anti-aircraft armament was provided with a 1.25cm base rangefinder for the 3.7cm guns and a hand-held, portable 0.7m rangefinder for the 2cm weapons. Both calibres of gun were later provided with Flakvisier 33 sights.

The torpedo armament was provided with its own sophisticated fire control system, including a separate torpedo transmitting station ('Torpedorechenstelle'). Primary control was exercised by the torpedo officer using one of the torpedo directors (stabilized in the Type 36A and later designs) in the bridge wings, and a rate of change of bearing instrument (TAM-Stand) on the bridge centre-line just forward of the range finder who normally kept the director on target by line of sight. Usually, enemy inclination and speed were visually estimated on the director, but this information could, if necessary, be obtained from the TS. Range was obtained either from the main rangefinders or, in later years, the radar, although the latter was never relied upon. In the director was a calculating box which, when fed with the target parameters, supplied the firing angles. Having set the torpedo firing circuits by means of selector switches in two boxes in the TS, one for the forward tubes and one for the after set, the torpedoes could be fired by pressing the 'Fire' switch, whereupon the salvo would be discharged automatically, with torpedoes launched at 2-second intervals. The transmitting station was more elaborately fitted than the director and was only used if time permitted. It duplicated the equipment in the director with, additionally, switchboards, remote power control units and a spread calculator (which was fed with length and inclination of the target, range and torpedo settings), as well as one firing selector switch for each tube.

Each bank of tubes was fitted with an open control position incorporating an elaborate binocular sight, its own calculator box for local firing, and power training controls, training being hydraulic for the Type 34, 34A and 36 designs and electric in the remainder. The torpedoes could be fired by compressed air or cordite, but the former was normally employed. It was the practice to fire torpedoes in salvoes of three ('Dreierfächer') or four ('Viererfächer').

As the Type 34 destroyers were being designed, anti-submarine technology in Germany lay with the depth-charge and hydrophone, although developments were under way in a new direction which will be described

shortly. The hydrophone system for detecting submerged submarines was essentially a 'passive' technique in that sound from the submarine was transmitted to the microphones installed underwater on the hunting surface vessel; no sound was emitted by the microphone itself; in other words it was a receiver only. Such systems had become well established during the First World War, and initially German technicians developed this system by producing a variable-resistance type microphone which proved to be very sensitive and did not require an amplifier. It was, however, unstable and not suitable for multi-units installations, and it was abandoned in the early 1930s. From this, however, an electromagnetic receiver was developed, in which the microphone receiver was replaced by an electromagnet. The diaphragm activated a smaller diaphragm to which it was coupled, the smaller one vibrating in a magnetic field and thus causing changes in the current flowing round the magnet. These currents were very small, necessitating an amplifier.

During the 1930s this equipment was replaced by the electrodynamic receiver, which worked on a principle similar to that of the generator in that the movement of a coil in a magnetic field caused an alternating current to flow in the coil. Further developments were the electrostatic condenser receiver, which may not have been put into service, and, finally, the crystal receiver.

All hydrophone systems produced by the Germans after the First World War were of the multiple receiver type and known as 'Gruppenhorchgerät' (GHG). Both the number of hydrophones and their arrangement varied from ship to ship: U-boats, for example, may have had 12 or as many as 24, whilst some surface ships had only 6, although the light cruiser *Nürnberg* had 32. The Type 34 destroyers were fitted with 36 receivers on each side of the hull. A typical installation would comprise one or more groups of receivers; a compensator; an amplifier with matched headphones; power supplies for receivers and amplifiers; and cabling. Two switchboards were included, enabling either one watchkeeper to listen to both sides alternately or two watchkeepers to have one side each. Listening frequencies were 500, 1,000, 3,000, 6,000 and 10,000Hz, and the groups of receivers could be arranged in various ways – linear, circular or planar arrays.

The linear array, with the receivers mounted in a line along the ship's side, was either a revolving directional type or fixed with a compensator, the compensator being an arrangement of inductors and capacitors designed to introduce a phase delay between individual receivers and the headphones. The fixed array, with its compensator, suffered from weakened or distorted signals, whilst the revolving type was difficult to install. The circular array, with receivers mounted in a circle on a single plane, was designed as a retractable unit in which each receiver was mounted in a 'sword' which could be lowered below the hull. This, however, exposed the receivers to a high level of self-noise and was abandoned in the 1930s, and the system was succeeded by the planar array which consisted of an array of horizontal semi-circular (or, later, elliptical) form, built into the ship on both sides, with the hull acting as a screen against the self-noise of the propellers. It is probable that it was this system, using electrodynamic receivers, that was fitted to the Type 34 and 36 destroyers.

Hydrophonic reception was dependent upon the loudness of the source relative to the sea state, self-noise, etc. A destroyer at medium to high speed would expect to hear a torpedo at 2,000m or more, whilst it would pick up a submerged submarine proceeding at high speed at 500–700m. U-boats are known to have located convoys at 20 miles by GHG and hear individual destroyers at 10 miles under good Atlantic conditions, although under poor conditions listening range would drop to half or less.

ENHANCED CAPABILITIES

It is appropriate to consider in this Chapter the various modifications which were made to these ships during the course of the war, since most were associated with fighting ability. As a result of the losses at Narvik, major modifications were carried out to only a few Type 34 or 36 ships, those sunk in the fjords being virtually in their peacetime guise. The first visual modification involved the fitting of tripod legs to the foremast. These legs extended well up the mast, in the case of Beitzen, Jacobi, Riedel, Schoemann and Galster to the crosstrees. The other four survivors after 1940 had rather lower tripod legs, except Heinemann whose tripod extended almost to the truck. War-completed destroyers commissioned with tripod masts.

The problem of submerged submarine location had received considerable attention from the Kriegsmarine's scientists, as will be evident from the description of the GHG apparatus. It should come as no surprise, therefore, that although the secrets of ASDIC were a closed book to the Germans, a similar system had been developed by the 1930s; indeed, it is only a short step from the echo-sounder principle, which was known, to its employment in a horizontal manner, especially since similar pulse/echo techniques were then being developed in the field of radar.

The German system, known as S-Gerät (Sondergerät, or special equipment) was developed by the Nachrichtenmittelversuchsanstalt (NVA) in the 1930s, with development trials being conducted by the tenders Strahl and Laboe. Its principle of operation was similar to the British ASDIC in that it was a horizontally polarized sword direction-finding device. It was manufactured by GEMA (Gesellschaft für Elektro-Akustische und Mechanische Apparate), and installation into operational ships began in 1938. Its basic components consisted of a 15kHz A.E.G. generator, cathode-ray tube, amplifiers and transmission/reception crystals. The transmission frequency could be either 10kHz, or 15kHz, in pulses of 300Hz. Since the velocity of sound in seawater was known to be 1,470m/sec,

range could be deduced from a simple formula utilizing the time differential between pulse transmission and echo reception. Accuracy of bearing was ±1°, and of range 1 per cent.

Deliveries of equipments were slow, only Zenker and Eckoldt being fitted by the end of 1939. It was expected that deliveries would be six per month in January and February 1940, seven in March and ten per month thereafter, until August when thirteen were expected and fifteen in September. The plans for installation were: January Z18; February Z10; March Z7 and Z15; April Z20 and Z14; May Z8 and Z3; June Z4, so that by this date, 50 per cent of destroyers would be fitted, the aim being to have at least one per division fitted. Not until late autumn would all destroyers be fully equipped.

Riedel had been fitted by August 1940, while Ihn was in Danzig in February 1941, running trials with S-Gerät under the guidance of the NVK, from which it might be inferred that this was her first fitment. When she returned to France two months later, on the sortie to bring in the returning raider Thor, she was stationed ahead to use her S-Gerät, suggesting that the other two destroyers, Heinemann and Steinbrinck were not so fitted or had defective sets. It is likely that later classes completed with S-Gerät already fitted. The installation of radar sets in 1940–1 resulted in an extension to the after end of the bridge where a cabin was built, on to the top of which the main rangefinder, as well as the radar aerial mattress, was transferred. This entailed a weight increase of 2.5 tonnes, for which the

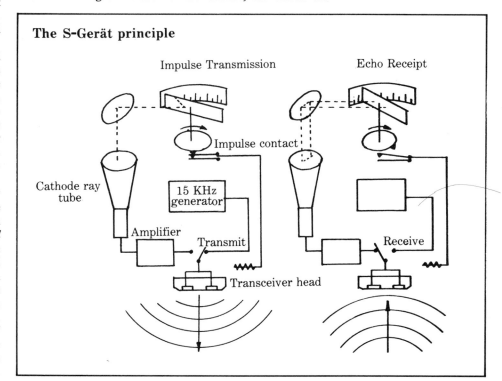

The S-Gerät principle

searchlight on the mast and the after director were landed, whilst the rangefinder was reduced to a 3m base. This totalled 4.4 tonnes compensation, but the addition of depth-charges and de-gaussing added another 17.9 tonnes, necessitating the removal of the motor boat and derrick as well as the electric capstan. Following these modifications, the net weight gain was 3 tonnes.

The pre-war destroyer's general appearance, then, remained more or less unaltered until 1942, when several units – *Jacobi*, *Riedel*, *Ihn*, *Lody*, *Steinbrinck* and *Beitzen* – all emerged from refits with the forward funnel cut down by 0.7m and the cowl by 1.2m; at the same time, the cowl on the after funnel was also shortened by 0.7m. In 1944 *Jacobi*, *Steinbrinck* and *Lody* underwent major refits, in the course of which the former received clipper bows and all three a 'goal post' foremast ('Tormast'), which allowed the radar mattress to sweep 360°. *Beitzen* received only the clipper bows.

Armament modifications were invariably concerned with enhancing anti-aircraft capabilities, but it is interesting to note that, unlike British practice, torpedo armament was in no instance sacrificed for this purpose, although by the time it became necessary to increase the flak armament the day had long since passed when there was much likelihood of the ships ever firing another torpedo offensively; in fact, it is doubtful if any of these ships fired a torpedo after mid-1944, other than for practice purposes, except during the 4th Flotilla's action in January 1945.

The poor rate of fire and mechanical unreliability of the 2cm C/30 gun had been appreciated for some time and steps were taken to rectify matters. The task of redesign was given to the Mauserwerke concern, a company well known in the small-arms field. The troublesome breech mechanism was revised and the rate of fire thereby improved to 420–480 rounds per minute, although in practice only 180–220 were achievable. The new design emerged in 1940 and was outwardly indistinguishable from the old. However, destroyers were not at the top of the priority list for the new weapons, and it was not until 1941 that they began to receive them, *Ihn* and *Heinemann* being fitted with theirs in April 1941. The original mountings were augmented by a single mounting on the forecastle just forward of No. 1 gun, one on the forward shelter deck under the muzzle of No. 2 gun and a third on the after shelter deck, under the muzzle of No. 4. Later in the war, the foremost of these three mountings was repositioned as a bow-chaser in the eyes of the ship, on a circular bandstand platform, the sides of which folded up when not in action. Until 1944 none of the AA armament, 3.7cm or 2cm, was fitted with gun shields, although a crude-looking shield was available for the 2cm weapons; the latter, however, seems mainly to have been fitted in auxiliary escort vessels, S-boats and R-boats, although *Z23* did show such shields early in the war.

The first major improvement to the flak armament was the replacement of the two single 2cm guns on the after shelter deck by a quadruple 2cm mounting. This extremely effective weapon was essentially four 2cm C/38 barrels on a special mounting and was known as '2cm Flak 35 im Vierling L/38'. It was developed by the Mauser company and produced by Rheinmetall from 1940. Installation aboard destroyers began in late 1941 or early 1942, and so none was available before Narvik. *Heinemann* had probably not received hers at the time of her loss, while *Z26* and *Schoemann* certainly still had their 2cm singles when they were sunk in April and May 1942 respectively. *Eckoldt*, however, going down in December 1942, had by then received her Vierling. *Beitzen* may have received the first mounting late in 1941, since she was so fitted at the time of the 'Channel Dash' in February 1942. Of the war-completed ships, it would appear that *Z23–31* completed without the Vierling and were retrospectively fitted. Ships which survived to receive their 15cm turret generally received a second Vierling on the handling room forward of the bridge, whilst *Z38* and *Z39* commissioned with it fitted there; conversely, *Z37* had not received her forward Vierling by the spring of 1943, but she carried the full 15cm armament.

As the war progressed and the Allies gained wide air superiority, the Kriegsmarine found that the 2cm gun was ineffective, especially as the RAF was now using rockets from medium altitude instead of cannon and machine-gun fire from low altitude. During 1944, therefore, plans were laid for increasing the flak outfits of all classes of ship by giving them a higher proportion of 3.7cm weapons, utilizing the new 3.7cm Flak M/42 gun, or, in the case of certain cruisers, the even newer Flak 43/M and captured Flak 28 Bofors guns.

The 3.7cm SK M/42 on the LM/42 mounting was yet another Rheinmetal-Borsig product and featured a monoblock barrel with a breech ring connected by a bayonet joint. Detailed design changes had been made to speed production, and the rate of fire had been improved to 250 (cyclic) and 180 (practical) rounds per minute. For the first time shields were to be fitted to the light weapons. This tardy appearance of shields is surprising, for even the thinnest protection helped morale.

At a meeting early in November 1944 the detailed provisions of the rearming (or 'Barbara' refit as it was code-named) were promulgated. In the case of destroyers and torpedo boats, each class was dealt with, and although the modifications differed in detail an overall pattern emerged. All the destroyers were to receive two twin 3.7cm LM/42 mountings before the bridge at No. 2 gun deck level, two more would replace the original 3.7cm SK C/30 weapons amidships, and three further mountings on No. 3 gun deck displaced that 12.7 or 15cm gun. The 15cm-gunned ships were to receive a further two single 3.7cm weapons on the midships deck in lieu of the former single 2cm weapons, as was the surviving Type 36 ship, *Karl Galster*. The Type 36B ships were also to be fitted with two single 3.7cm mountings on the upper bridge, where they supplanted the original Vierlings. *Z28*, with the extensive deckhouse aft, was dealt with rather differently and could not accommodate as many extra guns. In addition, all the single 2cm C/38 guns were to be supplanted by LM/44 twin mountings positioned in the bows and bridge wings and on the quarterdeck, with the Vierling being retained aft, the refits to be carried out as and when the ships came in for overhaul. In the final event, only *Jacobi*, *Lody*, *Steinbrinck*, *Z25*, *Z29* and *Z39* received the full 'Barbara' refit. Certain other ships received extemporized augmented flak outfits from local sources. These were *Z24*, *Z28*, *Z32*, *Z33* and *Z34*, and in the case of the last two the weapons came from the sunken *Lützow* in 1945. *Z24* and *Z32* were not part of the 'Barbara' programme, whilst *Z35* and *Z36**★** were sunk before being rearmed; the state of *Z43* at the time of her loss is not known.† *Z29* was caught in dockyard hands, part way through her refit at the war's end.

As was to be expected, the programme did not go quite according to plan, and the final position was that the various survivors were re-armed as follows:

Jacobi (10 x 3.7cm, 13 x 2cm):
Two twin 3.7cm abaft No. 2 gun at shelter-deck level
Two twin 3.7cm abreast after funnel

★The latter is reported as having been re-armed between 29 November and 8 December 1944, but with what is not known.

†One of her former officers states that all light flak had been landed by the time of her scuttling.

Two single 3.7cm on platforms at former No. 3 gun position
Twin 2cm mountings on forecastle, bridge wings and on No. 3 gun position, plus Vierling and one single mount

Lody (14 x 3.7cm, 10 x 2cm)
3.7cm outfit in seven twin mounts
2cm armament in one Vierling and three twins

Steinbrinck (14 x 3.7cm, 10 x 2cm)
3.7cm outfit as *Lody*
Twin 2cm mountings on forecastle and bridge wings, plus Vierling

Z25 (10 x 3.7cm, 16 x 2cm)
Two twin 3.7cm mountings on deckhouse aft of turret
Four single 3.7cm mountings abreast after funnel
Two single 3.7cm mountings on after shelter deck abreast No. 3 gun position
Twin 2cm mountings abreast forecastle 3.7cm mountings and in bridge wings
Two Vierlings on extended deckhouse, replacing No. 3 gun

Z29 (2 x 5.5cm, 9 x 3.7cm, 20 x 2cm)
Two single 3.7cm abreast former No. 3 gun position
Vierling and single 3.7cm on extended deckhouse in No. 3 gun position

Below: Twin Automatic 3.7cm guns on *Z39* installed under the 'Barbara' programme. Note also the covered 2cm twin and the radar outfit. (USN Historical Center)

Two twin 3.7cm mountings abreast after funnel on former 2cm position

Possibly two prototype single 5.5cm mounts on the vacated 3.7cm position amidships

Two Vierlings before the bridge

Twin 2cm mountings on quarterdeck, bridge wings and forecastle

Z39 (14 x 3.7cm, 14 x 2cm)

Two twin 3.7cm forward of bridge, abreast after funnel and abreast former

No. 3 gun position

Two single 3.7cm on after funnel platform and two twin 2cm in bridge wings

Two Vierlings, plus two single guns on extended deckhouse in No. 3 gun position

Z33 did not undergo a 'Barbara' refit but obtained extra flak guns from the wrecked pocket battleship *Lützow* in 1945. No. 3 gun was landed and given to *Z34*, and her 3.7cm outfit was increased to ten guns by the close of the war. These were probably disposed two twins before the bridge, two twins on the midships platform and one twin on the vacant No. 3 position. Twelve 2cm guns (one Vierling, two twins and four singles) were also fitted.

Ihn appears to have undergone a partial or interim refit, in the course of which No. 3 gun was landed, but instead of receiving 3.7cm guns she was fitted with shielded twin 2cm weapons. Two were shipped on the forecastle, abreast No. 2 gun, two abreast the former No. 3 position, and one on an extended Vierling deckhouse. It is probable also that two further mounts were shipped in the bridge wings, making eighteen 2cm guns in all, in addition to the four 3.7cm weapons already carried.

Riedel augmented her flak outfit to fourteen 2cm (one Vierling, two twin and six single), but *Beitzen* appears to have received no additions at all. *Z34* received at least one 4cm Bofors (before the bridge) and possibly two others, and she was fitted with Föhn rocket launchers. *Z38* finished the war with six 3.7cm and sixteen 2cm, while *Z31*, which had been fitted with a single 10.5cm gun in lieu of the forward turret after action damage in 1945, had a final flak outfit of fourteen 3.7cm and at least twelve 2cm guns.

The siting of the close-range armament was good, particularly forward, where the modified ships could now bring four 3.7cm and one or two 2cm guns to bear in what was usually a 40–50° blind spot. All mountings had a good field of fire, most having arcs of over 120°. However, although the volume of fire was impressive, the Germans had by this time lost considerable ground in HA gun control, all the flak armament being hand-controlled without RPC and no gyro gunsight having been developed. No gunnery (air) radar was available, and in consequence there was no attempt at aircraft target indication by radar.

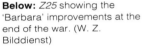

Below: *Z25* showing the 'Barbara' improvements at the end of the war. (W. Z. Bilddienst)

It would seem, too, that although the pre-war 3.7cm mounting had been stabilized, the problems associated with it had led to its abandonment in the LM/42 mounting, for by the end of the war *Z33* was reported as having no stabilized flak positions.

CONCENTRIC FIRE ZONES

Throughout the 1930s and during the war years, Germany had been at the forefront of rocket technology, and it was inevitable that this expertise would be diverted to military projects as her military situation became even more desperate. In a surprisingly short period of time, a wide range of rocket weapons was developed, of which the V-1 and V-2 are perhaps the best known. There were, however, numerous other projects, including surface-to-air and air-to-air missiles. Fortunately for the Allies, the very number of projects initiated led to a conflict of priorities, and only one or two types saw brief operational service in the closing stages of the war. As far as the Kriegsmarine was concerned, there were two main projects, the 7.3cm Föhn and the 8.6cm RAG; the latter was the more important as regards the destroyers and torpedo boats. This weapon began to enter service in mid-1944 with patrol craft operating in areas of high air attack risk, such as the coast of Norway and the Skaggerak, and was later fitted to some larger units.

The equipment itself was basically an unguided surface-to-air and surface-to-surface missile, firing an 8.6cm rocket by means of a simple tube launcher. It was primarily a barrage-type weapon, with a range of ammunition designed to provide zonal protection as an attack approached closer to the vessel in question. After trials aboard *Möwe*,* the weapon was issued to Commander Norwegian Escort Forces, in order to gain operational experience and establish tactical operational techniques. Further trials were conducted aboard *U994*.

The original intention to develop nine different types of ammunition was criticized by operational commands as confusing and unnecessary. The types were Rkt Drahtseil (R.Dg.) 400 and 1000 (wire cable); Rkt Sprenggranate (R.Spg.) 400, 600 and 800 (HE); Rkt Leuchtgeschoss (starshell); Rkt Signalgeschoss (signal); Nebelraketen (smoke); and Doppelraketen (double rocket). For operational employment, however, use was restricted to R. Dg. 400 and 1000 and R. Spg. 400 and 800.

Each HE rocket (R. Spg.) had the equivalent destructive power of an 8.8cm shell. The R. Dg. round was an idea similar to the British PAC of 1940 whereby a forest of suspended wires was fired in front of attacking aircraft to destroy wings and propellers and hence bring the aircraft down. All ammunition was propelled by black powder, and each wire round could remain airborne for over 30 seconds.

The operational technique involved the establishment of

*An auxiliary trials vessel, not the torpedo boat.

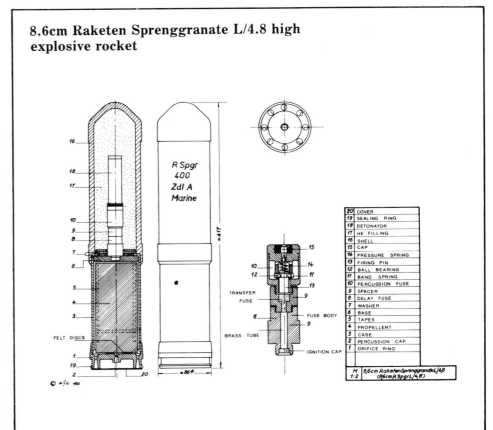

8.6cm Raketen Sprenggranate L/4.8 high explosive rocket

20	COVER
19	SEALING RING
18	DETONATOR
17	HE FILLING
16	SHELL
15	CAP
14	PRESSURE SPRING
13	FIRING PIN
12	BALL BEARING
11	BAND SPRING
10	PERCUSSION FUSE
9	SPACER
8	DELAY FUSE
7	WASHER
6	BASE
5	TAPES
4	PROPELLENT
3	CASE
2	PERCUSSION CAP
1	ORIFICE RING

three concentric fire zones around the vessel under attack, each being allocated a specific type or types of ammunition, for which ready-use ammunition lockers were stowed close to the launcher according to zone requirements. Each locker contained three rows of five rockets: Row 1 had R. Dg. 1000 for Zone 1; Row 2 R. Dg. 400 or R. Spg. 800 for Zone 2; and Row 3 R. Spg. 400 for Zone 3. Zone 1 was 4,500–3,000m distant, Zone 2 3,000–1,500m, and Zone 3 less than 1,500m, and changes of ammunition type inside a zone were to be avoided. It was estimated that, with a salvo every 2–2½ seconds and an aircraft speed of 120m/sec, each aircraft would receive 5 or 6 shots from each RAG per zone. If fire were opened early enough, therefore, the 'fire zone' could be saturated with 25–30 R. Dg. 1000, 12–15 R. Dg. 400, 12–14 R. Spg. 800 and about 25 R. Spg. 400. Low-flying aircraft required a launcher elevation of 25–40°, dependent upon ammunition type, whilst for sea targets R. Spg. was fired at 20° and R. Lg. at 35–40°.

According to the intentions of the 'Barbara' programme, destroyers were to receive four RAG outfits but later this was increased to six, with 28 rounds per launcher, and the torpedo boats operating in the Skaggerak eventually received many more launchers. The success achieved with this equipment is not known.

Right: *Hans Lüdemann*, showing the midships arrangements and symmetrical positioning of the 3.7cm guns. (W. Z. Bilddienst)

5. BEFORE THE STORM: OCTOBER 1929 TO AUGUST 1939

With the commissioning of *Möwe* at Wilhelmshaven in October 1926, the Navy could at last see some concrete evidence of a replacement programme for the elderly First World War boats which still remained in service. The new ship had an adequate armament and performance, making 32.65 knots on trials, about average for her class. *Seeadler* proved a knot faster at 33.69 knots, whilst *Albatros* only managed 31.75 knots. By October 1928, the first of the Type 24 boats, *Iltis*, commissioned, followed shortly by *Wolf* until by August 1929, all twelve of the new ships had joined the fleet. The Type 24 were faster by two knots, mean speed of the class being 34.3 knots, with the fastest and slowest being *Leopard* (34.91) and *Jaguar* (32.94) respectively.

For the next few years, they were used to develop tactics with the new light cruisers and train a new generation of destroyer men. At this time, torpedo boat organization was still based on the old half-flotilla system, there being four of these formed into the 1st (1st and 2nd half) and 2nd (3rd and 4th half) Torpedo Boat Flotillas. Before the eventual replacing of all the older veterans by the new boats, the flotilla organization was as follows:

1st Flotilla (Based in Swinemünde)
1st half Flotilla – *G7*, *G8*, *G10*, *G11*
2nd half Flotilla – *T151*, *T153*, *T156*, *T158*
2nd Flotilla (Based in Wilhelmshaven)
3rd half Flotilla – *Iltis*, *Jaguar*, *Tiger*, *Wolf*
4th half Flotilla – *Albatros*, *Falke*, *Kondor*, *Möwe*

Of the other older boats still extant, *S23* and *T155* were serving with the SVK. By 1934, the post of Flag Officer (Torpedo Boats) had been created and all the older boats diverted to secondary duties, *T196* as senior officers ship FdM, the Gunnery school had *T153*; SVK, *T190* and *T155* whilst the Submarine School had *T158*. At about the end of 1936, the organization was altered in view of the imminent entry into service of the new Type 34 destroyers. The 1st Destroyer Division was formed and the torpedo boats reallocated into three flotillas:

2nd – *Albatros*, *Leopard*, *Luchs*, *Seeadler* (Swinemünde)
3rd – *Iltis*, *Jaguar*, *Tiger*, *Wolf* (Wilhelmshaven)
4th – *Falke*, *Greif*, *Kondor*, *Möwe* (Wilhelmshaven)
Betweeen 1936 and 1939, these flotillas participated in

the various deployments of the fleet to Spanish waters during the Civil War. It proved to be an extremely active, if relatively uneventful, period for the torpedo boats, as they patrolled the Atlantic and Mediterranean coasts of Spain. Apart from *Seeadler* running aground leaving Cadiz in November 1936 and having to limp back to Germany on her starboard engine escorted by *Albatros*, the only incident of note was the bombardment of Almeria by *Deutschland*, when *Seeadler* and *Albatros* opened fire for the first time in anger and the former was near-missed several times by shore batteries.

It had been intended gradually to replace these ships in the front line flotillas by the new destroyers and the Type 35 torpedo boats, whereupon they could be converted to escort vessels by the removal of one bank of tubes, the after gun and rangefinder. Fitted with extra depth-charge equipment, they would replace the totally unsatisfactory F-boote in that role. However, because of the serious delays

in the new construction programme, the Fleet Commander, Admiral Boehm, was forced to request OKM in the early spring of 1938, that they be kept in commission instead. This was agreed to by OKM, who in June promulgated the new flotilla organization for torpedo boats:

3rd Flotilla (to be numbered 6th from 1 July 38) – *Tiger*, *Iltis*, *Wolf* (Wilhelmshaven)

4th Flotilla – *Leopard*, *Luchs*, *Seeadler* (Wilhelmshaven)

5th Flotilla – *Greif*, *Albatros*, *Möwe* (Wilhelmshaven)

The remainder being in reserve or re-fitting. This formation lasted until the outbreak of war, when the 4th Flotilla was disbanded and its boats distributed to the 5th and 6th Flotillas. Eventually in April 1940, by which time four boats had been lost, all the remaining boats were allocated to the 5th Flotilla.

Leberecht Maass, the first Type 34 destroyer, began boiler tests and basin machinery trials alongside the fitting-out pier in the Deutscher Werke yard at Kiel during December 1936. Builder's sea trials were commenced in the Baltic early in the New Year, and upon successful completion the ship was commissioned under Korvettenkapitän F. T. Schmidt on 14 January 1937; she also became the flagship of the Führer der Torpedoboote (FdT),* under whose authority destroyers were placed at this time. *Maass* was to be based in the Baltic, and she sailed for her home port, Swinemünde, towards the end of January. During the next six months most of her time was occupied in training, trials and torpedo-firing exercises, in the eastern Baltic around Pillau and Swinemünde or at the torpedo establishment at Eckernförde in Schleswig-Holstein. Since 1 February she had been part of the 1st Destroyer Division, but this formation would not be an effective fighting unit for some time to come, destroyer organization at this time being based upon three-ship divisions. By the close of the year, however, six more sister-ships had been commissioned and a second destroyer division formed. Exercises were carried out with the Fleet, both in the Baltic and the North Sea, and during the manoeuvres off Heligoland in September of that year, very bad weather was encountered, giving the destroyers a taste of what was to come and, no doubt, highlighting their seakeeping problems.

The pattern in 1938 was broadly the same as for 1937, with more ships commissioning and further divisions being formed - the 3rd, 5th and 6th. Towards the end of the year sufficient units were available to form flotillas, the 1st and 3rd Divisions constituting the 1st Flotilla, the 2nd and 4th Divisions the 2nd Flotilla and the 6th and 8th Divisions the 4th Flotilla; the remaining formation was the 5th Division.

Much of the time was again spent on trials and working up, and this year the first cruises were made to foreign countries. In April *Jacobi* and *Heinemann* sailed from Wilhelmshaven for Norwegian waters, an area which was to become very familiar to them in a few years' time.

Heinemann had been fitted prior to sailing with four 15cm guns in single mountings in Nos. 1, 2, 3 and 5 positions in order to conduct trials of the proposed armament for the Type 36A destroyers (*Z23–30*). Off Ålesund gunnery trials were conducted, and the effects of such heavy guns on destroyers assessed. Following completion of the trials the ships returned to Wilhelmshaven where the 15cm weapons were landed and the 12.7cm replaced. The first visit to a foreign port took place on 6 April 1938 when three units of the 1st Division, *Schultz*, *Beitzen* and *Thiele*, entered Hardangerfjord and anchored off Ulvik. On their return from Norway the three ships proceeded to Kiel, where they were taken in hand by Deutscher Werke for alterations to their bows and bridges; *Maass*, having visited Gothenburg in Sweden at the same time, followed for her rebuilding.

Practical experience with these ships had shown that they were very tender, i.e., quick to roll but quick to recover, and as a result, in order to assist stability, oil fuel levels were not allowed to fall below 30 per cent, which had an obvious effect on radius of action. During the Norway operation in 1940 rolls of 50° were recorded without any danger of the ships capsizing. The destroyers were inclined to bury their bows into the sea and, further, with a following sea they tended to carry weather helm and as a consequence steered very badly. Under these conditions they tended to turn broadside on to the sea and would only be returned on to course with considerable effort on the part of the helmsman, often with the assistance of engine manoeuvring. The Type 36 destroyers were an improvement in this respect since they were given twin rudders in parallel, which went some way to curing the steering problems. During this refit the round-fronted upper bridge was replaced by the square front and the bows raised by about 0.5m (20in) and lengthened by about 0.3m (1ft), which had the effect of increasing the sheer of the bows and imparting a slight rake to the stem. The object was to improve seaworthiness, and the alterations were reported to have been partially successful.

Meanwhile, in the North Sea, units of the 2nd Division were carrying out manoeuvres in the vicinity of Heligoland when, as a result of a navigational error, *Riedel* ran hard aground on rocks off the island. The ship's bottom was heavily damaged in several places, as were the port turbine and both propellers. Initial efforts to refloat the ship using her own power and with the help of tugs failed, and she was finally pulled off using old First World War 'M' class minesweepers and towed to Wilhelmshaven for repairs. The defects in the turbine could not be successfully repaired, and the ship thereafter suffered thrust bearing problems until a new turbine was fitted in 1942–3.

EXERCISES, TRIALS, MANOEUVRES

Adolf Hitler made one of his few sea voyages in July 1938 when he and his staff, including Göring and Keitel, boarded *Schoemann* at Kiel for the short journey up to

*This post can be compared with Rear-Admiral or Flag Officer (Destroyers) in the Royal Navy.

Eckernförde, presumably on a tour of inspection. Following this *Schoemann*, with her sisters of the 2nd Division *Riedel* and *Jacobi*, left for a week's cruise to Norway, visiting Sognefjord and Øye. Further exercises, trials and manoeuvres followed, including, on 19 August, a review of the Fleet by Admiral Raeder, after which the whole Fleet was inspected by Hitler and the Hungarian Regent Admiral Horthy (who had just launched the heavy cruiser *Prinz Eugen*), embarked in the yacht *Grille*. The Fleet flagship was *Gneisenau*. Also present were all three pocket battleships, the cruisers *Nürnberg*, *Leipzig* and *Köln* and the destroyers of the 1st (*Thiele*, *Beitzen*, *Schultz*), 2nd (*Riedel*, *Jacobi*, *Schoemann*), 3rd (*Ihn*, *Steinbrinck*, *Eckoldt*) and 6th (*Heinemann*, *Zenker*) Destroyer Divisions. *Maass* wore the flag of FdT and was accompanied by several torpedo boats, escorts and S-boats. After the review the Fleet proceeded to sea for manoeuvres, accompanied by *Grille*, and these continued until 30 August. The previous day had seen the commissioning of the first of the Type 36 destroyers, *Diether von Roeder* (Kapitänleutnant Holtorf), as leader for the 5th Destroyer Division; Holtorf was formerly first lieutenant on board *Thiele*.

The autumn of 1938 brought the Sudetenland crisis, and the Fleet was put on alert between 28 and 30 September, after which the 2nd Division (*Jacobi*, *Riedel* and *Schoemann*) accompanied *Admiral Graf Spee* when she sailed from Wilhelmshaven bound for Spain and the Mediterranean on 6 October. The squadron sailed north around the British Isles and three days later anchored in Irish waters to meet the tanker *Dithmarschen* from which oil and provisions were obtained during the night. On the 11th *Admiral Graf Spee* and *Jacobi* resumed their journey southwards, *Dithmarschen*, *Riedel* and *Schoemann* having been detached to Lough Swilly because of machinery damage in the supply ship. On completion of the repairs, the two destroyers followed the squadron and rejoined it by the 15th when anchored in Tangier Bay. The Spanish Civil War was still in progress, and although the destroyers did not take part in the neutrality patrol (which was undertaken by cruisers and torpedo boats) they did carry national identification stripes across No. 1 gun at this time. Two days later the destroyers left Tangier, passed through the Straits of Gibraltar and secured alongside the pier in Ceuta where leave was given once again. On the 19th the division sailed for home, calling briefly at Vigo to refuel from the tanker *Samland* before shaping course northwards across the Bay of Biscay. Passing through the English Channel, the destroyers arrived in Wilhelmshaven on 23 October.

Early in December a number of the destroyers sailed from Swinemünde westwards, through the Kattegat and Skagerrak, northwards through the North Sea and into the Atlantic. Here, off Iceland in very bad weather, further secret trials were conducted. On 22 December the ships returned home. The destroyer strength of the Kriegsmarine had been steadily growing as new ships commissioned and worked up: by the turn of the year, eleven Type 34s and

two Type 36s had been commissioned.

In January 1939 the problems of the high-pressure steam plant were becoming apparent. These troubles were known as 'rickets' by the engineering staffs and were the cause of much extra and arduous work for them. To investigate more fully the problems, *Heinemann* was allocated to trials with reduced steam pressures, and during the next couple of months was employed in the Baltic on these duties. It would seem, however, that no major breakthrough was achieved, since the problems persisted throughout the war, certain ships seemingly more trouble-prone than others.

SABRE-RATTLING

War clouds were rapidly growing over Europe whilst the Navy continued its programme of construction and training. Although it has often been stated that the Kriegsmarine was unprepared for war with England (and in respect of numbers it was), numerous exercises were mounted during the period to bring the Fleet to a high level of efficiency, which was of the utmost value during the early years of the conflict. In May 1939 a strong squadron, including the pocket battleships *Deutschland*, *Scheer* and *Spee*, accompanied by the cruisers *Leipzig*, *Köln* and *Nürnberg* and escorted by the destroyers *Maass*, *Beitzen*, *Thiele*, *Schultz*, *Ihn*, *Eckoldt* and *Künne* as well as light surfaces forces, sailed from Baltic ports to occupy Memel. Embarked in the *Deutschland* were Adolf Hitler and the Admiral commanding scouting forces, Hermann Densch.

At that time Memel belonged to Lithuania, one of the Baltic states which had gained its independence from Russia in 1920, but prior to 1914 the town had been part of East Prussia. It was detached from Germany by the Treaty of Versailles and then seized by Lithuania. Accordingly, by the same sort of sabre-rattling that had brought him the Sudetenland, Czechoslovakia and Austria, Hitler then forced Lithuania to cede Memel and its environs to Germany, which it did on 22 March 1939 - indeed it could hardly do otherwise, given its isolation, the hated USSR to the east and its almost non-existent armed forces. The Lithuanian Navy at this time consisted only of the ex-German First World War minesweeper *Prezidente Smetona*, with two 75mm guns, plus a few customs launches. The German Fleet could be certain, therefore, that there would be no last-minute military hitches. Only a few days later, even before the Fleet occupied Memel, the German press began an anti-Polish campaign.

The journey eastwards was hampered by bad weather and high seas, but by 24 March the squadron had reached Memel where the major units anchored in the bay and the destroyers and smaller craft went alongside in the harbour. The bad weather in the Baltic continued, and when *Künne* was ordered west to the North Sea to provide an honorary escort for the new 'strength through joy' liner *Robert Ley*, she ran into a severe storm during which a man was washed overboard. Despite a four-hour search, he was not found.

Above: *T11* in Kiel Fiord. Note lack of radar, paucity of flak guns and stylized bow wave. (Archiv Gröner)

Künne suffered from the heavy seas, her cutter being smashed and other damage being incurred on the starboard side, but following quick repairs she passed through the Kiel Canal en route for Hamburg where she met the liner. After escorting her to Wilhelmshaven, where the launching of *Tirpitz* by Hitler took place on 1 April, she was joined by *Diether von Roeder* and together the pair provided the escort whilst Hitler, taking a great interest in his Navy at this time, made a short trip to Heligoland where there was yet another Fleet Review. On return to Hamburg, the liner and destroyers took part in a large reception and remained at the port for several days.

Further measures followed, of which the most important was the large spring exercise which began on 18 April. Taking part were *Admiral Graf Spee* (Admiral Boehm) and the cruiser trio *Leipzig*, *Köln* and *Nürnberg*, together with *Maass* (FdT, Konteradmiral Lütjens), units of the 1st (*Beitzen*, *Thiele*, *Schultz*) and 3rd (*Ihn*, *Steinbrinck*, *Eckoldt*) Divisions, and *Roeder;* also participating were U-boats and replenishment ships. The fleet steamed southwards once again into southern Spanish and Moroccan waters, where numerous exercises were carried out. During this time at least one of the destroyers suffered machinery problems. Visits were made to various Spanish and Moroccan ports,

induding Ceuta, Pontevedra and Vigo. After refuelling in Vigo and Pontevedra the squadron sailed for Germany on 13 May, being joined by *Deutschland*, also returning from a foreign cruise, on the way; reaching Germany on 15 May, the ships of the squadron dispersed to their home ports.

WAR WATCH

In the meantime, on 28 April, having already (on the 3rd) instructed his armed forces to prepare plans for an attack on Poland in the autumn, Hitler denounced the Anglo-German Naval Treaty and the Polish Non-Aggression Treaty of 1934, which left the Poles in a very invidious position. During May, however, numerous pacts were made all over Europe, one of which was the Anglo-Polish Treaty signed in London on 25 May. This reassured Poland to some extent, but Hitler was already at the door, and in recognition of the fact that the Polish Navy could not hope to survive the onslaught of the German Fleet plans were laid for certain units to escape to England should war between Germany and Poland break out. Whilst the political manoeuvring was going on, however, the Kriegsmarine continued its war training – which now had to take into account conflict with England, since the

Naval and Air Force Staffs had by this time been instructed to prepare plans to attack British shipping. Admiral Raeder's famous 'Z' Plan, with its scheduled completion date of 1947–8, was now in ruins, and it was obvious that the Fleet would have to go to war with what it had; in the case of the destroyers, this meant that instead of the planned 68 or so vessels, only 22 at the most would be available.

At the end of June *Lüdemann* and *Künne* sailed from Swinemünde bound for Norway, but in the course of so doing the latter suffered a machinery failure resulting in a loss of electric power, the steering motor going off the board and the ship colliding with the pier. She was put into dry dock for examination, but the damage was found to be negligible and so later the same day the cruise was recommenced. For the next ten days or so the ships, which had been joined by *Diether von Roeder,* completing the 5th Division, sailed along the Norwegian coast, passing Stavanger and Bergen, visiting Loenfjord and Balholmen at the eastern end of Sognefjord; *Karl Galster* also was in Norwegian waters at this time, visiting Andalsnes in Romsdalfjord some 150 miles to the north. This was to be the last peacetime excursion to Norway for the destroyers: they would not return until eight months later, and then under very different circumstances.

On 23 August Hitler gave orders that 'Y Tag', or invasion day, would be 28 August at 0415 hours or 0430 hours, but as a result of diplomatic machinations between England and Poland this was then postponed whilst the implications were studied. The destroyers took on ammunition and warheads for their torpedoes, and sailed for patrol positions in the eastern and western Baltic. *Ihn, Steinbrinck* and *Eckoldt* (3rd Division), with FdT embarked, took up positions between Bornholm and the Bay of Danzig, and *Beitzen, Thiele* and *Schultz* (1st Division) patrolled the western end of the Baltic. It was during these operations that the Kriegsmarine lost its second ship since the scuttling of the High Seas Fleet in 1919. (The first had been the sail training ship *Niobe.*) The 1st Destroyer Division was patrolling and exercising east of the island of Bornholm on 26 August, *Schultz* being a few miles north-west of the small island of Christiansø, which itself lies about 10 miles east of Bornholm, at 0813 hours that morning. The day passed uneventfully, until at 2000 hours the division assembled on the cruiser *Nürnberg,* which was flying the flag of the Commander Scouting Forces, Vizeadmiral Densch. The ships were sailing with war watches set and under darkened conditions. Owing to problems in No. 1 boiler room, *Schultz* was proceeding on Nos. 2 and 3 rooms only, until at 2100 hours the senior engineer, Kapitänleutnant (Ing) Winter reported No. 1 operational again. The squadron remained in company at night cruising stations, steering various courses at the direction of the captain of *Nürnberg,* but in the early hours of the 27th, whilst on a heading of 215° and at a speed of 12 knots, *Schultz* received a signal over the short-wave net

ordering the 1st Division to refuel from the oiler *Samland.* Unfortunately, this signal must also have contained further instructions to other ships, ordering them to close up on the *Nürnberg,* but the full text was not passed up to Korvettenkapitän Trampedach, the destroyer's CO; consequently, having satisfied himself that no ships other than those of the 1st Division were visible near the cruiser, course was altered to 115° and speed increased to 17 knots towards the oiler. A few minutes later, at 0234 hours, two torpedo boats were sighted on the starboard bow and a third on the port bow. The distance was estimated at about 300–400m, and barely a minute later *Schultz* rammed the darkened *Tiger,* which quickly began to sink. Survivors were hauled aboard the destroyer, herself badly damaged about the bows, which had been bent back up to the collision bulkhead and had sprung a leak in the tank spaces in the adjacent compartment XIV. *Tiger* sank at 0313 hours, with two of her company dead and six seriously wounded; there were no casualties aboard the destroyer.

By 0520 hours *Thiele* had *Schultz* under tow, stern first, and was making 4 knots on a course of 200° for Swinemünde. Two tugs, *Jomsburg* and *Taifun,* arrived on the scene after half an hour, taking over the tow from *Thiele* which then began A/S screening. Two more tugs, *Storm* and *Norder,* arrived, following behind the tow. By late afternoon four R-boats appeared on the scene to take over the A/S screen, releasing *Thiele,* and with the minesweepers disposed in diamond formation the little convoy plodded its way southwards, arriving in Swinemünde at 0625 hours on the 28th. Here the war watch was stood down, although the AA guns remained manned. That same afternoon the crippled destroyer was passed through the Stettiner Haff to Stettin, where she was docked in the Oderwerke yard at 0800 hours on 29 August. Repairs lasted until late September and prevented *Schultz* from participating in the Polish Campaign.

Two days before war with Poland broke out, *Ihn, Steinbrinck, Eckoldt* and *Heinemann* sighted the Polish destroyers *Blyskawica, Grom* and *Burza* on passage westwards from Gdynia towards the Skaggerak. After shadowing the Polish ships for some time, and since a state of war between the two countries did not as yet exist, the German ships broke off the chase and returned to Swinemünde. The Polish destroyers reached England in due course, where they were a welcome addition to the Royal Navy, subsequently serving with distinction in the Mediterranean, Atlantic and Arctic theatres. *Grom* was sunk by air attack off Norway in May 1940, but the other pair survived the hostilities.

Meanwhile peace was slipping away very fast, and despite last-minute political moves war was now inevitable. At 0630 hours on 31 August 1939, Hitler, as supreme commander of the German forces, ordered the Army to take up its positions for the attack on Poland. The Wehrmacht issued their final instructions at 1600 hours, setting the time of attack for 0415 hours on 1 September.

6. NORTH SEA OFFENSIVE: SEPTEMBER 1939 TO FEBRUARY 1940

At the start of the Second World War the Kriegsmarine had completed sixteen Type 34 and 34A destroyers, together with five Type 36, *Anton Schmitt* being due to enter service on 24 September, although not all the commissioned destroyers were yet fully worked-up. More destroyers (carrying five 15cm guns) were planned, but of these only *Z23–26* had been laid down prior to the outbreak of war; there would thus be little reinforcement of the meagre destroyer strength until late 1940 at the earliest, even discounting any early war losses. In fact, owing to repairs and refits, there were only thirteen operational destroyers, of which three of the 5th Division remained in the west, the remainder all being allocated to Naval Group East.

It was not expected, at the start of the Polish campaign, that the conflict would spread westwards, so the Kriegsmarine was able initially to concentrate its overwhelming force against the determined but tiny Polish Navy, without regard to its western defences. The naval forces allocated for the campaign were under the sea-going authority of the Commander Reconnaissance Forces, Vizeadmiral Densch, in his flagship *Nürnberg*; two other light cruisers, *Leipzig* and *Köln,* made up the cruiser force. The Führer der Torpedoboote, Konteradmiral Lütjens, aboard *Maass,* had with him *Thiele, Beitzen, Ihn, Steinbrinck, Eckoldt, Heinemann, Zenker, Arnim* and *Lody,* and included in the force were six MTBs, five escort vessels, twenty-one minesweepers of various types and ten U-boats; against this fleet the Polish Navy, under Rear-Admiral Unrug, could only muster the destroyer *Wicher,* the minelayer *Gryf* and the submarines *Orzel, Sep, Rys, Wilk* and *Zbik,* together with some small auxiliaries.

It was soon apparent that the forces employed by the Kriegsmarine were unnecessarily, and in fact dangerously, large, since the main threat from the Polish forces was the submarines. These had put to sea early, and the cruisers operating close inshore in confined waters were easy targets. This having been realized, the three cruisers and three of the U-boats were withdrawn to the west by 2 September, the second day of the conflict.

The destroyers, ordered to conduct mercantile warfare off the Polish coast near Hela and the Gulf of Danzig, sailed from Pillau at 0332 hours on 1 September. It was a fine night, with light, freshening winds from the north-west and good visibility – ideal conditions for detecting blockade-runners in those pre-radar days. By 0500 hours the blockade positions had been reached, and in the course of the day a number of ships, including neutral Norwegian and Greek steamers, were stopped and searched. These operations occasionally resulted in the destroyers being only a few miles off the Polish coast at Hela. Polish submarines were active in the area, and throughout the day numerous submarine alarms were received from *F7,** *Ihn* and *Steinbrinck*; the last was attacked by *Wilk,* but the torpedoes missed and the submarine was damaged by depth-charges during the destroyers' counter-attack, although the damage was insufficient to prevent the submarine from continuing operations.

The important Polish base of Hela was being valiantly defended by Admiral Unrug (it did not surrender until 1 October), and on 3 September *Maas* and *Zenker* received orders to reconnoitre the naval harbour and identify the warships present. They located the destroyer *Wicher* and minelayer *Gryf* in port and prepared to open fire. *Maas* took *Wicher* and *Zenker* engaged *Gryf* at a range of 12,700m (14,000 yards), both Polish ships replying, together with a shore battery of two or three 6in guns. The Poles made good shooting, forcing the two German destroyers to take sharp evasive action and increase speed to 27 knots, which, with the laying of a smokescreen by the destroyers, hindered their fire control considerably. At 0657 hours the 6in shore battery obtained a hit on *Maass* at the starboard forward corner of No. 2 gun deck, the exploding shell throwing splinters against the gun shield and cutting down the gun crew, killing four and wounding another four, one seriously. All electric power to the mounting was severed by splinters, although the gun itself remained serviceable. The action continued intermittently, but at 0735 hours Flag Officer (Torpedo Boats) ordered the action to be broken off and the destroyers to proceed to Pillau to refuel. Seventy-seven rounds of 12.7cm ammunition had been expended by *Maass* in the engagement. No. 2 gun was repaired by the ship's own staff but was only capable of

*A fast escort vessel or Geleitboote.

local control, whilst the shell hoists could not be repaired with the means on board.

By 1015 hours on the 3rd, *Maass* was secured alongside the Dalbenplatz in Pillau, where the dead were landed and the wounded discharged to the hospital ship *Berlin*. A day or two later *Maass* sailed for Swinemünde for repairs to her ammunition hoists, the replacing of No. 2 gun and repairs to tubes in No. 3 boiler room, the machinery defects having limited the ship's speed to 28 knots. Following these repairs and the taking on of replacement crew members, *Maass* was again serviceable from 10 September. After the two destroyers had broken off their bombardment the port of Hela was subjected to a heavy air attack, during which the Ju 87s of 4/Trägergruppe 186 sank *Wicher* and the bombers of 3/Küstenfliegergruppe 706 from Kamp-bei-Kolberg destroyed the minelayer *Gryf*.

THE THREAT FROM THE WEST

The situation in the Baltic now no longer required the presence of the destroyers: only the submarines of the Polish Navy still posed a threat, and they were best left to the minesweepers and patrol craft in the area. Accordingly, over the next three weeks the 1st, 3rd and 5th Divisions were passed through the Kiel Canal to Cuxhaven and Wilhelmshaven to meet the new threat from the west – Great Britain having declared war on Germany on 3

September. The 4th Flotilla, with some torpedo boats, was ordered into the Skaggerak and Kattegat to commence mercantile warfare against British and French vessels attempting to return home from the Baltic.

The main task of the destroyers, however, was to help lay the defensive minefield (known as the 'Westwall') which was to extend from the island of Borkum at the German-Dutch border as far as the latitude of Limfjord on the Jutland peninsula, a minefield designed to protect the German Bight from the offensive sorties of the British Home Fleet. Whilst loading mines for the start of this operation on 4 September, *Lody* suffered the accidental explosion of an anti-sweep device, which killed two men and wounded six others as well as causing some light damage to the ship's stern. During the same day, the first attacks on German warships by aircraft of the RAF took place, and in the course of these *Diether von Roeder* suffered a near-miss whilst lying in the Schillig Roads off Wilhelmshaven. This particular attack, by Blenheim aircraft of Nos. 107 and 110 Squadrons, was in fact aimed at *Admiral Scheer* and *Emden*, also lying at anchor nearby. No damage was caused to the destroyer, but the pocket battleship was hit by three bombs which failed to explode and the cruiser by a crashing aircraft, whilst the attacking aircraft suffered heavy losses to the ship's anti-aircraft fire. Minelaying began the following day, the ships sailing in the evening. They were divided into three groups: Group 1

Left: An early wartime view of a Type 23/24 torpedo boat. (Bundesarchiv)

comprised the cruisers *Köln* and *Königsberg* with the destroyers *Roeder* and *Lüdemann*, Group 2 the escort *Grille* and the destroyers *Künne* and *Galster*, and Group 3 the minelayers *Roland* and *Cobra* with the destroyers *Giese* and *Riedel*.

The laying of the 'Westwall' occupied much of the surface fleet until 20 September. In all, sixteen destroyers of the 1st Flotilla (*Thiele, Beitzen, Ihn, Steinbrinck* and *Eckoldt*), the 2nd Flotilla (*Riedel, Schoemann, Heinemann* and *Maass*), the 4th Flotilla (*Arnim, Lody* and *Giese*) and 5th Division (*Roeder, Lüdemann, Künne* and *Galster*) participated, usually on more than one occasion. Apart from the accident to *Lody* described earlier, the whole operation was conducted without loss. Meanwhile other destroyers, led by the FdT, Lütjens, were conducting mercantile warfare in the Skaggerak. Lütjens' flag was in *Heidkamp* which, on completion of working up, had replaced *Maass* as the destroyer leader. By 6 October the destroyer patrols including, at times, Beitzen, *Lody, Ihn, Steinbrinck, Arnim, Giese, Roeder, Lüdemann* and *Galster*, together with supporting torpedo boats, had stopped and searched about 130 merchantmen, some of which were escorted into Kiel as prizes. One other valuable prize, however, escaped, for just before midnight on 14 September *Beitzen* sighted a submarine proceeding without lights close in on the Swedish shore. Believing her to be Swedish, the destroyer did not attack, but in fact the submarine was the Polish *Wilk* in the course of breaking out of the Baltic for England. The submarine arrived safely and subsequently served successfully with the British forces. After 30 September the search forces in the Skaggerak were reduced, the 5th Division (*Roeder, Lüdemann, Künne* and *Galster*) being detached to Swinemünde whilst *Heinemann, Arnim* and *Giese* returned to Kiel.

In the western command area *Jacobi* and *Heinemann*, having completed refits and repairs at Wilhelmshaven, were ordered into the Baltic for exercises and training. On passage through the German Bight towards Brunsbüttel the two ships were attacked by eleven Hampden bombers of Nos. 61 and 144 Squadrons from RAF Hemswell whilst south-east of Heligoland. The destroyers so successfully defended themselves with their anti-aircraft armament that the attack was beaten off and the 1st Destroyer Flotilla, which had been prepared to come to their assistance from the Jade, was not in fact sent to sea. The British bombers were caught by German fighters and lost five of their number. Both ships continued their passage, transiting the Kiel Canal and entering the Baltic on 1 October. Leaving Kiel, they sailed eastwards to Swinemünde where, together with *Schultz*, they commenced exercises, which had very shortly to be interrupted in order to help bring into port the prizes taken by patrol boats. Mercantile warfare was again briefly conducted by the 2nd Flotilla (*Schoemann, Ihn* and *Steinbrinck*, together with the torpedo boats *Greif, Falke* and *Albatros*) in the Baltic approaches to the Kattegat between 3

and 5 October, but after searching the Skaggerak the flotilla returned to Wilhelmshaven, sailing round the Skaw and down the North Friesian islands.

In the North and South Atlantic, the pocket battleships *Deutschland* and *Admiral Graf Spee* had begun to operate, the latter with rather more success than the former. The appearance of these two raiders put a considerable strain on the resources of the Royal Navy, which nevertheless managed, with French assistance, to form eight hunting groups consisting of battlecruisers, aircraft carriers and cruisers between Brest and Ceylon. In order further to strain the British resources, an operation was planned by the OKM to relieve pressure on the pocket battleships and to attempt to entice out the Home Fleet into a submarine and air attack trap. Scheduled to take part were *Gneisenau* (Flagship of the Fleet Commander, Admiral Boehm), *Köln* and ten destroyers. The 5th Division, with *Heidkamp* (FdT), *Roeder, Lüdemann, Künne* and *Galster*, passed through the Kiel Canal from the Baltic on 6 October to join the 1st Flotilla (*Schultz, Beitzen* and *Arnim*); *Lody* and *Giese* were also to have participated but were unable to do so and were replaced by *Ihn* and *Steinbrinck*, already lying in Wilhelmshaven.

On 7 October the 5th Division moved into the Elbe, where boarding parties and prize crews were taken on, and the following day, less *Lüdemann* (which had developed machinery defects) but reinforced by *Steinbrinck*, it met the flagship and sailed into the German Bight. Here the cruiser and the remainder of the destroyers (*Riedel, Schultz, Arnim* and *Eckoldt*) joined. The squadron's orders were to sweep off the south coast of Norway and allowed light forces to be attacked but required superior forces to be avoided. This type of order was to become a serious restriction on the actions of commanders at sea in future years, but in this case, since the whole object was a diversionary one, it was justified. The squadron steamed northwards along the Danish coast and remained free from discovery until 1320 hours (British time) on the 8th, when a Hudson of No. 224 Squadron from Leuchars sighted and reported it; by this time the ships were on the latitude of the Lister Light, steaming northwards at about 20 knots.

The British sighting report certainly had the effect the Germans had intended. The battlecruisers *Hood* and *Repulse*, together with cruisers and destroyers, sailed from Scapa Flow for a position north-west of Stadlandet, light cruisers and destroyers of the Humber force for the entrance to the Skaggerak, and the main body of the Home Fleet (Admiral Forbes) for a position north-east of the Shetlands. The German squadron continued northwards, and although RAF Coastal Command remained in touch until early evening on the 8th, neither the searching warships nor the Wellingtons of Bomber Command managed to make contact. Similarly, although the Luftwaffe did manage to attack the British ships, the 127 He 111s (KG 26 & LG 1) and 21 Ju 88s (1/KG 30) failed to inflict any damage. The reason why the British forces were unable to locate the German ships was that Admiral Boehm had reversed course during the night of the 8th, having succeeded in drawing out the British forces. However, although his plans had matured, the operation failed in that none of the U-boats or aircraft deployed achieved the hoped-for success. Passing the Skaw, the squadron steamed down the Kattegat, arriving safely in Kiel on the 10th, with the exception of *Eckoldt*, which was detached to Swinemünde.

VULNERABLE WATERS

There now began a period of intense activity for the German destroyer flotillas which lasted until February the following year: operating during full-moon periods, the destroyers conducted eleven successful sorties. Each of the Type 34, 34A and 36 destroyers was capable of carrying 60 contact mines which, allied to the ships' very high speed (and conveniently ignoring their machinery problems), made them very formidable minelayers. The North Sea, particularly on the English East Coast and in the mouth of the Thames, is very shallow and unusually suited to minelaying, and it was through these waters that large numbers of ships sailed every day, moving supplies vital to Britain's war effort. The waters were vulnerable not only to offensive mine warfare but also to air attack and attack from light surface forces (S-boats) in view of the close proximity of the German bases in the Ems, Weser and Elbe estuaries.

These facts were only too obvious to the British Admiralty, but whilst the latter correctly assessed the dangers of air and surface attack they failed to appreciate the potential of the surface forces for minelaying and attributed such operations to U-boats. Mines certainly were laid by the U-boats, fourteen Type IIB and IIC boats being involved up to the end of 1939, but since each submarine only carried eight mines, the total number laid, even with some boats carrying out more than one operation, can only have been small in comparison with that for which the destroyers were responsible. A few mines were also laid by the seaplanes of Naval Air Command West, whose obsolete He 59s, He 60s and He 115s operated from bases in the East Friesian islands, but these efforts proved disastrous to the German minelaying offensive since one aircraft, as is well known, dropped a new and secret magnetic mine on to the mudflats of the Thames estuary, whence it was recovered with great gallantry and its secrets revealed. Thus destroyer-laid mines were the cause of the bulk of the East Coast shipping losses up until about February 1940, a fact which remained unknown to the British until after the war since none of the minelaying sorties was detected. Britain herself had declared a mined area on 23 September, 25 miles wide and 25 miles offshore along the East Coast, extending from the Humber to the Tyne and intended to protect the inshore convoy routes between the Tyne and Thames down which passed the vital coal traffic. However, as a result of a shortage of both mines and minelayers, the

only mines in this area up to the end of 1939 were German, the first British fields not being laid until January 1940.

During the week following their sortie with *Gneisenau*, the destroyers assembled in Wilhelmshaven Navy Yard. *Eckoldt* returned from Swinemünde and Konteradmiral Lütjens took his leader, *Heidkamp*, through the Kiel Canal to join the group. After taking mines on board *Galster*, *Eckholdt*, *Lüdemann*, *Roeder* and *Künne* (*Heidkamp*, as escort, carried none), the squadron sailed from the Schillig Roads at about midday on 17 October. The target area was the mouth of the River Humber, an important focal point for the coastal convoys. A direct course from the Jade to Spurn Point gives a distance of some 250 miles, which, even for a ship steaming at 30 knots, requires a passage time of some 8 or 9 hours. In order to lay the mines and make part of the return journey under cover of darkness, it was necessary to sail from German ports during daylight hours. This of course involved a considerable risk of detection, because the RAF were flying reconnaissance sorties over the Heligoland Bight; accordingly, a northwards course was steered initially as a deception, but towards dusk course was altered and a high-speed westwards run made to the dropping point. In the early hours of the 18th, the five mine-laden ships began their task, between the Humber Estuary and Withernsee Light, *Heidkamp* standing by. Nothing untoward occurred, however, and on completion of the task the destroyers steamed for home at high speed. The field claimed its first victim, a 1,692grt steamer, a few days later on the 22nd, and a total of seven ships, two British, two Norwegian and one each Danish, Finnish and Swedish, totalling 25,825grt, were lost on these mines.

The 1st Flotilla (*Ihn*, *Steinbrinck* and *Schultz*) was now ordered to patrol the Heligoland Bight, much as its predecessors had done twenty-six years before. The 2nd Flotilla (*Jacobi*, *Riedel* and *Schoemann*), the 5th Division (*Roeder*, *Künne*, *Lüdemann* and *Eckoldt*) and *Heidkamp* with Konteradmiral Lütjens were passed through into the Baltic to Swinemünde for exercises, whilst the 4th Flotilla, consisting of *Lody*, *Arnim* and *Giese*, remained in the west for anti-mercantile duties.

On 21 October Lütjens was posted away and responsibility for the destroyer flotillas was transferred to a new post, known as Führer der Zerstörer (Flag Officer Destroyers) or FdZ. The first incumbent, Kapitän zur See Bonte, was appointed on the 26th when he embarked, with his staff, in *Heidkamp*, then lying in Swinemünde. Torpedo boats and S-boats remained under Führer der Torpedoboote, now Korvettenkapitän Bütow.

The weak points in these ships' machinery plant were becoming evident even at this early stage of the war and on occasion even threatened the safety of the ships themselves. One incident occurred during a sweep by the 1st Flotilla (*Ihn*, *Schultz* and *Steinbrinck*) and 4th Flotilla (*Lody*, *Arnim* and *Galster*) off the Skaggerak and south coast of Norway on 27/28 November 1939. In search of merchant shipping,

the destroyers pressed on in the face of a strong north-easterly gale and high seas, pitching and rolling heavily. The weather prevented air reconnaissance, without which much of the effect of the sortie would be lost, so that early the next morning Naval Command West ordered the operation to be broken off. Reversing course, the destroyers were making for home in the heavy seas when *Schultz* suffered a blockage in the main feed pump to No. 1 boiler room. Luckily, the watchkeeper had spotted the failure and started the standby pump almost immediately, but it was too late. Seawater entered a turbine, causing an instant explosion as it came into contact with superheated steam. The boiler room filled with scalding steam very quickly, but the duty watch managed to escape from the inferno, although the chief mechanician later died from his injuries. In the steam-filled boiler room, a bilge pump valve had been left open, with the result that the abandoned space began to flood. Water entered the other two boiler rooms and also short-circuited many electrical cables. All telephone communications failed, and to add to the problems both the remaining boiler rooms lost pressure.

By 2205 hours steam pressure had halved to 35kg/cm² and things were desperate: rolling heavily with no power, unable to anchor or be towed, and with her crew unable to keep their feet whilst they tried to effect repairs, *Schultz* was helpless. By good fortune, however, there remained a chance that No. 3 boiler room could flash up again, and by dint of much effort and experience the chief mechanician

there managed slowly to build up pressure until, forty minutes later, there was sufficient to supply and drive one turbine. This gave the ship 17 knots and saved her. Painfully, she crawled her way back to Germany for repairs, but she was out of action until late January 1940.

PENNY PACKETS

The next two mining operations, which were to have been conducted against the Thames and Humber estuaries on the nights of 8/9 and 10/11 November by the 5th Division (*Galster*, *Lüdemann* and *Künne*), the 6th Division (*Eckoldt* and *Ihn*) and the 2nd Flotilla (*Jacobi*, *Riedel* and *Schoemann*) under the command of FdZ, were both broken off because of machinery difficulties aboard *Künne* which had seawater contamination in her fuel oil. A number of successful operations then followed, beginning with a sortie into the Thames estuary on the night of 12/13 November by FdZ with *Heidkamp*, *Lüdemann*, *Künne*, *Galster*, *Giese*, *Riedel* and *Schoemann*. All except the first were carrying mines, the leader acting as group escort. The 2nd Flotilla (*Giese*, *Riedel* and *Schoemann*) had to turn back because of machinery breakdowns, *Giese* escorting the damaged pair, but the remaining four destroyers pressed on, steaming to the North Foreland and up to the Goodwin Sands and the Tongue Lightship, using the three deep-water channels 'South', 'Edinburgh' and 'Sunk' – that served the Thames estuary and the port of London.

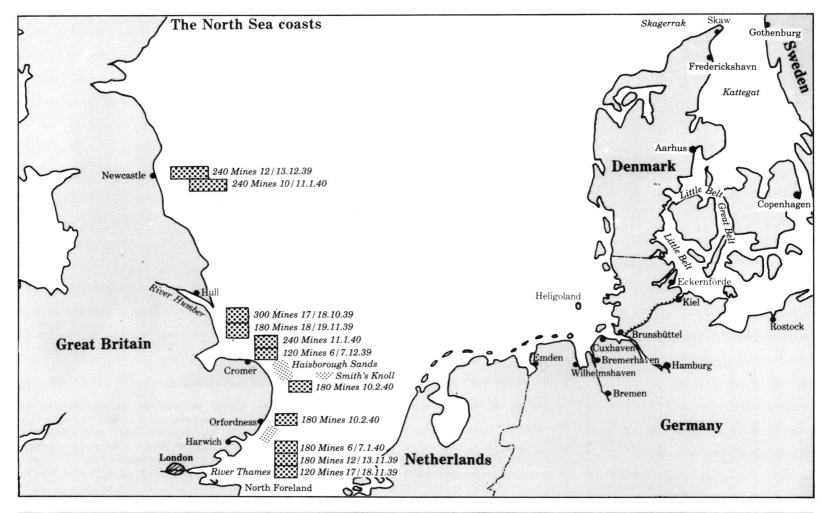

The North Sea coasts

Skagerrak — Skaw

Gothenburg

Frederickshavn

Kattegat

Sweden

Aarhus

Denmark

Little Belt

Great Belt

Little Belt

Copenhagen

Eckernförde

Rostock

Newcastle

240 Mines 12/13.12.39
240 Mines 10/11.1.40

Kiel

Brunsbüttel

Heligoland

Cuxhaven

River Humber — Hull

Emden

Bremerhaven

Wilhelmshaven

Hamburg

Great Britain

300 Mines 17/18.10.39
180 Mines 18/19.11.39

240 Mines 11.1.40
120 Mines 6/7.12.39

Bremen

Haisborough Sands

Smith's Knoll

Cromer

180 Mines 10.2.40

Germany

Orfordness

180 Mines 10.2.40

Harwich

180 Mines 6/7.1.40
180 Mines 12/13.11.39
120 Mines 17/18.11.39

Netherlands

London

River Thames

North Foreland

Most of the mines were of the new magnetic type which lay on the sea-bed. Germany had put a good deal of effort into the development of this weapon, but only 1,500 were available at the outbreak of war, whereas there were over 20,000 of the ordinary contact variety. The temptation to use these devastating and then unsweepable mines before large stocks were on hand proved too much for the Germans, however, with the inevitable result that they were dropped in penny packets. This not only alerted the British that something new was being used but also, as already noted, presented them with an unexploded sample, thus allowing counter-measures to be designed.

The German mine reacted to a change of magnetic field in the vertical plane as a ship passed over it. It could be activated by either a north pole down or a south pole down (i.e., it was bi-polar) and was designed to operate at a field strength of between 5 and 30 milligaus. Later mines incorporated a number of devices designed to render sweeping more difficult. These included a delay mechanism which did not arm the mine until a preset time clock had been run off, during which time it could not be swept except by counter-mining, and a 'ship counter', which allowed a certain number of ships to pass over before the mine was activated. These mechanisms could be used singly or together, and it was obvious that magnetic mines with these devices sown in association with contact mines and explosive sweep cutters presented the minesweeping forces with formidable problems.

During the sortie of 12/13 November the three minelaying destroyers laid 288 magnetic mines in the 'Edinburgh' and 'South' channels, causing severe disruption to traffic in the Thames, especially as a few nights later, 17/18 November, a further sortie by *Künne*, escorting the minelayers *Arnim* and *Galster*, sowed the 'Sunk' channel with about 180 more magnetic mines. By the middle of the month the problem was acute: only one channel was open and traffic almost, but not quite, stopped. During the month of November, 120,958 tons of shipping were sunk, of which approximately 79,000 tons (23 ships) were attributable to destroyer-laid mines. Included in this total were two British destroyers, *Blanche*, mined in the Thames close to the Tongue Lightship on 13 November, and *Gypsy*, off Harwich a week later; *Blanche*, had the doubtful distinction of being both the first British destroyer loss of the war and the first loss on this field. Having successfully laid their mines, the destroyers headed for home at full speed. Off the Terschelling Bank they were met by the cruisers *Leipzig* and *Nürnberg*, together with the torpedo boats *Leopard*, *Seeadler*, *Iltis* and *Wolf* of the 6th Flotilla. This practice of escorting destroyers with cruisers was to have serious consequences for the Kriegsmarine before the end of the year.

The minelaying sorties continued, and, as the incoming destroyers berthed, the 4th Flotilla, consisting of *Steinbrinck*, *Lody* and *Eckoldt*, were taking on mines for their operation the following night (18th/19th) against

Left: An unidentified Type 34 destroyer with a full mine load, sometime in 1940. (Author's Collection)

traffic in the Humber estuary. Their operation, too, was undetected and successful, seven ships totalling 38,710 tons eventually being sunk, including the Polish liner *Pilsudski* (14,294 tons). Met again by *Leipzig* and the torpedo boats, the destroyers were safely escorted into Wilhelmshaven. No further minelaying by the destroyers took place that month: instead, the ships were employed in mercantile warfare in the Skaggerak and on screening duties with *Scharnhorst* and *Gneisenau* during the early part of the sortie in which the *Rawalpindi* was sunk (21-27 November).

SITTING TARGETS

Some reorganization of the destroyers took place early in December, when the 3rd Destroyer Flotilla was formed, under Fregattenkapitän Hans-Joachim Gadow, from the existing 4th and 5th Divisions, all the ships of the flotilla (*Roeder*, *Künne*, *Galster*, *Schmitt* and *Lüdemann*) being Type 36s. This flotilla had an even shorter existence than its predecessors, since, with the exception of *Galster*, all its ships were lost in April the following year.

The importance of the British East Coast traffic was by no means lost on the German High Command, who instigated further measures against it. Mines were the obvious weapon, and another sortie into the area by the destroyers was planned. *Lody*, *Giese* and *Arnim* were detailed, under the command of the leader of the 4th Flotilla, Fregattenkapitän Bey aboard *Lody*, which was acting as escort. In accordance with FdZ's orders of 4 December, the ships sailed from the Jade on the morning of the 6th. The weather was calm and overcast with some haze as the destroyers steered a feint course towards 'Point I'. In explanation, it should be mentioned that the German Navy used a chart overlaid with a grid system for positional reporting purposes, so that instead of using latitude and longitude a ship merely reported that it was in, i.e., 'square 8231'. This did not give a unique reference, since there were other squares so numbered, but where there was any doubt the full code, with its two-letter prefix, would be employed. Hence 'AN8231' would refer to a point in the southern North Sea, whilst 'AF8231' was located somewhat north-west of Kristiansand in Norway. This system was obviously more secure, provided the enemy did not have the grid charts. Furthermore, during sorties of this nature, several navigational points were usually established to define the area of operation and to act as 'sea-marks'. These were usually labelled 'Point I', 'Point II', etc., but were often allocated names, particularly of German towns; thus in 1941 Vardo, near the North Cape in Norway, was 'Berlin', whilst 'Leipzig' was a point at sea, 69° 23' N 35° 08' E, in the same operational area.

From 'Point I' the destroyers steamed down swept channel 'Red' along the Friesian Islands to 'Point II', some 20 miles west-north-west of the island of Terschelling, and from there altered course almost due west, steaming at 27 knots, towards 'Point III', about 40 miles off the Wash. By this time, however, *Arnim* was having trouble with her boilers and had to shut two down; furthermore, both a boiler room fan and a generator failed, so that at 1835 hours the flotilla commander ordered her to return. He decided to continue the lay using *Giese* alone but altered the laying point in view of the reduced number of mines now available. The lay was now to begin some 4.2 miles off the Cromer Light, with the light bearing 271.5°. Course was altered to port to transit the various navigation points until the laying point ('Point Y') was reached. En route several darkened vessels, either patrol vessels or merchantmen, were seen by, but did not spot, the German ships.

After midnight, under a clear, starry night, with some haze over the coast, two more darkened ships were sighted approaching, west of the Cromer Knoll Lightvessel. These two ships suddenly reversed course at 0205 hours, and it was feared aboard the German destroyers that they had been sighted, but despite the very good, 9-mile visibility they were not detected. This proved an extremely lucky escape, since it is almost certain that the ships were the Royal Navy destroyers *Jersey* and *Juno* on patrol between the Humber and the Outer Dowsing, having sailed from the Humber on the afternoon of the 6th, and *Giese* would certainly have been in an unenviable position had she been caught with her mines still aboard. Throughout the night of 6/7 December the two British destroyers had patrolled their beat, steaming 145° down to the Haisborough Lightvessel and then returning on 325°, and it was at the southern turn on the second patrol that they were sighted by the intruders.

At 0212 hours the lay commenced, position-finding being a little complicated by the absence of shore lights, but the Haisborough Lightship, only about 3 miles away, was showing a dimmed beam, as was a buoy eastward of the Cromer Light. Despite the proximity of the lightvessel, and the noise of two premature detonations, no alarm was raised, and the lay was completed at 0239 hours without further incident, whereupon *Giese* closed with *Lody* standing to the north. Visibility was improving, particularly to the north and north-east, when at 0255 hours, as the two destroyers were retiring, two darkened ships were detected bearing 010°, about 8,000m (8,700 yards) distant. It was some minutes before the bridge director sight correctly identified them as destroyers. Being in an unfavourable tactical position for a torpedo attack, Bey increased speed and turned to run parallel with the enemy, *Lody* leading and *Giese* in line astern.

By 0310 hours the destroyers were in position, having closed the range to 4,600m (5,800 yards) and passed the target data into their torpedo target calculators. *Lody* took the leading ship (*Juno*) as target and *Giese* took *Jersey*, and at 0314 hours the German ships fired three and four torpedoes respectively. *Giese* calculated her firing data from an estimated target speed of 26 knots at a range of 4,600m, launching with a 5° spread and a 20° deflection angle and

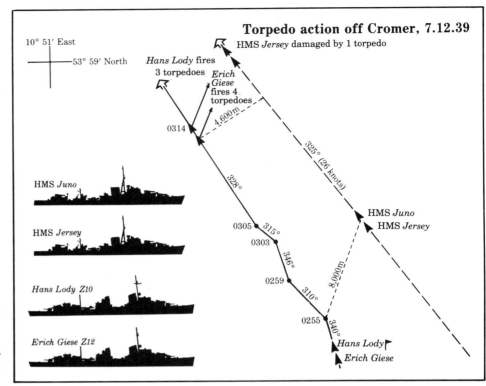

Torpedo action off Cromer, 7.12.39

setting the weapons to run at 40 knots. *Lody* set her torpedoes to run at 3m, which might account for her missing a sitting target, since the draught of the 'J' class destroyers was 9ft.* *Giese*, however, did not miss, one of her torpedoes striking *Jersey* on the port side abreast the after torpedo tubes in the fuel bunkers and wrecking the gear case room. Immediately a huge oil fire started, cutting off the after section of the ship. *Juno* turned to assist her stricken consort, laying a smokescreen as she did so; *Jersey* meanwhile lowered her whaler to rescue the doctor and other men trapped aft.

The two German destroyers, still not seen, briefly considered gun action, but decided against it in view of the distance home and the fact that the British ships had still not realized that surface vessels and not submarines had fired the torpedo. *Juno* must have remained a good target, however, and it is difficult to understand why further torpedoes were not fired: *Giese* may have carried only four torpedoes in view of her mine load, but *Lody* must have had a full outfit. Turning for home, the German ships crossed the North Sea at high speed, and by 1335 hours that afternoon they were passing the Jade minefields and were safe. *Giese* then proceeded to the Germaniawerft yard at Kiel for a refit, together with *Arnim*, the latter having had machinery repairs at Norddeutsche Lloyd in Bremerhaven following her abortive sortie on the 7th.

*But see comments on torpedoes and magnetic pistols in Chapter 4.

Back in the North Sea, *Juno* had taken *Jersey* in tow in the forenoon and shaped course for the Humber, the tug *Yorkshireman* helping shepherd the cripple into Immingham. After a month's temporary repairs in the Humber Graving Dock, where false frames and plating were fitted, she was moved over to Hull, where she remained under repair by Amos Smith & Co. until 23 September 1940.

A PRECARIOUS POSITION

The convoy route from the Thames to Scotland contained three focal points for shipping: two of these had already been dealt with and now it was the turn of the third. The Tyne was the assembly point for south-bound East Coast convoys for the period between November 1939 and February 1940, during which time it received the attentions of German destroyers on more than one occasion. The first operation occurred during the second week in December and was conducted by five vessels, of which *Künne* as leader (FdZ) carried no mines and acted as escort. The other four ships, *Steinbrinck*, *Heinemann*, *Ihn* and *Beitzen*, each loaded with 60 contact mines, constituted the laying group.

Künne sailed from Wilhelmshaven on 12 December, proceeding down the Jade and being joined by *Steinbrinck* and *Heinemann* in the Schillig Roads; later the same day the final pair, *Ihn* and *Beitzen*, joined the group as they passed through the German Bight. After the usual feint course during daylight hours, the destroyers crossed the North Sea at high speed and laid their mines without incident off the Tyne. Incomprehensibly at this stage in the war, with all the problems so evident in the Thames and Humber estuaries, the coastal lights in the Tyne area were still burning and the destroyers were able easily to fix their positions by the lights on Coquet Island, Curry Point, North Shields and elsewhere.

Turning for home at high speed, course was set for the entrance to the Skaggerak where, according to current practice, the cruisers of Commander Scouting Forces, Konteradmiral Lütjens, would meet them and cover their withdrawal to Germany.

The susceptibility of these destroyers to machinery damage manifested itself once again, however, and shortly after commencing the return journey *Heinemann* suffered a serious fire in No. 2 turbine room, necessitating the ship being stopped whilst it was extinguished. *Steinbrinck* stood by for over an hour as the fire-fighting parties aboard her sister got the outbreak under control. On the other side of the North Sea, the cruiser squadron, comprising the light cruisers *Nürnberg*, *Leipzig* and *Köln*, was awaiting the returning destroyers. Unseen below the surface not far away was another participant: HM submarine *Salmon*.

Salmon (Lieutenant-Commander Bickford) had already torpedoed *U6* nine days earlier off Stavanger, and now, at dawn on the 13th, she sighted the three cruisers at a great distance. It appeared, at first, that the cruisers would

remain out of range, but then an alteration of course put an attack into the realms of possibility. Two He 115 aircraft had just joined the cruisers as A/S air escort when Bickford fired six torpedoes still at long range. At 1124 hours the unfortunate *Leipzig* shuddered under the impact of an explosion amidships, her forward boiler room destroyed. Admiral Lütjens ordered a 90° turn to starboard to comb the tracks of any further torpedoes but when two more torpedoes were sighted they were, to his dismay, approaching from such an angle that the turn was presenting the starboard beam to them. Despite another emergency rudder order, this time hard to port, one of the torpedoes hit and blew *Nürnberg*'s bows off. The three cruisers, two of them crippled, were now in a precarious position. However, *Salmon* had gone deep to avoid the expected counter-attacks by aircraft and was unable to launch any further torpedoes.

The five destroyers, after being subjected to attack in error by German aircraft at 1120 hours, were still some 130 miles away, and received the information about the attack on the cruisers at about midday. They were ordered to proceed to the spot with all despatch, but shortly afterwards *Ihn* and *Steinbrinck* had to be detached to Wilhelmshaven because of machinery breakdowns and fuel contamination problems. The remaining destroyers reached the cruisers by 1357 hours and formed an A/S screen together with two 'F' class escort vessels and four 'M' boats.

Steaming slowly on zig-zag courses down the Danish coast, the crippled cruisers were shepherded towards the Elbe and safety, but before the security of the German ports could be reached they were sighted by another submarine, *Ursula* (Lieutenant-Commander Phillips), on patrol in the dangerously shallow waters of the Elbe estuary. Diving beneath the escorting destroyers, she fired a salvo of six torpedoes at close range towards *Leipzig* whilst the cruiser was some 8 miles to the south of Heligoland. Two of the torpedoes struck the escort vessel *F9* at 1233 hours, the unfortunate ship sinking three minutes later with heavy loss of life. *Beitzen*, the nearest destroyer, was only 400m from the explosion, but sighted no tracks. She was ordered not to depth-charge and concentrated on rescuing survivors, fifteen of whom, mostly (and unusually) engineering personnel, were picked up by the escort vessels.

Whilst the rest of the flotilla continued onwards, *Beitzen* and *Heinemann* conducted an A/S sweep but without result. *Ursula* had in fact come up to periscope depth to assess her results but quickly submerged again on seeing the two destroyers and stole quietly away. After some time the two destroyers abandoned their hunt and followed their comrades back into Wilhelmshaven.

The final results of this minelaying sortie were thus of mixed benefit to the Germans: eleven ships totalling 18,979grt had been sunk by the mines, but against this two light cruisers had been seriously damaged – one of which (*Leipzig*) was never again operational – and an escort vessel sunk; furthermore, the employment of cruisers to escort destroyers led to a serious disagreement between Admiral Raeder and the Commander-in-Chief, Admiral Boehm, as a result of which the latter resigned.

A DISAPPOINTING 'DOUBLE EVENT'

One further minelaying operation was planned before the end of the year. The 1st Flotilla, with *Ihn*, *Eckoldt* and *Schoemann*, sailed from Wilhelmshaven on 18 December for a sortie against the channels off Orfordness. By this time, as has been noted, all lights in the Thames and its approaches had been extinguished. As a result, when the destroyers reached the English East Coast they were unable to ascertain their position with the degree of accuracy demanded by minelaying operations, and they abandoned the sortie. No further operations of any significance took place during 1939: several ships were in dockyard hands, some on patrol duties in the German Bight and the rest running trials or training in the Baltic.

In the New Year minelaying resumed, the first target being once again the Thames estuary. On 6 January *Steinbrinck*, *Eckoldt* and *Ihn* (lst Flotilla) took on mines from the tender *Lauting* and sailed from Wilhelmshaven to join the support group consisting of *Galster* (FdZ), *Beitzen* and *Schoemann*. The lay was concluded without event, some 170 magnetic mines being dropped, and the destroyers again returned without having been detected. Six merchant ships totalling 21,617 tons were subsequently sunk on this field, as well as the destroyer leader *Grenville* with the loss of four officers and 73 men on 19 January.

The second operation of the year was a double event, with simultaneous lays in the Newcastle and Cromer areas. Taking part were *Heidkamp* (FdZ), *Eckoldt*, *Schmitt*, *Galster*, *Beitzen* and *Ihn*, the last four carrying mines destined for the approaches to Newcastle. The 4th Flotilla, consisting of *Heinemann*, Zenker and *Koellner*, were to mine the channel off Cromer. Both operations proceeded smoothly other than the now familiar machinery problems, this time aboard *Ihn*, which suffered tube failures, reducing her top speed to 27 knots, and, escorted by *Beitzen*, was detached to make her own way home. During the lays in January, 345 contact mines were dropped in the Newcastle and Cromer areas. The result from the Newcastle field was very disappointing, only the fishing trawler *Lucida* (251 tons) falling victim on 11 January. Off Cromer the mines were a little more successful, claiming three merchant ships totalling 11,153 tons.

By this time winter had set in with a vengeance, that of 1939-40 being particularly hard. Ice was many feet thick in some estuaries, and the sea froze off the English coast. The situation was no better (indeed, it was probably much worse) on the German side of the North Sea, with the Elbe, Weser and Jade all choked with floating ice, hindering ship movements and restricting warship operations. The old predreadnoughts *Schlesien* and *Schleswig-Holstein* had to be pressed into service as icebreakers, but many ships remained trapped in the Baltic, where the ice prevented training programmes from being carried through. The ice also hampered the crucial investigation into the problem of torpedo failures, since most of the work on torpedoes was conducted at the experimental establishment at Eckernförde near the Danish border. This was to affect the operational success of the U-boats for some further period to come and might well also have been a contributory factor in the low success rate of the torpedoes fired in the subsequent Norwegian campaign. It also seriously delayed the identification and rectification of the many defects and problems aboard the Type 35 torpedo boats considerably postponing their achieving operational status.

In view of the prevailing weather, therefore, it is hardly surprising that the next two sorties, planned for the nights of 17/18 January and 7/8 February, were aborted shortly after sailing. Severe icing, snow and rough weather rendered mine-carrying, let alone minelaying, extremely hazardous, storms causing damage to the ships themselves and washing mines overboard with ease. However, it was possible to carry through two operations during February, both on 9th/10th, one by *Eckoldt*, *Beitzen* and *Schultz* off the Shipwash, during which 110 magnetic mines were laid accounting for six ships totalling 28,496 tons, with a further vessel damaged, and the second by *Heinemann*, *Zenker* and *Koellner* off the Cromer Knoll near the Haisborough Lightvessel during the same night, in which 157 contact mines were laid, this latter field catching three ships of 11,855 tons. Both sorties were covered by a support group consisting of *Heidkamp*, *Riedel* and *Schoemann*. As things turned out, this was to be the last offensive sortie against the east coast of England because the operation planned for 15 February again had to be cancelled due to the weather.

Most of the Kriegsmarine's available destroyer strength was employed in these early sorties, seventeen out of a possible twenty-two ships taking part: *Eckoldt* participated in five operations, *Künne* and *Heidkamp* in four and *Beitzen*, *Heinemann*, *Ihn* and *Galster* in three each.

So ended a period of success, the like of which was never again to be enjoyed by the destroyers; riding high on the crest of confidence and optimism, their crews looked forward to 1940 to gain further laurels. It was not to be, however, and although the ships laid many more mines during the war the results did not compare with those obtained during the first five months. In point of fact, after 1941 most if not all of the minefields laid were of a defensive and not offensive nature as the fortunes of war turned inexorably against Germany: having begun the conflict so successfully, the destroyer force was now to be dealt two crippling blows from which it was never to recover.

7. WIKINGER AND WESERÜBUNG: FEBRUARY TO APRIL 1940

The North Sea has always been an abundant source of fish, and the rich waters have been worked by the fishing fleets of many countries, not least Britain. During the war the trawlers of the east coast ports continued to harvest their crop, providing a vital proportion of the food supplies of an embattled nation. One of the most popular grounds was the Dogger Bank, a shallow area some 90 miles out, and frequent sorties by the Luftwaffe across the North Sea on bombing and reconnaissance missions had not failed to notice the concentration of fishing vessels there and had reported the fact to Naval Group West. Not only was the fleet a reasonable target in itself, but the reconnaissance reports also indicated that some of the vessels were acting suspiciously and thought to be co-operating with submarines. This seems to have been a throw-back to the days of the First World War, when, as a result of submarine attacks on defenceless fishing vessels, some trawlers were equipped to tow a submarine, usually one of the small 'C' class boats which, when the fishing fleet was threatened, could be released to hunt the attacker. However, although used successfully in the earlier war, it is doubtful whether the same ploy was ever tried during the Second World War; moreover, apart from a few attacks by U-boats on fishing vessels in the first few days of the war, the biggest threat came from the air.

Nevertheless Naval Group West decided that an operation against the trawlers would sting the British psychologically, might capture some valuable auxiliaries and could force the Royal Navy further to dissipate its escort strength by having to guard the trawlers. Planning went ahead, the project being code-named first 'Kaviar' but later 'Wikinger'. The Luftwaffe had promised fighter cover and bomber support, and the German destroyers, which would spearhead the operation, did not anticipate any reaction on the part of British naval forces during the short sortie, so that everyone concerned believed that it would turn out to be a simple exercise. Events were to prove them very wrong.

'A HEAVY BLOW TO MORALE

Assembled for 'Wikinger' were six Type 34 destroyers: *Eckoldt*, as leader, had Fregattenkapitän Berger – Captain

(Dl) – aboard, and she was joined by *Beitzen*, *Riedel*, *Schultz*, *Maass* and *Koellner*. Each ship carrying a prize crew, the flotilla sailed from the Schillig Roads at about midday on 22 February 1940, passing to the south-west of Heligoland, from where the air escort had to return because the weather had closed in. Altering course to west-north-west, the destroyers approached the 'Westwall' barrage, through which they intended to pass by using swept channel '1'. This channel, some six miles in width, was normally swept frequently by the 1st Minesweeper Flotilla to provide a secret, safe passage for German warships requiring to reach the North Sea. However, many minesweepers had been trapped in the Baltic because of the severity of the winter, and yet more were in dockyard hands: only three 'M' boats and two torpedo boats were available to the local minesweeping command to keep the safe channels clear.

Entering the minefields at 1900 hours, the flotilla formed line ahead, *Eckoldt* leading, followed in order by *Beitzen*, *Koellner*, *Riedel*, *Schultz* and *Maass*, with 200m between each ship, and, steering 300° with revolutions for 26 knots, the destroyers forged on, the bridge look-outs and upper deck personnel huddled in their watch-coats, collars turned up against the bitter cold. Apart from the cold, with air temperatures hovering around freezing point, the weather was good. A light south-westerly blew and there was a low sea mist, but what was disconcerting was that the full moon, almost dead astern, made the ships that much more detectable.

The passage proceeded without incident until, at 1913 hours, *Eckoldt*'s lookouts sighted a twin-engined aircraft abeam of the ships flying at an altitude of about 60m up and down the line of destroyers as if carefully identifying them. The wakes of the ships stood out clearly in the moonlight and Berger, rather apprehensive of the aircraft's intentions, reduced speed to 17 knots in order to keep the trails to a minimum. At 1921 hours the aircraft appeared again, and the destroyers went to anti-aircraft action stations: as the aircraft made another pass, *Beitzen* and *Koellner* opened fire with 2cm guns. The aircraft replied and sheered off, having been positively identified as German by the first lieutenant of *Maass* and as a hostile by *Koellner*, but it was unfortunate for the destroyers that they opened fire because it tended to confirm to the aircraft that the vessels were hostile.

The intruder was not sighted again until 1943 hours, when *Maass* reported it in the moon astern; a minute later it became obvious to *Maass* that the aircraft was on an attacking run, and two bombs were dropped. The destroyer opened fire but did not hit the plane. One bomb struck the ship and exploded between the bridge and forward funnel, whereupon she dropped astern, slewing round to starboard and signalling for assistance. *Eckoldt* went about and stood by *Maass* but could detect no outward sign of damage. The other ships started to turn back too, but were ordered off by the flotilla leader, which, standing off from *Maass* by 500m, began breaking out and preparing towing gear. Suddenly *Maass*'s anti-aircraft guns opened up again as two bombs fell astern and amidships. There was the flash of an explosion followed by a column of flame and smoke as the destroyer was mortally hit. One of the bombs appeared to have struck near the after funnel, and when the smoke had cleared the bows and stern remained starkly visible in the moonlight, pointing vertically upwards, the lower parts resting on the shallow sea-bed.

At 1958 hours the flotilla leader ordered all the ships to lower boats and rescue survivors. *Koellner* closed the wreck, where men were struggling in the oil-covered freezing water, dropping liferafts and lifebelts. Her motor pinnace was swung out, lowered, and secured to the starboard propeller guard to help the survivors. *Eckoldt* and *Beitzen*, too, lowered boats, whilst *Riedel* and *Schultz* circled watchfully on an anti-submarine sweep. At 2002 hours a new explosion to the north-west was heard aboard *Riedel*, some 1,000m from *Schultz*, from which direction the explosion came. As *Riedel* turned to assist, the hydrophone room sent up a warning: 'Submarine, strength 5 decibels, 200°, on starboard side'; at the same time the crew of No. 1 gun reported seeing torpedo tracks. At 0208 hours a pattern of four depth-charges was dropped, of which one did not explode, but *Riedel* was not moving very fast and the three that did detonate caused her considerable damage, the gyrocompass, rudder motor and all command elements being temporarily knocked out by the shock. Korvettenkapitän Böhmig ordered the depth-charging stopped and instructed all hands to put on life-jackets because of the presence of submarines and the destroyer's lack of manoeuvrability. Whilst the steering motors were being repaired, hand-steering was employed.

The reports of submarines, the depth-charges, the mysterious aircraft and the general ignorance of what was going on all combined to generate panic amongst the remaining destroyers. Submarines and torpedoes were sighted everywhere, and no one had a clear idea of what was happening. *Koellner*, on seeing the depth-charges dropped by *Riedel*, ordered her picket-boat cast off and, under the mistaken impression that this had been done, worked up speed, dragging the boat under and drowning its unfortunate occupants. *Koellner* circled and arrived at the

wreck to find that there were no survivors clinging to the hull. Had they all been rescued? If so, by whom? Was this in fact *Maass* at all?

As she nosed into the wreck another report reached the bridge: 'Torpedo approaching, submarine to port'. Panic again ensued. The time was now 2030 hours, and Fregattenkapitän Schulze-Hinrichs, *Koellner*'s captain, believing that he himself had seen two torpedo tracks, ordered full ahead and turned to port, abandoning the helpless men in the water. Suddenly, as she made to ram the 'submarine', its 'conning tower' revealed itself to be the bows of *Maass* still protruding in ghostly fashion from the surface of the sea. It was now obvious that two destroyers had been sunk, and the facts were quickly transmitted to the flotilla leader, whereupon the surviving ships were ordered to steer 120° and retreat back to Wilhelmshaven at 17 knots.

When the casualty toll was finally counted, there were found to be only 60 survivors from *Maass* (24 on board *Koellner*, 19 on *Eckoldt* and 17 on *Beitzen*) out of a ship's company of 330; there were no survivors at all among the 308 men aboard *Schultz*. The freezing waters and the lack of a co-ordinated rescue attempt resulting from the submarine panics were responsible for the high figures.

A disaster of such magnitude demanded an explanation, but such was not easily come by at first because all the reports from eye-witnesses differed. Initially, it was believed that the aircraft had been British and had sunk both destroyers, but this was not a convincing answer since British aircraft had so far been singularly unsuccessful in their attacks and that they could sink two ships together in one night was a little difficult to believe; further, *Maass* had definitely identified the aircraft as German. It was not until reports began to come in from Fliegerkorps X that one of their aircraft had attacked a ship steering 300°, 20 miles north of the Terschelling Lightship, that the awful possibilities dawned upon Naval Group West.

Could the destroyers have been sunk by friendly aircraft? At first discarded, this theory grew and eventually reached the ears of Hitler, who ordered an immediate enquiry, which was convened aboard the heavy cruiser *Hipper* on 23 February. Statements were taken from the survivors, the destroyer crews and the air crews. After much deliberation it was concluded that one aircraft, an He 111 from 4/KG 26, had made two bombing runs, sinking first *Maass* and then *Schultz*. The aircraft was part of a force sent out to attack shipping in the North Sea, an operation about which the Luftwaffe notified the Kriegsmarine but about which the latter did not see fit to warn its own destroyers; furthermore, the Kriegsmarine did not notify the Luftwaffe that its destroyers were at sea.

The conclusions reached by the court of enquiry did not result in anyone being punished, and the incident further widened the rift between the Kriegsmarine and the Luftwaffe. There seems to be little doubt, however, that the losses can be attributed to the Navy's gross inefficiency.

Above: Destroyers at Cuxhaven on 6 April 1940, in readiness for 'Weserübung' (Bundesarchiv)

The court's finding in 1940 can probably now be disputed in the light of post-war evidence, since although no British submarine was anywhere near the spot in question, British Intelligence had located the position of the swept channel and had sent two destroyers to mine it on the night of 9/10 February, and these mines, given the weak minesweeping forces available, would probably have still been there on the night of the disaster. It is a strong possibility, then, that whilst *Maass* was definitely sunk by bombs, *Schultz* may have been mined after bombing, because the ships became disoriented following the first attack and she may well have strayed into the British field. Thus ended Operation 'Wikinger' – a heavy blow to the destroyers' morale and a sortie which resulted in the ships' first losses. It was shortly to be followed by an even bigger catastrophe.

MAJOR BENEFITS

The weather continued to be very cold and during March 1940 prevented any major operations being undertaken. Behind the scenes at Hitler's headquarters and in the high commands of the three services, however, detailed planning was well under way for an operation which would rank as perhaps the most important Kriegsmarine undertaking of the whole war – 'Weserübung', the invasion of Norway. The strategic importance of that country both to the Allies and to Germany, and its relation to events in the Baltic, Finland and Russia and to the German war economy, are complicated questions, and a detailed appreciation is outside the scope of this book. Some brief explanation is, however, relevant.

To the Germans, possession of Norway would confer several major benefits. First, the valuable iron ore traffic which passed down the Norwegian coast from Narvik during the winter months when the Gulf of Bothnia was iced up could be securely protected, indeed totally appropriated, for the German war effort. Second, the acquisition of naval bases in northern Norway would greatly facilitate the break-out by capital ships and raiders into the Atlantic Ocean for mercantile warfare, and third, any possession of Norway by Germany naturally denied the country to the British.

Britain's interest in Norway was two-fold. From a naval point of view it was desirable that a mine barrage be placed in Norwegian territorial waters, in order to force the ore traffic out into the open sea where it could be attacked, although this could not be done without violating Norway's neutrality. The second reason was political. The Russo-Finnish war had broken out on 30 November 1939 and the British Government was considering ways to support the Finns in their struggle, consideration being given to sending troops and supplies across Scandinavia to the Gulf of Bothnia. At first, both British and German governments were reluctant to take any step against Norway, but Germany, having wind of British plans in that direction, then decided on a pre-emptive strike.

To support the Army's invasion of Norway (and of Denmark, which was to be taken at the same time), the Kriegsmarine gambled almost its entire strength. Without seaborne support the operation would have been doomed to failure, and even so, had the British reaction been quicker, better conceived and more confident, the German Navy might well have been almost wiped out as it withdrew from the landings.

To convey the troops and cover the landings, all the serviceable units down to torpedo boats were employed; only *Admiral Scheer* and the cruisers *Nürnberg* and *Leipzig* of the major units did not participate. All sixteen operational destroyers were allocated to the invasion force, the remaining four (*Ihn*, *Steinbrinck*, *Galster* and *Lody*) being in dockyard hands under refit. The invasion force itself was divided into eleven groups, of which Groups 1 to 6, formed mostly by the heavy units and destroyers, were to subdue Norway, Groups 7 to 11, composed in the main of light forces, being despatched to deal with Denmark. Almost the whole of the destroyer force was allocated to Group 1, whose task it was to transport General Dietl and his Mountain Division to occupy the port of Narvik. Eleven destroyers were allocated to this group, although one, *Beitzen*, was held in reserve. *Heidkamp*, *Koellner*, *Zenker*, *Thiele*, *Arnim*, *Künne*, *Giese*, *Schmitt*, *Lüdemann* and *Roeder* were each scheduled to carry about 200 men together with their arms, ammunition and some light transport equipment. General Dietl embarked in the leader, *Heidkamp*, together with Kommodore Bonte.

All the ships of Group 1 assembled in Wesermünde during the first week in April and began embarking troops whilst alongside the Columbus Quay on the 6th; none of the destroyers had to stand down for any reason, so *Beitzen* was not required – a stroke of good fortune in the event. The remaining destroyers, allocated to Group 2, consisted of *Eckoldt*, *Riedel*, *Heinemann* and *Jacobi*, *Schoemann* having to be replaced by *Eckoldt* because of machinery defects. Group 2, together with the heavy cruiser *Hipper*, was charged with the occupation of Trondheim and embarked its troops at Cuxhaven on 6 April. *Hipper* took her group to sea at 2200 hours that day, navigating the narrow channels of the River Elbe down to the open sea. Passing the islands of Neuwerk and Scharhörn to port, the group continued course out into the German Bight, where it was to join with Group 1 and the battlecruisers *Scharnhorst* and *Gneisenau*, Group 1 sailing from Wesermünde at 2300 hours. Forming line ahead in the narrow, deepwater channel between the Würsterwatt and Langlützen sands, the destroyers steamed out into the German Bight for their rendezvous with the battlecruisers. Though none of the men aboard could know it, they were leaving Germany for the last time.

MOUNTAINOUS SEAS

On meeting the battlecruisers, *Hipper* and the fourteen destroyers took up their cruising stations around them and set off on the great adventure. During their passage through the German Bight and along the Jutland peninsula the weather was calm and the sky cloudless, and no doubt a few prayers were said for a veil of mist or rain. As a result of the fine weather, the force was sighted by twelve Bomber Command Blenheims from No. 107 Squadron RAF whilst standing to the west of the Skaw on the 7th. *Hipper* gave a timely warning and the attacking aircraft were met by a dense screen of anti-aircraft fire from all the ships, and, faced with such conditions, not one of the Blenheims was able to score a hit whilst the destroyers twisted and turned to avoid the attackers' bombs. Although Squadron Leader Embrey had radioed a warning and a sighting report, the signal was not picked up owing to a change in wavelengths, about which the aircraft had not been informed; the only station to receive the report was RAF Drem, but nothing was done since the report was addressed to Bomber Command, to which Drem did not belong.

The attack lasted no longer than 20 minutes, and the force pressed on. Meanwhile the weather had begun to deteriorate, the wind veering south-south-westerly and increasing to Force 5, with rising seas and poor visibility. All ships secured for heavy weather, double-lashing deck cargoes and rigging lifelines. Conditions on board for the soldiers were terrible. Trapped in a strange environment, confined in the fetid atmosphere of the mess decks and unable to keep their feet, most just lay down and succumbed to seasickness.

By 1800 hours the wind had increased to Force 6, and under the overcast, leaden skies, the destroyers began to feel the effects of the wind and waves badly: pitching and rolling, the ships lifted their stems in the following seas, plunging their bows deep into the water, which threw the green seas over the forecastle and bridge, and course could only be maintained by prodigious efforts on the part of the helmsmen. During the night the wind reached storm Force 7, scattering the destroyers and washing a number of embarked troops and crewmen overboard; rescue attempts were plainly impossible and the force continued. Equipment was lost overboard, and the heavy seas broke lashings on the depth-charges, which exploded in the destroyers' wakes as they corkscrewed onwards.

By early morning on the 8th the wind had veered southwest but the weather remained atrocious. A heavy sea caught *Heidkamp* amidships, cascading into No. 1 boiler room through the fan intakes, extinguishing the burners and shorting electrical circuits. Below decks, as the destroyer rolled on her beam ends, confusion reigned in the darkness. The engine room staff managed to restart the boiler and mend the lighting, and order was gradually restored.

At 0815 hours *Lüdemann* sighted an unidentified destroyer through the gloom, on an opposite course. It was the British *Glowworm*, which had been detached from escorting the battlecruiser *Renown* to search for a man overboard. *Glowworm* challenged the German and the latter replied 'Swedish destroyer *Göteborg*', but the ploy failed to deceive and *Glowworm* opened fire briefly as *Lüdemann* turned away into the murk. The British vessel was by now on full alert and when, 45 minutes later, she was again seen, this time by *Arnim*, fire was quickly exchanged. Not surprisingly, in the heavy seas running, neither ship obtained hits, although *Glowworm* was coping much better than the German.

Arnim signalled to her consorts *Jacobi* and *Eckoldt*, but the former was caught by the seas, which flooded the boiler rooms and swept five men overboard, and with only one boiler alight, she was forced to look to herself and ignore the fight; neither could *Eckoldt* engage, as she could not approach in time. *Arnim* attempted to lead *Glowworm* to *Hipper*, which had been detached at 0922 hours in response to *Arnim*'s signal, and the British destroyer willingly complied, hoping for bigger fish. Steaming through mountainous seas, *Hipper* sighted the antagonists; neither could correctly identify her, but a 20.3cm (8in) salvo aimed at *Glowworm* soon cleared up the problem. Twisting and turning in the heavy seas, the British destroyer made smoke to conceal her movements and endeavoured to work herself into a good torpedo attack position: hit by *Hipper*'s shells, but still moving, she fired her torpedoes without effect. Realizing that his ship was doomed, Lieutenant-Commander Roope manoeuvred to ram *Hipper*, inflicting severe damage. *Glowworm*, fell away, bows crumpled and on fire, sinking shortly afterwards.*

*Roope was posthumously awarded the VC for this action.

Later that day *Hipper* and her destroyers were detached to Trondheim whilst the rest of the force continued northwards. The weather continued to deteriorate, with the wind now Force 8 and a long swell running. At 2100 hours on 8 April the ships had reached the latitude of the Lofoten Islands, where all the destroyers of Group 1 were to be detached to Narvik whilst the battlecruisers continued northwards as a diversion. As midnight approached, the destroyers, running up Vestfjord, began to feel the protection of the Lofotens to port, the seas reducing and the rolling becoming less. Speed could now be increased to 27 knots, but the storms had taken their toll of the destroyers' oil tanks: forced continually to manoeuvre, the ships had consumed enormous quantities of fuel, particularly *Giese*, which now trailed far behind, steaming slowly, in an effort to conserve her remaining bunkerage.

At 0300 hours on 9 April the destroyers had passed the pilot station at Tranøy whose light was still burning on the black and white striped tower, providing a valuable navigational beacon. Ten minutes later a Norwegian coastguard vessel hove in sight, but although the destroyers went to action stations no attempt was made to interfere with their progress. The sea was now calm and the embarked troops were thankful to see daylight again after 2½ days confined below decks. Altering course eastwards, the flotillas rounded the island of Barøy and entered Ofotfjord.

Dawn was now approaching. A driving snowstorm cut visibility, and, forming line ahead and switching on their navigation lights, the invaders began feeling their way up the twisting fjord towards the first obstacles, the batteries on the Ramnes narrows. Suddenly, out of the snow appeared two Norwegian patrol vessels, *Michael Sars* (300 tonnes, two 47mm guns) and *Kelt* (one 47mm). *Roeder* ordered the Norwegians to heave to but they disregarded the command and radioed a warning to the coast defence ships in Narvik. *Roeder* again ordered them to return to Narvik, but it was not until several 3.7cm rounds had been fired that they reluctantly complied; outnumbered and outgunned, there was little else that they could do.

Continuing up the fjord at 27 knots through the snowstorm, the destroyers approached the narrows, where *Lüdemann* and *Schmitt* were detailed to land their troops, the 1st and 6th Companies, 139th Mountain Regiment, to secure the positions. Whilst they slowed and swung out their boats the remainder of the destroyers pressed on up the fjord towards Narvik, but the information concerning the batteries had proved false and the troops, after searching fruitlessly for some time, were re-embarked at about 0800 hours. Whilst their troops were ashore the destroyers had apprehended the fishery protection vessel *Senja* (243 tonnes, one 47mm) and sent her back into Narvik under guard; in the meantime Bonte had detached the 4th Flotilla (*Zenker*, *Koellner* and *Künne*) to proceed up Herjangsfjord to Elvegard at the head of the inlet, where the regional depot for the Norwegian Army's 6th Division was situated. Here the ships were to land more troops from the 139th Regiment and then act as fire support in the absence of any of the Army's own artillery.

Leaving *Roeder* on patrol at the entrance to Ofotfjord, Bonte continued eastwards with his remaining ships, *Heidkamp*, *Thiele* and *Arnim*, *Giese* not having yet entered the fjords. Shortly, through the snow ahead, loomed the bulky outline of the coast defence ship *Eidsvold*, which had anchored outside Narvik harbour the previous night when it was clear that an invasion was about to take place. The Norwegian look-outs had sighted the German destroyers and a shot was fired across their bows whilst the signal 'Heave to immediately' ran up the Norwegian yardarm. *Thiele* and *Arnim* swung out of line and continued on whilst the leader slowed and lowered a boat to take the commodore's 2nd Staff Officer, Kapitänleutnant Gerlach, across to present the Germans' demands.

The situation was tense as the boat crossed between the ships, for although *Eidsvold* had been built in about 1900 she nevertheless mounted two 21cm and six 15cm guns. Gerlach informed Captain Willoch of *Eidsvold* that they had come as friends and defenders but that he must immobilize his ship, but the demands were obviously unacceptable to the Norwegians and Gerlach was sent away. *Eidsvold* trained her guns on to *Heidkamp* but trickery was afoot: on leaving the coast defence ship, Gerlach's boat cleared the range for the destroyer and fired a Very light, indicating lack of success in the negotiations. *Heidkamp*, in readiness for the signal, had already trained her tubes on to the Norwegian and quickly fired four torpedoes. Two hit, and the captain and 174 men perished with the old ship.

Inside Narvik harbour, warned and ready, lay a second coast defence ship, *Norge*. This ship, a sister of *Eidsvold*, was equally elderly, having been first commissioned in 1901. Her captain, Askim, challenged the two destroyers as they entered the harbour but received no reply. *Norge* opened fire with her ancient 21cm guns but her shells landed in the water beside the Germans as they ran alongside the pier for the troops to leap ashore. *Arnim* replied with her 12.7cm guns, and for a few minutes battle continued as the two ships traded shots across the crowded harbour. After the initial salvo, however, most of the Norwegian shells were over, and fell into the town. *Arnim* then quickly took an opportunity to fire her torpedoes and launched seven. Five malfunctioned and missed, but although the other two ran on the surface they hit the old coast defence ship. *Norge* rolled over with, again, heavy loss of life; as she sank, *Thiele* arrived to land her troops, followed shortly by *Heidkamp*.

ATTACK AT DAWN

Narvik was occupied without resistance and the depot of Elvegard taken without trouble, and *Giese* finally managed to reach Herjangsfjord and anchor at its head at 0830 hours. *Lüdemann* and *Schmitt* re-embarked their troops at the narrows and proceeded to join their comrades in Narvik harbour, while *Roeder* was recalled from patrol and sent up to Elvegard to land her troops.

By early afternoon the first destroyer was ready for oiling, and by 1430 hours *Heidkamp*, as senior ship, was secured alongside the oiler *Jan Wellem* (11,776grt) to fuel. This

Below: An unidentified Type 36 destroyer at Narvik. (Author's Collection)

ship, a converted whaler, was one of three oilers allocated to the Narvik force and had put in there before the invasion commenced, having sailed down from Murmansk under the guise of a merchant ship. However, this was the Achilles' heel of the German plan because no special measures had been taken to protect the two oilers en route to Narvik, while the converted whale ship had neither the capacity nor the right pumping arrangements to deal with the ten destroyers quickly on her own. It was vital that the destroyers be fuelled and away before the British reaction caught them trapped in the fjords. Bonte waited anxiously for his other two oilers to arrive. One, the 6,031grt *Kattegat*, had sailed from Kopervik, north of Stavanger, on 6 April but had been detained by the Norwegian patrol vessel *Nordkamp* (a sister of *Senja*) whilst south of Bødø: dissatisfied with the German's reactions, *Nordkamp* sank her with her 47mm gun. The other, *Skagerrak* (6,043grt), had been captured by the patrol vessel *Stegg* and sent into Bergen on 7 April, where she still remained.

The Germans were unaware of these events, and the oiling of the destroyers in Narvik proceeded very slowly: by midnight on the 8th only *Heidkamp* had fuelled, and *Zenker* and *Koellner* were still alongside. In the early hours of the following morning, these two completed oiling and were dispatched to anchor at Elvegard, their places taken by *Künne* and *Lüdemann*. At 0400 hours the destroyers were positioned at various stations in the fjords; *Heidkamp* and *Schmitt* were both anchored in Narvik harbour, while *Künne* and *Lüdemann* remained alongside *Jan Wellem*. Bonte's plan called for the destroyers to oil in pairs, with another always on picket duty out in Ofotfjord in case of surprise attack; the remainder would be dispersed about the fjords. At this time, *Roeder* was the picket destroyer and *Thiele*, together with *Arnim*, was in Ballangenfjord; *Giese*, in Herjangsfjord, had been joined by *Zenker* and *Koellner*.

The British were aware that something was afoot in Norway and had sent units of the Royal Navy to intercept the German forces. Out to sea, beyond the Lofoten Islands, was the 2nd Destroyer Flotilla under the command of Captain Warburton-Lee in *Hardy*. With him he had three other destroyers, *Hotspur*, *Havock* and *Hunter*, all 1,340-ton 'H' class ships mounting four 4.7in (12cm) guns and eight 21in (53.3cm) torpedo tubes; *Hardy*, as leader, carried five 4.7in guns. Warburton-Lee had been ordered to patrol the approaches to Vestfjord to prevent a German landing, but later, on the 9th, his orders were changed and instead the Admiralty ordered him into Narvik to destroy any enemy shipping there. Not knowing that the Germans had already landed in Narvik, he was very surprised to be informed, whilst stopping at the pilot station on Tranøy, that six large enemy destroyers had gone up the previous day. The Norwegian pilots also told him that a submarine had gone in, that the fjord was probably mined, and that the Germans held Narvik in considerable strength. Despite the fact that their flotilla had been boosted by the arrival of *Hostile*, the odds appeared to be very much against the

British in that the German ships were much larger and more heavily armed. Warburton-Lee decided to gamble on the advantage of surprise and signalled the Admiralty that he intended to attack at dawn, even though further warned by London that the Norwegian coast defence ships might also be in the hands of the enemy.

The British flotilla began to thread its way up the twisting fjord through driving snow which cut down visibility to 400 yards. Meanwhile Kommodore Bonte was hoping that he would be able to give his destroyers sufficient fuel for their return journey to enable them to escape to the south the following night. Dawn broke at about 0520 hours, with the weather still cold, windy and snowing, to find *Roeder* picking her way cautiously into Narvik harbour. *Roeder* had been the duty picket, but a misunderstanding of her orders led her to assume that the coming of dawn released her to return to harbour. As a result, instead of being able to surprise the British ships as they groped their way up the fjord the German camp was now undefended and the positions were reversed: as *Roeder* moved slowly into the harbour and prepared to anchor, her cable party cursing the snow and the cold, the British destroyers were only yards behind.

Barely ten minutes after *Roeder* had anchored to await her turn to oil and her upper deck parties were on their way below to the warmth of the mess decks, the British flotilla arrived at the harbour entrance. *Hardy* led *Hunter* and *Havock* across the harbour mouth, whilst *Hostile* and *Hotspur* were detailed to engage any shore batteries present. Surprise was complete. Sweeping round the entrance, *Hardy* fired three torpedoes at a destroyer, probably *Heidkamp*, and four more at the harbour installations; *Hunter* fired her full outfit of eight at destroyers in the harbour and *Havock* five more, all three ships opening up with their 4.7in guns at the same time.

Chaos reigned aboard the German destroyers. Hardly had the 'Action stations' bells sounded aboard *Heidkamp* at 0535 hours than a torpedo from *Hardy* stuck her port side in compartment III, exploding the after magazines, hurling the three after guns into the air and destroying the ship as far forward as No. 1 turbine room, Bonte, most of his staff and many others being killed. With the mangled stern awash, the ship's company managed to secure the wreck alongside a neutral steamer whilst the fight raged on. No sooner had *Heidkamp* exploded than *Schmitt* received a torpedo from *Hunter* in her port side on No. 2 turbine room, jolting Korvettenkapitän Böhme awake and trapping him in his cabin. Freeing himself, he rushed up on deck only to be blown overboard by a second torpedo explosion in No. 3 boiler room. The destroyer broke in two and went to the bottom in a few minutes. Not a shot had been fired at the British ships until now, the Germans believing that an air raid was taking place. The destroyers' flak armament fired fruitlessly into the sky until gun flashes were sighted off the harbour mouth, whereupon the situation became clearer. *Hotspur* fired a further four torpedoes into the harbour, and then Warburton-Lee took his ships around for a second attack.

Künne and *Lüdemann*, alongside *Jan Willem*, hurriedly slipped their wires, but *Künne* had suffered severe shock damage to her machinery as a result of the torpedo explosions on *Schmitt*, which had been only a few metres away. Both her engines seized, immobilizing her, but her armament was serviceable and she fired back at the British gun flashes though achieving no hits. After an hour or so she was able to limp across to the Post pier, where she secured alongside. *Lüdemann* suffered too. As she was coming astern from the tanker, without slipping wires or hoses, a shell destroyed the steering motor, causing a fire which necessitated flooding the after magazine, whilst a second hit knocked out No. 1 gun and caused casualties among the crew. Her fire was also ineffective.

It was, perhaps appropriately, the unfortunate *Roeder* which suffered most from the British gunfire: the nearest target, she received a rain of shells, one of which wrecked her cable gear, preventing her from either weighing or slipping her anchor, whilst two other hits in the port side oil bunker in No. 2 boiler room caused serious fires and dense choking smoke in the compartment, further hits in compartment XII, No. 3 gun and No. 3 boiler room all adding to her plight. Training her torpedo tubes to port, she launched her full outfit, angled to run out of the harbour entrance. None hit, probably because of faulty depth-keeping mechanisms, although several ran under the British destroyers, *Hardy*, *Hunter* and *Havock* all being able to avoid every one of the eight torpedoes. It is probably true to say that but for the faulty torpedoes *Roeder*'s salvo might have gone down in history and reversed the result of the Narvik battle; as it was she had shot her bolt, and by going astern and dragging her anchor she, too, reached the Post pier, where Korvettenkapitän Holtorf ordered her to be abandoned.

The second attack on the harbour caused further damage, and then Warburton-Lee decided to retire. The action had lasted less than an hour but the harbour was littered with sunken, sinking and damaged vessels. As the British withdrew, *Lüdemann* fired four torpedoes out of the harbour mouth towards the retiring ships, and one ran under *Hostile*. Not one of the five German destroyers remained undamaged, whilst little or no damage had been sustained by the 2nd Flotilla.

CAUGHT IN THE CROSSFIRE

Believing that he had dealt with all the enemy destroyers, it was an unpleasant shock to Warburton-Lee to find himself confronted with three more enemies off the entrance to Herjangsfjord. These were *Koellner*, *Zenker* and *Giese* of the 4th Flotilla (Kapitän zur See Bey) which had received the alarm and weighed anchor at about 0630 hours. Running down the fjord in echelon, *Giese* on only two boilers because of a shortage of fuel, the Germans opened fire with their six forward guns at a range of about 6,500m (7,000 yards). *Hardy* replied with a full broadside, and a running fight ensued in the poor visibility when two more ships appeared ahead of the British Flotilla. At this juncture, unknown to Warburton-Lee, the 4th Flotilla's ships had broken off their chase and turned hard to port to avoid *Lüdemann*'s torpedoes as they fanned out across the fjord.

Identifying the two ships ahead as friendly cruisers, *Hardy* challenged them and received gunfire in return. They were in fact *Thiele* and *Arnim*, which had been anchored for the night in Ballangenfjord; hampered by thick fog, these two only succeeded in getting under way at 0640 hours, but they arrived on the scene in the nick of time. *Thiele* opened fire on *Hardy* at 0657 hours at a range of 3,700m (4,000 yards), straddled with her fourth salvo and then began to hit. Caught in the crossfire, the leading British ship began to suffer heavily, and, hit in the bridge and wheelhouse and with her forward guns destroyed, she careered out of control at 30 knots as the two Germans crossed the British line and swung west to run parallel for a time. *Thiele* fired two single torpedoes, *Havock* five and *Arnim* one – all without effect.

Hardy, rapidly reduced to a wreck, was run ashore on the south side of Ofotfjord, blown up and abandoned. Some revenge was exacted by her flotilla-mates, however, since *Thiele* had been hit seven times, losing No. 1 gun, the transmitting station, No. 1 boiler room and a steering motor and suffering numerous fires. She lost way and continued to fire her remaining four guns in local control whilst *Arnim* raced by, firing as she went, although she also had been hit, five times in all. It was now *Hunter*'s turn to suffer as the two German ships reversed course and ran back down towards Narvik. Hit by 12.7cm and 3.7cm shellfire, *Hunter* had been reduced to a flaming wreck when *Thiele* fired three torpedoes, hitting the damaged vessel in the bows. She quickly lost way, only to be rammed by her next in line, *Hotspur*, whose bridge had been badly hit, wrecking the steering. Locked together, the two British destroyers continued to take heavy punishment until *Havock* and *Hostile*, as yet undamaged, turned back to assist their comrades. *Hotspur* managed to extricate herself from the wreck of *Hunter* and make her escape down the fjord, *Hunter* later sinking. *Zenker*, *Koellner* and *Giese* continued to chase, but they broke off the action after a short while and returned to Narvik, rescuing 50 men from *Hunter* on the way. Whilst *Giese* must now have been running almost on the smell in the tanks, both the other destroyers had fuelled, so that, even though fuel shortage is generally quoted, the reason for breaking off the fight is not clear.

On their way out of the fjords the British ships struck an indirect but nevertheless serious blow against the remaining German destroyers. To the Germans' misfortune, entering the fjord at that moment was the supply ship *Rauenfels* with supplies of ammunition for the destroyers and artillery and for other weapons for the troops ashore. Two rounds of HE

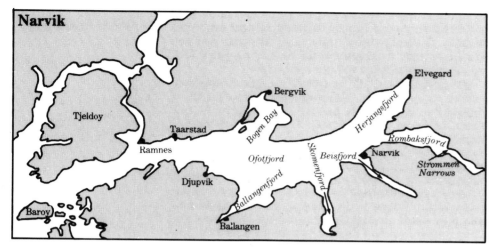

Narvik

from *Havock* converted her from an 8,460grt cargo steamer into an enormous, exploding column of smoke.

The echoes of guns and torpedoes died away, and peace returned to the fjords. Korvettenkapitän Bey, upon whom command now devolved, took stock of the situation. *Heidkamp* was slowly sinking and *Schmitt* had sunk. *Roeder* (five hits, immobilized), *Thiele* (seven hits, one boiler out) and *Lüdemann* (No. 1 gun destroyed, magazine flooded) had all been damaged to various degrees. *Künne* was undamaged and had now repaired her engines, and *Zenker*, *Koellner* and *Giese* remained unscathed and these had shot away 50 per cent of their ammunition. By late morning on 10 April *Zenker* and *Giese* were alongside *Jan Wellem* for fuel whilst the remainder still afloat began emergency repairs. The ship's company of *Heidkamp* returned to the wreck and began to salvage guns and ammunition. Naval Group West ordered Bey to break out that night with *Zenker* and *Giese*, and at 2040 hours the two destroyers, having fuelled, sailed from Narvik with Bey aboard in an attempt to break back to Germany.

Although darkness was approaching, conditions were not ideal, for the sky was cloudless and the visibility good. Passing down the fjord, Bey ordered *Thiele* and *Künne* out from Narvik when abreast the wreck of *Hardy*, in order that a second search be conducted whilst he continued westwards. As the two destroyers reached the end of Ofotfjord a smoke cloud, thought to be more British destroyers, raised a false alarm – in fact, it turned out to be the still smouldering wreck of *Rauenfels* – and course westwards was continued until 2205 hours, when, after passing Bary, shadows were sighted which were identified as destroyers. A larger shadow which was thought to be a cruiser was just that, the British *Penelope*. These ships, stationed here for the express purpose of preventing the Germans' escape, did not sight the two destroyers, but their presence nevertheless undermined Bey's confidence and, incredibly, he laid smoke, reversed course and took his ships back into the fjord.

Throughout the next day, 11 April, the destroyers continued their repairs and oiling, and by late afternoon *Zenker*, *Koellner*, *Lüdemann* and *Künne* were fuelled and operational, but still no further attempt at escape was made. *Heidkamp* had finally rolled over and sunk during the morning and *Roeder*, written off as irreparable in the time likely to be available, was de-stored, had her weapons and ammunition landed, and was prepared for scuttling. *Thiele* and *Giese* were alongside *Jan Wellem*, making use of her workshop facilities whilst they endeavoured to repair their battle damage; *Arnim*, likewise, continued her repairs. Still Bey hesitated and did not sail his four serviceable vessels. At sea, in open water, with room to manoeuvre and with the opportunity to use their superior speed, they would at least have had a chance, but here in the narrow, blind fjords they were caught like rats in a trap, and the fates of the remaining destroyers were sealed.

Even without the presence of the enemy, the German destroyers were not safe, because the poorly charted fjords featured many rocks and ledges lying just below the surface. It was the unfortunate *Koellner* which first found one. Moving to her dispersal point in Ballangenfjord, she ran heavily aground and, as she was brought up all standing, her bottom was ripped open as far as No. 3 boiler room, flooding the transmitting station, torpedo warhead room and Nos. 2 and 3 boiler rooms. Shortly afterwards *Zenker*, too, touched bottom, luckily with much less damage; even so, her port screw suffered, thus affecting her speed. His indecision had now cost Bey two of his only four seaworthy and battleworthy destroyers.

ENTER *WARSPITE*

It would seem that by 12 April all hope of escape had been abandoned, and no further attempts were made. *Koellner* was little more than a wreck following her grounding and could only be employed as a floating battery. She transferred her oil fuel to the other ships to eke out their meagre supplies, and it was decided that she would be sent down the fjord to Taarstadt just east of the Ramnes narrows, where she could be camouflaged close inshore in a suitable position to use her torpedoes in ambush.

Eight destroyers now remained to Bey, but of these only *Künne* still possessed all her guns and torpedoes and was mobile. *Lüdemann* had four guns and four torpedoes left; *Zenker*, her propellers slightly damaged, still had her full outfit of torpedoes; and *Giese*, repairing machinery damage, had eight as well, two having been taken from *Heidkamp*. *Arnim* was good for 33 knots and had all her guns in order, plus six torpedoes (from *Heidkamp* and *Koellner*). *Thiele*, good for 28 knots, had four guns serviceable and six torpedoes, four of the latter having been taken from *Koellner*. *Roeder* had been stripped as a floating battery with only Nos. 1 and 2 guns manned, whilst *Koellner*, a wreck but with five guns and two torpedoes remaining, completed the sorry flotilla. At 1846 hours the peace was shattered as Swordfish aircraft of Nos. 816 and 818 Squadrons FAA from the carrier *Furious* flew in on a bombing attack, the noise of their Pegasus engines reverberating around the narrow, rocky fjords. The weather, however, was unfavourable, and only nine aircraft found the target, causing no damage except to some of the destroyers' crewmen ashore.

The ability of the German code-breakers to decipher British messages warned Bey that an attack was in the offing, so he moved his destroyers to meet it as best they could. On the morning of the 13th *Künne* escorted the damaged *Koellner* down the fjord towards her ambush position at Taarstadt, where part of her crew were to be taken off since they would not be required to steam the ship again. Moving slowly down-fjord, they had only reached Djupvik when *Künne*, at 1156 hours, sighted the vanguard of the British attacking force, comprising nine destroyers – *Bedouin, Eskimo, Cossack, Punjabi, Hero, Icarus, Forester, Foxhound* and *Kimberley* – supported by the battleship *Warspite* with her eight 15in (38.1cm) guns. All the destroyers were armed with 4.7in (12cm) guns, having between four and eight weapons each.

As she steamed up the fjord *Warspite* catapulted off her Swordfish scout plane to reconnoitre the route ahead and examine the various inlets. *Koellner*, unable to offer battle and unable to reach her original ambush position, turned to port and ran into Djupvik, hoping to surprise the British force from there instead. *Künne* radioed a warning to Bey, but pressed on closer in order to estimate the enemy strength more fully and then went about, laid smoke and retreated back to Narvik, exchanging shots through the snow falls with the leading British ships as she did so. Bey, on receipt of the alarm from *Künne*, sailed his destroyers at 1215 hours, *Lüdemann, Zenker* and *Arnim* slipping anchor and proceeding into the open fjord from Narvik harbour. *Giese*, lying with cold boilers, could not be sailed for some time, while *Roeder* remained alongside the pier as a floating battery, ready to use her forward guns against the harbour entrance.

Warspite's aircraft, returning to her nest after having sunk *U64* with her puny anti-submarine bombs, spotted *Koellner* lurking in her ambush position and alerted the oncoming destroyers by radio to the danger, so that when *Bedouin* and *Eskimo* rounded the point they did so with guns and tubes already trained to starboard. At 1309 hours both sides opened fire with shells and torpedoes at a range of only 3,500m (about 2 miles). Even *Koellner*'s 3.7cm guns joined in, but it was a hopeless fight for the German ship: a stationary target, without the advantage of surprise, she was shot to pieces by the British, managing only one salvo in return and firing her two torpedoes. *Warspite*, too, joined in the target practice, firing two 15in salvoes at the unfortunate destroyer. Hit in No. 1 boiler room and No. 2 turbine room by shellfire and then having her bows blown off by a torpedo, *Koellner* was doomed. Her ready-use ammunition was expended and the shell hoists destroyed, and Fregattenkapitän Schulze-Hinrichs ordered her to be scuttled, a depth-charge detonation in the auxiliary machinery space sending her to the bottom soon after. Her casualties were 31 killed and many wounded.

Having dealt with one destroyer, the British squadron pressed on up the fjord. *Künne* had by now met her three compatriots from Narvik harbour and swung into line astern with them to await action. There now took place a confused destroyer action, both sides manoeuvring in and out of the snow squalls, firing guns and torpedoes, whilst another Fleet Air Arm attack brought further havoc, but, once again, no serious damage was done to the German destroyers as they twisted and turned at high speed. In the poor visibility, most of the shooting was also ineffective, and as the Germans withdrew they reached the entrance to Herjangsfjord, where *Thiele* joined them from Narvik. She fired four torpedoes without scoring any hits and then joined Bey as he ordered a retreat up Rombaksfjord, the destroyers having by now expended most of their ammunition. *Künne*, however, was standing to the north of the other vessels and withdrew up Herjangsfjord instead, her ammunition gone. Her crew prepared her for scuttling, ran her ashore and abandoned her; moments later, a depth-charge exploded in the torpedo warhead room, breaking her in two. Her wreck was later torpedoed by *Eskimo*, but *Künne* had suffered neither hits nor crew losses during the day's action.

As *Künne* was running ashore, *Giese*, with steam on her engines at last, got under way at about 1405 hours. As she approached the harbour entrance, however, her port engine failed, preventing her from turning and leaving her stopped for thirteen minutes. Whilst stationary, both she and *Roeder* engaged whatever targets could be located, initially *Eskimo* and *Punjabi*. *Giese* fired three torpedoes and the British destroyers three and two respectively, all without effect, but both *Giese* and *Roeder* engaged *Punjabi* with gunfire, hitting her hard. The 'Tribal' had her transmitting station wrecked, forcing the guns into local control, and then received two serious hits forward, causing fires, and a fourth, aft, necessitated the flooding of the after magazine; yet another shell destroyed the starboard motor boat and punctured steam pipes. Neither of the British destroyers managed seriously to damage either of the two Germans.

Giese got her engines going again by 1405 hours and left harbour at 12 knots to be greeted by heavy and accurate fire from *Bedouin* and *Warspite*, although the latter's shells passed straight through the thin plating. *Giese* fired her last torpedoes at *Punjabi*, which narrowly avoided them, and after firing her last shells was abandoned, adrift and on fire. She sank later, having been hit at least twenty-one times.

Following the destruction of *Giese*, *Cossack* nosed her way into Narvik harbour, only to be met by heavy and accurate gunfire. Shells hit her bridge, wrecking the steering and telegraphs and putting her out of control, so that she ran aground on a wreck at the south side of the

Above: *Georg Thiele* aground during the action on 13 April 1940. (IWM)

fjord. Here she remained for the next twelve hours, until she could be towed off by *Kimberley* after the action. It was thought at first that a shore battery had been responsible, but in fact her assailant was *Roeder*, using her Nos. 1 and 2 guns. Retribution rained in on *Roeder* from the other British destroyers, torpedoes wrecking the jetties and shellfire setting her ablaze. She exploded and sank just as *Foxhound* was about to board her.

As this action was taking place in the harbour, the rest of the British destroyers were pursuing the remainder of Bey's ships up Rombaksfjord. *Zenker* and *Arnim*, already out of ammunition, steered up to the head of the fjord, but *Thiele* and *Lüdemann* took up a strong position behind the Strommen narrows, whence they could ambush the British ships as they came through. *Thiele* had four guns operable (all except No. 1) but only two torpedoes left, and her fire control system for both guns and torpedoes had been destroyed. The brief lull was utilized to bring up ammunition and then, as the British came through the narrows, both sides opened fire at a range of about 5,000m (3 miles). British fire concentrated on *Thiele*, which was hit repeatedly. Her two torpedoes, fired personally by Leutnant zur See Sommer, the torpedo officer, left the after tubes. One failed to run, but the second ran true and blew off *Eskimo*'s bows as far back as 'B' gun. *Thiele* herself was, however, badly hit, receiving shells on her guns, W/T office, bridge and superstructure, and, with her ammunition expended, she was run ashore, where she broke in two and capsized. *Lüdemann* had also fired torpedoes, but without success, and then retreated up the fjord, being repeatedly hit on the stern as she did so. She joined up with *Arnim* and *Zenker*, and all three set demolition charges and their crews abandoned ship, although the charges aboard *Lüdemann* failed to explode properly and when the British destroyers *Hero* and *Icarus* arrived she was still afloat and seemingly intact. After a few salvoes, however, it became apparent that she was

abandoned, and each British ship sent across a whaler with boarding parties. The white ensign was hoisted and it was hoped to tow her off as a prize, but in view of the dangers of air attack this plan was vetoed by *Bedouin*'s CO, who had now arrived on the scene. *Hero* then destroyed *Lüdemann* with a torpedo, the wreck burning for some time.

Quiet descended on the fjords once more as the British withdrew, taking the damaged *Eskimo* and *Cossack* with them and leaving the wrecks of ten German destroyers littered around, wrecks that would remain mute witness to the disaster until the end of the war.

HEROIC DEFEAT

Surprisingly, no one was censured for the defeat on the German side. Bey's career seems to have been unaffected by his timid handling of the affair, although a little more enterprise on his part could have ensured the escape of at least two and possibly four destroyers; similarly, all the destroyer COs subsequently received further destroyer or flotilla commands, except, for some reason, Korvettenkapitän Friedrichs of *Lüdemann*. In fairness, however, the individual ships probably fought as well as the tactical situation allowed in a predicament caused by poor overall command strategy.

The action was seen as an heroic defeat in Germany and medals were struck to commemorate the battles; furthermore, the new Type 36A destroyers were thereafter popularly known as 'Narviks' and the flotilla to which they belonged was dubbed the '8th Flotilla (Narvik)'.*

In contrast to the misfortunes of Group 1, the destroyers of *Hipper*'s group fared much better and, indeed, had an almost uneventful time. Detached from the battlecruisers at

*Many of these large war-built destroyers did, unofficially, adopt the names of destroyers lost at Narvik, e.g., Z24 (*Georg Thiele*) and Z27 (*Erich Giese*).

about 1300 hours on 8 April, they were sighted at 1450 hours at 64° 12' N, 06° 25' E by a Sunderland on reconnaissance, but they were wasting time and steaming west when sighted, which confused the British Command. They were not intercepted, and by 0030 hours the squadron had Halten Light at the entrance to the Frohavet on the beam. Trondheim was occupied without much resistance, except from a shore battery which *Hipper* engaged with her after turrets, *Jacobi*, *Riedel* and *Heinemann* landing their troops to subdue it while she continued into Trondheim with *Eckoldt*.

All four destroyers had suffered a good deal of storm and sea damage during the passage north, and here, too, the fuel problem was acute: only about 40 tonnes remained aboard each destroyer, and there were no supplies to be had in Trondheim. *Riedel* ran aground, damaging her hull; her company was sent aft and she was beached in Strommen Bay, where she remained as a battery until 20 April. *Hipper* left for Germany on the 10th, accompanied by *Eckoldt*, whose bunkers had been replenished by other destroyers for the journey.

The Fleet Air Arm put in another appearance from *Furious* the next day, when Nos. 818 Squadron (Lieutenant-Commander P. Sydney-Turner) and 816 Squadron (Lieutenant-Commander H. Gardner) flew their Swordfish against Trondheim, this time equipped with torpedoes. *Riedel*, on her sandbank, spotted nine aircraft on a southerly course at 0717 hours and opened fire with all her armament, including her 12.7cm battery. The Swordfish flew in low at about 20m and launched their torpedoes at the three destroyers from a range of about 3,000m (3,300 yards), but the torpedoes were set to run too deep and they hit the bottom or grounded on the sandbanks, thus frustrating the attack. *Heinemann* and *Eckoldt* (the latter having abandoned her return with *Hipper* owing to the bad weather) left for Germany on 14 April, arriving two days later, whilst *Jacobi* remained in Norway until early May; *Riedel*, with damage to repair, did not sail for home until June.

A TORPEDO BOAT MYSTERY

The year 1940 saw the torpedo boats engaged in operations in the Skaggerak, with occasional requirements to act as fleet screen vessels. It began badly, however; on 31 January *Iltis* had the misfortune to ram *U15* which was on its way to another patrol off the east coast of England. The U-boat sank with most of its crew. *Iltis* was sent to the Seebeckwerft for repair and thus missed 'Weserübung'. In April eight were allocated to the invasion of Norway, making up parts of three groups. *Leopard* and *Wolf*, in Group 3, were assigned to take Bergen; *Greif*, *Luchs* and *Seeadler*, in Group 4, to capture Kristiansand; and *Albatros*, *Kondor* and *Möwe*, Group 5, Oslo. Of the last group, *Albatros*, whilst attempting to force her way into the narrow Pappelallee to land her troops, met with heavy fire from the minelayer *Olav Tryggvason* moored inside the harbour, and, able to reply only with his single forward 10.5cm gun (which developed defects after only eight rounds), Kapitänleutnant Strelow decided that it was not possible to take the harbour with one torpedo boat armed with a single gun and withdrew. In more open waters, she once again traded shots with the minelayer, whose fire continuously straddled, causing injuries amongst the embarked troops. Resistance was fierce, and the torpedo boat was then ordered to land her troops in Somsbugten to take the shore batteries at Bolarne. After trans-shipping the soldiers to *R21*, *Albatros*, under fire from the shore batteries, ran heavily aground and became a total loss.

The force sustained a third loss at the end of the month when *Leopard* was rammed and sunk by *Preussen* in the course of escorting a force of minelayers in the Skaggerak, and in May *Möwe* was badly damaged by a torpedo from the British submarine *Taku* off south-west Norway, requiring repairs at Wilhelmshaven until October. By midsummer the 2nd Flotilla had joined in operations, and in July both were engaged in escorting the minelayers whilst they laid fields in the eastern approaches to the Channel. Further fleet screening duties followed, in the course of which, on 26 July, *Luchs* was sunk off the south-west coast of Norway. There is some mystery as to the circumstances surrounding her loss, which happened whilst she was acting as an A/S screen for *Gneisenau* and *Nürnberg* with other destroyers and torpedo boats. *Luchs* exploded and quickly sank without any alarm having been raised. As the explosions occurred, the flagship reported sighting torpedo tracks and a periscope, while at least one of the destroyers sighted floating mines. Subsequently several more mines were sighted. What, then, was the agent of her destruction?

A British submarine, *Thames*, ought to have been on patrol in this precise area at the time, and this boat is generally listed as 'missing believed mined' on or about 23 July. However, there is no definite evidence for this date. If this boat were still operational by the 25th she would have received orders over the radio to proceed to 58° 40' N, 03° 30' E en route to a new patrol position, which would have taken her from a position west-south-west of Lindesnes on a north-westerly course which was bound to intercept the south-bound German squadron – indeed, the course was almost the exact reciprocal of the intended German one. In view of recent Intelligence revelations, this may or may not have been coincidental. No serious A/S hunt was made by the Germans, and no claim of a sinking, but it is not impossible that *Thames* was herself sunk by one of the drifting mines some time later. No signals had been received from the submarine since she had sailed, but this fact is not of great significance for it could have been a technical problem.

So ended 'Weserübung', at a cost to the Kriegsmarine of ten destroyers, three torpedo boats and the cruisers *Blücher*, *Karlsruhe* and *Königsberg*, not to mention many other ships damaged.

8. CHALLENGE IN THE CHANNEL: MAY 1940 TO OCTOBER 1942

At the end of April 1940 only ten destroyers remained on the strength of the Kriegsmarine, nine Type 34 or 34A and a solitary Type 36, *Galster*. Of these, only *Beitzen*, *Schoemann*, and *Heinemann* were operational, the others all being in dockyard hands, except for *Riedel* on her sandbank in Norway. With the loss of all the destroyers at Narvik, the 1st, 2nd, 3rd and 4th Flotillas were dissolved and two new flotillas raised, the 5th, comprising *Eckoldt* (leader), *Steinbrinck*, *Ihn* and *Beitzen*, and the 6th, made up of *Galster* (leader and FdZ), *Schoemann*, *Heinemann* and *Lody*; other vessels were not allocated for the time being.

No major operations were conducted during May, except minelayer escort and a couple of defensive minelaying sorties by some of the destroyers. During May *Lody*, *Galster*, *Steinbrinck* and *Ihn* all completed their refits and began extensive work-up for, despite the desperate shortage of ships of all classes, the Kriegsmarine maintained its peacetime training routines, with the result that six months often elapsed before a ship was considered battleworthy and sent into an operational area. To counterbalance this increase in strength, however, *Jacobi* and *Heinemann* went into dockyard hands for extended refits the same month.

Early in June an offensive sortie by the Fleet was planned against British shipping supplying the Allied landing forces in northern Norway. Under the command of Admiral Marschall aboard *Gneisenau*, the squadron consisted additionally of *Scharnhorst*, *Hipper* and four destroyers – *Lody*, *Schoemann*, *Steinbrinck* and *Galster* – though because of the chronic shortage of ships the post-refit work-ups of the first three destroyers had to be cut short in order to give the Fleet a screen. This operation, code-named 'Juno', was intended to entice out the Royal Navy from its close support of the weakly held bridgeheads in the Vestfjord area and threaten the supply lines.

Marschall sailed from Kiel on the morning of 4 June, intending to strike at Harstad on the night of the 8th/9th. Led by the barrage-breaker *Sperrbrecher 4* (the 6,757grt converted merchantman *Oakland*), the squadron sailed northwards through the Belts and the Kattegat, escorted also by the torpedo boats *Jaguar* and *Falke*, the tender *Hai* and R-boats as far as the Skaggerak. By noon on the 5th the squadron had reached the open sea and turned north-

westwards to round the southern tip of Norway. Steaming at 24 knots through poor visibility, Marschall continued up the Norwegian coast throughout the 6th, refuelling his destroyers and the heavy cruiser from the fleet oiler *Dithmarschen* from midnight onwards, a slow process that was not completed until the evening of the following day when *Hipper* slipped the hoses from the tanker. The Admiral had meanwhile received air reconnaissance reports of two groups of ships and decided to attack the southernmost, the tanker *Oil Pioneer*, escorted by the trawler *Juniper* and, sailing independently, the empty troopship *Orama* and the hospital ship *Atlantis*. Marschall signalled his intention, but Naval Command West ordered him to leave the attack on the convoys to *Hipper* and the destroyers and to continue northwards himself to execute the planned assault at Harstad. This order Marschall chose to ignore and spread his ships out in a long line abreast.

Hipper located *Oil Pioneer* at 0555 hours on 8 June, and the heavy cruiser opened fire on the tanker's escort, being joined shortly by *Lody* which opened up on the unfortunate *Juniper*. Leaving *Lody* to rescue survivors, *Hipper* turned her attention to the tanker, which was set on fire and then torpedoed by *Lody*, *Schoemann* this time rescuing the eleven survivors. At 0940 hours *Atlantis* was sighted by *Scharnhorst*, which allowed her to proceed unmolested, but the trooper *Orama* was not so lucky: sighted by *Galster* and chased by her and *Lody* (which called up *Hipper* because the destroyers believed that she might be an auxiliary cruiser), the luckless *Orama* was shot up by both *Hipper* and *Lody* and then torpedoed twice by the destroyer. *Galster*, *Lody* and the cruiser rescued the survivors, 274 men in all. Shortly afterwards, *Hipper* and the four destroyers were detached to Trondheim and thus missed the battlecruisers' action with the carrier *Glorious* and her destroyers. En route *Lody* captured a trawler, and by the afternoon of the 9th all the destroyers were safely in Trondheim.

During the course of the next few days both *Scharnhorst* and *Gneisenau*, and the light cruiser *Nürnberg*, had rejoined the Trondheim force, making quite a respectable target for the RAF and the Fleet Air Arm, although only the latter managed to get in an attack, with Skuas of Nos. 800 and

803 Squadrons from *Ark Royal*, and it was an expensive failure. *Lody*, *Schoemann* and *Steinbrinck* escorted the damaged *Scharnhorst* home to Germany between 20 and 24 April, attacked on the way by six Swordfish of Nos. 821 and 823 Squadrons from Hatston and also by nine Beauforts from No. 42 Squadron RAF. However, the ships put up a strong anti-aircraft defence and shot down two of the Swordfish, none of which secured any hits. The Beauforts, on the type's first sortie and each carrying two 500lb (227kg) bombs instead of torpedoes, dived down to 4,000ft (1,200m), receiving as they did so long-range barrage fire from the battlecruiser and destroyers. The latter, anticipating a torpedo attack, opened out their protective formation to about 1,400m radius and put up an intense fire with their close-range weapons; *Scharnhorst* meanwhile had turned hard to starboard and then to port to avoid the bombs, which she succeeded in doing. Disengaging, the Beauforts were set upon by the Bf 109s of the air escort and lost three of their number. Having safely escorted the battlecruiser home, *Schoemann* went into refit at Wilhelmshaven, whilst the other two returned to Norway, where they rejoined *Galster* and *Ihn* in Trondheim: all four were required to escort *Gneisenau*, which, after temporary repairs following her torpedoing by the submarine *Clyde* on 20 June, was to return home for full repairs.

The battlecruiser, accompanied by *Hipper* and *Nürnberg* as well as by the destroyers, sailed for home on 25 July, *Hipper* being detached that night for an anti-shipping foray in the Barents Sea. In the afternoon of the next day, torpedo boats of the 5th Flotilla joined the escort, but a short while later, whilst the squadron was some 40 miles east of Karmøy, the torpedo boat *Luchs* exploded and sank as recounted in the previous chapter. Leaving two torpedo boats to rescue survivors, the remainder of the squadron arrived in Kiel on the morning of the 28th.

In August the 5th Destroyer Flotilla moved through the Kiel Canal to Wilhelmshaven, from where, between 14 August and 6 September, it assisted the minelayers *Roland*, *Tannenberg* and *Cobra* in the laying of barrages 'SW0', 'SW2' and 'SW3' in the south-western corner of the North Sea. *Galster*, *Jacobi* and *Steinbrinck* participated in these operations, as did torpedo boats of the 1st, 2nd and 5th Flotillas.

HEAVY FLAK

With the fall of France, all the ports and harbours down to Bordeaux now became available to the Kriegsmarine: U-boats soon moved to Brest and Lorient, and the surface forces were not far behind them. It was with the object of striking at Britain's coastal traffic between Land's End and the Straits of Dover, therefore, that FdZ, Kapitän zur See Bey, was ordered to take the 5th Destroyer Flotilla westwards early in September 1940. Bey left Wilhelmshaven with *Lody* on 9 September, accompanied by *Galster* (D5, Kapitän zur See Berger), *Eckoldt*, *Ihn* and *Riedel*. After putting into Le Havre the next day, the flotilla continued westwards but were caught by RAF Blenheims on the morning of the 11th whilst crossing the Seine Bay. The only anxiety was a near-miss on *Ihn*, and no damage was suffered by any of the destroyers, which continued on and by early afternoon were secured alongside in Cherbourg.

There was by now an enormous concentration of barges, tugs and makeshift landing craft in French Channel ports, intended for 'Seelöwe', the planned invasion of England, and this was, of course, an important target for the RAF, who were continually raiding the ports. The newly arrived destroyers experienced one of these attacks scarcely a week later, when in the early hours of 18 September the RAF mounted a two-pronged strike on Cherbourg. There was a moon, but it was cloudy and the night was dark, and the plan therefore involved high-level Blenheims (53 and 59 Squadrons) first bombing the docks with incendiaries so that the resultant fires would silhouette the shipping in the port for the low-flying, torpedo-carrying Beauforts of No. 22 Squadron.

The attack developed as planned, with the six torpedo aircraft weaving low over the harbour. Both bomber and torpedo aircraft were met with heavy flak from the shore guns, destroyers, escort vessels and merchantmen in the inner roads, which was particularly undisciplined in the case of the merchantmen and Vp-boats. Although several Beauforts attacked the destroyer flotilla, no hits were scored and, in fact, it is doubtful whether the Germans were aware that torpedoes as well as bombs had been used, since no mention is made to that effect in their official records.

Three or four bombs fell on the Transatlantic harbour, opposite the Quai de France, and two more fell some 120m from *Ihn* without doing any damage. However, the steamer *Johann Blumenthal* was sunk, her crew being rescued by a boat from *Lody*, and the torpedo boat *T11* received splinter damage in one of her turbine rooms, causing some casualties. *Eckoldt* sent a boat across with her doctor to assist the wounded. One of the Beauforts (L4508) was shot down by the ships' defensive gunfire.

Leaving Cherbourg, the destroyers moved then to Brest, where they were to be based for the next couple of months. Their first operation was once again an offensive minelaying sortie, this time into the Falmouth area. Taking part were *Lody*, *Galster*, *Ihn*, *Jacobi* and *Steinbrinck*, carrying mine loads, with *Eckoldt* and *Riedel* as escort. Sailing on the evening of 28 September, and accompanied initially by the minesweeper *R26*, the destroyers steamed across the Channel, and, despite a scare when *Galster* detected a darkened patrol vessel at 0145 hours, the field was successfully laid between 0202 and 0240 hours on the 29th. The flotilla returned to France at high speed, was met by *R26* and *M4001* at 0717 hours, and was back at its moorings again by 1000 hours the following morning. Five small ships totalling 2,037 tons were subsequently lost on these mines.

Whilst at Brest Navy Yard following this operation the destroyers, dispersed about the harbour, once again suffered air attack, and some damage was sustained. The assailants on this occasion, in the early hours of 10 October, were Swordfish of No. 812 Squadron FAA on detachment to Coastal Command. Attacking with bombs, they scored no direct hits, but two missiles fell 30–40m from *Eckoldt*, one abreast the forecastle and the second abreast the after tubes, causing shock and heavy splinter damage. One member of the ship's company was killed and three others wounded. As a result of the damage, including leaks in an oil bunker in No. 1 boiler room, the destroyer was out of action for three or four days. *Lody* and *Riedel* were also damaged by splinters, which caused casualties among their crews, though *Ihn* and *Steinbrinck* escaped. Another attack developed at 2247 hours, but no further damage was caused, despite near misses on *Eckoldt* and *Riedel*.

A CRITICAL POSITION

Although two destroyer flotillas, the 5th and 6th, were in existence at this time, their organization was somewhat loose and ships from both commonly operated together in a seagoing capacity under the FdZ's overall command. Thus the next operation undertaken – an offensive sweep into the South-West Approaches – involved both flotillas and was commanded by Bey aboard *Lody*. Weighing anchor at 0503 hours on 17 October, *Lody, Steinbrinck, Ihn, Galster* and *Riedel* cleared the Chateaulin Roads and steamed a feint south-westerly course into the Bay of Biscay. The night was moonlit but cloudy, and there was a light south-easterly wind and a slight swell. At 0600 hours *Riedel* suffered five tube failures in No. 1 boiler room, having to shut off both boilers with the result that her maximum speed was reduced to 25 knots. She remained in company for a while, but at 0648 hours was ordered to return to Brest. A little later five torpedo boats of the 5th Flotilla joined as reinforcements. Course was altered due west at 0745 hours, but at 0830 a Blenheim aircraft was sighted to the north-east by *Steinbrinck*, whereupon course was altered once again, this time to the south-east.

Visibility had remained disturbingly good throughout the morning, so that it was with no great surprise that at 1056 hours Bey received a decoded British signal timed at 0820 and warning of four destroyers steering west at 48° 24' N, 6° 33' W; the Blenheim had obviously seen them and radioed a sighting report. Bey continued his operation,

Right: *Lody, Ihn* and *Riedel* with the oiler *Brossen* at Cherbourg in 1940. (Author's Collection)

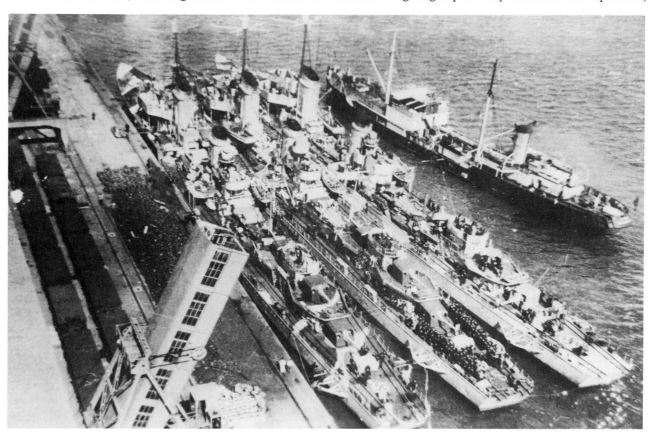

although by this time another of his destroyers, *Steinbrinck*, was experiencing machinery problems, her port manoeuvring valve having become blocked by a foreign body and the port turbine getting revolutions only for 22 knots. Nevertheless, the flotilla turned north at midday to run into the Western Approaches, and at 1533 hours Naval Group West passed an air reconnaissance signal timed at 1300 reporting that seven destroyers were south of Plymouth and steaming westwards at high speed. *Steinbrinck* was still having problems, this time with her starboard turbine as a result of tube failures in No. 1 boiler.

By 1700 hours the destroyers were some 40 miles southwest of the Scillies. Visibility remained very good, with a light east-north-easterly wind. Course had just been altered round to 190° when five shells suddenly landed astern of *Lody*. All ships rushed to action stations and connected all boilers, except *Steinbrinck*, which had only five operable. No enemy ships could be observed yet, but the shells had actually been fired by the light cruiser *Newcastle*, which on receipt and assessment of the 0820 hours Coastal Command report had sailed from Plymouth at 1121, accompanied by the cruiser *Emerald* and the 5th Destroyer Flotilla (*Jackal, Jupiter, Kashmir, Kelvin* and *Kipling*), to intercept the German force. The British ships (Force 'F') had been sighted and reported by German reconnaissance, but the presence of the cruisers was not mentioned. At 1445 hours Force 'F' received information to the effect that the German destroyers were at 48° 20' N, 6° 10' W, steering west at high speed, and altered course to cut them off. Then, at 1700 hours, *Newcastle* sighted a *Maass* class destroyer bearing 201°. She altered course to 200°, worked up to full speed and went to action stations. Seven minutes later *Newcastle* opened fire at extreme range with 'A' and 'B' turrets, and hoisted the general signal 'Chase'; *Emerald*, stationed astern of the cruiser, opened fire several minutes after her consort.

The four German destroyers retired towards Brest at 29 knots in line ahead, with 600m between each ship. By 1715 their attackers could be observed on the port quarter, at a range of about 28,000m (17½ miles), but the individual ship types could not be distinguished. There was, however, no doubt that at least one cruiser was involved, and twenty minutes later a *Southampton* class vessel was identified. Bey ordered the sortie to be broken off at 1738 hours, and the four destroyers worked up to full speed in order to outrun the British ships. Steering 180°, *Steinbrinck* led *Ihn* and *Galster* in starboard line of bearing formation, her companions making smoke; *Lody* was abreast of *Steinbrinck*, to port.

Newcastle had meanwhile catapulted her Walrus to port to provide air reconnaissance, and Force 'F' forged onwards, less *Jupiter* which had dropped astern with engine trouble. Intermittent fire was maintained, most of the salvoes landing in the vicinity of *Galster* and *Lody*, which, owing to their evasive action, were not hit. A north-north-easterly wind, Force 2–3, favoured the smokescreen; this

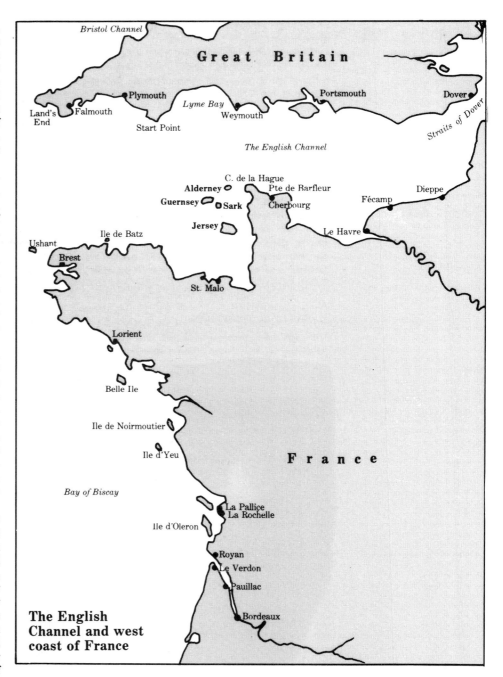

The English Channel and west coast of France

effectively protected *Steinbrinck*, which had not as yet come under fire. However, despite the Germans' theoretically superior speed, the range dropped steadily from 18,600m to 16,000m (11½–10 miles) by 1800 hours, and fifteen minutes later *Steinbrinck* received isolated fire for the first time. The British gunnery was good, the destroyer being bracketed fore and aft and straddled with columns of water only 10–20m distant. Some splinters came aboard, but

Above: *Karl Galster* seen in Brest in 1940, now fitted with tripod mast and radar. (W. Z. Bilddienst)

before any serious damage was sustained she regained the safety of the smokescreen from *Lody*. The latter now led *Ihn*, *Galster* and *Steinbrinck* in starboard quarter-line at speeds of up to 35 knots, but the position was becoming critical.

The British ships were now clearly visible to the naked eye, their large battle ensigns streaming in the wind, and in an attempt to delay their progress *Lody* and *Galster* fired three torpedoes each with their tubes trained hard astern; *Steinbrinck* turned to port to run parallel with Force 'F' and fired four torpedoes, estimating enemy range and speed to be 14,500m (9 miles) and 32 knots. Returning to course, there was jubilation on her bridge and congratulations for her torpedo officer when, at 1900 hours, a column of smoke arose twice mast height on a cruiser. Oberleutnant zur See Sommer, who had fired the torpedoes, already had something of a reputation, having been *Thiele*'s TO at Narvik when he torpedoed both *Hunter* and *Eskimo* during the battles in the fjords. German records still note this 'hit', but the log of *Newcastle* gives the probable explanation.

The cruiser's Walrus had been spotting for the guns and reporting the enemy's movements since take-off, and she signalled a warning of approaching torpedoes to her parent ship at 1841 hours, whereupon *Newcastle* altered course to 196° in order to comb them. A little later, a Do 17 bomber, which had been shadowing the British force in turn, made a run on *Newcastle*, which replied with her 4in (102mm) AA. At 1901 the Dornier dropped a stick of bombs astern of the cruiser and was engaged by all the force – including the Walrus. Coincidentally, it is probable that the splashes observed were from the bombs and that the smoke was 4in gunfire in reply.

The range had now opened and there was no chance of the Germans being caught, so that at 1921 hours, just as a Blenheim aircraft had dropped four or five bombs on *Steinbrinck*, missing by 30–50m to port, Force 'F' abandoned the chase, altered course to 070° and reduced

speed to 26 knots because of a defect in *Newcastle*'s No. 3 boiler room. By 0905 the next day the cruiser was back in Plymouth. The German destroyers, too, had an uneventful passage after that, reaching Brest before midnight.One Blenheim (T2319) failed to return from these attacks.

The focus of torpedo boat activity also moved south-west once more during the last few months of 1940, when almost all the operational ships took part in intensive mining sorties around the Straits of Dover. In September, the 1st and 2nd Flotillas were ordered to Cherbourg for operations in the Channel, but on the 12th *T2* was damaged by bomb splinters when attacked off the Scheldt by a Blenheim and put into Vlissingen for repairs. The 2nd Flotilla carried out the mine-laying sorties 'Walter Hanalore' and 'Bernhard' in the same month, whilst the 5th Flotilla (*Greif*, *Kondor*, *Seeadler*, *Falke* and *Wolf*) caught and sank the Free French submarine-chasers *CH6* and *CH7* and the trawlers *Listrac* (778 tons) and *Warwick Deeping* (445 tons) off the Isle of Wight on the night of 11/12 October, but *T11* had been hit and damaged by a bomb in her forward turbine room on 18 September. In the same month *T3* was bombed and sunk whilst in Le Havre; she was raised in 1941, but not fully repaired and recommissioned until 12 December 1943.With the postponement of 'Seelöwe', the 1st and 2nd Flotillas were ordered home, the 5th to St. Nazaire and the 6th to Le Havre.

During the latter half of 1940 the number of U-boats entering service in the Kriegsmarine was beginning to rise. As a consequence there were manning problems, since, despite popular belief, there were never enough volunteers for this service. To fill the vacancies all the other arms were scoured for suitable crewmen, the destroyer and torpedo boat forces being no exception. In October both the torpedo and gunnery officers of *Ihn* and *Eckoldt* were 'commandeered' for U-boat duty, and the two destroyers were practically non-operational as a result of these and

many other crew changes. FdT temporarily countermanded the order; both he and Naval Group West made strong protests to OKM, but to no avail, and the officers had to be given up. Crew changes were to be a frequent and continual problem throughout the war, particularly from 1943 when restricted sea time slowed up the training of new crew members and therefore reduced the efficiency of many units.

At the beginning of November 1940 both the 5th (Kapitän zur See Berger) and 6th (Kapitän zur See Schulze-Hinrichs) Destroyer Flotillas were based in Brest and disposed eight ships: *Galster* (FdZ), *Jacobi* (D6), *Eckoldt* (D5), *Ihn*, *Beitzen*, *Lody*, *Steinbrinck* and *Riedel*, *Beitzen* having only recently arrived in French waters. These vessels constituted all the available operational destroyers: only *Schoemann* and *Heinemann*, both refitting or working up, and the new *Z23* and *Z24*, on trials, remained in home waters. Of the torpedo boats, seven were stationed in French waters, *Falke*, *Greif*, *Kondor* and *Seeadler* at St Nazaire, and *Iltis*, *Jaguar* and *Wolf* at Cherbourg; the remaining boat, *Möwe*, was still under repair at Wilhelmshaven.(The Type 35 boats of the 1st and 2nd Flotillas were all in Norway.)

This strong concentration of destroyers and torpedo boats was, however, short-lived. After an abortive sortie into the Bay of Biscay and off the Basque coast, *Jacobi*, *Eckoldt*, *Ihn*, *Steinbrinck* and *Riedel* sailed for refits in Germany on 5 November. The weather during the passage up-Channel was once again bad, giving the destroyers

considerable trouble in steering and at one stage causing *Eckoldt* to stop engines. Reaching German waters two days later, the 5th Flotilla's *Eckoldt*, *Ihn* and *Steinbrinck* went into Blohm und Voss (Hamburg), Oderwerke (Stettin) and Blohm und Voss respectively for short refits, while *Jacobi* and *Riedel* of the 6th Flotilla were to refit in, respectively, Wilhelmshaven and Deutscher Werke–Kiel.

ENORMOUS FLASH

Machinery problems continued to plague the Type 34 and 34A destroyers, particularly *Heinemann* and *Schoemann* (6th Flotilla), whose catastrophic engineering condition resulted in a conference involving the Führer der Zerstörer, the ships' captains, senior engineers, the flotilla commander and Admiral Raeder late in 1940. After about seven months' repairs neither ship was yet seaworthy, and an investigation was ordered.

In western France only *Beitzen* of the 5th Flotilla and *Lody* and *Galster* of the 6th remained, under the command of FdZ aboard the latter. No operations took place until the last week in November owing to breakdowns and bad weather, after which two sorties into the Plymouth area were planned. All three ships sailed from Brest on the evening of 24 November and set course north-westwards towards Land's End. Shortly after midnight a number of darkened boats, thought to be patrol vessels, were sighted. In fact this was a fishing fleet of some thirteen trawlers and smaller craft working about 12 miles south-west of Wolf

Rock, and it was attacked by gunfire at about 0015 hours. The destroyers claimed a vessel sunk, but although two Belgian trawlers were reported missing they later turned up safely.

Unbeknown to the Germans, however, there was a strong force of British destroyers at sea, not far away. This was once again the 5th Destroyer Flotilla (Captain Lord Louis Mountbatten), which was under orders to patrol south of Prawle Point but had subsequently been diverted to intercept an enemy convoy to Cherbourg. The flotilla at this time comprised *Javelin*, *Jackal*, *Jersey*, *Kashmir* and *Jupiter*. Officers and men on the bridges of both *Javelin* and *Jupiter* sighted gun flashes to the west, but since this bearing put them over land Captain (D5) was not informed, even though it is almost certain that these flashes were caused by the gunfire aimed against the trawlers. No action was taken, and the destroyers continued their patrol between longitudes 4° and 5°. Meanwhile, to the west, the three German destroyers, having disengaged from the fishing vessels, located by radar a small convoy south of the Lizard consisting of three merchant vessels, *Appolonia*, *Stadion II* and *Fernwood*, together with a tug and two barges. It had sailed from Plymouth at 1730 hours on 24 November, and by 0030 the next morning was abreast the Lizard, steering 280° at 8 knots. The convoy had sighted gunfire ahead, and a short while later a destroyer put a searchlight on to *Appolonia* (2,156grt), opening fire as she did so. The merchantman received hits on the bridge and upper deck which started fires and blew her funnel away. Her crew took to the boats as *Galster* put two torpedoes into her, sending her to the bottom with her engineer offficer and thirteen Chinese crew.

Having despatched one vessel, the destroyers turned their attention to the others, but were only able to locate *Stadion II*, which was left in a damaged but salvageable condition as the Germans withdrew. Meanwhile the British 5th Flotilla, having seen these last gun flashes, finally put two and two together: coupled with a report (five hours old) of German destroyers off Wolf Rock, Mountbatten realized that they would return to Brest, and he altered course to cut them off as they steered for Ushant. The Germans were not to be caught, however, and by 0720 the British had reversed course in view of the danger of dive-bomber attack.

Three nights later, on the evening of the 28th, a second sortie was mounted, in the same area but a little further to the east, by the same three destroyers. The weather was clear and the sea calm with a light swell as the destroyers steamed north at 21 knots towards Prawle Point. Over Plymouth an air raid was in progress, and the ships could clearly see the fires burning. Turning west and increasing speed to 24 knots, they were about sixteen miles south of the Eddystone when shadows were observed to port. At 0439 hours, having turned south to investigate, the objects were identified as two tugs, *Aide* and *Abeille XIV*, the former towing the lighter *BHC10*. The tugs carried only

five Lewis guns between them as armament, and they had just altered course towards Falmouth when two shells landed alongside from two destroyers which had appeared on the starboard beam. The three destroyers then fired on the British group from a range of about 300–400m, having turned to run parallel and reduced speed to 9 knots. After the lighter had sunk, both tugs rescued the crew whilst under heavy fire, the accuracy of which, in the words of the tugs' captains, was 'disgracefully bad'. *Aide* sank after 20 minutes, but *Abeille* escaped, although damaged.

The destroyers ceased fire at about 0514, continued westwards, and shortly afterwards located a small vessel steaming towards Falmouth. This proved to be the diminutive *Pilot Boat 4*, which had left Plymouth shortly before the tugs, in company with two drifters. Coming up astern, the German ships sent up flares and then opened fire at 0606 hours. Once again shooting was poor, 50 to 60 rounds being fired for about only twelve hits, which nevertheless sank the cutter. Her survivors were rescued by *Jackal* later in the forenoon. The destroyers then broke off their sortie, altered course to the south and worked up to 29 knots to return to Brest. In the darkness, the sizes of the ships sunk had been grossly overestimated, *Lody*, for example, believing the lighter to have been about 1,000grt and the pilot vessel 1,000–1,500 tons. In fact, the sunken tug and lighter in total grossed only 424 tons, whilst the pilot vessel must have been very small indeed since she is not mentioned in offficial loss records.

On the British side, the 5th Flotilla had once again been alerted, this time early enough to intercept the retiring German ships. At 0630 hours *Lody* received warning over the short-wave radio of two objects bearing 148° which could not be clearly identified because of the darkness; they were, however, approaching rapidly. *Galster* was leading *Beitzen* and *Lody*, steering 180° at 29 knots, while the British flotilla, consisting of *Javelin*, *Jupiter*, *Kashmir*, *Jackal* and *Jersey*, were steering 310° at 28 knots in line of bearing 100°. The German force was thus crossing ahead of the British, from starboard to port, at a range of about 1,500m. Initially only the two leading British ships were visible, one of which was wrongly identified as a 'Tribal'.

Galster gave permission to use torpedoes and turned her group on to 230° at 0643 hours; at exactly the same moment, the British flotilla altered course to 220° in order to run parallel. This was a most unfortunate decision on the part of Captain Mountbatten, because not only did his flotilla's directors and guns swing off target during the 50° turn but he also presented his beam to the enemy – and the Germans' preference was always for the torpedo. At 0644 all three German destroyers fired four torpedoes each in 9° fans, set to run at 40 knots and a depth of 2m, using estimated data since there was insufficient time to utilize the transmitting station.

There was a delay of about a minute on the British side before fire was opened while the directors re-acquired target, and then a 4.7in (12cm) salvo was loosed off. The

Above: Two torpedoes hit *Javelin*, lighting up the night and illuminating one of her assailants to starboard. Note the short range of the action. (PRO)

Left: The severely damaged bow of HMS *Javelin*. (IWM)

2pdr pom-poms, which had also trained with the director, were unable to see the target and did not open fire until starshell was available. The British gun control officer had greatly overestimated the range, but so had the Germans, and both sides' opening salvoes were long. The second British salvo was correct for range, but hardly had it been fired than *Javelin* leapt bodily upwards under the detonation of two torpedoes from *Lody*. An enormous flash lit up the night, starkly illuminating the three German ships.

The first torpedo hit on the starboard side aft, abreast station 70, blasting the after magazine in a distinct double explosion. The other, seconds later, hit forward abreast station 15, throwing a column of water and debris up which drenched personnel on the upper deck. No. 2 gun remained in action, firing two more salvoes before the training jammed. Engine room personnel, hearing the explosions forward, shut the ahead manoeuvring valves and closed emergency bulkhead valves. The ship lifted, listed 30° to port, then settled with a 5° list. Everything forward of station 30 had disappeared, and the stern aft of bulkhead 64 had dropped and was hanging down. Forward, flooding was uncontrolled as far aft as station 35, with further slow flooding in No. 2 magazine, whilst the engine room was flooding through bulkhead 61 but was under control. Fire was a serious hazard, however, since the after hit had ignited Nos. 5 and 6 oil tanks, setting stations 64–68 ablaze. The port 4in ready-use locker was on fire, but all

S 1581 (10)

VIEW SHOWING DAMAGE AFT

VIEW SHOWING DAMAGE FORWARD

H.M.S. JAVELIN Torpedoed - 29.11.40

Damage Control saved H.M.S. Javelin

" ...was towed safely to harbour "

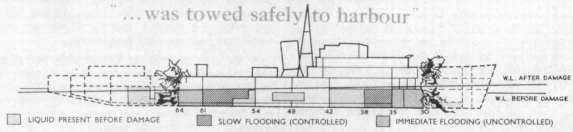

W.L. AFTER DAMAGE

W.L. BEFORE DAMAGE

64   61   54   48   42   38   35   30

☐ LIQUID PRESENT BEFORE DAMAGE   ▨ SLOW FLOODING (CONTROLLED)   ▦ IMMEDIATE FLOODING (UNCONTROLLED)

JAVELIN, steaming at 28 knots, was struck by two torpedoes at about 15 and 70 stations.

The forward torpedo destroyed the bows and caused rapid flooding back to 35 bulkhead.

The after torpedo destroyed the stern abaft 64 bulkhead and caused rapid flooding to 61 bulkhead.

The ship heeled considerably, but recovered to 5° to port and then became upright when the stern dropped off.

Fire at the after end, caused by oil fuel from Nos. 5 and 6 tanks, was brought under control largely by the use of saturated steam.

Ready use ammunition was extinguished by Foamite.

Topweight was jettisoned, 35 bulkhead shored and slow flooding controlled by pumping.

The ship was towed safely to harbour.

NOTE
Ships' ability to withstand considerable damage at its extremities.

C.B.H.3068

the other explosives were jettisoned, as were the remaining torpedoes. Bulkheads were shored up and steam hoses rigged as the damage control parties fought to save the stricken ship. Twenty minutes later the stern fell off, leaving just 155ft (47m) afloat.

Javelin's consorts swept by at full speed in pursuit of the German ships, firing large numbers of starshell to illuminate the targets. *Lody*, as the trailing ship, received the most attention, the British salvoes straddling her several times and the closest shells only about l0m to port abreast the after shelter deck. All three German ships returned fire with their after 12.7cm guns, made smoke, dropped smoke floats and weaved about to avoid splashes. Speed was worked up to 35 knots at times, and flames were visible from all the funnels. Gradually, under the protection of the smoke and with the advantage of speed, the range was opened until the German ships were out of danger.

The British flotilla abandoned the chase at about 0900 hours and returned to stand by *Javelin*. By midday on the 29th the stricken hulk was under slow tow by the tug *Caroline Moller* towards Plymouth, where she arrived the next day. Three officers and 45 men had been killed in the attack and the destroyer was under repair for 13 months. Little damage had been caused to any German destroyer. *Lody* had received 2pdr hits in the forward funnel and in the torpedo TS, whilst all three vessels had been hit by splinters which caused no damage. No casualties were sustained by the crews.

The success of this sortie was a further considerable fillip to the morale of the destroyer force, a fact fully appreciated by Naval Group West, whose commanding officer, Generaladmiral Saalwachter, reported: 'The sortie has been a complete success because of the torpedo hits on both destroyers and the sinking of the steamers and the tugs, and has inflicted a serious defeat on the enemy. Especially gratifying has been the lack of damage to our destroyers. The performance of the destroyers against a superior force deserves the highest recognition and will have re-established confidence in crew and equipment after a period of forced inactivity owing to weather, personnel changes and machinery breakdowns.'

The sortie effectively marked the end of the destroyers' first deployment in western France, for both *Galster* and *Lody* sailed for home and refit early in December, leaving *Beitzen* as the sole representative of the destroyer flotillas. She remained until March 1941, being engaged in minelaying in the Channel and escorting *Hipper* in and out of Brest on her forays into the Atlantic. *Beitzen* eventually returned to Kiel on 18 March, whereupon she too passed into dockyard hands.

A VARIETY OF TASKS

Whilst the 5th Torpedo Boat Flotilla remained in France, the 1st and 2nd Flotillas moved north once more, to Stavanger in Norway. Air reconnaissance reports had located two north-bound coastal convoys off the British coast which, it was estimated, would pass between Kinnaird's Head and Smith's Bank at about 0200 hours on 7 November. Both flotillas, with *T1*, *T6*, *T7*, *T8*, *T9* and *T10*, sailed on the 6th, aiming to pass through a gap in the British minefields shown on charts captured when the British submarine *Seal* had been taken in May. Closing up to action stations shortly before midnight, the torpedo boats approached the target area. The night was dark and cloudy, with a light north-westerly wind, and the flotillas forged on in the North Sea swell until they were only 40 miles off Kinnaird's Head. A little after midnight the leader of the 2nd Flotilla, *T6*, was shaken by a large explosion on her starboard quarter. Ready-use ammunition and signal flares ignited, causing a serious fire aft. Both engines quickly stopped and the ship lay down by the stern, listing 10° to starboard. Neither T2 (Korvettenkapitän Riede) nor *T6*'s CO (Kapitänleutnant Wolfram) had a clear idea of the damage, because all telephone lines were disrupted and fire-fighting parties were rushing aft. Steam and smoke poured out of the ship. The captain, since he believed the ship to be sinking fast, ordered all hands on deck and went aft to assess the damage. By this time the forward turbine room had begun flooding and the list increased, and it was now obvious that the ship could not be saved. After all rafts had been launched, 'Abandon ship' was ordered. T6 sank quickly by the stern until her bows were in the air, then slid out of sight. T7 and T8 rescued the survivors, including Captain (T2) and the CO, but forty-eight men were lost. As the result of this disaster, the sortie was called off and the ships returned to Stavanger. It was not until after this loss that Admiral Carls received information from the abandoned Norwegian *MTB5* (which had gone ashore near Quineville on 1 October) that the British east coast mine barrier had been extended further north.

At the close of 1940 the Kriegsmarine had eight of the older types of torpedo boats and ten of the newer Type 35 craft in commission, although not all were fully worked-up. Both the 2nd and 5th Flotillas opened the New Year with minelaying operations, the former still in Norwegian waters. The 5th Flotilla, however, lost *Wolf* on a mine north of Dunkirk on 8 January, whilst returning from an operation. Then, with the commencement of the invasion of Russia, attention was transferred to the Baltic, and T7 and T8 moved south to join T2, T5 and T11 in the 'Baltenflotte'. During September and October all the torpedo boats supported the cruisers in operations against Osel Island, the Sworbe and Dagö.

During the same period there was not a single German destroyer operational: all thirteen commissioned vessels (including *Z23–25*) were either in dockyard hands or working-up on trials. Of the 5th Flotilla, *Eckoldt* at Hamburg was scheduled to complete her refit at the end of December, and *Steinbrinck* and *Ihn* (Stettin) by late January 1941. All refits were completed on time, but once again a hard winter had set in in the Baltic: *Eckoldt* was trapped in

Kiel, while *Steinbrinck* and *Ihn* could not get out of
Swinemünde. No icebreaker was available in the Eastern
Baltic as, for some reason, *Castor* had been sent to the
Great Belts, and it was not until 12 February that two such
ships, *Stettin* and *Preussen*, were available to try to force a
passage through the ice. The attempt failed, however,
because the ice was too thick, and it was not for a further

week that the two destroyers managed to sail for
Gotenhafen for work-up; hampered by ice and foggy
weather, it was not until late March that they were
operational again.

On 5 April 1941 Kapitän zur See Berger, aboard
Steinbrinck, sailed for a second Channel deployment;
accompanying him was *Ihn*, from his own flotilla, and

Heinemann, detached from the 6th. Thick fog covered the first day of the passage, necessitating the posting of extra bridge and radar look-outs and reducing the passage speed. Boulogne was passed on the following day, but the weather worsened, with heavy seas giving the destroyers considerable problems in maintaining course. During the morning a Blenheim scored two near-misses on *Ihn*, and in the afternoon *Heinemann*, the last in the line, was attacked by aircraft, two torpedoes being launched at her. Turning hard to port and listing heavily, she strove to avoid them, smoke pouring from her funnels. One passed ahead and one astern as her AA guns opened fire and the escorting fighters chased the attackers. Unharmed, the destroyers returned to Brest for a short while, then moved down to La Pallice, and for the next five months or so the three ships operated on the French Atlantic coast in a variety of roles but not seeing any real action.

Many of their duties were associated with the movements of raiders, supply ships and blockade-breakers through the Bay of Biscay. The first such operation was mounted late in April, when, on the 22nd, *Ihn*, *Heinemann* and *Steinbrinck* weighed anchor from La Pallice to escort in *Hamburg*. Their rendezvous was in the south-west of the Bay of Biscay, north of Cape Ortegal, where they met the incoming ship at 1132 hours the next day after having been directed further west by a reconnaissance aircraft. 'Hamburg' was a cover-name, and in fact the ship was the raider *Thor* (Kapitän zur See Kahler) returning from a successful 322-day cruise in which she had sunk or damaged 138,933 tons of Allied merchant shipping. Forming a protective screen around the auxiliary cruiser, the destroyers escorted her to Cherbourg, whence she continued onwards to Germany whilst the destroyers returned to Bordeaux. Next it was the turn of the supply ship *Nordland*, again met in the Bay of Biscay but escorted this time to Le Havre between 17 and 20 May. After this the destroyers stood by to perform a similar service for the naval tanker *Ermland*.

During the first days of June they met the heavy cruiser *Prinz Eugen* (Kapitän zur See Brinkmann) far to the south after her escape from the *Bismarck* hunt and brought her safely into Brest. During their return, *Ihn* caused a momentary scare with a submarine report, both she and *Heinemann*, depth-charging the suspected position. It was, however, a false alarm. The remainder of June and July were quiet, apart from the occasional air raid.

On 16 July the flotilla strength was increased to five ships by the arrival of the new Type 36A ships *Z23* and *Z24*, after which the whole flotilla provided escort for *Scharnhorst* (Kapitän zur See Hoffmann) during her infrequent trips into the open sea. *Ihn* left Brest to return to Germany for refit on 27 July, being attacked during the afternoon by five MTBs of the 11th Flotilla from Dover whilst off Calais. At this stage of the war the effectiveness of the British MTBs was poor, and attacks were often badly executed. This one was no exception: two boats almost collided and the

torpedoes were launched at too great a range, not only missing *Ihn*, but almost finding one of the British boats. The German destroyer replied with ineffective gunfire, and passed safely up the Channel and through into the Baltic to the Oderwerke yard at Stettin for overhaul.

The four remaining destroyers in Western France escorted the homeward-bound raider *Orion* (Fregattenkapitän Weyler) into the Gironde on 21 August following her 510-day cruise, but by this time a refit for both *Steinbrinck* and *Heinemann* was long overdue, the former suffering from numerous tube failures and blockages and needing a boiler clean. Both had been ordered home on 8 August, but first the *Orion* operation intervened and then *Steinbrinck* ran aground, so that it was not until 6 September that the two ships left La Pallice to return home. Passing Ushant in darkness, they put into Le Havre the next day and remained there until dusk so that the Straits of Dover could be transited in darkness as well. No attacks occurred and they reached Germany without incident. *Heinemann* was scheduled to be refitted by Deschimag at Bremen and *Steinbrinck* at Blohm und Voss in Hamburg. This was to be the last time that these destroyers were to be based in France.

The torpedo boats, however, continued to work the Channel Waters and on 16 November 1941, *T7*, *T4* and *T11* left Copenhagen for Kiel, passed through the Kiel Canal the following day and put into Wilhelmshaven. Staging down-Channel, the boats reached Cherbourg in the forenoon of the 25th after oiling at Vlissingen. Their task was to escort '*Sperrbrecher 52*', alias the returning raider *Komet*, back to Germany after a cruise of 515 days. The raider, with an escort of two minesweepers, arrived in Cherbourg in the afternoon of the 26th. She sailed again just after midnight with the torpedo boats and the two minesweepers (*M10* and *M153*) as escort. The hours of daylight were spent in Le Havre before passage was continued at 1924 hours on the 27th. The escort had now been increased to six R-Boote and five minesweepers as well as the torpedo boats. The raider's passage had not gone un-noticed by the Admiralty who had sailed a number of MTBs in an attempt to sink her. The two sides made contact between Boulogne and Dunkirk at about 0400 hours on the 28th, when a confused night action took place. With the MTBs weaving at high speed and the escort turning quickly to engage under the ghostly illumination of star shells, it is not surprising that mistakes occurred. *T12*, turning at speed whilst attacking an MTB, accidentally hit *T4* with gunfire causing some injuries, and claims were made for MTBs sunk which were not. One of the MTBs also managed to rake *T4* with machine-gun fire, wounding four men on the bridge, including the CO, Oberleutnant zur See Sommerlatt, whereupon the flotilla commander took over the ship. Twenty minutes later *T4* was shaken by an explosion amidships, the engine room reporting steam leaks in No. 2 boiler room. Riede initially feared a torpedo hit, but it soon transpired that the ship had been struck by a dud 10.5cm star shell fired by one of the minesweepers. This had hit the forward torpedo tubes, shell splinters piercing the main steam lines in No. 2 boiler room below. Both the tubes and torpedoes were put out of action, fortunately without exploding a warhead. No casualties were incurred but speed was reduced to 24 knots. The action petered out without success by either side and by 0710 hours the ships had reached Dunkirk. *T7* had suffered some machine-gun damage and had three dead and three wounded, but the raider passed safely up to Germany. On the 30th the flotilla arrived back in Wilhelmshaven.

Only a couple of days later a new operation was mounted, this time in the opposite direction, to get 'Sperrbrecher 53', alias *Thor*, down-Channel for her second raiding cruise. On 2 December *T2* and *T12* stood by the raider in the Schillig Roads providing flak cover and the following day were joined by *T4*, *T7* and *T14* from Wilhelmshaven. Fog greatly hindered their passage so that the squadron did not reach Vlissingen until after midday on the 4th. Here passage was once more delayed for the ships did not sail again until the 7th, reaching Zeebrugge that same day. After a further sojourn in this port, passage was resumed once more on the afternoon of the 13th, Le Havre being reached the following day until the torpedo boats were relieved by the boats of the 8th Minesweeper Flotilla off Brest during the evening of the 15th. *T2* and *T4* remained in Brest whilst *T7* and *T12* sailed for Germany on 17 December, the former for refit and overhaul at Wesermünde, the latter at Kiel.

In the meantime, manpower shortages forced the OKM to request that a ship of the 2nd Flotilla be paid off in order to man new construction. Riede chose *T8* on the grounds that her Deschimag machinery was defective and unreliable. This ship was, on 12 December, en route from Gotenhafen to Bremerhaven for a machinery overhaul. Her orders were cancelled, the ship paying off at Kiel on 30 December and was later towed to Königsberg.

CHANNEL BREAKTHROUGH

The surviving Types 34 and 36 destroyers spent the remainder of their operational careers in Norwegian waters, except for a brief return to Brest for a special operation early in 1942. This special operation, code-named 'Cerberus', was of course the Channel breakthrough by the Brest squadron. Ordered by Hitler, against the wishes of the Naval High Command, it succeeded brilliantly, but despite this it was a strategic defeat because the threat of another Atlantic foray by the battlecruisers was removed. As 'Cerberus' was being planned, there were only eighteen commissioned destroyers available to the Kriegsmarine, of which eleven were operational: five of these, *Z23–27*, were based in the Arctic at Kirkenes, and the remainder, *Beitzen*, *Jacobi*, *Heinemann*, *Schoemann*, *Ihn* and *Z29* were in home waters or southern Norway. *Riedel*, *Galster*, *Lody*, *Eckoldt*

and *Z28* were in dockyard hands, whilst the final pair, *Z30* and *Steinbrinck*, were working-up in the Baltic.

The 5th Flotilla, consisting of *Beitzen*, *Schoemann*, *Heinemann* and *Jacobi*, sailed from Kiel on 24 January, passed through the Canal, and cleared Brunsbüttel locks by 1800 hours that day. After steaming down the deep-water channel past Cuxhaven, the flotilla reached the open sea and turned westwards for France. The weather was very cold, the sea rough, and icing conditions were encountered. During the night passage off the Friesian Islands *Jacobi* had her bows damaged by the heavy seas, necessitating an unscheduled stop at Rotterdam in order to effect temporary repairs, but these were completed by evening and the passage westwards resumed.

The weather remained poor, with the destroyers steaming into a Force 5, moderating westerly wind, under cloudy skies and with temperatures down to -4°C. Towards evening on the 25th the flotilla was approaching the Dover Narrows, steaming at 18 knots in line ahead some 20 or so miles off the Belgian coast. At 2113 hours a heavy explosion occurred under the bows of *Heinemann*, and she sheered out of line, badly damaged. *Beitzen* reversed course in order to find out what was wrong, but on being signalled 'Mine explosion' from the stricken destroyer she stood off. *Heinemann* informed her flotilla commander of the extent of the damage – Nos. 2 and 3 boiler rooms knocked out – but before any further action could be taken a second mine exploded, blowing off the bows and leaving her well down by the head. D5 (Kapitän zur See Berger) ordered the destroyer captain to abandon ship, and as he did so he received hydrophone reports of fast-moving screws judged to be either torpedoes or MTBs. *Beitzen* went full ahead and turned hard to port but could see nothing. Ordering *Jacobi* to rescue survivors, *Beitzen* and *Schoemann* continued the search. Further hydrophone reports resulted in starshell being fired, but once again nothing was sighted. Finally, after nearly ramming the wreck of the sinking destroyer, Berger presumably decided that things were becoming unpleasantly similar to the *Maass/Schultz* débâcle and called off the search. *Beitzen* joined in the rescue operation, her cutter remaining in the water for about an hour and a quarter until rescue operations were concluded at 2325 hours. She had on board 200 survivors, five of whom subsequently died; *Jacobi* had 34, and 93 were lost with the ship. The remaining three destroyers set course for Le Havre, experiencing navigational difficulties on the way since they had been unable accurately to determine their position for some time. They arrived safely by 0920 hours on the 26th, and the survivors were landed.

It was thought that the destroyers had been sighted by aircraft from Vlissingen or that their presence had been reported by agents, thus enabling the British to mine their likely passage, but there is no real confirmation of this. Berger pondered at some length on the loss. He believed that the water had been too deep for influence mines, yet the first explosion had pressed in the lower compartments and caused severe shock, although there were few leaks. He concluded that a moored mine with an influence mechanism had been responsible, or else a torpedo; no torpedo tracks were sighted, but that was not surprising in the conditions prevailing.* He further commented that the experience in rescue operations obtained during the loss of the two destroyers in February 1940 helped greatly in this present rescue. The 5th Flotilla reached Brest without further incident and were there joined by *Ihn* and *Z29* as well as *Z25*. The initial escort for the heavy ships would thus consist of six destroyers, with torpedo boats, S-boats, R-boats and minesweepers joining en route.

Preparations for the breakout had been under way in great secrecy for some time. The minesweepers of the 1st, 2nd, 4th, 5th and 12th Flotillas, as well as the 2nd, 3rd and 4th R-boat Flotillas, had swept a channel from Brest to Holland in the preceding weeks, and a complex system of air cover had been set up. *Scharnhorst*, *Gneisenau* and *Prinz Eugen* left habour late on the night of 11 February during a lengthy air raid which effectively disguised their departure. The destroyers, awaiting them outside the harbour, weighed anchor at about 2320 hours and formed up around the heavy units.

The sea was calm as the squadron sailed at 18 knots towards navigation point 'Bruno 11', after which speed was increased to 24 knots and course altered towards 'Point 30a'; reaching this marker, speed was further increased to 27 knots for the passage up-Channel. Around midnight the flagship *Scharnhorst* detected strange signals on her radar, and spirits fell as the Admiral's staff assumed that the force had been discovered. However, it was soon noticed that the bearing of the transmissions remained constant and appeared to emanate from one of the destroyers in the screen. It turned out to be a faulty piece of electrical equipment on one of *Beitzen*'s gun mountings which was quickly located and rectified.

The heavy ships were sailing in line astern, the flagship leading, *Gneisenau* astern and the heavy cruiser bringing up the rear. *Z29* (FdZ) led *Scharnhorst* by some 2,500m, *Jacobi* was abreast *Gneisenau*'s starboard side and followed by *Beitzen* abreast *Prinz Eugen*, whilst on the port side of this column *Ihn* was abreast *Gneisenau*, followed by *Schoemann*. In this formation the squadron passed the Channel Islands, swept in close to Cherbourg and crossed the Seine Bay, as yet undetected. The first four Bf 110s of the air escort joined at 0845 hours, followed by seven Bf 109s three-quarters of an hour later. At 0945 *Schoemann* had the nine torpedo boats of the 2nd (Korvettenkapitän Erdmann) and 3rd (Korvettenkapitän Wilcke) Flotillas in sight, whose ships, *T2*, *T4*, *T5*, *T11*, *T12*, *T13*, *T15*, *T16* and *T17*, joined at about 1000 hours. Overhead, a further fifteen Bf 110s bolstered the air umbrella.

There was still no reaction from the British, whose radar patrols had all failed for one reason or another. The weather remained disappointingly good, with a westerly wind Force 3, sea State 2, a temperature of 4°C and medium visibility. Off Le Touquet four minesweepers of the 1st Flotilla joined to escort the squadron through a minefield, during which time speed was reduced to 10 knots and line ahead formed. At about 1120 hours a British aircraft finally located the German ships, and was engaged briefly by the flagship's after 10.5cm guns. Steadily the ships approached the narrows between Dover and Calais, their crews tensed for action. The weather began to turn in the Germans' favour, the wind backing to south-west and increasing to Force 6, sea State 5, and the S-boats of the starboard screen began to lay smoke to conceal their passage.

Suddenly, at 1320 hours, the first attacks developed, just

*In fact a minefield laid by *Plover* had been responsible.

Below: *Paul Jacobi* during the 'Cerberus' operation. In the background is one of the whalers converted to a Flakjäger, acting as a marker boat. (Bundesarchiv)

as the torpedo boats of the 5th Flotilla (Korvettenkapitän Schmidt), *Seeadler*, *Falke*, *Kondor*, *Iltis* and *Jaguar*, had joined the escort. There appeared to be two groups of MTBs, consisting of four and five boats, which were sighted on the port bow at a range of about 8,000m (8,750 yards) from *Schoemann*. The craft were in fact *MTB44, 45, 48, 219* and *221* and *MGB41* and *43* from Dover. *Ihn* turned towards them, followed by *Schoemann* in her wake, ordered by Admiral Ciliax to drive them off. As *Ihn* passed through the S-boat smokescreen the MTBs fired torpedoes and the destroyer fired red and green flares to warn the heavy units. *Schoemann* opened up her guns at 1340 hours at a range of 6,000m (6,570 yards), then turned hard to starboard to avoid one of the torpedoes. *Ihn* avoided a

torpedo to port then opened fire herself three minutes later on two MTBs ahead of her, switching target shortly to three more on her port bow. Her firing was inaccurate due to her twisting and turning, the short seas coming aboard in the stiff wind and an unserviceable forward director. She avoided another torpedo and continued to chase the MTBs, still without securing any hits. *Schoemann* heard a number of torpedoes, one of which appeared to explode only 500m ahead of her, although this was probably one of the shells which began to land around *Ihn* at 1344 hours, throwing up columns of water as close as 400m to the destroyer. Initially, *Ihn* thought that these were 'shorts' from her companions, but she quickly realized that they were in fact from unseen British shore batteries.

The accuracy of the shelling, a feint torpedo attack by the two torpedo-less MGBs and the close proximity of the Goodwin Sands all combined to cause *Ihn*'s captain, Korvettenkapitän Wachsmuth, to break off the chase, which he did at 1347 hours. The inability of *Ihn* to sink any of the MTBs later drew unfavourable comment from Berger, commander of the 5th Flotilla.

As the two destroyers turned to rejoin *Jacobi* the last of the coastal battery salvoes landed and then six Swordfish torpedo aircraft of No. 825 Squadron FAA (Lieutenant-Commander Esmonde) came in low in a suicidal attack. Met by a dense barrage of fire from the escorts, and attacked from above by the fighters of the air escort, the Swordfish were all shot down, *Ihn* accounting for one with her starboard 3.7cm mounting and another with Nos. 3 and 4 2cm guns. By 1407 hours all the MTBs were out of sight. *Schoemann* had suffered in the air attack, having been hit about fifty times in the stern by 2cm cannon fire as the fighters dived into the Swordfish, though damage was relatively light, but *Ihn* was good for only 25 knots, having no reserve feedwater left.

Three more MTBs, from the Ramsgate Flotilla, were sighted by *Schoemann* 50° on her starboard bow at 1443 hours, both she and *Ihn* astern opening fire a few minutes later. Their shooting was good but again not decisive, and both ships ceased fire at 1449. However, the squadron suffered its first setback at 1530 hours, when *Scharnhorst* was mined off the mouth of the Schelde. Immobilized, the battlecruiser was passed by the other ships whilst *Z29* took on board Admiral Ciliax. Leaving four torpedo boats to stand by, *Z29* sped off after the rest of the squadron.

Between 1600 and 1730 hours the ships of the squadron were subjected to a series of uncoordinated air attacks by the RAF: Beauforts of Nos. 42, 86 and 217 Squadrons unsuccessfully launched torpedo attacks, whilst Hudsons from Nos. 407 and 500 Squadrons were equally out of luck with their bombs; many aircraft from Bomber Command also took off to attack, but few found the target. The destroyers replied continuously with all their flak armament, but at 1638 hours a new threat developed when *Beitzen* sighted two destroyers through the murk, bearing 320°; shortly afterwards another was seen to their left, as

well as a fourth ship which was identified as a cruiser. Kapitän zur See Berger flashed the alarm and opened fire. The ships were British destroyers, *Campbell* and *Vivacious* of the 21st Flotilla (Captain Pizey) and *Mackay*, *Worcester* and *Whitshed* of the 16th (Captain Wright), which attacked at 1645, launching their torpedoes at a range of about 3,200m. *Jacobi* opened fire, got off six salvoes which straddled the British ships, and then cleared the range for the big ships' guns; *Beitzen* meanwhile had launched four torpedoes in a counter-attack and likewise cleared the range. *Gneisenau* and *Prinz Eugen* avoided the torpedoes and then severely mauled the British flotilla, particularly *Worcester* which barely got home.

At 1700 hours, *Beitzen* received a near-miss by a bomb from a Blenheim which dropped out of the clouds, the pattern falling only 30m from the stern and causing shock damage and leaks in compartment I. Opening fire with her light armament, she brought down the attacker; hits were observed from the 3.7cm guns in the starboard engine, but the major contributor to the success was the newly installed 2cm Vierling. *Jacobi*, too, was under heavy attack, twisting and turning whilst firing back, but the destroyer successfully evaded all the bombs.

Z29, with Admiral Ciliax aboard, had meanwhile struck trouble. One of her 15cm guns had suffered a premature explosion which sent splinters into the machinery spaces, severing oil lines and immobilizing her. She called up *Schoemann* to take off the admiral, which the latter did at 1825 hours, and whilst the transfer was taking place the two destroyers were passed by *Scharnhorst*, which had managed to get under way again. For the destroyers, the remainder of the passage was uneventful. *Scharnhorst* was mined again at 2235 hours and *Gneisenau* met a similar problem at 2055, but all the ships of the squadron reached German harbours safely.

The torpedo boats of the 3rd and 5th Flotillas remained in the Channel theatre, engaged on convoy escort duties and in minelaying and escorting armed raiders down-Channel, *Michel* 13–20 March and *Stier* 12–19 May. *Stier*'s passage proved particularly tough. She left Rotterdam with an escort of six R-boats, six vessels of the 2nd Minesweeper Flotilla and four more of the 8th, as well as *Seeadler*, *Iltis*, *Kondor* and *Falke* of the 5th Torpedo Boat Flotilla. Proceeding down-Channel, the R-boats took the lead in a 'V' formation, followed by a single sweeper; then came the 2nd Flotilla and 8th Flotilla in similar 'V' formations, the raider herself being closely boxed in by the torpedo boats, *Seeadler* ahead, *Falke* astern, *Iltis* to starboard and *Kondor* to port. It was impossible to disguise the movement of the convoy, and the Dover batteries detected and shelled it, albeit without success. British MTBs then attacked, and a fierce, confused fight developed. At 0400 hours the look-outs on *Iltis* saw a torpedo track to port, whereupon Kapitänleutnant Jacobsen instantly ordered both engines full astern. It was to no avail. The torpedo (from *MTB 221*) struck amidships, just abaft the forward funnel, breaking the ship in two. The fore-ends listed heavily over to port, then sank bows up, the stern half quickly following. Nine minutes after *Iltis*, *Seeadler* was also torpedoed (by *MTB219*) from the coastward side. Hit amidships, she rolled over to port, throwing the captain off the bridge and into the sea where he saw his ship break in two and vanish. Both vessels suffered heavy loss of life, among the victims being Jacobsen. On the British side, *MTB220* was sunk, but the raider successfully passed out into the open sea.

A second operation in October was less successful when, on 13 October 1942, *T4* and *T10* sailed for Le Havre with the leader of the 3rd Torpedo Boat Flotilla *T14*, and *T19* as escort for the raider *Komet* which was attempting to break out on a second raiding cruise. In command of the escort was Korvettenkapitän Wilcke (Captain T3). The torpedo boats were disposed in diamond formation around *Komet* with *T14* in the van, *T10* to starboard (or seaward), *T4* to port (inshore) and *T19* bringing up the rear. Five hundred metres separated each ship and the passage speed was 13 knots, not far off the maximum speed of the raider. *Komet*'s passage had been in trouble right from the start because of bad weather and already she had lost four of her escorting minesweepers (*R77*, *R78*, *R82* and *R86*) to mines on the 8th after leaving Vlissingen. Her movements became known to British Intelligence and the Admiralty put in hand air and sea counter-measures. As the raider moved down-Channel, five destroyers, *Cottesmore*, *Quorn*, *Glaisdale*, *Eskdale*, and *Albrighton* (all 'Hunt Class') under the command of Lieutenant-Commander J. C. A. Ingram were transferred west to Dartmouth whence they sailed with eight MTBs to patrol off Cap de la Hague. All were armed with four 4in guns as were the second group, *Fernie*, *Tynedale*, *Brocklesby* and the Polish *Krakowiak* which sailed from Plymouth. The German force was therefore outnumbered and outgunned.

First contact was made with the German force by an aircraft which dropped flares as the squadron was off Barfleur, but despite the fact that a British attack was inevitable, Kapitän Zur See Brocksien, CO of *Komet*, made no attempt to put into Cherbourg to evade it. This was a fatal decision which can only be accounted for by assuming that the delays already experienced had frustrated him so much that he had resolved to fight his way out into the Atlantic. In the early hours of the 14th, Ingram's destroyers and MTBs made contact and action was joined.

T10, the outboard ship, was quickly smothered by shell fire, receiving two hits in No. 2 turbine room, causing fires and steam escapes. Speed rapidly fell off until she was reduced to 8 knots. Kapitänleutnant Sommerlatt turned his ship hard to port and made smoke, intending to fire his torpedoes on the turn. However, mistakes on the tubes had them trained the wrong way and the chance was missed. With her stern to the enemy, the next hit struck No. 3 depth-charge rack on the starboard quarter which blew up.

Five minutes later, the engine room had just reported that the engines were now good for 24 knots when a fourth shell hit the midships deckhouse and flak gun, exploding ready-use ammunition and causing fires. Soon after, a fifth hit the funnel and boiler room fan intakes knocking out the starboard engine and reducing the port to 9 knots. *T10* was now in a bad way, the depth-charge explosion having set both compartments I and II below decks on fire. Finally, she was struck a sixth time in the mast just below the search-light platform. With only a couple of machine-guns left in action and the after tubes unserviceable due to fires below, *T10* was no longer in any condition to fight and withdrew inshore. She had suffered eleven killed and a similar number wounded.

T4, in an unfavourable tactical position, was unable to fire her torpedoes as she was 'wooded' by *Komet* and *T10*. As she manoeuvred to avoid two torpedoes, *T4* found herself under fire from two directions. *Komet* opened fire to starboard with her 15cm (6in) guns but at the same time, wild machine-gun fire from the raider hit *T4*, *T14* and *T19* which caused several casualties, including Korvettenkapitän Wilcke. *T4* was perhaps fortunate in that, she, unlike the others, was fitted with an armoured bridge and deckhouse. At 0215 hours, *Komet* was seen to be on fire forward after an explosion; the fire quickly spread to the forebridge and was followed by a dull explosion and a column of fire and smoke. She blew apart and sank very quickly, leaving only smoke and burning oil on the surface. None of her crew survived and after damaging *Brocklesby*, the torpedo boats escaped without further harm. *Komet*'s loss is generally attributed to torpedoes from *MTB236*.

This disastrous action led to a proposal by Captain (2nd Flotilla) Korvettenkapitän Erdmann that consideration should be given to the fitting of a 10.5cm gun on the forecastle of the torpedo boats as they were severely limited by the after mounting of their only gun. Konteradmiral Bey (Flag Officer-Destroyers) disagreed, however. In his view, it was not the job of torpedo boats to give gun protection to an auxiliary cruiser armed with 15cm (6in) guns. This was a little unfair because the raider was not designed or intended to fight such an action – she did not have the gunnery control, gun disposition or manoeuvrability to do so. Nevertheless she was fitted with radar and the question must be asked, why did she not detect the British forces and avoid them? This and the reason why no attempt was made to run for Cherbourg after they had been discovered will remain unknown because Brocksien did not survive the action. Thus the torpedo boats' job *was* to protect *Komet* and there is little doubt that their inability to do so was due in part to their poor armament as well as their lack of good radar. In addition, since an attack was to be expected from seaward, the disposition of the escort was not ideal. It is also probable that had the escort been comprised of the older but better armed Type 26 torpedo boats, the battle would not have been so one-sided, but there were only three of these useful ships in service at the time.

9. THE FREEZING NORTH: MAY TO DECEMBER 1941

After the invasion of Norway in the spring of 1940 that country did not feature a great deal in the Kriegsmarine's plans for its surface warships until 1941, except as a convenient staging post for ships breaking out into the Atlantic on raiding forays. As far as the destroyers were concerned, the first such operation was 'Rheinübung', the well-known sortie by *Bismarck* and *Prinz Eugen*, for which both the battleship and the heavy cruiser had been working-up in the eastern Baltic for some months in preparation. The two heavy ships sailed unescorted from Gotenhafen on 18 May 1941 and set course westwards. They were met off Cape Arkona by *Eckoldt* and *Z23*, which, together with *Sperrbrecher 13* and *31* had sailed from Swinemünde to form part of the escort; *Lody* joined later, off the southern entrance to the Great Belts, with minesweepers from the 5th Flotilla. Altering course to pass through the Kattegat and Skaggerak, the destroyers took up their anti-submarine screening positions, *Lody* leading with *Eckoldt* to port and *Z23* to starboard, all steering a zig-zag course at 30 knots. At midday a Swedish ship, the cruiser *Gotland*, was sighted 15 miles to starboard and made a report which subsequently reached the British Admiralty; shortly afterwards, an air escort of two He 115s and six Bf 110s joined, and for the rest of the day the passage was continued without serious incident. Leaving the minefields off Kristiansand, the line ahead formation, assumed for the transit of the mined area, was opened out into a screen, and shortly before midnight the air escort bade farewell and returned home.

By 0400 hours on the 21st the ships were some 50 miles west-south-west of Boknafjord. The weather could not have been worse for the Germans: the sea was calm, with a north-north-easterly wind Force 1, and although it was cloudy, visibility was good. Dawn broke to find the squadron off Bømlo, where an air escort of four Bf 110s joined, and during the forenoon it entered Korfjord near Bergen for fuelling, where Admiral (West Coast) ordered *Lody* and *Eckoldt* to replenish from tanks to the north and south of Byfjord while *Z23* anchored off Kalvenes and oiled from the tanker *Wollin* in the fjord itself. The cruiser oiled too, but in the light of later events it remains a mystery why Admiral Lütjens failed to take the opportunity of topping up *Bismarck*'s tanks as well.

The stay in Bergen was brief, and after dropping the pilots at the exit of Hjeltefjord at 2000 hours, the squadron resumed its passage northwards through the Scharen at 17 knots, with the destroyers in screen formation once more. They remained undetected and had now reached the latitude of Trondheim. The destroyers' task was now at an end, for at 0502 on 22 May Admiral Lütjens signalled to D6 (Kapitän zur See Schulze-Hinrichs) 'Destroyers dismissed, with thanks', whereupon the three ships altered course for Trondheim as the two heavy units gradually pulled out of sight. No one was then to know that only five days were to elapse before the proud battleship lay on the sea bottom.

The destroyers anchored in Trondheim that evening, having been escorted in through the minefields by patrol boats. Here they remained for two days, before sailing for home on the 24th. *Lody* put in to Wesermünde, where Schulze-Hinrichs boarded *Ihn* for passage to Wilhelmshaven to make his report to FdZ.

CRIPPLED POCKET BATTLESHIP

The next excursion to Norway was rather more eventful. This operation, code-named 'Sommerreise', was the passing of *Lützow* (Kapitän zur See Kreisch) to Trondheim in preparation for a planned foray into the Atlantic. The pocket battleship, formerly named *Deutschland*, sailed from Kiel on the evening of 11 June, accompanied by the light cruisers *Leipzig* and *Emden*, together with five destroyers. The destroyers were in two divisions: the first comprised *Lody* (D6), *Z23* and *Z24*; *Eckoldt* and *Galster* formed the second. Passing northwards through the Kattegat, the destroyers were ordered into screen formation. *Lody* was stationed about 2,000m ahead and *Z23* and *Z24* 70° to port and starboard of the leading cruiser, whilst *Eckoldt* and *Galster* were similarly disposed about the rear cruiser. During the day an air escort of Ar 196s, He 115s and Bf 110s flew above the ships at various times. The British Admiralty had known on 10 June that an important ship was due to move to Norway, and by the 11th their Intelligence sources had correctly identified her. Despite this knowledge, and the increased air patrols, the ships

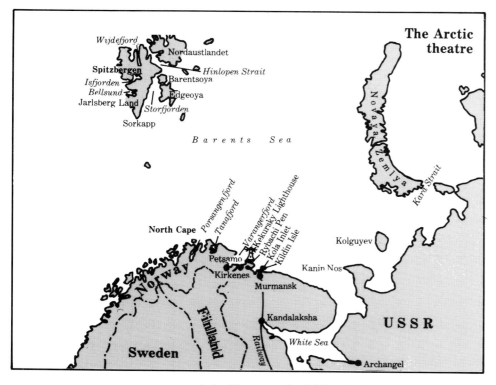

The Arctic theatre

Wijdefjord

Nordaustlandet

Spitzbergen

Hinlopen Strait

Isfjorden   Barentsoya

Bellsund   Edgeoya

Jarlsberg Land   *Storfjorden*

Sorkapp

B a r e n t s   S e a

Kolguyev

North Cape

Porsangenfjord

Tanafjord

Varangerfjord

Kekursky Lighthouse

Rybachi Pen

Kola Inlet

Kildin Isle

Petsamo

Kirkenes

Kanin Nos

Murmansk

Kandalaksha

Railway

White Sea

U S S R

Sweden

Finland

Norway

Archangel

Kara Strait

Novaya Zemlya

passed the Skaggen minefields early in the afternoon of the 12th without having been sighted. Wind and sea conditions in the entrance to the Skaggerak caused the destroyers to experience difficulties in station-keeping as they closed in on *Lützow* after the departure of the light cruisers to Oslo, and by late afternoon they could not maintain speeds over 21 knots, although conditions improved by 2000 hours and the squadron was able to work up to 24 knots. Off Kristiansand escort officers came aboard both *Lützow* and *Lody* for the passage north, and at 0040 hours the ships rounded the Naze and altered course to 325°, whereupon, once again, the weather affected the destroyers, bridge windows being broken on *Lody* and speed having to be reduced to 21 knots. The German ships were now warned, through a decoded British signal, that an RAF aircraft (Blenheim W of 114 Squadron) had reported them, but no attack developed as yet.

Two hours later *Lützow* and her destroyers were about 25 miles off the coast, in the vicinity of *Karmøy*. It was a dark night, with eight-tenths cloud. Here and there the moon shone brightly through the gaps, illuminating large pools in the black sea. A west-south-westerly blew Force 2, the light breeze merely ruffling the surface of the sea, but the peaceful scene was deceptive, for, above the clouds, fve Beaufort torpedo-bombers from RAF Wick (No. 22 Squadron) and nine from No. 42 Squadron flying from Leuchars had been fruitlessly searching the Norwegian coast between Stavanger and the Lister Light throughout the night. Suddenly, quite by chance, an aircraft from No.

42 Squadron, which had already turned for home, caught sight of *Lützow* as she sailed through one of the illuminated pools of light on the sea.

The solitary Beaufort crossed astern of the ships and then turned eastwards to begin her run in. Flying at 140 knots only 60ft above the water, Flight Sergeant Lovett released his torpedo on the unsuspecting ships. As he flashed low over *Z23* the destroyer fired a Very light in challenge, but no ships opened fire until the alarm was sounded at 0220 hours. It was too late: the aircraft escaped and its torpedo ran true, exploding on *Lützow*'s port side and throwing a column of water high into the air. The ship stopped, listing to port and enveloped in smoke and steam. She signalled 'Torpedo hit, quad 3186' and ordered *Eckoldt* to take her in tow towards Egersund for protection under the shore batteries. One more No. 42 Squadron aircraft attacked without success, whilst a third could not release its torpedo. *Eckoldt* towed for a while, with *Lody* stationed north, *Z23* south, *Galster* east and *Z24* west of the crippled pocket battleship. At about 0330 hours *Lützow* managed to start her starboard engine and made 12 knots under her own power; later, at 0424, one of No. 22 Squadron's aircraft finally managed to find the ships, but the torpedo missed and in the dawn sky the plane was caught and shot down by one of the Bf 109 escorts. Soon Kreisch decided to abandon his attempt to reach Norway and reversed course for Germany, which, despite a bombing attack by Blenheims when two bombs fell close to *Z24*, the ships reached safely. *Lützow* would need six months for repairs.

VALUABLE OBJECTIVES

On 21 June 1941 Hitler launched Operation 'Barbarossa', his invasion of Russia, and by so doing opened up two new operating areas for the Kriegsmarine: one was obviously the Baltic, and the second, less obviously, the Arctic. Here, close to the border with Finland, lay the only ice-free Soviet port in the region, Murmansk, and also the valuable nickel mines at Petsamo. General Dietl's mountain divisions, in company with the Finnish Army, were to capture these valuable objectives and also cut the Kirov railway which ran between Leningrad and Murmansk and was therefore of great strategic importance, having also some propaganda value to the Germans since 25,000 German and Austrian POWs were reported to have died whilst building it during the First World War. Then, as now, the sustenance of armies in the field in such areas was considerably difficult, especially in view of the paucity of roads and other communications, and as a consequence most of the supplies had to be convoyed by sea around the North Cape and into Kirkenes. This in its turn required escort vessels for the convoys and fire support ships for the troops in the coastal strip.

Murmansk was not only an important commercial port, it was also the base for the Soviet Northern Fleet (Admiral Golovka). This fleet was not a balanced one, nor was it particularly strong, except in terms of its fifteen submarines, which, it was apparent to the Kriegsmarine, might constitute a significant threat to the supply convoys. Apart from the submarines, there were three aged First World War destroyers, *Karl Liebknecht*, *Kuibishev* and *Uritzky*, together with five modern Type 7 ships, *Gremyashchy*, *Gromky*, *Grozny*, *Sokrushitelny* and *Stremitelny*; in addition, there were three torpedo boats of dubious value and some escort vessels. Only the Type 7 destroyers and a few of the submarines could be considered effective fighting units, and even the former, Italian designed, did not take kindly to the rough northern waters; nevertheless, they had to be countered.

There were fifteen commissioned destroyers available to the Kriegsmarine late in June 1941. Four of these, *Heinemann*, *Steinbrinck*, *Z23* and *Z24*, were with the 5th Flotilla in western France. *Riedel* and *Jacobi* were in the Baltic working-up, as were the new ships, *Z26* and *Z27*, whilst *Z25* had run aground in Norway and required repairs in Germany. This left, initially, only three ships of the 6th Flotilla, *Galster*, *Schoemann* and *Eckoldt*, available for duty in northern waters, although two more, *Beitzen* and *Lody*, would soon be ready also. It is interesting here to compare the losses and building rates of the Royal Navy and the Kriegsmarine in terms of destroyers for the period from April 1940 to June 1941. During those fourteen months Britain had lost forty-six ships of this type, whilst completing ten new vessels; in comparison Germany had lost twelve and built only five more (*Z23–27*). Thus, despite the disruption of air raids, British destroyer output was double that in Germany, where the inconvenience of raids was, at that time, much less significant.

The 6th Flotilla (Kapitän zur See Schulze-Hinrichs) was ordered to the Arctic and the three available ships sailed from Kiel on 20 June. Escort officers were taken aboard *Galster* and *Schoemann* off the Skaggen for passage through the 'Westwall' minefields, and pilots later came aboard to take the ships into Bergen, where they arrived early in the evening of the 21st. Here their passage was delayed by defects in *Schoemann*'s main feed pump, which needed dockyard assistance. Schulze-Hinrichs was apprehensive of air attacks and wanted to disperse his ships about the fjords, but *Schoemann* could not move and the available tugs were too weak to shift her. He also had no intention of ever again being caught in closed fjords. Desperate to have the destroyers move north, Admiral (West Coast) sent his personal car to Oslo airfield with engineering staff in order that the latter could be flown over to Germany to obtain spares. *Beitzen* and *Lody* had meanwhile arrived in Bergen, but it was not until 4 July that all five ships were able to continue their passage.

Calling at Trondheim the next day for fuel and supplies, the Germans found the Norwegians less than accommodating and had trouble obtaining pilots. At Tromsö the flotilla split into two divisions, *Lody*, *Schoemann* and *Galster* (1st) and *Eckoldt* and *Beitzen* (2nd),

and oiled from the tanker *Weissenburg* by divisions. On leaving the port the 1st Division escorted the transports *Barmbeck* and *Hercules* while their flotilla-mates convoyed the tanker northwards, all arriving safely in Kirkenes by the 10th. The destroyers anchored in the fjord around the island of Renøy, remaining at three hours' readiness whilst Schulze-Hinrichs and his staff went ashore for an important conference with Konteradmiral Schenk – Admiral (Polar Coast) – General Dietl and General Stumpff, the commander of Luftflotte 5, during which operational policy was discussed. In brief, the destroyers' objectives were to attack the Russian destroyers and surface craft supporting the various Soviet forces in the Litsa Bay area and to hinder any landings by the Red Army; in addition, flank attacks on the exposed coastal Soviet positions were to be made in support of the German Army in its advance to Murmansk. The German XIX Mountain Corps and the 2nd and 3rd Mountain Divisions had begun their push forward on 29 June, but progress was slow as a result of poor roads and fanatical Soviet resistance. The Soviet Navy had been very active in supporting the hard-pressed Army, both by shelling and by landing troops behind the German lines, and it was hoped by the Germans that the arrival of the 6th Flotilla would alter things.

The operating area, the Barents Sea, was an unenviable spot: the common enemy, as anyone who has served here will confirm, was the weather. In winter the ice moves south as far as Bear Island, the days shorten to a couple of hours in length, and the cyclonic winds ('Bora') in the Kara Sea to the east of Novaya Zemlya whip up the snow over those islands and drive it across the Barents Sea in fierce storms. The thaw does not occur until May, and the summer is noted for cloud and fog. By September, the temperatures are already falling again. The cold pervades everything, freezing the seas as they come aboard, coating equipment and superstructure in thick layers of ice, adding dangerous topweight to ships so that it has to be chipped off to prevent capsizing. Guns and machinery seize up as the ice chokes training gear or increases the viscosity of the lubricating oils. The decks become treacherous with ice, and once in the sea a man not rescued in two minutes will be dead, even if his heart had withstood the initial shock of being plunged into the freezing water. Cold and inhospitable in peacetime, the Arctic is even worse in war.

Little time was lost in preparing for the first sortie, and in the morning of 12 July the five destroyers sailed from Kirkenes for a strike against the Murman coast. The weather was poor and Varangerfjord blanketed by thick fog as the destroyers picked their way out to the open sea. Out in the Barents Sea, they spread into a reconnaissance formation and swept eastwards but sighted only a trawler. Towards evening the weather improved but the sweep remained fruitless, and by midnight the sortie had been called off, all ships concentrating on *Lody* for a run in to the Russian coast. At 0200 hours Cape Teribersky was in sight and then, half an hour later, off Voroni Lighthouse, some

Above: *Hermann Schoemann* in arctic Norway, February 1942. (Bundesarchiv)

shipping was at last spotted. It proved to be a small convoy which consisted of the auxiliary escort vessel *Passat* (*SKR22*), the trawler *Molotov* (*RT67*) and one other trawler, *RT32*. Each of the trawlers was towing peculiarly shaped barges, the purpose of which could not be identified by the Germans. *Passat*, herself a former fishing trawler, carried two 46mm guns, but the armament of the other vessels was negligible. Both sides opened fire at 0248 hours, but it was not until half an hour later, after spirited resistance, that *Passat* went down. Ten minutes later the 558-ton *Molotov* followed her, but *RT32* escaped. The destroyers had fired away four-fifths of their outfit, plus an unauthorized torpedo from *Galster* which ran amok on the surface.

Breaking off the action to return to Tanafjord, the ships were first seen and challenged by an aircraft which fired four red flares. *Lody* replied with four white and opened fire. The visitor was a friendly Ju 88, but the only damage

sustained by either side was to some radio equipment aboard *Lody* which was rendered unserviceable by her gunfire. Later, another attack developed from two Russian floatplanes which dropped six to eight 100kg (220lb) bombs near *Lody*. The bombs fell 200m to starboard and 150m to port, and the destroyer reported three hits on the aircraft. Opening out into reconnaissance formation once again, the flotilla steamed north-eastwards to clear the coast. Three more aircraft were seen from *Lody* but their attention was centred on *Eckoldt*. The destroyer successfully evaded all six bombs and managed to shoot down one of her attackers. No more attacks developed, and despite being hampered once more by the fog the flotilla was back in Tanafjord by the evening.

The results of the sortie hardly justified the prodigious expenditure of fuel and ammunition. It was an action similar to that off Plymouth in November 1940, illustrating once more the generally poor gunnery of the German ships, and the ammunition would have been better spent in assisting the German Army directly through fire support ashore. The 2nd Mountain Division had begun a push forward on the 13th which was brought to a standstill by Russian reinforcements fetched up to Litsa Bay by four destroyers and smaller craft. It is surprising, therefore, that the German destroyers made no attempt to intervene, especially as the Army's position must have been known to them and, close to German-held territory, air cover would have been available. Moreover, it is hardly conceivable that the German forward positions were unaware of the origin of these reinforcements, and Luftwaffe reconnaissance flights could surely not have missed them completely. It remains a fact, however, that despite frequent and widespread use of destroyers and other surface vessels by the Russians for the purpose of landing reinforcements, the German destroyers never attempted to engage them. In fact, Schulze-Hinrichs was very apprehensive about approaching the coast, being wary of mines and air attack; more significantly, he would have preferred S-boats to have been allocated his tasks, although these could not have undertaken shore bombardment and were not entirely suited to harsh northern conditions.

INEVITABLE AIR ATTACKS

The 6th Flotilla made a second sortie, following the lines of the first, on 22 July. Initially all five ships were to take part, but before the sortie could begin *Lody* had trouble with her condensers, necessitating the whole flotilla anchoring off Renøy whilst her engineering staff endeavoured to rectify the problems. Whilst it was at anchor the Soviet Air Force put in an appearance, dropping two bombs just astern of *Lody*. The condenser problems were not to be solved quickly, and Schulze-Hinrichs decided to shift his flag to *Galster* and send *Lody* into Kirkenes for repairs.

The flotilla sailed out into the Barents Sea, which was, for once, calm and clear. The conditions assisted the Russians considerably, and their aircraft found the flotilla in the early evening and made a concerted attack on *Beitzen* and *Eckoldt*. Unable to exceed 30 knots because of boiler problems, the destroyers opened fire with 12.7cm guns and light flak, upsetting the bombers' aim and causing the twelve to sixteen bombs to miss. Later that evening a signal was received that a large Russian flotilla leader was off the Murman coast, and the destroyers altered course to intercept, but there were no *Leningrad* class leaders in the Arctic at this time and so the identity of the ship in the reconnaissance report remains a mystery.

The German flotilla's interception attempt was thwarted because all next day thick fog blanketed the area, forcing the four destroyers to reduce speed drastically. It was not until midnight, therefore, that the coast was raised, and an hour later the only vessel found was not a destroyer but the naval survey ship *Meridian* near the Isle of Lietskie. She was taken under fire by *Schoemann* and by the third salvo was in

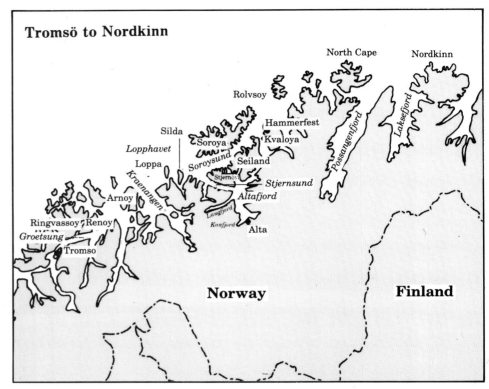

Tromsö to Nordkinn

flames. When she sank, the smoke was visible for two hours. *Beitzen* then sighted a flying-boat on the water under the coast and sank it with a few salvoes. These brief actions stirred up the expected hornet's nest, and as the destroyers withdrew they were attacked out of the sun by flying-boats which dropped bombs close to *Galster*, forcing her to take violent avoiding action; half an hour later a second attack was successfully avoided. Two further attacks by six DB3s from Archangelsk, which were seen only at the last minute, were also unsuccessful, although some twelve bombs near-missed the same destroyer. No more attacks developed, and by late afternoon the Flotilla was back in Bokfjord.

A third sortie on 29 July to the White Sea was broken off the next day when an He 111 reconnaissance aircraft signalled to her base 'Aircraft carrier, Square 9111, course E, speed 27 knots'. This was *Victorious*, accompanied by *Furious*, in the course of launching aircraft attacks on Kirkenes and Petsamo. The German destroyers were well to the east, and although they reversed course they had little chance of catching the carriers. Even so, their absence from harbour denied the Fleet Air Arm four valuable targets, with the result that, robbed of surprise, eleven Albacores and two Fulmars were shot down for little return.

What was to prove the final offensive sweep in this phase was launched the following month. On 9 August *Galster* and *Schoemann* were engaged upon convoy escort duties and so the sweep was conducted by only three destroyers.

After oiling from the tanker *Tiger*, *Lody*, *Beitzen* and *Eckoldt* sailed from Boknafjord at 2140 hours for their target area, this time the Kola Inlet. The sky was cloudy but the temperature was quite high and visibility about twelve miles as the destroyers sailed eastwards. In the early hours of the next day *Lody* sighted a patrol vessel bearing 203° at a range of 16,000m (10 miles), sailing north-west under the coast near Kildin Island at the entrance to the Kola Inlet. She was estimated to be 600–800 tons and in fact she was the 574-ton converted trawler *SKR12* (*Tuman*), armed with two 45mm guns. On being sighted *SKR12* turned south to close the coast, the destroyers increasing speed to attack. At 0342 hours, when the range had dropped to 5,100m, *Lody* and *Beitzen* opened fire. *SKR12* made smoke and turned south-east, replying gallantly with her puny armament. All three destroyers were now firing alternately, and the target was covered in smoke and surrounded by shell splashes. After ten minutes the destroyers ceased fire and then located a second patrol vessel in the entrance to the Kola Inlet but she was out of range. *SKR12* sank seventeen minutes after fire had been opened on her. Thirty-seven from her crew of 52 were rescued.

The German ships were now very close to the Russian coast, and at 0410 hours two shore batteries on the Pogan Peninsula and Medreji opened fire at a range of about 23,000m (14½ miles). There appeared to be one 4-gun and one 5-gun battery. Most of the shells fell astern of *Beitzen*, whereupon Schulze-Hinrichs quickly took his flotilla out to sea and opened the range, working up speed to 31 knots. *Beitzen* and *Lody* dropped smoke floats to cover their withdrawal, but of the ten French-manufactured floats dropped by *Lody* only one ignited, probably as a result of sabotage.

The inevitable air attacks developed, one of which caught *Beitzen*. Three DB-3 or SB2 bombers dived out of the clouds, dropping four to six bombs in *Lody*'s wake which severely shook up her consort *Beitzen* in line astern. Following this attack Schulze-Hinrichs detached *Beitzen* and *Eckoldt* to Narvik for overhaul and continued to Kirkenes alone with *Lody*. Whilst on passage south *Eckoldt* was attacked by a single aircraft whose bombs straddled the destroyer, near-missing abreast No. 1 gun. The shock of the explosion damaged the steering and stopped the starboard engine, but both could be repaired. During the engagement *Lody* had fired eighty-nine 12.7cm shells, *Eckoldt* eighty-seven and *Beitzen* ninety-four – a rather better performance than in previous engagements.

Beitzen was examined in Narvik by the engineering staff in order to discover the extent of the damage caused by the bombing on the 10th. Compartments XIV and III had cracks and leaks, whilst her turbines were very noisy above 24 knots; various components of her auxiliary machinery were also defective. It was decided to send her home to refit immediately, but before departure she took on fuel from *Eckoldt* and in return passed over her ammunition to both *Eckoldt* and *Lody*; in the early evening of 14 August she sailed for Bergen on the first leg of the trip home. *Beitzen*, actually belonged to the 5th Flotilla, whose ships were at this time operating from western France.

EFFECTIVE SUBMARINE WORK

The 6th Flotilla was now to be engaged upon convoy escort duties between Tromsö and Kirkenes, reinforcing the minesweepers and patrol craft on that route, the reason being greatly increased submarine activity against the vital supply convoys to the German Arctic battle front. The Soviet Navy had about fifteen boats operating against this traffic, but most of the effective work was done by the British submarines *Trident* (Commander Sladen) and *Tigris* (Commander Bone) which had been sent to operate from Polyarny in north Russia in August. The German coastal convoy organization became so hard-pressed for escorts that there was no option but to use the destroyers as well. Morale aboard the destroyers was, incidentally, rather low at this time, for the crewmen had had no mail from home for several weeks, enquiries later establishing that all the flotilla's letters had been sent to Helsinki.

Schoemann obtained a submarine contact on 22 August off Loppa whilst escorting a convoy to Tromsö with *Galster*, and although the destroyer reported seeing a periscope and hearing propeller noises, three depth-charge attacks produced oil flecks, bubbles and some scratches on the hull but no definite evidence of a sinking. It is uncertain as to which submarine this was, since although HMS/M *Trident* was in the Lopphavet on this day her log does not record depth-charging by any destroyer: she had broken off an attack on the merchant ship *Nordsterner* in the morning and sunk the *Ostpreussen* in the afternoon when she was depth-charged, but this, according to her log, was by two trawlers. *Tigris* was in the Svaerholt at this time and is unlikely to have been involved, while no Soviet submarine was off Loppa.

The next day, however, *Schoemann* suffered severe damage in her starboard gearing because of broken teeth and required dockyard assistance in Germany, landing 200 rounds of 12.7cm and 500 of 3.7cm shells preparatory to the move home. Meanwhile a reinforcement for the flotilla was on its way north, having sailed from Kiel on the 9th. This was *Riedel*, but as she was making her way northwards she ran heavily aground in the Scharen. Her double bottom was ripped in compartments IV–X and both shafts seized, and she was towed into Bergen, where it was intended to repair her with help from Kiel and Horten. *Schoemann*, sailing home for repairs on the 27th, took with her the flotilla engineer, Korvettenkapitän (Ing) Karbe, as far as Bergen to inspect *Riedel*.

There now remained only three ships with the 6th Flotilla in the Arctic, *Lody*, *Galster* and *Eckoldt*. The convoy operations continued, and at 0900 hours on 30 August a convoy of four merchantmen sailed from Tromsö bound for Kirkenes. Consisting of the steamers *Donau II* (2,931

Above: *Z26*, probably in Norwegian waters, in the condition in which she was lost. Only one single 2cm has been added, on the forecastle. (Bundesarchiv)

tons), *Bahia Laura* (8,561 tons), *Cornouaille* (3,290 tons) and *August Bolten*, the convoy was escorted by *Lody* (with Schulze-Hinrichs aboard), *Galster*, *UJ178*, and the Vp-boats* *Gote* (*V6113*) and *Franke* (*V6111*); two more escorts, *UJ176* and *UJ177*, were to join off Nordkinn. Interestingly, both *Gote* and *Franke* were captured British trawlers, the former *Cape Siretoko* and *Larwood* respectively, taken in April 1940 during the Norwegian campaign. The convoy's initial route lay from Tromsö down Groetsund, passing east of the island of Renøy, through Kaagsund and into the Kvaenangen. Here, at the entrance to the fjord, lay the open sea, where submarines could lurk in the Lopphavet. To reduce the danger the normal route passed between the islands of Loppa and Silda, keeping as close inshore as possible, then through the sheltered waters of Stjernsund and eventually passing eastwards of Hammerfest. All went well at first, and an He 115 joined as air escort, but problems soon arose because *Donau II* had machinery breakdowns which delayed the passage of the convoy, with the result that Schulze-Hinrichs decided to save time and cut straight through the Sørøysundet. This involved a much longer passage in the deep waters of the Lopphavet, and it was a decision he later regretted. Schulze-Hinrichs' other problem was the fact that the convoy's speed of 10.5 knots could not be maintained because of the low speed of *Cornouaille* and the Vp-boats.

In the late afternoon, whilst to the east of Loppa, the

convoy passed four R-boats of the 7th Flotilla and their depot ship, the former fishery protection vessel *Weser*, southbound for Tromsö. This group of ships had unknowingly been the intended target of a submarine, the British *Trident*, then on patrol in the Lopphavet. *Trident* had sighted what she identified as a minesweeper and four R-boats at 1524 hours and started an attack, but she broke it off forty-two minutes later. Shortly afterwards she sighted the air escort of the *Lody* convoy and closed to attack the ships. *Trident* was at the end of her patrol and had only two torpedoes remaining. At 1714 hours she fired these at the two leading merchantmen, then went deep and shut off in anticipation of depth-charging. At the moment that the attack was launched, the convoy had Silda Light bearing 213°, 2–5 miles distant, and had just altered course for the Sørøysundet. The four merchant ships were in line ahead, *Donau II*, *Bahia Laura*, *Cornouaille* and *August Bolten* with the escort in line ahead to port; *Lody* led *Galster*, with one of the Vp-boats between them. *Lody* in fact saw the torpedoes fired, only 100m on her port bow, the tracks clearly visible running ahead and astern of her. In the words of Schulze-Hinrichs, it was a 'skilled and cold-blooded attack': both torpedoes struck home, one on *Donau II*, which sank five minutes later, and the second forward of *Bahia Laura*'s bridge, setting ammunition on fire.

Lody turned hard to port and dropped a marker buoy, but the general unhandiness and slow turning characteristics of these destroyers cost valuable minutes. A periscope was sighted about 100m west of the marker buoy

*'Vorpostenboote': coastal patrol vessels.

and *Lody* fired three patterns of three depth-charges. Whilst part of the escort milled around dropping depth-charges, mostly singly (which later drew adverse comment), *Galster* and some of the smaller escorts rescued survivors. The convoy lurked under the coast for safety. *Bahia Laura* was listing to starboard and slowly sinking as one of the Vp-boats attempted to take her under tow for beaching. It proved to no avail, and *Galster* went alongside to take off survivors. There were two hundred horses in the stern, but nothing could be done for them.

By 1900 hours *Galster* had over 500 rescued aboard and the Norwegian steamer *Mittnattsol*, which had come on to the scene, about 200. *R153* arrived with the 7th Flotilla's doctor, and *Lody* sent hers across to *Galster*. At 2000 hours *Galster*, *Mittnattsol* and *R153* were detached to Tromsö whilst the air escort, Vp-boats and submarine-chasers continued the hunt and *Lody* shepherded the remains of the convoy to Hammerfest, where it arrived in the early hours of the 31st. Meanwhile, at the scene of the attack, it was becoming obvious that the damaged vessel could not be saved, and at 2055 *Gote* and *Franke* were ordered to sink her by gunfire. This took the best part of an hour, and it was not until 2155 hours that the Hamburg-South America line vessel disappeared below the waves. *Lody* took on depth-charges from the Vp-boats to replenish her outfit and in the afternoon of the 31st sailed from Hammerfest with the convoy, arriving in Langfjord on the evening of 1 September.

The two torpedoed ships had between them been carrying 1,598 soldiers and marines as well as 78 crew members. When the survivors were counted, it was found that *Galster* had 490 (plus 47 wounded and 46 dead), *Lody* 38, *Franke* 178, *Gote* about 360, *Mittnattsol* about 200 and *R153* 21. This made a total of some 1,334 survivors out of 1,676, and the high percentage was undoubtedly due in part to the fine weather and also to the fact that *Trident* had expended all her torpedoes.* *Trident* had sustained some minor damage in the counter-attacks, which lasted over two hours, but the precise number of depth-charges dropped is uncertain: German records give 39 (six from the Vp-boats, three from the He 115 and 30 from destroyers), whilst *Trident*'s log records 56. In any case, the number of charges dropped was small in relation to the length of the counter-attack.

By the beginning of September 1941 only two ships of the 6th Flotilla were operational. *Schoemann* was under refit at Deschimag (Bremen) and not expected to complete until November, *Jacobi* at Deutscher Werke (Kiel), *Heinemann* at Norddeutsche Lloyd (Wesermünde) and *Riedel* at Bergen. To add to the difficulties, Korvettenkapitän Schemmel, commander of *Eckoldt*, had gone down with jaundice and been flown to Stuttgart for treatment; as a temporary

*Four had been fired at *Ostpreussen* (3 hits); two at the tanker *Tripp* (misses); two at the merchantman *Levante* (misses); and four at *Bremse* (all misses).

replacement, the captain of *Riedel* was to be flown over from Berlin.

When the minelayer *Bremse*, escorting the transports *Barcelona* and *Trautenfels* carrying 1,500 men of the 6th Mountain Division, was attacked by the British cruisers *Aurora* and *Nigeria* in the Barents Sea on 7 September, none of the three destroyers was operational, although *Eckoldt* could have been provided with an emergency CO. Schulze-Hinrichs decided, however, that in view of the paucity of the information available it was useless sending a single destroyer out. *Bremse* went down fighting, alone in the Arctic waters, but the transports escaped to the safety of the fjords. Her commander and most of her crew were lost.

Lody was now in need of refit and was experiencing serious water losses. The flotilla commander shifted to *Galster* and on 27 September *Lody* sailed for home. The flotilla strength continued to decline, for on 12 October *Eckoldt* was rammed by a Norwegian steamer in Tromsö. The Norwegian hit the destroyer on the port side, compartment V, flooding the starboard turbine room, although the port turbine remained serviceable. It was at first believed that the Norwegian had deliberately rammed the destroyer, and her crew were arrested on a charge of sabotage though later released. *Eckoldt* was put into the floating dock at Trondheim on 22 October and required twelve days of repairs before she was seaworthy enough to go home, arriving for refit at Germaniawerft on 9 November. *Galster*, as sole representative of the 6th Flotilla, remained in the Arctic until relieved by the 8th Flotilla, whose first two ships, *Z24* and *Z26*, arrived in Tromsö at the end of November. *Galster* had a very good record for serviceability, but she too was now due for a refit and by the beginning of December had arrived at Deschimag (Bremen) for overhaul. The last ship of the 6th Flotilla had now left Norway, but only temporarily.

In the final analysis, the achievements of the 6th Flotilla in the Arctic during its six months' tour were disappointingly few. The destroyers had failed to find any important Russian warship, let alone sink one, and had provided no shore bombardment support for the Army ashore; in fact, the Soviet Navy's only serious loss during this period, apart from submarines, was the destroyer *Stremitelny*, and she succumbed to air attack. Mines and bombs were, it is true to say, two very real hazards to any operation by the destroyers, since the Soviet Navy set great store by mining operations and had sown many between the entrance to the White Sea and the Rybachiy Peninsula. The Soviet Air Force, too, was very active, if not effective, so Schulze-Hinrichs' caution can to some extent be understood. There were other targets to be found in these waters at this period, but the important word is 'found', since although five outward-bound PQ convoys had sailed to Russia and three return QP convoys for the United Kingdom up to December 1941, none had been located by the Germans – who were not even aware of their sailings.

SERIOUS CONCERN

The 8th (Narvik) Flotilla which replaced the 6th in the Arctic had been formed at Wesermünde on 1 December 1940, under the command of Kapitän zur See Pönitz, with the destroyers *Z23*, *Z24* and *Z25*, all Type 36As, the 'Narvik' appellation having been decreed by Hitler in recognition of the April 1940 battles. However, the first two ships were engaged on trials and work-up, whilst *Z25* had only commissioned on 30 November. Until March 1941 the destroyers of the flotilla continued their lengthy training routines in the comparative safety of the Baltic, hindered only by the bad weather, ice and air raids on Bremen and Kiel, during one of which Pönitz was injured by a splinter and was temporarily replaced by Korvettenkapitän Smidt. By the beginning of March the flotilla's strength was increased by the addition of *Z27*, although she still had work-up and training to complete.

On 19 March, while still not at an acceptable level of training in the eyes of Pönitz, the 8th Flotilla was ordered to return forthwith to Kiel from Gotenhafen and to make operational all armament, including depth-charges (but not mine gear), whilst on passage west. Any deficiencies were to be made up in Kiel Dockyard, where full war stores and ammunition were to be embarked. Charts of Bergen, Stavanger and Kristiansand were taken on, so there was little doubt as to the ships' destination. Their task, in fact, was to escort home the heavy cruiser *Hipper* following her operations in the Atlantic whilst based at Brest.

Both destroyers sailed from Kiel on the morning of 21 March. The weather was bad, and in the German Bight the winds, Force 6–7, whipped up the seas, throwing water over the destroyers' bows, preventing No. 1 gun from being worked and damaging radar gear. Speed was forced down to 12 knots at times, and by the early hours of the 22nd, off Esbjerg, the north-westerly had risen to Force 8 when Pönitz decided to run in under the Danish coast for shelter. *Z23* had lost a cutter, ready-use ammunition and depth-charges overboard, whilst a torpedo davit had been damaged and cracks formed in the upper deck; *Z24* had lost her gyrocompass and was making water in two compartments. Kristiansand was safely reached, however, and by the afternoon of the 24th the destroyers had reached Bergen. Both sailed again two days later with *Hipper*, escorting her as far as Anholt before being ordered back to Bergen again to perform the same duty for the homeward bound *Admiral Scheer*. They were assisted in this task by the torpedo boat *Iltis*.

Whilst the two destroyers were repairing their sea damage much discussion was taking place amongst Captain (D8), FdZ and Commander-in-Chief (Fleet) concerning the destroyers' part in the operation. Pönitz considered that the employment on such an operation of ships not fully worked up and inadequately trained was foolhardy, and that only the fact that the British did not locate the ships prevented a major débâcle. Admiral Carls disagreed most strongly, rightly pointing out that the capital units were of major importance and that in view of the critical shortage of destroyers Captain (D8) should have realized this.

The other major topic of comment was the weatherly qualities of the new destroyers. Quite obviously, the hoped-for improvement over the Type 34 and 36 designs had not been fully achieved, and the fore-ends were still too fine and still had inadequate buoyancy for good seakeeping. It was feared that without a major redesign of the fore-ends the destroyers would remain handicapped in bad weather; furthermore, it had not escaped notice that the poor rough-weather performance was still evident even before the fitting of the twin turret forward.

The flotilla returned to the Baltic to continue its training, which extended to June 1941 when *Z23* and *Z24* were ordered to France under the command of the 6th Flotilla. In May *Z27* had collided with *U652* in the Bay of Danzig, damaging both vessels. The destroyer's propellers and starboard shaft were wrecked, necessitating her docking at her builder's yard in Bremen for repairs, during which time the opportunity was taken to install heating in the oil bunkers. *Z25* was ordered to Norway in June, but she ran aground in Hagesund and was then sent home again for repairs. *Z26* and *Z27* were both in dockyard hands or on training in the Baltic until September 1941. During the last week of September the flotilla, consisting of *Z25*, *Z26* and *Z27*, was attached to the 'Baltenflotte', together with *Tirpitz*, *Scheer*, *Köln*, *Nürnberg* and four boats of the 2nd Torpedo Boat Flotilla. This strong force had been concentrated to contain the Soviet Fleet in Leningrad should it attempt to sail on the invasion of Russia by Germany. No such move was made, however, and, after cruising around the Åland Islands and anchoring in Föglofjord for four days, the squadron returned to Gotenhafen.

In October the 8th Flotilla was ordered by Fleet Command to have *Z23* to *Z27* fully operational by 1 November and to prepare to move to Norway. Naval Group North ordered *Z23*, *Z24* and *Z26*, with *Jacobi*, to sail for Norway on 2 November, *Z25* and *Z27* being in dockyard hands. However, *Z26* developed defects in her boiler blowers, *Jacobi* tube failures in two boiler rooms and *Z24* defects in the starboard astern manoeuvring valve, and the orders were changed and the destroyers sent to Swinemünde. A second attempt to sail on the 9th was only partially successful, since *Jacobi* got a rope around her propellers and as there was no dock large enough for destroyers in Kristiansand she had to return to Kiel again, leaving Pönitz with only *Z24* and *Z26*. His main cause of concern was the availability of torpedoes in the Arctic bases, for he intended to use his ships offensively against targets worthy of such weapons, and he estimated that he would require fifty or sixty.

The passage north was another rough one, the heavy stern seas causing the ships to yaw badly. Equipment and depth-charges broke loose, making conditions on the upper deck hazardous in the extreme. Aboard *Z24* one man was badly injured and later died, while another was lost overboard from *Z26*. From Bergen the destroyers sailed through the inner leads, passed Ålesund and on the 17th entered Trondheim to find the port blanketed in smoke from a serious fire in the army stores ashore. The following day the flotilla was ordered to Tromsö by Generaladmiral Boehm (Admiral Norway) for service with Admiral Polar Coast (Konteradmiral Nordmann).

Before the destroyers sailed, however, the question of torpedoes was once again discussed, this time with the Torpedo Director (Trondheim), Fregattenkapitän Benfer. Pönitz was concerned to learn that although there were twenty-two torpedoes at Bergen, twenty-four in Trondheim and nineteen at Narvik, the only means of transport were two small Norwegian motor-sailers. One, *Harriet*, was fitted with radio but the other, *Ingeborg II*, was not. Neither could get beyond Narvik in winter because of the ice problem, so as a temporary measure it was arranged that those torpedoes in Trondheim would be shipped to Narvik, whose store would then be full up, and that further supplies would be requisitioned from Germany; in the meantime, efforts would be made to obtain a suitable vessel locally and equip her with compressors and racks for 50–60 torpedoes.

Continuing their northward journey, the destroyers called briefly at Narvik to show the battleground to the ships' companies and to hold a memorial service, passage then being resumed to Tromsö. Here the first signs of enemy activity were noted, for the Norwegian merchant ship *Vesco* had recently been torpedoed and sunk by the British submarine *Sealion*, then operating out of Polyarny in North Russia. In Tromsö *Z26* developed lubrication problems in the starboard LP turbine, wrecking the rotor. A delay was necessary to effect repairs, but to the south three other members of the flotilla, *Z23*, *Z25* and *Z27*, had now begun their long haul north.

Admiral Boehm, Konteradmiral Nordmann and Kapitän zur See Pönitz were all concerned with deciding what tasks the 8th Flotilla could undertake, bearing in mind that only two ships were as yet on station. The senior officers realized that large-scale operations were not feasible with only two vessels, and Pönitz too considered that it had been a hasty decision to send only two ships at first. More importantly, however, the Admiral was seriously concerned with the flotilla's state of readiness, since *Z23* and *Z24* had had only limited battle training and *Z25* and *Z26* none at all, whilst *Z27* had exercised for only one week. This, taken together with the personnel changes which were still plaguing the destroyers, meant that for the time being the flotilla would be employed on escort duties, a task for which they were really too big and fast although one which would provide valuable training.

Z23, *Z24*, *Z25* and *Z27* sailed from Tromsö on 10 December, escorting the depot ship *Tanga*, all the destroyers except *Z24* carrying 50 mines each. The cold polar conditions hindered the passage, with driving snow at first preventing any entrance into Kirkenes, but finally the weather abated a little and, guided by the minesweeper *M30*, the little convoy entered its new base, where the destroyers disembarked their mines to the merchantman *La France*. Four days later the flotilla mounted its first operation in the Arctic, 'Zange', a sweep off the Murman coast. *Z26* developed machinery defects again, this time in the port HP turbine through lubrication failure once more, and had to be withdrawn. Pönitz therefore transferred with his staff to *Z25*, mainly because she was the only unit of the remaining four with her radar serviceable.

The flotilla steamed eastwards to a position some 100 miles north of Kanin Nos, then turned south, formed into a line-abreast reconnaissance formation and swept down to Kanin Nos but without sighting anything. Re-forming again, Pönitz then began the second stage of the sortie by moving into the coast towards Murmansk. Suddenly, in the fog, two shadows were sighted off Cape Bol Gorodezki and confirmed by radar, bearing 240°, at a range of 37,500m (23½ miles) and moving quickly aft on the starboard side. In the poor visibility of the early evening the German flotilla identified the two enemy ships as Russian destroyers, but in fact they were the British minesweepers *Speedy* and *Hazard* (850 tons, two 4in guns). The flotilla received permission to open fire at 1732 hours, and three minutes later *Z25* fired three torpedoes (of which only one launched) and *Z27* eight (of which only one of the second 'Viererfächer' launched). The gun action lasted barely fifteen minutes, with targets appearing and disappearing into the murky weather, and despite, once again, prodigious expenditure of ammunition by the German ships, neither of the British ships was sunk. The Germans broke off the sortie and returned to Kirkenes.

This first operation could hardly have been considered a success, and it drew criticism from Naval Command over a number of points. Thus, although Pönitz believed that *Z27* should not have expended a full outfit of torpedoes, the Admiral disagreed on the grounds that ships must take advantage of surprise. Incidentally, *Z27* was another destroyer whose torpedo officer had been transferred to U-boats and replaced by someone 'green'. The flotilla was also criticized for not using starshell for illumination, for abandoning the second part of the task and for not economizing on fuel after the disengagement, but it was acknowledged that this was the first operation by a new and only partly trained flotilla operating in an unfamiliar area. Technical problems with radar and radio communications had not helped, and the unserviceability of the leader (*Z26*) further aggravated matters. However, it was early days yet and the flotilla looked forward to better success in 1942.

Hazard had 'A' gun disabled by a hit on its elevating gear after firing only one round whilst 'X' gun was badly damaged. Her foremast and wireless were shot away by two direct hits and her motor boat destroyed before she and her consort became lost to view.

10. ARCTIC ADVENTURE: JANUARY TO DECEMBER 1942

The 8th Destroyer Flotilla remained in the Arctic at the beginning of 1942 and now consisted of only four serviceable ships, Z26 still having problems with her port turbine. Then Z27 too developed defects in her shafts, part of the problem being associated with the use of synthetic materials to replace white metal in the bearing blocks, and in consequence a minelaying operation scheduled for the first week of the year had to be reduced in scale, with only Z24 and Z23 detailed as layers and Z25 as escort. Severe cold, down to −12°, delayed the start of the sortie until the air temperatures improved, but the three ships sailed from Kirkenes on 13 January. This sortie, code-named 'Kussel 1'/'Zauber', was a two-part operation, first the lay off Katschkowski-Huk, and then an armed sweep along the Murmansk coast. The lay was successfully completed, both Z23 and Z24 dropping fifty EMC type mines, but 'Zauber' was not carried through because D8 believed that this would jeopardize the security of the field – a decision for which he was later taken to task by Admiral Nordmann.

Z26 had meanwhile left for home and refit, escorted by Z27, and she was followed on the 29th by the rest of the flotilla, now withdrawn from the Arctic theatre, Z24 to refit and Z25 to take part in 'Cerberus'. The flotilla returned to the Arctic by late March (although Pönitz had not expected to sail north again until mid-May), Z24, Z25 and Z26 arriving back in Kirkenes on the 27th.

The year 1942 was the one in which Norway became Hitler's 'zone of destiny', and for the first time the Kriegsmarine began to base its strike force of capital ships in her deep and sheltered fjords. The first of the heavy ships to move up was Tirpitz, following the path of her ill-fated sister. Admiral Raeder and the Naval Staff still wanted to send Tirpitz out into the Atlantic on raiding forays, but Hitler, shaken by the loss of Bismarck, refused to hear of it; instead it was proposed that she be sent to Norway to attack the Allied convoys to North Russia, a plan to which Hitler readily agreed.

Tirpitz (Kapitän zur See Topp) had been undergoing trials and then an extended period of training and work-up in the Baltic since her commissioning on 25 February 1941. It has been mentioned that the Kriegsmarine adhered to the long peacetime work-up routines even in war: the contest between the barely commissioned Prince of Wales and Bismarck shows the contrasting policies of the two navies. Tirpitz sailed across the Baltic to Kiel, where she transited the Canal to Wilhelmshaven. The Naval Staff were not going to risk her being sighted off the Swedish coast as Bismarck had been, and she was met in the German Bight by an escort of four destroyers under the command of D5 (Kapitän zur See Berger) aboard Beitzen. The other destroyers were Heinemann, Jacobi and Z29, the first two actually belonging to the 6th Flotilla.

Under the code-name 'Polarnacht' the ships sailed north on the evening of 14 January 1942 and reached Trondheim on the 17th without incident, except for the sighting of two unidentified vessels on the 15th which, on investigation by Z29, proved to be harmless fishing boats. The destroyers remained alongside at Hoppla-Elven in Trondheimfjord that night, but early the next day they had to sail home again as they were required in Brest in connection with 'Cerberus'. This voyage south, as has already been described, resulted in the loss of Heinemann whilst the destroyers were on passage through the English Channel.

Following the successful conclusion of 'Cerberus' the destroyers were once again required to escort heavy units up to Norway, this time Prinz Eugen and Admiral Scheer. Beitzen (Captain D5), Jacobi, Schoemann, Ihn and Z25 were given the task of escort, and in the early hours of 21 February the squadron sailed from the Elbe and set course northwards. Yet again, however, the British Admiralty had received Intelligence of the move, and reconnaissance planes were out searching. One of these located the ships later in the morning, whereupon the German squadron reversed course, a ruse that was successful in avoiding the expected air attacks. During the evening the passage north resumed as the weather worsened. Throughout the dark and cloudy night, the east-south-east wind, blowing at up to Force 8, gave the destroyers considerable trouble and caused rolls of up to 35°, Schoemann moving so heavily that her port 3.7cm platform was under water and two crewmen washed away into the night. Two depth-charges broke loose to explode in the destroyer's wake and the heavy seas damaged one of the throwers. On the morning of the following day, 22 February, two British bombers located and attacked the ships. They were unsuccessful, but five bombs fell only 150m off Schoemann's starboard bow. After

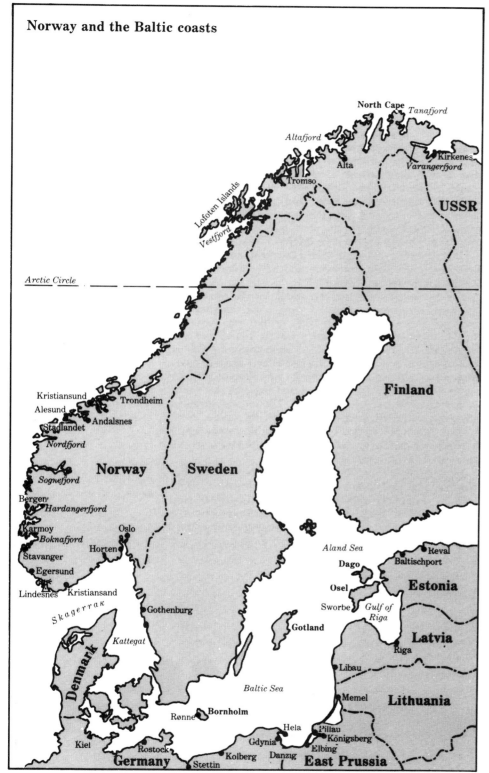

Norway and the Baltic coasts

halting at Bergen for fuelling the ships sailed north again in the evening, bound for Trondheim.

The bad weather continued, with the result that the destroyers were unable to match the speed of the heavy cruisers. *Beitzen*, *Jacobi* and *Ihn* lost touch and returned to Bergen, leaving only *Schoemann* and *Z25* with the two larger vessels. At 0703 on the 23rd, just as dawn was breaking, a large explosion occurred in the water some 40m off *Schoemann*'s port bow. The destroyer thought a bomb had been dropped and altered course hard to starboard to avoid the column of falling water, whilst 400m away to starboard the shock of the explosion alerted the bridge watch aboard *Prinz Eugen*, who considered that, since the water was too deep for mines, it might have been a depth-charge washed overboard. Two minutes later the puzzle was solved as a torpedo struck the cruiser's stern, blowing off her rudder but miraculously not touching the propellers. Wreathed in a cloud of steam, the heavy cruiser lay stopped with her stern hanging off as the destroyers began a submarine search. The torpedoes had been fired by HMS/M *Trident*, which had by now turned over her Arctic assignment to two 'S' class boats and moved south. She was not damaged following her attack and withdrew after the destroyers returned to the stricken cruiser. Escorted by the destroyers, *Prinz Eugen* finally arrived in Trondheim just before midnight on the 23rd. Repairs were undertaken on the spot by the repair ship *Huascaran* but were not completed until May.

SEARCH FOR A CONVOY

Even without *Prinz Eugen*, there was now a reasonable strike force available to the Kriegsmarine in central Norway for attacks on the Russian convoy route, of which the Germans were now aware. *Tirpitz* and *Scheer* were supported by five destroyers, *Beitzen* and *Ihn* of the 5th Flotilla, *Jacobi* and *Schoemann* of the 6th, and, operating with the 5th flotilla although nominally belonging to the 8th, *Z25*. In Trondheim, the destroyers' base was alongside piers at Hoppla-Elven, where in later years they were to lie inactive, their guns covered in tarpaulins made rigid by the freezing weather for weeks on end; for the moment, however, the weeks were fairly eventful.

The first operation against the Russian convoys was to be aimed at PQ12, whose sixteen ships had sailed from Iceland on 1 March. Acting on information received from air reconnaissance, *Tirpitz* set off with four destroyers, *Jacobi*, *Schoemann*, *Ihn* and *Z25*, and two torpedo boats, *T5* and *T12*, early in the afternoon of the 6th, but, steaming down the Frohavet, *Ihn* developed a defect in No. 2 boiler room which reduced her speed to 21 knots, although this was eventually corrected later in the afternoon. The destroyers and torpedo boats were disposed in screen formation about *Tirpitz*, with *Jacobi* leading, *Schoemann* and *Z25* to port, *Ihn* and *T5* to starboard and *T12* astern. There was a light wind from the south, the sea was calm, and visibility was very good. Overhead was an air escort of Bf 109s, Ju 88s and Bv 138s, and during the afternoon a reconnaissance message was received giving details of the convoy and its weak escort.

At 2010 hours that evening the squadron was abreast the island of Vikna, at which point *Jacobi*, *T5* and *T12* were ordered to return to Trondheim. *Z25* moved over to a position on *Tirpitz*'s starboard bow, with *Ihn* ahead and *Schoemann* opposite *Z25*. The weather became worse during the night and a swell developed. Heavy seas began to break over the destroyers, making conditions difficult, and by the morning, when the ships were to the north-west of the Lofoten Islands, the waves broke bridge windows, damaged the shield and jammed the training gear of No. 1 gun, and fused signal lamps aboard *Ihn*.

Admiral Ciliax ordered his remaining three destroyers to form a reconnaissance line and steer 345° at 25 knots until evening, and then to rendezvous with him again; *Tirpitz* would sweep to the north-west, then turn east in an endeavour to locate the convoy. Kapitän zur See Schulze-Hinrichs (D6) was unhappy about the weather conditions, however, and signalled that the reconnaissance line ordered would be difficult to maintain in the seas then running. A new rendezvous was given by *Tirpitz*, and at 1020 hours she altered course to the north-west and disappeared into the mists whilst the destroyers turned on to their search course. The northerly wind was moderating but a fairly high swell was running from the north-east, and it was cloudy and bitterly cold, with driving snow and low visibility.

Things had improved by early afternoon, and at 1615 hours *Z25* signalled 'Smoke in 350°'. Course was altered to intercept until the steamer could be identified as a Russian freighter sailing in ballast to Iceland. She was the 2,815grt *Ijora*, a straggler from the homeward-bound QP8 convoy. *Ihn* ordered her to heave to and not use her radio, emphasizing the point by firing a 3.7cm shot across her bows. *Ijora*'s crew manned their single gun aft and trained it on *Ihn*, at the same time radioing 'RR gunned, gunned *Ijora* gunned RRRR, 72.35N 10.50E *Ijora*'. On hearing this

the destroyers opened fire, hitting the freighter in the hold and on the bridge and setting her on fire; the two rounds from *Ijora* fell short of *Ihn*. After a few minutes Berger ordered 'Cease fire', *Ihn* having expended 43 rounds of 12.7cm and 82 of 3.7cm ammunition. *Z25*, on the other hand, had hardly fired a shot.

Despite the fires aboard the Russian steamer, she was not sinking very fast, and to hurry things on *Ihn*, from a rather unfavourable position, fired a torpedo, which ran amok, turning 90° and passing only about 10m astern of the destroyer. *Schoemann* had no luck with her torpedo either, and she was then ordered to sink the freighter by gunfire and drop a depth-charge close by. Her cargo of timber made her slow to sink. *Tirpitz* hove in sight two minutes after the burning ship sank, and was joined by the destroyers, but by now the latter, especially *Ihn*, were short of fuel. That evening *Ihn* was detached to Harstad, where she was to refuel from the oiler *Pelagos*. *Tirpitz* attempted to oil the remaining two ships during the night, but heavy seas and icing made this impossible and both *Schoemann* and *Z25* had to be sent to Tromsö.

The battleship continued the search for the convoy and the three destroyers completed their oiling, but only *Ihn* managed to rejoin *Tirpitz*, at 0745 on the 9th. Assuming station ahead of her, she began a zig-zag course and anti-submarine screening routine. Later in the morning *Ihn* had moved over to a position on the battleship's starboard bow when two aircraft were sighted. An Arado 196 was catapulted off while *Tirpitz* turned east and then east-north-east, increasing speed as she did so. The sea was turbulent and the destroyer shipped water, which rapidly froze, hindering the gun crews. There was a fresh north-easterly blowing and the heavy cloud base was estimated at 600m, although visibility was very good.

At 10.20 hours five Albacores were sighted on the port quarter, and the aircraft attacked with torpedoes, *Tirpitz* replying with her heavy flak and then her lighter guns. Attacking from both sides, the aircraft were obviously aiming for the battleship, but two torpedoes dropped close to *Ihn*'s starboard side forced the latter to alter course hard

Below: A contrast in silhouettes between the Types 35 and 37 torpedo boats in Norway, 1942. In the foreground is *T15* and behind, *T7*. (Archiv Gröner)

to starboard as the tracks passed very close under her stern. *Ihn* shot down one attacker with Nos. 3 and 4 2cm guns, the aircraft crashing 800m away to starboard. *Tirpitz*, too, by means of violent course alterations, managed to avoid all the torpedoes, having fired over 4,500 rounds of flak ammunition as well as two 38cm broadsides, but *Ihn* had been unable to use her 12.7cm weapons in barrage fire owing to the course alterations. Two hours later the ships were safely back in Vestfjord, where they were rejoined by *Schoemann* and *Z25*.

A ROGUE TORPEDO

The next major destroyer action took place farther north, in the Arctic, when Kapitän zur See Pönitz weighed from Varangerfjord with the 8th Flotilla (*Z26*, *Z25* and *Z24*) during the afternoon of 28 March to begin a sortie against convoy PQ13, which had been sighted by a Bv 138 of 2/KüFlGr 406 the previous day. Ordering torpedoes to be set for a running depth of 3m, the flotilla commander took his ships out into the Barents Sea. East of Vardø the flotilla increased speed and steered almost due north, then altered around to a north-east heading to find the convoy, a northerly course being assumed once more from about 2200 hours. The weather at this time was kind, with a light west-north-westerly and a calm sea; overhead the sky was light, with good visibility apart from occasional snow showers, but it was very cold, ice forming on guns, wires and upper decks and making conditions hazardous. Before midnight the ships' companies were sent to action stations on receipt of a signal from Admiral (Nordmeer) giving information about the convoy's position. Their first contact with any part or former part of the convoy came at 2338 hours when a light was sighted off the starboard bow. Closing to investigate, the destroyers found several lifeboats from the freighter *Empire Ranger* which had been sunk by air attack three hours previously. Sixty-one seamen were rescued, but, no doubt grateful for their rescue from the bitter arctic night, they gave rather more details about the convoy than they should have done.

Armed with this information, Pönitz took his flotilla north-westwards, spread out into a line-abreast reconnaissance formation. In the early hours of the 29th *Z24*'s radar developed defects, leaving only the leader with an operational set. This hampered things somewhat, but at 0143 hours a steamer was sighted which proved to be the Soviet freighter *Bateau* (4,687 tons), a straggler from the convoy. *Z26* engaged her with gunfire and then despatched her with a torpedo, hitting amidships. The merchantman sank in five minutes while *Z25* and *Z26* rescued the survivors, who only numbered seven. *Z24* took no part in this sinking. Then, rescue operations complete, the flotilla resumed its search for the convoy.

By now there were signs that the weather was deteriorating: the wind had veered north-easterly, snow showers became more frequent and the visibility was becoming more changeable, and under such conditions the absence of radar was a severe handicap. For three hours the flotilla forged north without success until a convoy position report from a U-boat was received. This placed it north-west of the destroyers and clarified the situation a little. Pönitz altered course once more, this time to the west, thus putting the now strong easterly Force 5 at his stern, which made the ships yaw badly; driving snow made conditions even more uncomfortable.

The escort for the convoy consisted of two British destroyers (*Oribi* and *Eclipse*) and two Soviet (*Sokrushitelni* and *Gremyashchi*), with the trawler *Paynter*. They escorted eight merchantmen, disposed in three columns, whilst, three miles ahead on the starboard bow, the light cruiser *Trinidad*, with the destroyer *Fury* astern, zig-zagged along at 20 knots. Shortly before midnight on the 28th the captain of the cruiser had received a signal from SBNO (North Russia) based on a sighting report from a Soviet submarine, warning him that a destroyer attack might be expected and, with the crew at second degree readiness (i.e., half the armament stood to), the cruiser swept the area with her Type 281 and 284 radar.

The 8th Flotilla had by now managed to work its way north of the cruiser's track, although it was not aware of her close proximity. At about 0940 the two antagonists detected each other by radar, visibility by now having closed down to less than two miles. The cruiser gained visual contact at 0950 but the destroyers had already sighted her a few minutes earlier and Pönitz had given his ships permission to open fire with guns and torpedoes at 0946. The cruiser appeared out of the mists 30° on the port bow when the range was already down to about 3,200m. *Trinidad* opened up at *Z26* with 'A' and 'B' turrets, tuned to ranges obtained by radar, as the destroyers opened fire and launched torpedoes. The cruiser's first salvo fell short as the German reply straddled her, but her second hit *Z26* hard, knocking out Nos. 2 and 3 guns, igniting ready-use cartridges and hitting the port turbine room. A large fire broke out between the after funnel and the mainmast, producing clouds of smoke. After five salvoes the cruiser shifted target to the second in line, *Z25*, which received three broadsides and one salvo from 'X' and 'Y' turrets. Hits were observed, and the port 4in (10.5cm) battery also joined in but had difficulty in spotting fall of shot. The German gunfire was less effective but *Trinidad* was hit twice, aft between stations 166 and 185, wrecking some cabins, and on the port-side platform deck, wrecking the admiral's office and causing some flooding.

Z26 had launched her seven remaining torpedoes, *Z25* eight and *Z24* four, and then the destroyers turned hard to starboard and steamed north into the driving snow. *Z24* had attempted to fire a second 'Viererfacher', but due to a mistake at the tubes in the heat of battle one was launched to starboard while the rest were not fired. *Trinidad*, anticipating the torpedo attack, turned away to starboard, successfully combing the tracks, one of which passed close down the port side and then circled back to the north again to find the enemy. Radar and visual contact was lost by the cruiser in the swirling snow and mist, whilst *Z24* and *Z25* had become separated from *Z26*.

Damaged but still steaming at 26 knots, *Z26* turned further to starboard and strove to escape from *Trinidad*'s devastating gunfire; with sleet, fine snow and spray freezing on to the binocular glasses and rangefinders, a ship fitted with gunnery control radar carried a decisive advantage. *Trinidad* regained contact again at 0956: tracking the contact and increasing speed to 30 knots, she closed to about 3,100m then altered course to pass under the destroyer's stern. First black smoke was sighted, and then the ship from which it was issuing appeared. 'A' and 'B' turrets opened fire again, hitting and straddling the destroyer, which made no reply. Pönitz signalled to *Z24* and *Z25* that he was badly damaged, but visual contact was not yet regained between the two detached ships and their stricken leader.

Men were already abandoning *Z26*, whether intentionally or otherwise is not known, for the cruiser passed a number, alive and dead, in the freezing sea. After being hit again *Z26* altered course to starboard and began to zig-zag violently, but the British ship turned to starboard to open the 'A' arcs and closed the range down to 1,800m. Further hits were registered on *Z26*, one under the bridge on the port side and two more further aft, and as the range fell the 4in (10.5cm) battery joined in once more and even the pom-pom opened fire. *Z26* was now clearly doomed: her speed fell away and she slewed to starboard, defiantly opening fire again with No. 1 gun as its range was cleared.

After firing 24 salvoes from 'A' and 'B' turrets and 13 from 'X' and 'Y' in this second engagement, *Trinidad* sent three torpedoes to finish off the damaged ship. Two failed to launch but the third reappeared minutes later off the port bow, heading for the cruiser herself. It was impossible to avoid despite emergency manoeuvring and the missile struck her between stations 71 and 79, causing serious flooding and a list of 17° and forcing her to break off the action.

Conditions aboard *Z26* were by now desperate. She was still manoeuvrable, but her speed had been reduced and all but one gun destroyed. Left alone by the cruiser, it seemed as if she might just have a chance of escape when a destroyer appeared to port. Assuming her to be *Z24* or *Z25*, she flashed her call sign, 'ZU', but in fact it was *Eclipse*,* which had been stationed ahead of the convoy but, in anticipation of a fight, had moved in to join the action. Searching with her Type 286P radar, she quickly picked up a contact and closed.

The weather was by now very poor and visual contact was not obtained until the range had fallen to about 800m. *Eclipse* opened fire with her forward guns as *Z26*, making

15 knots, turned to starboard and increased speed, attempting to work south under cover of smoke. A running fight then developed through the murk, *Z26* making only a feeble reply whilst being repeatedly hit by all calibres from the British ship. Reaching 25 knots, she did manage to lose *Eclipse* once or twice, but a trail of oil in her wake soon brought up her antagonist again. Finally, *Z26* was hit by six shells and brought to a halt at 1120 hours. By this time she had her stern awash, clouds of smoke and steam were issuing from amidships and black smoke was pouring from her forefunnel. Listing to port, with the icy seas sluicing over her upper deck, *Z26* could no longer fight or run.

Eclipse manoeuvred to give her the *coup de grâce* but suddenly the snow stopped and visibility increased dramatically to reveal *Z24* and *Z25* at last coming to the aid of their leader. They both quickly opened accurate fire on the British ship at a range of 10,000m, and *Eclipse* broke away and ran for a snow squall. Neither of the German ships gave chase, but they managed to land two hits on the retiring destroyer's after deckhouse, exploding under 'X' gun and causing casualties and a fire among the ready-use cartridges; two more shells landed on the water under the flare of the starboard bow, causing splinter damage. *Z24* fired her last three torpedoes but missed.

Z24 and *Z25* then took off as many survivors as possible as Korvettenkapitän Berger ordered *Z26* to be abandoned and scuttled. Eighty-eight men, including Berger and Pönitz, were rescued, whilst eight more were later picked up by *U376* (Marks); however, 243 seamen perished. *Z26* disappeared below the Barents Sea as her former consorts retired to the south, arriving in Kirkenes that evening. She was the first Type 36A ship to be lost.

FRANTIC EFFORTS

At the end of March 1942 only *Ihn* of the 5th Flotilla and *Schoemann* and *Jacobi* of the 6th were operational and based in Trondheim, the remaining ships of the class again all being in dockyard hands. This situation continued until May, by which time *Beitzen*, *Riedel*, *Lody*, *Steinbrinck* and *Galster* had left the yards and were working-up in the Baltic. In Norway, *Schoemann* had been despatched up to Kirkenes to join 'Destroyer Group Arctic' as a replacement for *Z26*. She arrived in Kirkenes on 9 April, Kapitän zur See Berger assuming command of the group which consisted of *Z24* and *Z25* as well as his own ship.

The group's first operation commenced on 11 April, *Schoemann*, *Z24* and *Z25* moving against convoy PQ14. Weather conditions were poor with snow showers and low visibility, and despite two attempts by the destroyers they failed to locate the enemy. The conduct of the sortie drew forth a good deal of criticism both from Admiral (Nordmeer) and from Admiral Carls, Commanding Officer Naval Group North. It was considered by the higher commands that operational orders were not sufficiently

Below: *Z25* off Trondheim on 16 May 1942. She differs in minor details from *Z24*, e.g., a seaboat at davits to starboard and extra life rafts, but is otherwise similarly armed. (Bundesarchiv)

*Interestingly, the British ship knew that this call sign belonged to Z26.

adhered to and that the flotilla commander broke off the search prematurely; he was also criticized for his search formation and for not attempting to locate any stragglers or damaged merchantmen on his return journey. The weather conditions were accepted as poor, but not sufficiently bad as to require the cancellation of the sortie. Admiral Carls went on to say: 'The order of Admiral (Nordmeer) about 0910 hours to continue searching obviously cancelled all the previous signals and intentions of Captain (D5) and should, as far as practicable, have been carried out. In case of doubt, it was possible to request new orders on account of the weather. Facts have proved that the visibility during the afternoon allowed air reconnaissance and therefore there must have been a possibility of success for the destroyers. In the absence of any further reasons from Captain (D5), agree with disapproving criticism by Admiral (Nordmeer). That the operation was conducted contrary to the clearly signalled intentions of Admiral (Nordmeer) must, as seen, have led to lack of success.' Admiral Carls ordered Admiral (Nordmeer) to inform Berger of his criticisms at their next meeting.

The next convoys, PQ15 and QP11, were, however, to be located. U-boats and reconnaissance aircraft signalled their locations, whereupon the U-boats attacked. *U456* hit the cruiser *Edinburgh*, part of the close escort for QP11, with two torpedoes and severely damaged her. On 30 April the three destroyers, then anchored off Renøy, were ordered out to attack the damaged cruiser, and at 2330 they sailed through icebergs and floes into the Barents Sea.

In the early afternoon of the following day, south-west of Bear Island, a destroyer was sighted on the starboard beam, flashing the challenge 'AA'. Three steamers and two more destroyers came into view, and it became apparent to the Germans that they had succeeded in finding the convoy. *Schoemann* identified three of the enemy ships as 'F' or 'H' class destroyers and a fourth as being similar to the French *Bourrasque* class; *Z24*, on the other hand, recorded the presence of a three-funnelled destroyer. In fact, the convoy's escort consisted of the destroyers *Bulldog*, *Amazon*, *Beagle* and *Beverley*, four corvettes and one trawler. The ex-USN *Beverley* would probably have been the ship difficult to identify: all three British-built destroyers had had their armament reduced to two 4.7in (12cm) guns whilst employed on escort duties, and *Beverley* carried only three 4in (10.5cm) guns. The escort was outgunned quite seriously, since the three German ships carried five 12.7cm and eight 15cm guns between them.

At 1405 hours *Schoemann* opened fire on one of the British ships, observing hits, and the British destroyer launched torpedoes, which were detected by *Schoemann*'s hydrophones and successfully avoided. Throughout the afternoon the three German ships made six attempts to get at the convoy, but they were driven off each time by the tenacious British escort. Fire was exchanged across the icy sea at ranges of between 9,000 and 14,000m; torpedoes were despatched by both sides, some to explode on the ice-floes littering the sea. Firing became intermittent as the British ships laid smokescreens, but the German ships hit *Amazon* hard, although she remained afloat. Torpedoes from *Z24* and *Z25* sank the 2,847-ton Soviet freighter *Tsiolkovski*, but no other vessel in the convoy was damaged. None of the German destroyers had been hit, but although *Schoemann* had fired 380 rounds and *Z24* 204, and *Z25* had in addition fired one and *Z24* three torpedoes, they had

failed to get at the convoy. Schulze-Hinrichs broke off the action at 1750 hours and decided instead to try to locate his original objective, the crippled cruiser. It was not, however, until the following day, 2 May, that he received a signal from a U-boat to the effect that the cruiser had stopped or was steaming very slowly, and escorted by only two destroyers, in Square 5863. This put the enemy some 200 miles north-east of the North Cape and well within striking distance of the searching German flotilla.

Schulze-Hinrichs intended to attack with his ships widely spread, in line abreast and with about 3,000m (16 cables) between each destroyer. The ships' companies went to action stations at 0500 hours, and just under an hour and a half later Schoemann sighted the crippled cruiser at a range of about 13,000m (8 miles); to the east of her was a large destroyer, identified as a 'Tribal', although in fact Edinburgh was at this time escorted by the destroyers Forester and Foresight as well as four minesweepers, Harrier, Niger, Gossamer and Hussar, and the Russian patrol ship Rubin was also present. Edinburgh was in a bad way. Of the two torpedoes from the U-boat, one had blown off her stern abaft 'Y' turret, peeling back the quarterdeck so that the latter was actually pierced by the guns of the turret, and the stern abaft armoured bulkhead 228 had broken off, taking with it the port inner 'A' bracket and propeller. The second torpedo had caused extensive flooding aft and put the gunnery control system out of action. With 'Y' turret jammed, only 'A', 'B' and 'X' turrets were usable.

Schoemann opened fire on the 'destroyer' (which was probably the minesweeper Harrier) and began a high-speed dog's-leg course towards the cruiser to obtain a good torpedo position. Her captain, Korvettenkapitän Wittig, had been ordered by his flotilla commander to retain two torpedoes against unforeseen circumstances, so preparations were made to fire two salvoes of three. Frantic efforts were being made on the tubes to alter the torpedo settings, which were still adjusted for the previous day's action against the convoy. Wittig gave permission to fire torpedoes when the range had reduced to 2,800m, and the destroyer approached the silent cruiser at 21 knots. Suddenly, Edinburgh's 'B' turret opened fire, her first salvo falling only 100m wide.* The destroyer increased speed to 31 knots, turned hard and began to make smoke, but the British ship was shooting extraordinarily well and her second salvo straddled and hit the hard-steaming Schoemann, two 6in shells landing in Nos. 1 and 2 turbine rooms. The third salvo fell 30m short, abreast compartment IV. Edinburgh fired a total of about 24 salvoes from her 6in guns, plus a few rounds of controlled 4in.

Aboard the destroyer all command elements, the director gear and both main engines were knocked out, immobilizing her. White smoke poured from the region of the after torpedo tubes as she turned away, dropped smoke floats over the bows and eventually stopped. The radio staff

managed to repair a short-wave set and call up help as messages came up to the bridge giving detailed reports of the damage sustained. Kapitänleutnant (Ing) Böhmer, the engineer officer, had to report that the hit in No. 1 turbine room had destroyed both the manoeuvring valves and the turbogenerator, as well as severing many fuel pipes and causing fires, although the latter were extinguished after gallant work by the watch officer, Kapitänleutnant (Ing) Scheiber. In No. 2 turbine room the hit had destroyed the second turbogenerator, the control platform and the HP turbine.

Because of the turn as Edinburgh opened fire, only one torpedo had been launched from the forward tubes, the remaining torpedoes being seized by the shock of the hits, one of which also jammed the after tubes. The torpedo officer ordered the tube crews to stand fast and fire on local control if any profitable targets presented themselves. No. 1 gun was out of action as a result of ice in the breech mechanism, whilst No. 2 fired in local control although the sights were iced up; No. 3 was wooded, but Nos. 4 and 5 fired on local control under the command of the torpedo officer. After some time, four torpedoes were launched from the after tubes at a British destroyer on the port side, but only three ran and they missed.

It became evident to Wittig that, even with the assistance of the other two destroyers, it was unlikely that he would be able to save his ship, so at 0730 hours he gave orders to clear it for scuttling, destroy all secret gear and launch the liferafts. Whilst this was being done Schoemann came under fire again, this time from the British destroyers. She received further hits, one on the port side in compartment XIII causing a fire in the mess decks, another underwater flooding Nos. 1 and 2 magazines, and a third in No. 2 boiler room causing it to flood slowly. The crew had assembled on the upper deck to port, where some were wounded by the shell hits. Afraid that a fourth hit would cause many casualties, Wittig ordered the ship's company into the liferafts. It was not possible to lower the motor boat because of the list and lack of power.

Z24 came alongside at 0750 hours, still firing her No. 1 gun as she did so. On her first approach she was only able to rescue twelve men from the snow-covered decks of the listing Schoemann, and she went round for a second attempt as Z25 laid a protective smokescreen. Alongside Schoemann's port side once again, she managed to take off a further 200 men, as well as ten from the floats. Meanwhile, below decks aboard Schoemann, the first lieutenant, Kapitänleutnant Loerke, set depth-charges in compartment XI above No. 2 magazine and in compartment III above No. 4, whilst Kapitänleutnant Temming searched the ship to ensure that all the crew had left. The seacocks in Nos. 1 and 2 boiler rooms, as well as a condenser intake, were also opened to assist the sinking.

After destroying the radar on the bridge, the captain and the remaining crew members transferred to Z24 while Loerke set the fuzes on the depth-charges and then

*'A' and 'X' turrets did not engage, owing to the poor visibility; 'B' turret was controlled from the bridge.

boarded a cutter. The abandoned destroyer, outwardly undamaged apart from a list to port, wallowed helplessly as *Z24* drew away. The Kriegsmarine's ensigns flew from the truck at both fore- and mainmast as the crews of *Z24* and *Schoemann* gave three cheers. After a few minutes the forward depth-charge exploded, damaging the bridge and setting her bows low in the water; the explosion of the second detached the stern forward of compartment III, and she rapidly disappeared below the icy waves.

Z24 and *Z25* broke off their action shortly after *Schoemann* sank, leaving 56 men in the cutter and on floats, including the first lieutenant. Happily, they were all rescued soon afterwards by *U88* (Bohmann). *Schoemann* sank in position 72° 20' N, 35° 05' E with eight of her crew killed and 45 wounded. Wittig was given command of *Z23* a few days later, whilst Loerke went on to command first the torpedo boat *Falke* and then the new *Z39*. *Edinburgh* had been hit by a third torpedo from either *Z24* or *Z25*, abreast station 93 on the port side, giving her a list of 17°. It being unlikely that she could be towed into Murmansk, orders were given for her to be sunk. 'B' turret was still engaging as *Harrier* and *Gossamer* went alongside to take off the crew, after which the former tried to sink the cruiser with her 4in guns and depth-charges. It took a torpedo from *Foresight* to send her to the bottom, along with two officers and 55 men.* Despite this success, it was probable that, with a little more aggressiveness, the German destroyers could have also sunk the two British destroyers, severely damaged as they were. Zerstörergruppe (Nordmeer) was disbanded on 9 May, and *Z24* and *Z25* were placed at the disposal of Admiral (Nordmeer).

STEAMING ON FOUR BOILERS

Movements of heavy units to and from Norway continued to occupy the meagre destroyer strength available, and in the middle of May two important operations took place. In Trondheim, temporary repairs had been made to *Prinz*

**Edinburgh's wreck was located 38 years later and salvage operations commenced to recover the gold bullion being shipped from Russia to the USA in payment for arms. The first gold bars were brought to the surface in October 1981.

Eugen following her torpedoing in February, but she had to return to Germany for a new stern; in Swinemünde, *Lützow* was ready to move northwards. The two operations, code-named 'Zauberflöte' and 'Waltzertraum', were to be almost simultaneous.

'Waltzertraum' began first and involved the Type 34s *Beitzen* and *Lody*, as well as *Z27* and *Z29* and the fast escort vessel *F1*; *Beitzen* had been having her turbines repaired since the middle of March, whilst *Lody* had been in dockyard hands since October 1941 following her return from northern Norway. *Beitzen*, *Z29* and *F1* sailed from Swinemünde on the morning of 15 May, joining *Lützow* in the Pomeranian Bight. It was a beautifully clear day, with a calm sea and almost cloudless skies as they sailed westwards, passing Rugen, through the Mecklenburger Bight and the Fehmarn Belt until they were joined off Kiel by *Lody* and *Z27* during the evening. The escorts were disposed about the heavy cruiser, with *Z29* (FdZ) leading, *Beitzen* and *Lody* to port and *Z27* and *F1* to starboard, as they zig-zagged up the Kattegat.

On the afternoon of the 16th *Beitzen* obtained a contact with her hydrophones and S-Gerät, dropping two depth-charges and sighting oil. Further depth-charges were dropped but the destroyer could not wait and had to pass the hunt over to the patrol vessel *Vp909*. At this stage of the war it was extremely unlikely that a British submarine would have been so far inside the Skaggerak (about 15km, or 25 miles, east of the Swedish coast), so if the contact were in fact a submarine it may well have been a neutral Swedish boat.

Kristiansand was reached without further incident, and the destroyers fuelled from the tanker *Marna*. Here there was to be a pause in the passage north, and the opportunity was taken to use the destroyers to reinforce the 'Westwall' minefields at the entrance to the Skaggerak. The four destroyers took on mines from the tender *Lauting* and sailed; whilst on passage they sighted the homeward-bound *Prinz Eugen* under heavy air attack but were obviously unable to assist. After successfully completing their lay, the ships returned to Kristiansand where, having re-oiled, they joined *Lützow* again, and at 2345 hours on the 18th the squadron sailed from Kristiansand, reaching Trondheim

Above: *Z28* (left) and *Beitzen* (inboard) at Narvik in 1942–3 with two minesweepers on the right and the minelayer *Skagerrak*. (USN)

without further incident two days later. The three other destroyers left *Lody* in Trondheim and escorted *Lützow* and the oiler *Nordmark* up to Bogen Bay in Narvik, where they arrived on the 25th.

Operation 'Zauberflöte' had meanwhile been successfully carried out between 16 and 18 May. *Prinz Eugen* had sailed from Trondheim in brilliant sunshine in the early afternoon of the 16th. The weather was ominously good, and no one aboard the German flotilla expected to get through to Germany without being attacked by the RAF. Escorting the heavy cruiser was a motley collection of 'lame ducks', all heading for refits in home dockyards: two destroyers, *Jacobi* and *Z25*, were accompanied by two Type 35 torpedo boats, *T11* and *T12*.

The passage to Kiel naturally took full advantage of the 'Indredled', the ships threading their way through a succession of straits and narrows. Initially, the course took the flotilla through the narrow Oksebaasen Straits, north of Ålesund and then through Aram Sound to the east of Stadlandet, where it was necessary to leave the sheltered waters for about an hour in order to round Stadlandet itself. Here, in the open sea, they were located for the first time by air reconnaissance. *Jacobi* was steaming on four boilers, with Nos. 2 and 3 boiler rooms on line, but in the early evening a tube burst occurred in the superheater on No. 3.2 boiler, shutting that boiler down. Both boilers in No. 1 boiler room were flashed up to replace it, whereupon boiler 3.1 was then also shut down. Nine cubic metres of feed water had been lost. The ship's engineering staff turned to to repair the defective boiler but it was only after six and a half hours of hot, arduous work that it was serviceable again.

The dangerous Nekoyosen narrows were passed at dawn the following day, with four Bf 109s overhead and the two torpedo boats forging ahead with their minesweeping gear. Bergen was passed in the forenoon, and by evening the flotilla had reached Egersund. Half an hour later the expected air attacks materialized, in the form of Coastal Command Beauforts from No. 42 Squadron, and at this point, off the Lister Light, the two torpedo boats were stationed ahead of the cruiser, whilst *Z25* was close in on her starboard side and *Jacobi* trailed some way astern. The Beauforts split into two groups to attack from port and starboard and were met by an intense barrage from all ships. *Prinz Eugen* used her 20.3cm (8in) guns and *Jacobi* her 12.7cm in barrage fire, and a combination of heavy flak, hard manoeuvring and the presence of a Bf 109 air escort resulted in the attacking aircraft, which included torpedo-carrying Beauforts of Nos. 42 and 86 Squadrons as well as Hudson bombers and a Beaufighter escort, failing to hit any of the ships: the cruiser outmanoeuvred all the torpedoes despite the jury steering whilst *Jacobi* was only shaken by near-misses. Three Beauforts of 42 Squadron and four of 86 Squadron were shot down. By now the flotilla was almost in home waters, and in the evening of 18 May *Jacobi* anchored off Friedrichsort near Kiel. Two days later, she went in to refit at Deutscher Werke in Kiel.

Her refit was to include stripping both LP turbines, the renewal and repair of various pumps, re-tubing all the superheaters and numerous other repairs, and she would be non-operational for the remainder of 1942, her completion being delayed first by an accident in No. 2 boiler room when escaping steam scalded to death one of the crew and a workman as well as injuring two others in September, and then, at the end of October, by an air raid which resulted in further damage from several near-misses. Repairs to the boiler room, changing the condenser pump in No. 1 turbine room and sealing leaks in the bunkers caused by the bombs put the completion date back from early October to the second week in November. However, further defects arose in her engines with the result that it was not until the second half of that month that she began post-refit trials.

A STRONG PROTEST

To return to May 1942, there were now only three serviceable Type 34 destroyers in Norway, *lhn* (D5, Kapitän zur See Berger), *Beitzen* and *Lody*; three others,

Galster (Type 36), *Riedel* and *Eckoldt*, the last with D8 (Pönitz) aboard, had sailed from Kiel bound for Norway on the 11th, but *Eckoldt* developed turbine problems and had to turn back, Pönitz shifting to *Galster* before he continued up to Trondheim with *Riedel*. Troubles continued to dog the destroyers, however, for *Lody* had suffered flooding in the starboard turbine room and auxiliary machinery spaces as a result of a fire main valve being carelessly left open; as a consequence, she was not operational for the first two weeks in June. During this period, with the arrival of the commanders of both the 5th and 8th Flotillas, D6, Schulze-Hinrichs, was temporarily attached to the staff of Generaladmiral Boehm (Admiral Norway).

On the strategic front, the war against Russia still assumed great importance and the Allied supply route to Arctic Russia continued to rank high on the priority list of the Kriegsmarine. In July it was intended that the 35-ship PQ17 convoy, which had sailed from Iceland on 27 June, would be the subject of a three-pronged attack by U-boats, aircraft and the surface fleet. The surface ships available for action were *Tirpitz*, *Hipper* and four destroyers – *Ihn* (D5), *Galster* (D8), *Lody* and *Riedel* – plus the torpedo boats *T7* and *T15* at Trondheim, while *Lützow*, *Scheer*, *Beitzen*, *Z28* (FdZ), *Z24*, *Z27*, *Z29* and *Z30* lay farther north in Narvik. Not surprisingly, the presence of such a powerful fleet caused considerable misgivings at the British Admiralty, and their movements, especially that of *Tirpitz*, was to result in one of the most controversial decisions made by the Admiralty during the war, the ordering of PQ17 to scatter.

The German surface-ship operation, code-named 'Rösselsprung', got under way during the afternoon of 2 July when the *Tirpitz* force, commanded by Admiral Schniewind and known as 'Force 1', sailed from Trondheim bound for Altafjord where it was to meet 'Force 2' under the command of Vizeadmiral Kummetz aboard *Lützow*. Kummetz left Narvik after midnight in thick fog, and whilst in the narrow confines of Tjeldsund *Lützow* ran aground, eliminating her from the operation. *Scheer* and her destroyers continued up to Altafjord, where they arrived the following morning. Trouble had also struck the *Tirpitz* group, for while the squadron was passing through the Gimsøy narrows in line ahead *Lody* struck an uncharted rock, causing serious damage to both propellers and shafts, as well as ripping open her double bottom in many places. *Galster*, next astern, moved out to pass her starboard side and ran aground also, damaging her port shaft, propeller and S-Gerät dome. Hardly had *Galster* struck than *Riedel* also ran aground, though less severely, her damage being confined to her propellers. *Ihn* alone escaped the obstruction and accompanied *Tirpitz* and *Hipper* to Altafjord, where the vessels arrived on the morning of the 4th.

The delays involved in obtaining Hitler's permission to send the big ships to sea, as well as the damage to three destroyers and *Lützow*, effectively nullified any chance of the surface forces taking part in the slaughter of PQ17, for although the remainder of Forces 1 and 2 did sail from Altafjord on the 5th the Luftwaffe and U-boats had wrought such havoc that their intervention was unnecessary. By the following day the surface fleet was back in its sheltered fjords, having caused the convoy to scatter, it is true, but without entering battle itself.

The three damaged destroyers crawled painfully back to Trondheim where they effected temporary repairs before sailing back to Germany. *Galster* left for Kiel on 12 June, escorted by *Ihn* and *Z24*. Steaming on one engine only, the crippled destroyer reached her destination two days later without incident. Shortly after the ship entered dockyard hands, her CO, Korvettenkapitän von Bechtolsheim, was posted away as 1st staff officer to FdZ and his ship was taken over by Korvettenkapitän Harmsen, the ship's company being released to help bring in the harvest. The other two damaged destroyers were not ready for home until two weeks later and had to make the passage under tow. They left Trondheim on 25 July, *Riedel* under tow by the tug *Titan* and *Lody* by *Arngast*.

At first all went well, and by the early hours of the 28th the little convoy was abreast Hillersøy, south of Stavanger. It was a calm, clear night, with a full moon and little cloud – hardly ideal conditions for a stealthy passage back to Germany. And so it proved, for at 0127 hours three Beauforts were sighted on the starboard quarter, obviously having seen the ships. The tows were hurriedly slipped as the destroyers endeavoured to gain some limited manoeuvrability, *Riedel* having revolutions for 7 knots on the starboard shaft and for 9 on the port. The three aircraft split up, two aiming for *Riedel* and the other for *Lody*, as both destroyers opened barrage fire with their 12.7cm guns, *Riedel* turning towards the island of Hillersøy with the intention of setting herself lightly aground. Two torpedoes passed within 100m of her starboard side but they were successfully avoided and went on to explode on the shore. One aircraft was observed astern and another forward, and both were engaged by all available weapons. Hits were observed on one aircraft, but because of stoppages in Nos. 1 and 2 2cm guns the situation could not be exploited. After being hit again by the Vierling, the aircraft passed into the darkness against the island and was not seen again. (This was probably AW290 of 86 Squadron.)

A second attack developed twenty minutes later, the attackers again being met by fire from all weapons and both destroyers avoiding the torpedoes. The Beauforts flew off into the night, leaving the two ships to continue their passage without further attack and arrive in Kiel on 29 July. Both were to undergo repairs in the Deutscher Werke yard in Kiel, where it was estimated that eight weeks would be required for *Riedel* and six months or longer for *Lody*. On hearing of the length of refit needed by *Lody*, the Skl ordered that she be paid off into reserve and her crew disbanded. Her CO, Korvettenkapitän Pfeiffer, protested most strongly at the break-up of a trained crew and sought ways of reversing the decision. He tackled the yard engineer, Dip. Ing. Severin, who was persuaded to say that delivery of new shafts could be expedited and the ship could therefore be ready by December, i.e., within a normal refit period. Armed with this information, Pfeiffer put the facts to Berlin and was rewarded on 22 August by the OKM's agreement for the ship to stay in commission.

The three Type 34 destroyers remaining in northern Norway, *Beitzen*, *Eckoldt* and *Steinbrinck*, under the command of the 5th Flotilla, operated in the Trondheim–Narvik–Kirkenes area in a variety of roles between August and December. At the end of August all three escorted the minelayer *Ulm* part way to the Barents Sea for an operation from which the minelayer did not return, being caught and sunk on the same day by the destroyers *Marne*, *Martin* and *Onslaught*; also in August, *Admiral Scheer* was escorted out on a foray into the Kara Sea, but once again the destroyers were detached very early on.

In September and October several minelaying sorties were conducted in the Barents Sea in which *Steinbrinck* could not participate as she had run aground at Kirkenes at the beginning of September and had been sent down to Trondheim. Between 5 and 8 September *Beitzen* (D5), with *Z29* and *Z30*, laid a minefield in the Kara Straits, and between the 24th and the 28th *Hipper*, *Z23*, *Z28*, *Z29* and *Z30* sailed on Operation 'Zarin', a sweep to the north-west coast of Novaya Zemlya. Once more the Barents Sea was in an angry mood, with winds and sea reaching Force 8. The air was filled with driving snow and the sky obscured by thick cloud, and *Z23*, newly fitted with her twin 15cm turret forward, made particularly heavy going in the rough seas. No results were achieved, however, and by the morning of the 28th the destroyers were back in Kaafjord. In October, between the 13th and 15th, *Eckoldt*, *Beitzen*, *Z27* and *Z30* laid more mines off the Kanin Peninsula at the entrance to the White Sea; then, early in November, the same four ships, accompanied by *Hipper*, made a sortie towards the White Sea against individually routed Allied ships but succeeded only in sinking the Soviet tanker *Donbass* and the submarine chaser *B078*.

With the departure home of *Steinbrinck* in September, only *Eckoldt*, *Beitzen*, *Z23*, *Z25*, *Z27*, *Z29* and *Z30* now remained in northern waters. Problems in the dockyards at home were causing serious extensions to refit periods owing to air raids, interrupted work and power supplies, and delays in the delivery of spares and reconditioned equipment. *Jacobi*'s situation has already been outlined, while *Riedel*'s completion had to be extended from 22 October to 21 November and that for *Lody* until the end of December. *Galster*'s work included changing the HP blades in No. 2 turbine, relapping the gears, and alterations to the Saake burners. Modifications were made to the condensers and boiler fans, as well as to the bows, and weather shields were fitted on the torpedo tubes. Finally, the tubes were cleaned in five of her boilers. This put back her

recommissioning date from the end of September to early November, although in the event she was ready for sea again on 23 October.

POINT-BLANK RANGE

In the Arctic, the last operation of the year in which the destroyers took part was a crucial one, and one which was to have repercussions from which the Kriegsmarine never recovered. Anxious to have the New Year brought in with a success, Raeder had planned to carry out a cruiser attack on the next Allied convoy to Russia. Under the command of Admiral (Cruisers), Vizeadmiral Kummetz, in the heavy cruiser *Hipper* and accompanied by *Lützow* and six destroyers, the operation was given the code-name 'Regenbogen'. The target was Convoy JW51B which had sailed from Loch Ewe on 22 December with fourteen ships and an escort consisting of the destroyers *Onslow*, *Oribi*, *Obdurate*, *Obedient*, *Orwell*, *Achates* and *Bulldog*, as well as a minesweeper, two corvettes and two trawlers; in command of the escort was Captain Sherbrooke aboard *Onslow*. The convoy was seen by *U354* (Herbschleb) on the 30th whilst south of Bear Island, and the submarine's report of six to ten ships with a weak escort seemed to present an ideal target for the German squadron.

Lying in Kaafjord, the German force raised steam in all boilers and prepared to sail. The six destroyers involved were *Eckoldt*, *Beitzen*, *Riedel*, *Z29*, *Z30* and *Z31*, *Riedel* having only just returned to northern waters following the completion of her refit, escorting *Lützow* to Norway at the same time; a seventh destroyer, *Z23*, was unable to participate as a result of defects. Aboard the leader destroyer, *Eckoldt*, a tragedy had occurred on 25 December when her CO, Korvettenkapitän Gerstung, died suddenly. He had only taken over command in August, and on his death command was temporarily assumed by the first lieutenant, Bachmann. Also aboard *Eckoldt* was D5, Kapitän zur See Schemmel, who had relieved Berger in July.

The German squadron sailed from Kaafjord in the late afternoon of the 30th and by evening were steaming down Sørøysundet in line ahead, *Hipper* leading *Lützow* and the destroyers astern. Visibility was poor as they passed Hammerfest and reached the open sea off Rolvsøy. Outside the shelter of the islands the sea was rough and a north-westerly wind was blowing Force 6. It was bitterly cold, with temperatures 4° below zero, and the weather conditions were making things very difficult for the destroyers. A later alteration of course improved matters somewhat, but the heavy seas and icing had damaged *Beitzen*'s No. 1 gun, rendering it unserviceable. The following day the squadron formed a reconnaissance line with *Hipper* to the north, *Lützow* to the south and the destroyers strung out between in an attempt to locate the position of the convoy.

Eckoldt, with *Beitzen* and *Z29* in company, sighted the

convoy through the gloom at 0759 hours, and by 0820 she could make out thirteen ships off the starboard bow although the Germans, despite having been sighted by a corvette in the escort, were not at first reported. However, *Obdurate* also spotted them and turned to investigate. Closing the three ships, it was not until 0906 that they proved to be the enemy by taking *Obdurate* under fire, but when the latter turned to rejoin the convoy she was not followed by Schemmel since he had just been ordered to rejoin *Hipper*. At 0929 *Z29* opened fire again, probably on *Obdurate*. *Lützow* and the other three destroyers had not yet made contact with the convoy, but at 0948 hours the pocket battleship, accompanied by *Riedel*, saw smoke ahead, as *Z31* and *Z30* were endeavouring to attack the convoy from astern.

Meanwhile *Hipper*'s destroyers had rejoined the cruiser and then run into the minesweeper *Bramble* which had been detached to round up stragglers. At 1101 hours *Beitzen* opened fire at a range of 9,000m, discharging four salvoes and observing hits, and Kummetz ordered the destroyers to finish the unfortunate minesweeper off whilst he engaged the convoy. *Hipper* had succeeded in severely damaging *Achates* and *Obedient* when she was caught unawares by the cruisers *Sheffield* and *Jamaica* which had moved in to support the beleaguered destroyers of the escort. *Hipper* was quickly hit in a boiler room, and after replying weakly she made smoke and turned away. *Eckoldt* had despatched *Bramble* by 1121 and was endeavouring to relocate *Hipper*, but in company with *Beitzen* astern she made the fatal mistake of believing that the gun flashes to the north were issuing from *Hipper*, she being unaware of the presence of the British cruisers. At 1145 hours the two destroyers blundered into the cruisers at point-blank range. *Sheffield* sighted one *Maass* class destroyer bearing 215° and quickly shifted target to her, opening fire on *Eckoldt* with 6in, 4in and pom-poms.

Total confusion must have reigned on *Eckoldt*'s bridge in those last few moments before the awful realization dawned, for she made frantic signals to *Hipper* asking her position and accusing the cruiser of firing on her. At such close range there was no escape. Hit repeatedly, she was last seen by *Sheffield*, stopped, burning and sinking; *Beitzen*, escaping into the darkness, thought that her after magazine had been hit. She herself was lucky, for despite other reports *Jamaica* did not open fire on her at all and she was able to elude the cruisers. Korvettenkapitän Schemmel and some 340 men perished in the icy seas when *Eckoldt* went down; there were no survivors.

Between 1140 and 1215 hours *Lützow* and her destroyers engaged the convoy, but with little effect on the merchant ships. The range was at first too great for *Riedel*'s 12.7cm guns, but she was soon able to engage one of the destroyers of the escort. Her second salvo was good, and the unknown destroyer turned away back to the convoy, but these were to be the closing actions of a battle which had lasted some four hours as Kummetz had already ordered a withdrawal. By 1540 hours on 1 January 1943, the destroyers were secured alongside the oiler *Nordmark* in Kaafjord again.

From a German point of view it had been a most unsatisfactory action. *Hipper* had sustained considerable damage, one destroyer had been lost and *Lützow* had been unable to start her planned Arctic sortie. They had been fought off by a handful of destroyers and two light cruisers, against which they had only managed to sink one destroyer (*Achates*) and one minesweeper, and damage one merchant ship. Admittedly, their orders were, as was usual for German operations, extremely restrictive, but the timidity of *Lützow* and the lack of dash shown by the smaller ships was almost unbelievable. On hearing the true details of the action Hitler flew into a monumental rage, the results of which were his famous order to scrap all the capital ships and the resignation of Grossadmiral Raeder.

Below: *Z38* in arctic Norway. (W. Z. Bilddienst)

11. FINALE IN FRANCE: JANUARY 1943 TO AUGUST 1944

Following the withdrawal of the 5th Destroyer Flotilla from the area in September 1941, western France and the English Channel had been left under the control of the torpedo boat and S-boat flotillas. The year 1943 would prove to be a period of mixed blessings for the torpedo boat force.

Both the 2nd and 5th Flotillas, now reinforced by the arrival of the first Type 39 boat, *T23*, operated in connection with the attempts to sail the blockade-runner *Himalaya* out of the Bay of Biscay in March and early April, and then in May the 2nd Flotilla moved back into the Channel on minelaying duties when *T22*, *T23*, *T18*, *T5* and *T12* laid three fields from Le Havre ('Dalie', 'Dornbusch' and 'Dotterblume'), whilst early in June *T22* assisted in the laying of 'Eiche', 'Birke' and 'Ulme' from Cherbourg. On the Biscay coast, the older boats of the 5th Flotilla were joined by the new *T22* on escort duties to inward- and outward-bound U-boats. By summer seven of the Type 39 craft had been put into commission, of which two were already deployed in western France and two others, *T24* and *T25*, sufficiently worked up to join them on operations. Both these boats sailed westwards from Germany on 3 July, two days after the arrival from France of *T18*, *T2* and *T5* of the 2nd Flotilla. On passage, *T24* and *T25* were shelled by the Dover batteries and, whilst off Ushant, engaged by three British 'Hunt' class destroyers.

The two torpedo boats had sailed from St-Malo on the night of 9 July, having been warned of the possibility of encountering enemy light surface forces on passage. At the same time, units of the 2nd Minesweeper Flotilla had left Lazardrieux to sweep the channel to Brest. On receipt of a sighting of enemy forces in the vicinity, the 3rd Security Division ordered the torpedo boats to close and cover the minesweepers, but the latter were intercepted before this could be done. A confused night action now developed off the Isle de Bas, between the Hunt class destroyers *Melbreak*, *Wensleydale* and *Glaisdale* and the sweepers (*M9*, *M12*, *M10*, *M153* and *M134*) in the course of which the latter were scattered and *M153* sunk. The arrival of *T24* and *T25* resulted in a sharp gun action between the destroyers and torpedo boats when *Melbreak* was badly damaged and *Wensleydale* slightly. *T25* received splinter damage from a near-miss off the starboard bow and some

one hundred holes were found in her upperworks but was not seriously hurt.

Operating from western French ports, the 4th and 5th Torpedo Boat Flotillas attempted to help the U-boats in and out of the Bay of Biscay at a time of increasing air and surface threat from British forces. Sometimes they were successful, sometimes not. Thus, in the early hours of 2 August, *T25*, *T22* and *T24* were sailed to assist *U383* which had radioed herself bombed and unmanoeuvrable in the Bay. After suffering numerous air attacks themselves, the torpedo boats came across and rescued the survivors of *U106*, a Type XB boat sunk by Sunderlands M/461 and N/228. *U383* was never found; she had gone down during the night with all hands. Later that month, they were successful in escorting the in-bound Japanese boat *I8* safely into port.

Torpedo boat organization as of 31 July was as shown on the next page. From this it will be apparent that of the seventeen Type 35/37 boats listed, only two were operationally employed, and as far as the torpedo boats were concerned, action now centred around the 4th and 5th Flotillas in France.

By this time, however, with the critical state of Germany's industry and its desperate need of raw materials, then unobtainable in Europe, the importance of the safety of blockade-breakers, inward-bound from the Far East, became paramount; furthermore, the escorting of U-boats across the increasingly hostile Bay of Biscay required larger and more heavily armed vessels to counter the threat from Allied air and seaborne forces. Thus it was decided, early in 1943, to transfer a flotilla of destroyers to the west to undertake these tasks and reinforce the torpedo boat flotillas. The flotilla concerned was the 8th, and the story of destroyer operations in this theatre for the remainder of the war is essentially the story of the 8th Flotilla.

PLANS AGAIN DISRUPTED

The unit had been ordered home from Norway on 7 February 1943 for service in the western theatre. In Germany, Korvettenkapitän Erdmenger (former CO of *Z28*) relieved Pönitz as captain (D8) in March, and the Flotilla now comprised *Z23*, *Z24*, *Z25*, *Z28*, *Z32* and *Z37*, the last two ships being of the Type 36A (Mob) design. At this stage of the war the passage down-Channel of a flotilla of destroyers was not an operation to be taken lightly, especially after the 'Channel Dash' of February 1942, following which fiasco the British were certain to have taken steps to tighten their hold on the narrow seas. Of this the German Navy was only too well aware, and as a consequence the breakthrough was planned with meticulous care.

Operational conditions in the Bay of Biscay were completely different from those obtaining in Norway and the Arctic regions, the dangers of air attack and mining being especially prevalent. A series of conferences was arranged involving Naval Group West in Paris, Naval Group North, Commander-in-Chief (Fleet), Flag Officer (Destroyers) and other interested parties to ensure the safe passage of the ships. Erdmenger harried officials on shore both personally and by telephone to obtain such special attention, equipment and modifications necessary for operations in the new theatre. Telephone communications were required to the new Vierling installed before the bridge, armour protection was needed on the bridges (although previously this had always been denied on grounds of stability), and protection was required over the rudder and engine telegraph positions. Because of shortages of materials, it was only possible to provide such protection on a temporary scale, and then only for Z23 and Z25; the others would have to wait. The opportunity was also taken to improve the ammunition arrangements in anticipation of a greater risk of air attack.

Late in February Erdmenger left on another trip to Paris for further talks on the operation with Naval HQ, staff officers of Luftflotte 3 and Jafu (Holland).* Generaladmiral Marschall and his Chief of Staff, Kapitän zur See Hoffmann, emphasized that the destroyers must reach Cherbourg by dawn at the latest, whilst the Luftwaffe officers pointed out the weakness of their service in that region. Nevertheless, it was agreed to have four aircraft over the ships at all times, with another four standing by. Having done all that he could, Erdmenger left for home by train; the latter was sabotaged on the way, but he arrived back safely in Kiel.

The operational orders envisaged a passage during the full-moon period of the night of 2/3 March, passing Dunkirk at 2130 hours at high water. Moonrise was at 0550 hours, and the passage westwards from Cherbourg would take place during the night of the 3rd/4th. Six destroyers were originally intended to be transferred, but in the event Z28 was undergoing a machinery overhaul and on completion was required to escort the battlecruiser *Scharnhorst* up to Norway (Operation 'Paderborn'), where she remained.

For the passage westwards, it had been intended that the destroyers would be divided into two divisions, 'A' and 'B', of which 'A' (Z23, Z24 and Z25), under the command of D8, would sail for Bordeaux while 'B', under Fregattenkapitän Reinecke in Z28, would sail for La Pallice with Z32 and Z37; 'A' Division would lead 'B' by 6–7 miles. After passage through the Kiel Canal, 'A' Division would anchor in Cuxhaven Roads and 'B' in Altenbruch Roads, where they were to oil by tanker during the night. Comprehensive orders running to ten pages in length covered the passage, and the details even included the number of binoculars to be carried. Against the possibility of disaster each destroyer was to have scuttling charges ready – three depth-charges, placed one in each shaft tunnel and one in the transmitting station – and four boats

Below: *Möwe* in the mid-war years. Note the addition of a Vierling in lieu of the after rangefinder. (W. Z. Bilddienst)

TORPEDO BOAT ORGANIZATION, 31 JULY 1943

2nd Flotilla (Wesermünde)
T2 Attached to 25th U-boat Flotilla (Libau)
T10 As T2
T7 Torpedo School (Travemünde)
T4 At Swinemünde
T5 Machinery overhaul (Wesermünde)
T11 As T5
T9 In dock (Elbing)
T12 In dock (Kiel)

3rd Flotilla (Gotenhafen)
T13 In dock (Danzig)
T14 In dock (Brest)
T15 In dock (Rostock)
T16 In dock (Kiel)
T17 In dock (Kiel)
T18 Torpedo School (Travemünde)
T19 Western France
T20 Torpedo recovery, U-boat flotillas (Norway)
T21 As T20

4th Flotilla (Brest)
T22 At Brest
T23 At Brest
T24 At Brest
T25 At Brest
T26 Working up (Baltic)
T27 As T26

5th Flotilla (La Pallice)
Möwe At La Pallice
Kondor At La Pallice
Falke At La Pallice
Jaguar At La Pallice
Greif Machinery overhaul (Cherbourg)
T28 In dock (Danzig)

---

*Jagdführer or OC, Fighters.

of the 3rd Torpedo Boat Flotilla were to move down the Channel just before the destroyers.

The German plans were once again disrupted by defects aboard the destroyers. In the shallow waters of the Channel, ground mines were a distinct danger, and the magnetic condition of both *Z23* and *Z32* was giving cause for concern. *Z23* and *Z25* passed through the Kiel Canal during the 3rd, then fuelled at Brunsbüttel and awaited *Z32* and *Z37* in Ostermoor, but the operation was already behind schedule, and with the further deterioration in the magnetic state of *Z23* the passage was postponed while the ship was degaussed; consequently, it was not until 5 March that the operation, code-named 'Karin', got under way, when *Z23* weighed from Brunsbüttel Roads at 0215 hours. Almost immediately, however, *Z25* had trouble with the HP stage of her port turbine and had to drop out. Later, *Z32* and *Z37* joined up and the four destroyers steamed towards the southern exit of the North Sea, paravanes streamed and with an escort of four aircraft overhead; by midday the flotilla stood north of the West Friesian Islands.

The weather was good, with calm seas and a clouded sky. Scheveningen was passed at 1830 hours, and by 2000 the Schelde estuary was close on the port beam. Flak was audible astern and the dangers of MTB action became more likely – propellers were heard to starboard but no attacks developed. Marker boats had been stationed along the Channel to guide the destroyers in a similar manner to those provided for Operation 'Cerberus', but this did not prevent a near-collision with the wreck of the torpedo boat *Wolf* (which had been mined north of Dunkirk on 8 January 1941 in a field laid by Royal Navy minelayers), whose shape was only seen at the last minute. As the narrows were approached, Dover radio was heard talking to MTBs, and at a couple of minutes before midnight the shadow of a darkened German vessel produced a few seconds of alarm.

At 0140 hours *Z23*'s port engine developed a fault, limiting her to 27 knots, and a few moments later *Z37* signalled that she was engaging three MTBs off Calais. Cap Gris-Nez was passed at 0156, and half an hour later, near Boulogne, shadows were sighted off *Z23*'s port bow. Motor noises were also heard, and the destroyer opened fire, followed by the Channel shore batteries and then *Z24*, but no hits were obtained by any of the participants. The passage had now fallen behind schedule, and as it was impossible to reach Cherbourg before dawn Erdmenger decided to put into Le Havre. Thick fog in the harbour made mooring conditions difficult, and in the process *Z37* grounded and needed to be pulled off by tugs.

The destroyers remained in harbour through the daylight hours until after midnight, when *Z23*, *Z24* and *Z32* slipped anchor and proceeded under a clear, starry sky. They were not challenged, and by 0322 hours Ushant was rounded and speed reduced to conserve bunkers. *Z24* was having problems with her twin turret, similar to those experienced by *Z23* in December 1942, but early in the afternoon

Sperrbrecher 5 was sighted off the mouth of the Gironde and led the destroyers up-river to Bordeaux, where they secured alongside early in the evening and rigged camouflage nets. The following day the flotilla staff went ashore for conferences with the local naval command and KG 40, the local Luftwaffe group at Bordeaux–Merignac, whose Fw 200 aircraft provided reconnaissance and anti-shipping strikes over the Bay of Biscay. For the rest of the month the flotilla remained at readiness in Royan Roads, during the course of which they were joined once more by *Z37*.

SHADOWS ON THE PORT BEAM

The flotilla's first operation got under way when all four destroyers sailed on 30 March to escort the blockade-runner *Pietro Orseolo*, inward bound from Japan. She was met by the destroyers some 140 miles west of Cape Finisterre and escorted back into the Gironde despite fierce attacks by RAF Beauforts and Beaufighters and despite being torpedoed by the US submarine *Shad*. Five aircraft were shot down by the destroyers' fire.

Another blockade-runner, *Himalaya*, which had attempted to break out to the Far East on 28 March but had had to turn back on being located by the RAF, was now to make a second try. Her escort group, under Erdmenger's command, consisted this time of *Z23*, *Z24* and *Z32*, together with the torpedo boat *T5*, the larger *T22* and the older *Kondor*. After sailing on 9 April, the ships were again located in the Bay by aircraft, whereupon the attempt was once more called off and the flotilla reversed course and headed back to the French coast, *Z23* leading the merchantmen with *Kondor* in line astern. *T22* was stationed ahead to starboard, and in a similar position on the port side was *T5*, the two other destroyers, *Z32* and *Z24*, being stationed on *Kondor*'s port and starboard quarters respectively. Closed up at action stations, the flotilla's crews awaited the air attack that the shadowing Sunderland had obviously called up.

It developed at about 2030 hours and was a combined attack by torpedo-armed Hampdens of No. 416 Squadron RCAF and Wellington bombers of No. 311 (Czech) Squadron. Five Hampdens swept in low from astern on the port side between *Z32* and *Kondor*, while two other torpedo attacks were made from the starboard beam and the port bow, the Wellingtons attacking from ahead and astern. All the ships put up a dense barrage of fire, including 15cm shells, around the merchantmen, effectively thwarting the RAF attacks. Several of the destroyers were shot up by the attacking aircraft, including *Z24*, which suffered a number killed and many wounded, but *Himalaya* reached the Gironde safely again.

The 4th Torpedo Boat Flotilla was further reinforced in August, when *T26* and *T27* sailed west from Kiel on the morning of the 30th, bringing the strength up to six vessels. After minelaying operations in September, the first of a number of clashes with British destroyers took place in early October, when the flotilla (*T22*, *T23*, *T25* and *T27*) sailed from Brest to act as distant cover for a small convoy.

In the early hours of the 4th of that month, the force was proceeding generally eastwards, in a position north of the Plateau des Triagoz, when they were alerted to the presence of an enemy formation to the north-west, and barely three minutes later two shadows, identified as destroyers, were observed broad on the port beam. The British formation – the 'Hunt' class destroyers *Limbourne*, *Wensleydale* and *Tanatside*, together with the fleet destroyers *Grenville* and *Ulster* – were as yet unaware of the presence of the German force, but the situation presented something of a dilemma for Korvettenkapitän Kohlauf since the British ships were clearly visible against the lighter northern horizon whilst his own flotilla was covered by the darker southern aspect. He was not yet in a good torpedo attack position, and his orders were to escort a convoy, not particularly to risk its security by offensive action. However, offensive thought won the day and the 4th Flotilla reversed course, ordering *T25* and *T27* (which were most advantageously placed) to fire six torpedoes each. *T25* launched only one and *T27* four before the flotilla turned away. No hits were achieved, whereupon Kohlauf took the flotilla about and ran parallel once again, still undetected. Then, to obtain accurate ranging, *T23* switched on her radar, which gave 3,400–3,600m (just over 2 miles), but the pulses were detected by *Limbourne*, which alerted her flotilla and caused it to alter its course to intercept, working up to full speed as quickly as possible.

T22 meanwhile, had launched a further six torpedoes, which failed to hit probably because the British force altered course and then swung eastwards again, but a running fight developed between the torpedo boats and the destroyers *Ulster* and *Grenville* (at 28 knots, the 'Hunts' were soon left behind). Under starshell illumination, the two sides traded fire, with the British getting the worst of it. *Grenville* was soon hit aft and set on fire, but she managed to get all her torpedoes away, although without effect. *T23* replied with three more but was equally unsuccessful, whilst *Ulster* launched four before receiving a hit in the waterline on the starboard side which flooded the forward magazines, although she was able to launch her four remaining torpedoes. The torpedo boats escaped unscathed, *T23* firing her last three 'fish' by the light of the starshell before the British destroyers broke off the chase. The German force continued eastwards, deterred from rounding on the damaged enemy ships by the presence of the 'Hunts', and by early evening was anchored in the Dinan Roads. It had incurred only minor splinter damage during the action.

ALIVE WITH TORPEDOES

Towards the end of October the torpedo boats achieved a great success, probably their most notable performance of the war. In the evening of the 22nd the flotilla (*T23*, *T26*, *T27*, *T22* and *T25*) assembled in Brest Roads, ordered to act as distant support for the movement of *Münsterland* and her escort of the 2nd Minesweeper Flotilla up the Channel towards Cherbourg. Later that night the flotilla sighted the convoy and took station to the north-west of it. At 0025 hours *T25* picked up a target north of the torpedo boats on her hydrophones, and sounding 'Action stations' Kohlauf took the flotilla towards it and then swung eastwards once more to take the expected skirmish away from the convoy. The enemy force was engaged upon an operation known as 'Tunnel', which had developed into a set pattern well known to the Germans and, accordingly, the German force expected that the British would run parallel to them in an ideal position for torpedo attack; moreover, the British force was once more against the lighter horizon and the torpedo boats against a dark background, and the Germans were further aided by a rain squall which was approaching from the south-west.

Visibility was poor, with low clouds, and there was a long, heavy swell on the sea. Moonrise was at 0125 hours, but shortly before this time *Limbourne* intercepted the German flotilla's manoeuvring instructions as it moved into a line-astern formation on an easterly course. The warning signals passed by *Limbourne* to the leader of the British force, the light cruiser *Charybdis*, were in turn detected by the torpedo boats, which now realized that surprise was lost.

The British ships – *Charybdis* and the destroyers *Grenville*, *Rocket*, *Limbourne*, *Talybont*, *Stevenstone* and

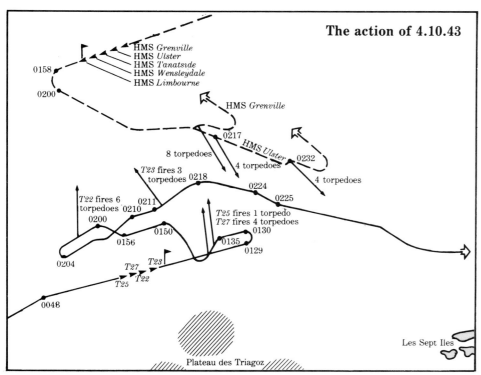

The action of 4.10.43

HMS *Grenville*
HMS *Ulster*
HMS *Tanatside*
HMS *Wensleydale*
HMS *Limbourne*

0158
0200

HMS *Grenville*

0217
HMS *Ulster*
0232

8 torpedoes
4 torpedoes
4 torpedoes

T23 fires 3 torpedoes 0218
0224
0225
T22 fires 6 torpedoes 0210
0211
0200
T25 fires 1 torpedo
T27 fires 4 torpedoes
0204
0150
0130
0156
0135
0129

T27 *T23*
T22
T25

0048

Plateau des Triagoz

Les Sept Iles

Wensleydale – made up an impressive force but one which had never worked together before, either by day or by night. At 0136 hours the cruiser obtained a radar contact at 8,100m then a few minutes later fired starshell which, however, must have burst above the clouds because no illumination developed. At the same time the torpedo boats gained visual contact on the cruiser and altered course to the south, increasing speed as they did so.

To Kohlauf the situation appeared critical, for the cruiser could inflict considerable punishment on his flotilla, but he was unaware that none of the British units had seen him, nor would they during the course of the short engagement. As the torpedo boats turned, all except *T25* launched their full outfits, a total of twenty-four torpedoes in all. Hardly had *Charybdis* fired her starshell when two torpedoes were reported approaching, and despite last-minute orders for full port rudder one struck her on the port side under the torpedo tubes. No. 2 dynamo room and 'B' boiler room flooded, the port electrical ring main failed and the ship took up a 20° list as she slewed to port and stopped.

The British were thrown into confusion as the sea became alive with torpedoes. *Limbourne* fired rocket flares, clearly illuminating the stricken cruiser as torpedoes narrowly missed *Grenville* and *Wensleydale*. Then a second torpedo struck the cruiser abreast station 135, again on the port side, and in five minutes her list had increased to 50°. The after engine room flooded, all electrical power failed and the whole upper deck structure had been loosened by the force of the explosions. Barely a minute later a torpedo struck *Limbourne* as she swung to port, hitting the forward LP room and exploding the forward magazine; she wallowed, listing heavily to starboard, her bows blown off. The British force raced about for some minutes, leaderless and in confusion, for the torpedoed destroyer was believed to have been *Rocket* and *Grenville*'s commander was unaware that he was now senior officer.

As the British destroyers rescued such survivors as could be found and sank the damaged *Limbourne* with a torpedo from *Rocket*, the German flotilla quietly withdrew unscathed and triumphantly rejoined the convoy. Kohlauf estimated that the first torpedo to hit the cruiser had come from *T23* and the second from *T27*, while *Limbourne* could have been hit from either *T22* or *T26*. The reason for *T25* not firing was due to personnel changes: her torpedo officer had only recently joined the boat after three years with the Luftwaffe, and in consequence he was unable to cope with the fast-moving night action.

This double success for the flotilla was a well-deserved achievement at this late stage of the sea war. It provided the Kriegsmarine's surface ships with a valuable piece of news for the home front, which by now was more used to U-boat press reports. In Paris, Admiral Krancke, commanding Naval Group West, was considerably heartened by the sinkings and recorded his feelings in his war diary: 'Especially to be emphasized is the skill and great prudence with which Korvettenkapitän Kohlauf has also led this

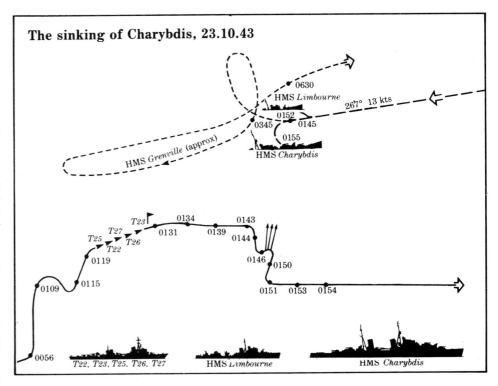

The sinking of Charybdis, 23.10.43

fight. In spite of the short time since he succeeded to the command of this flotilla, he has, in this second engagement, again proved his energy, dash and battle-readiness. I have recommended him for the Knight's Cross of the Iron Cross. The success has shown, furthermore, the extraordinarily good co-operation with the monitoring service.' This last sentence was a reference to the fact that the German radar and radio stations had established a good understanding of the workings of the British patrols and had helped to alert the 4th Flotilla to the presence of the *Charybdis* group.

Kohlauf did indeed receive his medal for the action, which marked the zenith of the torpedo boats' achievements. From this time onwards, however, their fortunes declined steadily in the face of overwhelming Allied sea and air superiority.

A RUNNING FIGHT

On the Atlantic coast, the 8th Destroyer Flotilla was engaged principally in escorting damaged U-boats across the Bay of Biscay during mid-1943, interspersed with exercises with the torpedo boats, routine refits and overhauls. Reinforcements arrived in November in the shape of *Z27* and *ZH1*, the latter the ex-Dutch destroyer *Gerard Callenburgh*, captured incomplete in 1940. Her commissioning by the Germans had been hindered at every turn by the Dutch and although she was finally taken into service on 5 October 1942 it took a further year of work for her to become fully operational on account of defects, machinery problems, etc., and she was only now sailing on her first operational deployment.

The two destroyers passed down-Channel between 2 and 4 November 1943, attacked by the Dover batteries and MTBs en route. In the engagement by the gun batteries both destroyers received some splinter damage, whilst several MTBs were damaged in that clash. The two destroyers' arrival in Bordeaux brought the flotilla's strength up to six, although *ZH1* was very much 'odd man out': smaller, slower and with a weaker armament than her flotilla-mates, she must have posed problems of deployment for the flotilla commander.

Kapitän zur See Erdmenger took the first opportunity to exercise his flotilla together when all six destroyers sailed into the Bay of Biscay on 20 November. The exercise was a large one, for the five Type 39 torpedo boats of the 4th Torpedo Boat Flotilla also joined in. Extending over two days, the exercises were intended to develop flotilla co-ordination and accustom the captains to working with each other; but a flotilla of ships could not be welded into an effective fighting unit in just a few days, and the skills would very soon be called upon.

In late December the inward-bound blockade-runner *Alsterufer* was expected to arrive in the Bay of Biscay from the Far East with more valuable raw materials. Erdmenger was ordered to sea with his complete flotilla, reinforced by the six large Type 39 torpedo boats of the 4th Flotilla, to escort the sorely needed cargo into a French port. The British Admiralty, too, were aware of the impending arrival of the ship and disposed its forces to intercept her: the light cruiser *Glasgow* had been sailed from Horta in the Azores on 24 December; *Penelope was* steaming north in the latitude of Lisbon; *Mauritius* had been ordered out from Gibraltar to reach a position 46° 01' N, 23° 20' W by the 30th; *Gambia* was in the Western Atlantic; and *Enterprise* was steaming to join *Glasgow*. The British intentions were three-fold: first, to sink any incoming merchantmen; second, to prevent any possibility of an outward-bound blockade-runner sailing; and third, to engage any German covering force.

Korvettenkapitän Kohlauf sailed from Brest in the morning of the 27th with *T23, T24, T26* and *T22*, and the 8th Destroyer Flotilla put out from the Gironde with *Z24, Z37, Z32* and *Z27*, accompanied by *T25* and *T27* (the torpedo boats would be detached to their flotilla the next morning). Operation 'Trave' was under way.

By 0400 hours the next day the 4th Flotilla was some 300 miles due south of Cape Clear, the 8th Flotilla standing to the south. Already the destroyers were beset with problems. *Z23*, whilst having temporarily repaired a leak in her bows, still had a defective S-Gerät and degaussing equipment, *Z24* had difficulties with her turbines, and *Z27* had problems in the forward turret. Unbeknown to them, their task was already fruitless, for the previous afternoon a Liberator bomber of No. 311 (Czech)

Squadron RAF had sighted and sunk *Alsterufer*, which had been unable to get off a signal to the German Command. This released the British cruisers, two of which, *Glasgow* and *Enterprise*, had rendezvoused at 0300 hours some 300 miles south-west of the German forces and were now steaming eastwards along the 45th Parallel.

In the outer bay a fresh to strong easterly breeze was blowing and the waves were beginning to build up white horses; overhead, the sky was cloudy. Conditions were becoming difficult aboard the destroyers and torpedo boats as they laboured in the rough seas. Already Allied aircraft had reported the position of the German ships, Liberator 'B' of No. 105 Squadron USN having sighted four destroyers steaming east at 0927 that morning and further reports having been received from Liberator 'V' of the same squadron. Armed with reasonably accurate information concerning the German forces, Captain Clarke, aboard *Glasgow*, took his cruisers northwards to intercept. Just after midday the 8th Destroyer Flotilla sighted the 4th Flotilla to the east, whereupon the torpedo boats turned east astern of the northernmost destroyers, taking station on their port wing. Erdmenger then took his ships eastwards in reconnaissance formation against the possibility that the blockade-runner had wandered in that direction.

In the meantime the British cruisers, which by 1130 hours were only 45 miles south of the German group, had worked north of the destroyers' eastward line of advance and then altered round to the south-east to intercept on the strength of position reports received from Commander-in-Chief Plymouth at 1240. As *Glasgow* turned she received a message from her consort reporting homing signals bearing 243°, whereupon the two ships altered course once more to 220°.

The German flotilla commander appears to have first received reports of the British cruisers at about 1258 hours, probably from a sighting signal by one of his ships, and he then ordered his ships to full speed whilst altering course to due east. Despite the fact that *Glasgow* and *Enterprise* had been under attack by the Luftwaffe at 1224, signals from Naval Group West warning the destroyers of the British presence were not received by the German ships until 1414, by which time action had been well and truly joined. Shortly after this initial sighting, Erdmenger altered course once more to starboard to bear away from the cruisers, which were threatening to interpose themselves between him and his base.

The destroyers were now steaming into the wind and sea, water being thrown up over their bows to cascade down over the forward guns, upper bridge and control platforms; the position of the gun crews serving the torpedo boats' open No. 1 10.5cm mounting and *Z27*'s forward gun must have been particularly unenviable. *Z24* sent off a signal to D8, '46° 40' N, 11° 40' W, cruiser course E, high speed', as Erdmenger signalled his intention to hold off the cruisers by torpedo attacks. With the cruisers on the port side, and

Above: *Z37* in June 1943 off the western coast of France. Note that she has not yet been fitted with a Vierling forward, making the original caption date questionable. (Archiv Gröner)

given the weather conditions, this was easier said than done, since by now the easterly wind had risen to near gale force, with sea State 5 and a high swell.

At 1304 hours the destroyers were ordered to cover the torpedo boats whilst they made a torpedo attack, an order which prompted Kohlauf to comment wryly that, whilst it was very comradely, none of his boats was in a position to fire torpedoes on account of the weather. He meanwhile put his flotilla in line ahead, to await events. Shortly afterwards D8 turned his squadron due south and reduced speed to 17 knots, presumably to assist in concentrating his force into divisions and to avoid running directly into the cruisers. As the ships turned, the torpedo boat flotilla, which had been stationed nearest to the cruisers, manoeuvred to take up a position between the two destroyer divisions with the 1st Division, *Z23* and *Z27*, nearest to the enemy; about a quarter of an hour later the German group altered course slightly further east and increased to 24 knots. Erdmenger was at this point informed by Captain (T4) that the torpedo boats could maintain 29 knots and that it was considered wise to gain as much easting as possible, to which he replied that this was not necessary until the situation was clarified. He was furthermore still hampered by *Z24*, which was steaming on

four boilers and good for only 27 knots maximum, with problems first in the port turbine and then in the starboard unit.

At 1340 hours *Z23* sighted and reported the cruisers on the port side, whereupon D8 ordered the 1st Division to close on the 2nd and was forced away westward again to 180°. The leader's signal to his squadron erroneously put the enemy on the starboard side, but all his ships were in no doubt as to where the enemy lay. It was not the last error by the flagship. Orders were given to fire torpedoes, but only the 1st Division, *Z23* and *Z27*, were in a position to do so, while the torpedo boat flotilla could not comply because it could not yet see the enemy. Heavy seas coming aboard rendered all rangefinders and binoculars useless, leaving only the naked eye for observation, whilst the 2nd Division on the disengaged side were obviously not yet able to reach a firing position.

Glasgow sighted the destroyers at 1332 hours at a range of 25,700m (16 miles) bearing 238°, and while Captain Clarke ate his action dinner of pea soup and corned beef sandwiches the two cruisers increased to full speed and altered course to cut the German ships off from their base. Sixteen minutes later *Glasgow* opened fire with 'A' and 'B' turrets at a range of 19,600m using her Type 273 radar for

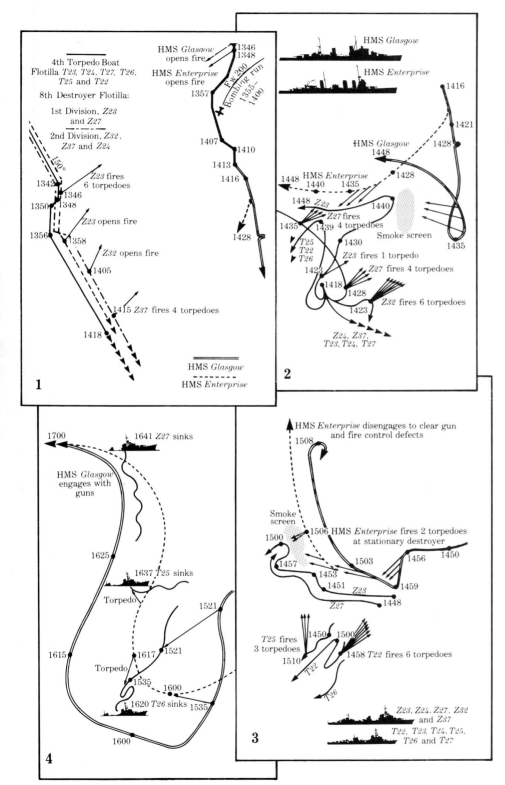

ranging, *Enterprise* following a few minutes later. The 1st Division, *Z23* and *Z27*, nearest to the cruisers, received eighteen broadsides from *Glasgow* as well as the attention of her consort between 1346 and 1400 hours.

Despite very good shooting by the cruisers ('fantastically close grouping', according to *Z23*), the two destroyers remained unscathed as shell splashes towered only 100-150m from their targets. *Z23*, complying with her earlier orders, launched six ineffective torpedoes, three from each bank of tubes, when the range was down to 17,000m, but *Z27* appears to have held fire. Both destroyers opened up with their 15cm guns and, making good shooting, landed their first shots only 200m over on *Glasgow*'s port quarter. The rough seas were already hampering the destroyers and even the crews in the turrets were not fully protected for the seas flooded *Z23*'s mounting through the ports. As the cruisers engaged the destroyers to starboard, a lone Fw 200 pressed home a bombing attack on *Glasgow* from the disengaged side, to be met by fire from the cruiser's 4in guns.

A running fight now developed in a generally southerly direction until about 1418 hours, during which time the 4th Torpedo Boat Flotilla was on several occasions ordered to attack with torpedoes. However, despite manoeuvring out of the line and closing with the cruisers, the attacks were frustrated by the heavy seas. All the torpedo boats were 'taking it green' over the bows, and it was impossible to serve their forward guns. The spray reached as far as the forward funnel, flooding the bridge and rangefinder positions and rendering any range-taking useless, even if the target could have been seen, and, abandoning the attack, Kohlauf turned south once more and rejoined the larger ships.

Z32 and *Z37*, initially stationed on the starboard, disengaged, side, were ordered by Erdmenger at 1356 hours to press eastwards for a torpedo attack. The two destroyers turned to port towards the cruisers, opening fire as they did so, although *Z32*, with a defective turret, was devoid of forward gunpower. Closing to 12,800m, *Z32* launched six and *Z37* four torpedoes, as the cruisers continued to rain down a heavy and accurate fire. The destroyers, too, were returning the fire with accuracy, and in fact it was they who obtained the first (and only) hit on *Glasgow* at about 1405 hours, although *Enterprise* was continually straddled by near-misses. Both destroyers laid smoke and then retired back towards the German line. As *Z32* turned away her forward funnel caught fire, causing the British ship to believe that a hit had been scored. The torpedo attack forced *Glasgow* to make an emergency turn to port as the track of one passed 30m from her port quarter and two more close down her port side. *Enterprise* had by this time parted close company with *Glasgow* and, acting independently, was not troubled by the torpedoes.

Whilst the 2nd Division was engaged in its torpedo attack Erdmenger made the decision to divide his forces into two groups. The reason for this move is not quite clear, and it was certainly not to the liking of Captain (T4) who considered it a mistake. It was probably not an attempt at a pincer attack on the cruisers, and although Naval Group West had signalled a warning of a further British force approaching from Cape Finisterre (*Penelope?*), it is questionable as to whether this had been received aboard the leader at the time the decision to separate was made; certainly, it was not passed to T4 until 1432. By about 1418 the German flotillas were spread in a long line in the order *Z32, Z24, Z37, T23, T27, T26, T22, T25, Z27* and *Z25, Z32* and *Z37* being off to port in the course of their torpedo attack. At this time *Z27, Z23* and the last three boats of the 4th Flotilla were ordered to turn to starboard on a reciprocal course. All the ships conformed to the order, with the exception of the flotilla leader herself, which veered to port in executing her 180° turn. As *Z23* turned she fired one of her last two loaded tubes on swinging, the training controls having become defective; a few minutes later *Z27* fired a Viererfacher, but neither attack produced any result.

Erdmenger now signalled to *Z32*, giving command of the southerly group to her CO, Korvettenkapitän von Berger, and ordering him to press to the east whilst his own group steered broadly northwards. The two cruisers, meanwhile, having avoided the torpedoes, continued southwards until it became apparent that the German force had split up, whereupon *Glasgow* reversed course at 1435 hours to chase the northern group of destroyers; *Enterprise* had already altered course to the west to head them off. Shortly after *Z27* had fired her torpedoes she received a shell hit, probably from *Enterprise*, which struck in No. 2 boiler room, passed through an oil bunker and caused a huge fire.

Clouds of steam gushed from her forward funnel as the leader's speed fell off. She was still fighting, however: after being hit she fired her second salvo of four torpedoes, again without effect, and was still engaging with three guns, No. 4 gun having been knocked out, but it proved impossible to reload the tubes owing to the movement of the ship.

As *Z27* was hit the three torpedo boats turned south once more, *T26* off *T22*'s port bow, with *T25* some 600m astern, although *Z27* and *Z23* were by now lost to view. *Glasgow* continued to engage, concentrating on *T25*. At 1454 hours the torpedo boat sustained hits in the region of the after torpedo tubes, the Vierling and the 3.7cm flak platforms, which killed or wounded all their crews. The port engine stopped, but when Kapitänleutnant von Gartzen ordered full speed on the starboard turbine his engineer officer reported that the oil lines to the after engine room had been destroyed and the boat rapidlly slowed down. Then a second hit struck near to the forward funnel, blowing the mast as well as the funnel into the air and overboard. *T25* was now clearly doomed and requested *T22* to attempt to come alongside and take off her crew. With her fire control damaged and unserviceable, with electrical power gone and with all low-angle ammunition expended, *T25* could now only fire slow salvoes of head-fuzed flak ammunition.

Seeing that her shells had had their effect, *Glasgow* shifted to *T26*, which was quickly surrounded by near-misses, and, manoeuvring frantically to escape, the torpedo boat requested, and was granted, detachment from the flotilla. *T22* had the enemy ships on her port quarter, and, in an effort to drive them off while she closed her damaged consort, she fired her full outfit of torpedoes and opened fire with her guns. The torpedoes, however, went

Left: *T26* in 1943, the year that she was lost in action with *Glasgow* and *Enterprise* in the Bay of Biscay. (Archiv Gröner)

unnoticed, and as *T22* turned to starboard towards *T25* she too was surrounded by shell splashes from the cruiser. The attempt was plainly suicidal and was abandoned: laying smoke and still engaging with guns, *T22* withdrew to the south-west, soon coming upon *T26*, still under fire and by now badly hit in the boiler room. As *T22* laid smoke to screen her, the damaged ship signalled that she was sinking and, now alone, *T22* turned northwards to break away. At about the same time that *T22* was attempting to cover *T26*, *Z23* was manoeuvring to go alongside the damaged flotilla leader, but the cruisers appeared at high speed and Erdmenger, thanking her for her efforts, ordered *Z23* away to the east. This move was impossible at that time, and so the destroyer laid smoke and made off to the west.

The two cruisers reversed course to a generally southerly direction, chasing and soon catching *T26*. *Glasgow* ordered *Enterprise* to finish her off while she turned north again to look for the other damaged enemy vessels, particularly *T25*. As the cruiser steamed northwards there came into sight, in the north-west, not *T25* but *Z27*, drifting and silent. Closing to point-blank range, *Glasgow* fired, exploding the destroyer's magazines. She sank quickly to port, taking with her Korvettenkapitän Erdmenger, his staff and the captain, who were still on her forecastle.

In the meantime *T25*, her bridge and upper deck over the forward boiler room a shambles and her after superstructure wrecked, remained afloat. Her engineer offficer was still hopeful that he could re-start the port turbine for low speed and thus have a chance of escape, but all thoughts were dashed when, at about 1635 hours, *Enterprise* hove into sight, having despatched *T26* with a torpedo; she closed to 3,000m, but her shells were met by only a feeble reply from two guns, and another torpedo sealed the fate of the German boat. Abandoned and on fire, *T25* soon sank out of sight.

Having accounted for three of the German squadron at no significant damage to themselves, and with no further enemy in sight, the two cruisers withdrew towards Plymouth, where they arrived on the evening of 29 December with little ammunition or fuel remaining. *Glasgow* had received only one hit, which had exploded in 'A' boiler room fan intake, killing two members of the port pom-pom crew; *Enterprise* had been continuously straddled but hit only by splinters which caused no real damage.

Of the remaining German ships, *T22* came across *Z23* at 1545 hours and was ordered to follow the destroyer as she escaped west and then turned to gain the safety of French ports, taking no further part in the action and finally putting into St. Jean de Luz, close to the Franco-Spanish border. The 4th Torpedo Boat Flotilla, with only *T23*, *T24* and *T27*, was ordered by *Z32* to break off east at 1515 and steered for Brest, the nearest safe port. *Z32*, with *Z37* and *Z24*, intended to return to assist *Z27* as this group still had considerable firepower intact: the leader had managed to reload only one torpedo owing to the seas, but *Z37* still retained four and *Z24* her full outfit of eight. *Z24*, however,

suffered tube failures in her superheaters and her starboard engine failed, and she requested permission to break off and join the 4th Flotilla which was retiring to Brest.

Z32 and *Z37* returned westwards and then probed north-west, but although they sighted the cruisers an attack was not carried through. By this time it was too late to save *Z27*, and in view of *Z37*'s fuel position the attempt was abandoned and the destroyers retired, suffering air attacks during the evening but reaching the Gironde safely. *Z24* finally managed to join up with the torpedo boats at 1721 hours, and the four ships returned to Brest that evening. Only 283 survivors of the 672 men on the three sunken ships were rescued, 93 from *Z27*, 100 from *T25* and 90 from *T26*. British and Irish ships, Spanish destroyers and German U-boats took part in the rescue, but Kapitän zur See Erdmenger and his staff, and Korvettenkapitän Schultz of *Z27*, his first lieutenant and his engineer offficer, perished.

INQUEST

The resounding failure of this second operation called for a detailed post-mortem on the part of the various flags and commands involved. Flag Officer (Destroyers), the newly appointed Admiral Kreisch, was of course greatly concerned at the losses and the failure to inflict any significant damage to the British cruisers. In his opinion, the initial conditions for the operation were themselves rather more unfavourable than for the previous one, partly because of the short time gap involved. This gap was dictated by the spacings in the Allied convoy cycle through which the blockade-breakers had to pass, but it meant that Royal Navy activity from the previous sortie had not yet dispersed and, furthermore, it allowed the ships involved little time between operations to rest and refuel. The weather also played a part in this early stage, for fog in the Gironde caused deployment problems, in turn necessitating much use of radio signals which FdZ feared might have compromised the impending sortie. Kreisch critically reviewed the operation from a number of standpoints:

1. Should an earlier abandonment have been ordered? After due consideration of the facts, he concluded that there was no evidence that an earlier decision could have been made.

2. How was it that the flotillas engaged in battle under such unfavourable conditions? Group West had been in no doubt that any contact with an enemy cruiser group would have had serious results and, in consequence, the Luftwaffe had been requested to provide air reconnaissance in such a way as to provide at least a few hours' warning of any enemy cruisers. Air searches were commenced on the 28th, between 43°–47° 20' N, and 7° 3'–16° 30' W by Fw 200 aircraft, whilst the area 47° 20'–48° 50' N was in the meantime searched by two Ju 88s. Kreisch noted that the late switching on of the Fw 200s' radar (see later) and the loss of 1½ hours on account of a machine being unserviceable left a gap through which the enemy cruisers

penetrated. In his opinion, the major factor was the unexpected appearance of these cruisers so close to the German ships.

3. Tactical leadership. The belief by the flotilla commander that two or more enemy groups were present – an impression built up as a result of faulty or insufficient signalling – had a major effect on his tactical employment. It had dictated his course, and the weather on this course affected his speed and his ability to fight the guns. Would it therefore have been better not to have separated, as in fact Captain (T4) thought? In analysing matters, FdZ noted that (a) the enemy fired for about an hour without effect; (b) in this phase, numerous torpedoes were fired from unfavourable positions without success; (c) when favourable situations then arose, there were no torpedoes left; and (d) after separation, only a few minutes passed before three ships were badly hit, the reason for this undoubtedly being the by now much reduced range.

4. Signalling. This left much to be desired, and in fact Kreisch apportioned a good deal of blame to this factor. Much use was made of the short-wave R/T net, so much so that it was overloaded and some signals did not get through; similarly, the radio net was hindered by inexperienced and partly trained personnel, leading to cipher errors and transmission failures. An important factor, too, was the allocation of the short-wave Channel 15 to the torpedo boats, whilst the destroyers used Channel 9: only the leader was fitted for both, and she had not exercised sufficiently as a leader in signalling practice.

5. The action. No commanding officer had a good overall view as to what was happening, and important information was either wrongly signalled or not signalled at all. For example, Kreisch quotes Z23 as having at one stage reported the presence of 'a cruiser and destroyer', thus leading Captain (D8) to believe that at least two enemy groups had made contacts. Z23 may, however, have been merely repeating an aircraft report of a similar nature received at about 1408 hours.

6. Co-operation with the Luftwaffe. The Navy had expected that any enemy intruding into the operation would at least be damaged by the shore-based aircraft. Twenty-five He 177 bombers had been detailed for air strike purposes, but on the day concerned only sixteen were operational. In the event, the weather, and in particular the low cloud base, restricted air operations considerably.

Admiral Kreisch summarized his conclusions. The defeat was due to: (a) the early and unknown loss of Trave (Alsterufer); (b) enemy knowledge of the operation; (c) inadequate air reconnaissance; (d) the encounter with cruisers without warning; (e) unsuitable weather for He 177 sorties; (f) unfavourable sea conditions for fighting the guns; and (g) the low speed of the torpedo boats. Admiral Krancke at Naval Group West, while not unnaturally dismayed at the losses, accepted the result as the consequence of a necessary gamble, bearing in mind the immense value of the cargo from the previous blockade-breaker Orsono; to continue the war successfully into 1944, it was vital that these cargoes be brought home. Nevertheless, he too apportioned much of the blame to the Luftwaffe for faulty reconnaissance. It would appear that the Naval Command was unaware that the Air Force's orders for reconnaissance patrols stipulated that radar would not be used until 12° W was reached on the outward flight, but the Navy had assumed that radar would be employed at all times, especially as the positions of friendly forces were accurately known. To the flotillas, Admiral Krancke sent a consolatory signal: 'Our Luftwaffe was numerically insufficient to prevent your being surprised by the cruisers, and weather conditions did not allow the operation to proceed according to plan. In attacking the enemy, your flotilla commander sought a favourable decision, which fate denied him. This will not make us waver. Duty fulfilled, and fulfilled with pride.'

Admiral Schniewind at Fleet Command broadly agreed with the other officers but made more of the training aspect. He considered that the British training was undoubtedly superior because of the longer time spent at sea, whilst the German ships were poorly trained in comparison on account of fuel shortages. This, in his opinion, was a vital factor in the engagement. His other main observation was that the eleven torpedo craft should have endeavoured to split the cruisers' batteries by separate attacks. At high speed, they should have been able to cross the danger zone before being seriously damaged, when their favourable positioning for torpedo attack would have forced the cruisers to take avoiding action. Whilst he agreed that a two-pronged attack was frequently successful, one gets the impression that he favoured smaller, multi-pronged attacks.

In view of the allegations made by the Navy against the Luftwaffe, Headquarters asked the latter two vital questions: why were the cruisers not detected until they were so close to German forces, and why did the Luftwaffe not intervene in the fighting? Fliegerführer Atlantik (Air Commander Atlantic), Generalleutnant Kessler, replied on both counts for the Air Force. On the first count, the air operations had been so organized that at dawn, the critical time, aircraft would be as far west as possible across the expected path of the incoming blockade-breaker. This followed the pattern of previous operations and was known to the Naval HQ. The 8th Destroyer Flotilla had themselves noted that the absence of early, accurate position reports during the previous sortie had been painfully felt. This was caused by equipment breakdowns and necessitated visual and not radar observation, and in consequence only a narrower strip could be searched by each aircraft. As a result, Kessler arranged for no fewer than ten radar-equipped machines plus two reserves to be available for this new operation. Thus it was calculated that, in the likely event that the blockade-breaker would be delayed, reconnaissance could be pushed farther west and thereby ensure an early sighting report for the Navy. At the same time, it was recognized that the area east of 12° W would not be overflown until the return flight some three hours later. If, therefore, an enemy force were in this area, there was a possibility that it could close the German flotillas during this time. Kessler held that to meet both demands, i.e., reconnaissance west of 12° W from dawn and east of 12° W in darkness, was impossible as there was no means of identifying friend from foe by radar, either in aircraft or in ships, and the Fw 200 Kondors were not fitted for flare dropping

On the second count, Kessler too attributed much blame to the weather, and with some justification. His main bomber force, 11/KG 40, with fourteen He 177 aircraft, was stationed at Bordeaux, whilst the Fw 200 reconnaissance bombers of 111/KG 40 were at Cognac. The latter were in the course of being fitted for launching glider bombs, and some had been hurriedly called back from Germany for the purpose. These bombs required at least 600m cloud base for effective use, but nevertheless the Air Force quickly flew off aircraft of 111/KG 40 in the hope that the base would rise from its current 200m during the flight. In the meantime, four Fw 200s of 111/KG 40, using homing buoys, made contact, but the weather was unsuitable for successful attacks. The Navy had requested aircraft standing by airborne in the area in case of hostile ships but this was plainly impossible because of assembly problems in darkness and the probability of having to return by midday and therefore having no strike potential left in the afternoon, whilst the splitting into two groups of the few aircraft available was not considered a good proposition. Thus the Luftwaffe thought that they had done all that they could with the forces at their disposal, a sentiment endorsed in fact by Admiral Krancke.

Turning now to the British forces, we find that, by coincidence, or more probably as a result of ULTRA Intelligence, they had intended to run up 12° W from the south to intercept the German vessels, which at 0940 hours had been reported at 46° 48' N, 10° 57' W. As their approach to 12° W was made from the west and was timed to arrive at that longitude at 0900 hours, they could not have been detected beforehand because the Fw 200s themselves had been ordered to reach 12° W at 0845 and commence radar search. Thus it is likely that had radar been used only half an hour earlier, aircraft 'AS' of 11/KG 40 might well have detected the cruisers at the moment they reached 12° W and thus gained an extremely vital extra 3½ hours' warning for the surface forces. As it was, 'AS' and the cruisers must have just missed one another in the half-light of dawn, possibly as the radar set was warming up, leaving the British ships undetected until the return flight of aircraft 'AR' crossed their track much further north at 1230 hours.

On the propaganda front, it was naturally embarrassing to the Kriegsmarine to report that eleven destroyers and torpedo boats with a combined firepower of twenty-four 15cm and twenty-four 10.5cm guns had been driven off with serious loss by two ships carrying only nineteen 6in (15.2cm) guns; furthermore, the German force had a torpedo firepower of 76 tubes plus reloads. There was no doubt that the weather severely handicapped the German ships, particularly the torpedo boats, and made the serving of their guns very difficult. The spray and spume obscured rangefinders and the absence of any effective gunnery radar put them at a great disadvantage compared with the British, whilst the co-ordinated control of eleven ships required a high degree of tactical training and long periods of working in close company, which the German squadron clearly did not have, and the absence of any Action Information Centre aboard the German ships merely emphasized this. Moreover, the fact that they were far from their bases clearly affected the decisions of the German commanders. Nevertheless, having considered all these factors, it is surprising that so little was achieved by the German ships, outnumbering the British force as they did.

It would appear that no real plan of action had been developed to counter attacks by British surface forces during these blockade-running operations, despite the fact that it was known that British cruisers were stationed in the approaches to the Bay of Biscay and were carrying out armed sweeps across it during the latter half of 1943. Reading the various ships' reports, it is difficult to escape the conclusion that the main concern of the German squadron was to return to their bases and that the torpedo attacks which were carried out were defensive and in pursuance of that aimed at delaying the cruisers rather than sinking them. As for Hitler, the news of the action merely confirmed his opinions as to the ineffectiveness of the Kriegsmarine, and his comments were quite scathing, but there was also widespread concern in the Fleet, and within the destroyer flotillas action was taken to improve their state of readiness and to devise tactics to counter such cruiser attacks. By June 1944, for example, the 5th Flotilla, then stationed at Horten for duties in the Skaggerak, was using the depot ship *Tsingtau* to represent *Glasgow*(!) in training exercises.

The question of the sinking of *Z27* received considerable investigation, for it was initially held that she had been lost through human error. *Z27* had been hit at 1435 hours by a shell which fell short, penetrated No. 2 boiler room underwater at frame 70, passed through oil bunker 3.1, severed the starboard main steam line to the turbines and exploded in front of the starboard boiler, K2.1; splinters pierced the bulkheads, causing further damage to the steam lines, and the whole boiler room watch was scalded and forced to evacuate the space. After the hit, the other two boiler rooms reported feedwater and oil fuel contamination problems as the steam pressure dropped rapidly in the starboard turbine. On questioning the survivors, the experts ashore held that because of incorrect valving procedures on the part of the engineering staff the steam supply to the port turbine was somehow cut off, leaving the destroyer helpless.

These findings by OKM were, however, disputed by FdZ, Vizeadmiral Kreisch, newly appointed after the death of Konteradmiral Bey aboard *Scharnhorst*. In his opinion, the engineer officer in question, Kapitänleutnant (Ing) Martin, was an experienced officer who had been a watchkeeper during the Narvik battles and was unlikely to make such a mistake. Martin did not survive and so could not defend himself, and the question remained unresolved until later in 1944 when two engine room personnel, Stabsobermaschinist Hasenbein and Maschinistmatrosen Kruskop, were repatriated from Spain after being rescued by a Spanish destroyer. These two had been stationed in No. 2 (starboard) turbine room close to Martin and confirmed that he had received the message giving the location of the hit in compartment XI and that they were aware of the breaching of the starboard main steam line in No. 2 boiler room. At this time the destroyer was clear on both boilers in No. 1 boiler room and on one in No. 3, and the port turbine was running. During the course of the next hour, the remaining boiler in No. 3 boiler room went out, probably as the result of water in the fuel oil, and the watch were unable to relight it; *Z27* now steamed on the port turbine, fed by No. 1 boiler room. Then, after about an hour, first the main feed pump and almost immediately afterwards the cruising feed pump failed in the port turbine room, and these problems were followed by the failure of the feed pumps in the boiler room, probably as a result of feedwater malfunction. Up to this time, an hour after the original hit, there was still 30kg/cm² of steam. These new facts provided sufficient evidence to clear the engineer officer's name.

Following the loss of *Z27* and the death of Erdmenger, Kapitän zur See Langheld took command of the 8th Flotilla, but he held the post only until 19 April 1944, when Kapitän zur See von Bechtolsheim took over. Von Bechtolsheim had been the first lieutenant of *Schultz* before the war, and had then commanded *Galster* before being appointed to the staff of Commodore (D) in 1942.

STEADY ATTRITION

At the end of January a further disaster struck the flotilla when, on the 30th, in the course of exercises in the Bay, *Z37* was rammed by *Z32* whose steering appears to have run amok. *Z32* cleaved into her flotilla-mate on the starboard side abreast the after torpedo tubes, causing a torpedo warhead to explode as well as flak ammunition. Both turbine rooms were put out of action and a serious fire developed amidships. *Z32* suffered damage to her bows, forward compartments and underwater hull, and the fires aboard both vessels were not extinguished for about an hour. *Z37* was a shambles amidships, blackened by fire and smoke and with a list to starboard. Immobile, with no propulsive power available, she was a sitting target for the RAF, which, however, did not appear on the scene on this occasion. Towed by *Z23* and escorted by the damaged *Z32*,

she was slowly brought into the Gironde and then down to Bordeaux where she was finally docked at the Forges et Chantiers de la Gironde yard. She required major repairs which would take at least twelve months. In fact it was the end for her. German shipyards were by this time no longer able to send out teams of specialists and craftsmen to occupied dockyards to supervise repairs, spares and replacements for major items were almost unobtainable, and the French workmen were not inclined to rush into repairing a Nazi destroyer at this stage of the war. In August, her main armament was taken out for shore defence purposes (the twin turret remained on the dockside), and a few days later the ship's company rendered her unusable by wrecking her machinery, fire control equipment and other fittings and setting fire to several compartments. *Z37* was formally paid off on 20 August, though not scuttled: she remained in the dry dock and was captured by the French when Bordeaux was evacuated.

To the north, in the Channel theatre, the torpedo boats had in the meantime been in action once more. Towards the end of January 1944 a number of torpedo boat movements had taken place when *T28* and *T29* passed down-Channel to France, arriving safely despite attacks by Albacores of Coastal Command and by the Dover batteries. *T28* sustained some leaks in a boiler room but remained otherwise unscathed. No reinforcement of the 4th Flotilla was intended, however, for *T23* and *T22* were both withdrawn eastwards to refit at the beginning of February. The flotilla's operational strength now consisted of *T24*, *T27*, *T28* and *T29*.

In the evening of 25 April, *T24*, *T27* and *T29* weighed anchor from St-Malo on a combined minelaying and convoy escort operation. After sowing mines north-west of Les Sept Iles, the three ships received reports of enemy units nearby and prepared for surface action. It was a moonless, starlit night, with a light breeze and calm seas, and visibility was about 3,000m. The enemy ships on this occasion were the cruiser *Black Prince*, in company with the destroyers *Haida*, *Athabaskan*, *Ashanti* and *Huron* – a decidedly superior force.

The cruiser's radar located the Germans before the latter obtained contact and the Allied vessels worked up to full speed in a chasing action. After opening fire with starshell and then a few rounds of 5.25in (13.3cm) from 'A' turret by radar, the cruiser took little further part in the action, leaving her destroyers to chase. A gun action now developed, with *T24* and *T27* being straddled continuously before *T27* was hit in the stern, reducing her speed to 12 knots, whereupon she was released to Morlaix. *T24*, replying with her after guns at targets weakly illuminated by starshell, was hit on the rangefinder platform and radio office, starting fires which were, however, quickly extinguished. She fired all her forward tubes without effect and, outpacing her pursuers, arrived in a damaged state at St-Malo.

Above: *Kondor*, one of the Channel 'work-horses', lost in the invasion air raids at Le Havre in 1944. (B.f.Z)

T29 meanwhile received a hit in the stern compartments, causing rudder failure, and swung about out of control. *Haida* and *Athabaskan*, thinking that she was about to break back, closed and engaged with every gun on board as well as torpedoes, and a hit on *T29* blew up the after funnel, set fire to ammunition and caused an explosion. She replied with what weapons she now had left, even using flak shells, and in the words of the British report 'fought with gallantry'. Further hits were rapidly sustained, the forward boiler room, forward turbine room, Nos. 3 and 4 guns, the bridge and the director all being knocked out, and a direct hit on the forward tubes blew them overboard as the after Vierling continued to engage the enemy. After a hit on the bridge had killed the captain, Kapitänleutnan Grund, the first lieutenant gave the order to abandon ship. *Haida* and *Athabaskan* withdrew northwards to allow *Ashanti* and *Huron* to give the *coup de grâce*, but at 0400 hours *T29* still remained afloat, whereupon all four returned to pound the burning wreck until she sank at about 0420, the Allied force having fired fifteen torpedoes without a single hit.

The steady attrition of the Kriegsmarine's surface forces continued as Allied task groups took the offensive in the Channel and on the coasts of Brittany in a continuous build-up to the forthcoming invasion of Europe. During the night of 26/27 April *T27* joined *T24* in St-Malo before both sailed for Brest in the evening of the 27th. Whilst off the Ile de Vierge they were intercepted by the destroyers *Haida* and *Athabaskan*, which had been ordered to patrol off the French coast. Surprise was achieved by the Canadian ships as starshell burst over the two torpedo boats; making smoke, the latter turned south, *T24* firing six torpedoes as

she went. Three of these were launched on the wrong side, but one of the others struck *Athabaskan* just as the two destroyers were turning to port for a chase. Shortly afterwards, there was a second, heavier explosion as a magazine went up.

T27 was hit and set on fire as she turned, working up to full speed and running south-east, *T24* breaking away to the east and escaping as *Haida* pursued her companion. The latter received two hits on the waterline in the forward boiler room and transmitting station, making water forward; further hits destroyed first the port Vierling and then the starboard, and these were quickly followed by two more shells forward as she strove to escape under the coast. Kapitänleutnant Gotzmann was endeavouring to reach L'Aber-Wrac'h but suddenly, off the port bow, the shore loomed up. Turning hard to starboard, the torpedo boat ran out of sea room and went aground. *Haida* continued to engage, exploding the ready-use ammunition on *T27*'s bridge and causing a large fire. The after Vierling continued to engage, but with no pressure on the mains the fires took hold and the ship had to be abandoned as *Haida* withdrew.

Despite efforts by *T24* and boats of the 24th Minesweeper Flotilla to tow her off, *T27* remained fast. On return to harbour, *T24* rescued 47 survivors from *Athabaskan* and was damaged by a ground mine; *T27* was later wrecked by air attacks. From the Allied point of view the Canadian destroyers were censured for failing to contemplate a torpedo attack, it being considered deplorable that the German force sized up the situation more quickly than they! The loss of *T27* effectively finished the 4th Flotilla, and *T24* was thenceforth attached to the 8th Destroyer Flotilla in Bordeaux for the rest of her career.

TOO FAR SOUTH

The major event of the year was of course the invasion of Normandy, to counter which the forces available to the Kriegsmarine were both pitifully small and poorly placed. No heavy units were deployed in the Channel theatre, nor had they been since early 1942: after the dissolution of the 4th Torpedo Boat Flotilla, only the 8th Destroyer and the 5th Torpedo Boat Flotillas remained to provide a surface striking force, together with the 5th and 9th S-boat Flotillas.

On 23 May, the 5th Flotilla was ordered to move from Cherbourg to Le Havre and sailed that night with *Jaguar*, *Kondor*, *Greif*, *Falke* and *Möwe*. In company were units of the 6th Minesweeper Flotilla. During the early hours of the following morning, they were surprised by an attack by a single aircraft from starboard, when *Greif* was struck by two bombs in compartments VIII and IX. The forward boiler room caught fire and the ship began to flood forward. The attacker, an Albacore of 415 squadron Coastal Command, was heard to signal 'I've had a good meal but it was damned hot!' Meanwhile the torpedo boat was in a bad way, with both No. 1 and No. 2 boiler rooms flooded. In her unmanoeuvrable state, she collided with *Falke*, though with little damage to the latter. *Greif*'s bows, however, were badly bent, making steering difficult, which *Möwe* discovered when ordered to take her in tow. The position was serious – already the minesweepers had been in action with MTBs, losing *M39* to torpedoes. Air activity was a constant menace and the tow recalcitrant. By 0435, the water was gaining on the pumps aboard *Greif*, who had only one boiler on line. Just over 1½ hours later, this last boiler failed and it was still more than 20 miles to Le Havre. Finally, at 0632, *Greif* sank. One minute later, *M84* was mined but made port, although her repairs were never to be finished. Fog now descended which, whilst making navigation difficult, did also protect the flotilla, but at 0743 *Kondor* touched off a mine about 10 metres off her starboard side, abreast the bridge. Taken in two by *Möwe*, the cripple was shepherded towards Le Havre, being met off that port by the 10th R-Boat Flotilla, which in turn had *R217* damaged by a mine. It had been an eventful passage with the expenditure of nearly 300 rounds of 10.5cm and more than 17,000 rounds of 2cm. *Kondor* was never operational again and having begun a long refit, was cannibalized for spares at the start of the Invasion.She was paid off on 28 June, then hit forward by bombs on 1 August, after which she was not considered worth repair.

When the Allies invaded France on 6 June, the 5th Flotilla could muster *Jaguar*, *Möwe*, *Falke* and *T28*, although the latter had only just completed a 4-month refit. During sorties against the invasion fleet on the nights of 6/7, 8/9, 9/10 and 12/13 June, some fifty torpedoes and large quantities of ammunition were fired, but their only success was the torpedoing of the Norwegian *Svenner* and the frigate *Halsted* but only the former was sunk. Kept away from the invasion area by MTBs, destroyers, mines and air power, their end was inevitable and in the course of a major RAF air raid on Le Havre on the night of 14/15 June, *Falke* and *Jaguar* were both sunk. *Möwe*, badly damaged, finally foundered on 16 June after some weapons and equipment were salvaged. *T28* and *Kondor* escaped damage. The former eventually managed to break out from Le Havre and fought her way across the invasion area to arrive safely in Germany by the end of July.

The destroyers of the 8th Flotilla were now positioned too far to the south to be able to intercept the invasion convoys, so on receipt of the news of the Invasion von Bechtolsheim sailed from Bordeaux on the 6th bound for his new base, Brest, where he would join forces with the 5th Torpedo Boat Flotilla. Only three operational ships were now left to him – *Z32*, *ZH1* and *Z24*, the last only a month out of a major refit. His intended departure from Bordeaux had been reported to British Intelligence with remarkable speed, for the large RAF Coastal Command station at Davidstowe Moor in Cornwall received orders in time to launch an attack, despite the fact that the passage to Brest took about twelve to fifteen hours at 25 knots.

In the evening of 6 June fourteen Beaufighter Mk Xs of No. 404 Squadron RCAF, armed with 25lb rocket projectiles, roared off the runways on the moor, quickly followed by seventeen more from No. 144 Squadron RAF, armed only with cannon for anti-flak duties. They were joined in the air by eight more aircraft from No. 248 Squadron, based at Portreath, as fighter escort. The strike force wave-hopped at about 50m, making landfall on Ushant and then flying south-west. Off Brest, four minesweepers and two trawlers were sighted, which put up an impressive flak display, while further south three more minesweepers were at first mistaken for their target. Then, having detached a number of aircraft of Nos. 144 and 248 Squadrons to attack a surfaced U-boat, the strike leader sighted the three destroyers at 2030 hours, although initially he did not realize that this was his target. Having cancelled the attack the truth dawned, and the strike force joined up for the attack.

The 8th Flotilla, steaming in line ahead with *ZH1* leading *Z32* and *Z24*, had reached a position some 30 miles west of the Ile de Noirmoutier when the aircraft, wrongly identified as Mosquitoes, were sighted. The attackers split up into sub-flights and dived out of the sun, to be met by flak only when close in. Four aircraft of No. 404 Squadron attacked *ZH1* with rocket salvoes and cannon fire, claiming underwater hits with the RPs although these were in fact short since otherwise the destroyer would have suffered serious damage. Nine No. 404 Squadron aircraft attacked *Z32*, firing full salvoes of RPs except P/404 which fired two at about 700m, then two pairs at 300m, before raking her superstructure with cannon fire; L/404, finding the centre crowded, attacked *Z24*.

Suddenly it was all over and the aircraft flew off, only to land, refuel and rearm for a second strike. Taking part in this second strike were six aircraft from No. 404 Squadron and five from No. 144. Further attacks were made on each of the three destroyers, hits being claimed on all; one aircraft, Q/404, ditched, but all the others returned safely. The destroyers suffered superstructure damage with three men killed and twenty-one wounded, but considering the strength of the attacking force the results for the RAF were extremely poor.

On the destroyers' arrival at Brest, Naval Group West began to issue operational instructions to the flotilla as the ships patched up the shell holes from the air attack. Mining operations were considered by the High Command, which asked if the flotilla still carried mining gear for EMC mines, but the answer was no and *ZH1* was never so fitted anyway. Memories of the air attack on the passage north plus the prospect of operations in the confined waters of the Channel, where Allied command of the air was unchallenged, were sobering thoughts. None of the destroyers had had any great augmentation of their flak outfit as yet, but von Bechtolsheim managed to obtain two single 3.7cm SK M/42 weapons on U-boat mountings from the local flotilla, and these were shipped on the midships flak platform of *Z32* in lieu of the two single 2cm guns formerly carried; two Vierlings were also obtained, and were fitted in a similar position on *Z24*. Both ships landed, besides the 2cm singles, the exercise loader and 8.8cm sub-calibre gun barrel, and, in the case of *Z32*, the after searchlight as well. *ZH1* received no extra armament: she was already equipped with four Vierlings.

THREE CRUISERS AND ONE DESTROYER

The 8th Flotilla was ordered out to attack the invasion forces on 8 June and sailed from Brest, escorted by the 40th Minesweeper Flotilla, that evening. All three destroyers departed, together with the torpedo boat *T24*, the last survivor of the now disbanded 4th Flotilla. (The latter had been damaged by a mine off Brest on 19 May.)

The squadron rounded Ushant, then steered approximately north-east to enter the Channel. By 0123 hours the destroyers were on an easterly course, when shadows were sighted off the port bow at a range of 4,000–5,000m. Von Bechtolsheim altered course northwards to intercept and ordered each ship to fire torpedoes. The enemy ships were the British 10th Destroyer Flotilla comprising the 19th Division, *Tartar* (D10), *Ashanti*, *Huron* and *Haidla*, and the 20th Division, *Blyskawica* (SO), *Eskimo*, *Piorun* and *Javelin*, which had sailed from Plymouth to intercept the expected German sortie. The British ships were steaming a south-westerly course in divisional formation, with the 20th broad on the starboard quarter of the 19th. Radar contact had been obtained by all British ships between 0116 and 0120 hours; at 0123 the 10th Flotilla altered course to starboard, which exposed their lightly camouflaged sides to the moon, and at this moment the German flotilla sighted them. *Tartar* opened fire with starshell and a running fight developed.

Z32, *ZH1* and *Z24* each launched four torpedoes, but the last ship, *T24*, could not yet see the targets and held fire. The British ships were by now equipped to monitor the German short-wave ship-to-ship command net and heard the German orders to fire; thus forewarned, they turned to comb the tracks. Despite using 'B' gun for starshell and having the 'A' arcs closed, thus reducing each destroyer to only two guns bearing, the British fire was extremely effective: As the German flotilla turned after launching torpedoes, *Z32* received a hit in compartment XV, causing a fire in the fore-ends, a second in No. 1 boiler room and

Right: *ZH1*, the odd man out. This ex-Dutch destroyer was sunk in the same action as *Z32*. (W. Z. Bilddienst)

splinter and 2cm hits in the radio room, damaging the aerials. *ZH1* suffered hits in the bows, side, boat deck and the GHG space, but the decisive shell penetrated the turbine room, destroying the main steam line and filling the room with scalding steam. The destroyer then received a further underwater hit in No. 1 boiler room, causing flooding, and as the steam pressure dropped the rudder motor failed, the engines refused to obey telegraphs and the turbogenerators ran down. Hand-steering was ordered, but despite both diesel generators being started all power was lost and the destroyer came to a stop, wreathed in smoke and steam which masked her from her assailants, *Ashanti* and *Tartar*.

These two ships then shifted their fire to *Z24*, quickly scoring hits. *Z24* had just fired her first salvo, and as her gunnery officer ordered a starshell shot a hit in the turret loading room caused casualties and severed all communications with the mounting. The range was now so close that both sides joined in with 3.7cm and 40mm weapons, and a certain degree of confusion reigned. A second hit on *Z24* destroyed the wheelhouse and charthouse, killing or wounding all the personnel in them; other shells hit the second funnel, forward turbine room and Vierling and set fire to the ready-use ammunition which had to be jettisoned overboard. Badly knocked about, *Z24* made smoke and turned away under its cover, receiving further shells as she did so. The after funnel was on fire, making a good target, and the engineer officer reported that the forward turbine room was making water. As she turned away under the protective smokescreen, *T24*, which was undamaged, followed her round and the two ships then lost contact with *Z32* and *ZH1*.

Z32 meanwhile had broken away to the north, then north-east, and had found herself alone with communication problems caused by her earlier hits. At 0211 hours four more enemy vessels were sighted off the port bow at a range of 7,000m. This was the 20th Division, led by *Blyskawica*, with *Piorun* astern to starboard and followed by *Eskimo* with *Javelin* on her port quarter. Von Bechtolsheim mistook the first three ships for cruisers and signalled to his flotilla: 'I have three cruisers and one destroyer before me – *Glasgow* class'. A fierce gun duel developed in which the British ships once again hit the German hard, *Z32* receiving 16 to 20 hits as she fired starshell, launched four torpedoes from her after tubes and then laid smoke and zig-zagged away. *Blyskawica*, straddled by *Z32*'s reply, turned away to avoid torpedoes circling right round to starboard and then steered east-north-east, throwing the remainder of the division into confusion astern of her. *Piorun* lost visual contact with the leader and reduced speed to 20 knots, while *Eskimo* and *Javelin*, assuming the turn had been made to launch torpedoes, followed round, firing three and four torpedoes respectively and eventually forming up again astern of *Blyskawica*.

Z32, having successfully lost the 20th Division, turned back to the west, still unsure of the flotilla's situation. She then ran into *Tartar* and *Ashanti*, whereupon a third action developed in which she managed to hit the former, forcing her to slow down, issuing clouds of smoke, to fight the fires. *Z32* was hit three times. One in compartment III, a magazine space, caused a dangerous fire and necessitated flooding, whilst two other shells hit the main sickbay and flooded No. 5 pump-room; on the upper deck, the after tubes and No. 2 gun were hit and damaged. *Z32* then broke away to the east again to reload her tubes and bring up ammunition. *Ashanti* turned to starboard to engage *Z32*, but at that moment *ZH1* appeared out of the smoke, wallowing and helpless.

The burning *Tartar* appeared on the German destroyer's port quarter and was promptly engaged by both after guns, although without power the ammunition hoists were not operating, but *Ashanti*, from her position on *ZH1*'s port bow, torpedoed her, blowing off her bows as far as the breakwater. The forward gun nevertheless continued to engage, and her remaining four torpedoes were launched singly from the after tubes under local control, although without effect. Seeing that his ship was now beyond assistance, Korvettenkapitän Barkow gave orders for her to be scuttled as *Ashanti* continued firing from port; *ZH1* replied with her port Vierling as the torpedo offficer and the first lieutenant, Kapitänleutnant Rieger, went below to set the depth-charges for scuttling.

At 0240 hours *ZH1* exploded and sank. Of her complement, the captain, first lieutenant, engineer offficer and thirty-six seamen were lost, whilst one boat with the gunnery offficer, Oberleutnant zur See Hansen, and 27 men finally managed to reach the French coast; 140 others were rescued by the 14th Escort Group under the command of Commander Currie RN.

Z24 and *T24* continued to steam west-south-west, as this was the last course ordered by D8. This was now taking them further away from the scene of the action, but most of the communication systems aboard the destroyer had been wrecked so she could not contact her leader. On the bridge, nine men had been killed and the wheelhouse was in ruins. The charthouse was a bloodied mess, all the charts and many of the signal books having been destroyed, and four men had been killed in the radio room which was also damaged and on fire, with both long-wave and short-wave communications sets out of action. *Z24* had been struck by five shells from the British destroyers, and there had been many pom-pom hits. Korvettenkapitän Birnbacher had no clear idea where he was as his navigating staff attempted to plot a course on the only remaining chart in the darkness of the shattered wheelhouse; requests to *T24* for a position were not answered (although *T24* does not record receiving any request). During the run to the south-west, turbine noises were heard astern by the hydrophones. These issued from the Canadian destroyers *Haida* and *Huron* which were giving chase. The Canadians pursued for some time, until *Z24* and *T24* had crossed a minefield safely, but were then ordered back to join *Tartar*.

The action of 9.6.44

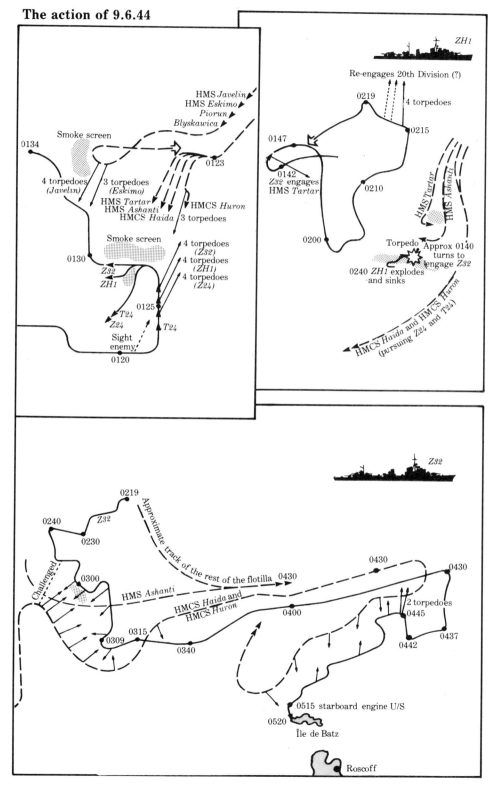

At 0239 hours the wayward pair were finally able to receive a signal from *Z32* which put the leader up to the north-east, and the two ships then reversed course to rejoin her. Sighting starshell in the distance, *Z24* turned west in order to range and then at last signalled her position to *Z32* with details of her damage and personnel losses and requested permission to detach to Brest. Von Bechtolsheim released the ships at 0420 but by then both were steaming away. By 0535 hours Birnbacher had turned over command to *T24* as he had no means of navigation, a decision which should have been taken very much earlier, and by evening *T24* and *Z24* were back in Brest.

Von Bechtolsheim, now alone with *Z32* and sadly concluding that he could probably not now continue his breakthrough to the east, was then sighted by the two Canadian destroyers, which were coming back to rejoin D10. Illuminating with starshell, the German destroyer was identified and a chase eastwards began with *Z32* working up to 31 knots. A British minefield barred her way, but she passed over it unscathed while *Haida* was forced to circumvent it, losing contact though regaining it twenty minutes later at a range of 10 miles. At 0430 hours *Z32* was still heading to pass between Jersey and Guernsey, with the Canadians 8 miles astern and the rest of their flotilla a further 12 miles behind. *Z32* now turned south-west, finally abandoning her breakthrough attempt, and fifteen minutes later starshell suddenly illuminated the sky and two 'cruisers with high superstructures' were sighted to starboard. *Haida* and *Huron* opened fire, forcing *Z32* to alter course away to the south.

By 0500 the Canadian ships were firing continuously and *Z32*, clearly, could no longer escape. A hit in the after turbine room slowed her down, and her forward turret received three heavy blows, knocking it out; she could now make only a feeble reply with No. 3 gun, using ammunition brought aft from the turret. She launched her last two serviceable torpedoes, and, since the torpedo davits had been destroyed and the last reserve torpedo could therefore not be loaded, she had now shot her bolt. At 0515 hours the starboard engine failed and, having fired the last of her ammunition, *Z32* was finished. Von Bechtolsheim ordered her CO, Korvettenkapitän von Berger, to run the ship ashore on the Ile de Batz and scuttle her. At 0520 the destroyer struck and for ten minutes was shot up by the Canadian ships before they withdrew, the crew finally being rescued by ships of the 2nd Vorpostenboot Flotilla later that morning.

FORMALLY DISSOLVED

This action destroyed the last major German force capable of damaging the invasion fleet. On the German side, FdZ, Konteradmiral Kreisch, was glowing in his praise of von Bechtolsheim, whom he described as brave, daring, experienced and resolute in his attempt to break through to

the Allied landing area. The captain of *Z24*, however, came in for some criticism over the handling of his part in the action, in particular over his failure to persevere and rejoin his flotilla leader, even though his action on breaking away under smoke after being hit was concurred with. Furthermore, considering the state of *Z24*, it was expected that he should have ordered *T24* to take over leadership much earlier than he did. Despite being outfought and outmanoeuvred, admittedly by a superior force, FdZ considered it a glorious page in the destroyers' story.

Naval Group West themselves had not been unaware of the slim chances of the remaining few destroyers making contact with the invasion fleet. Admiral Krancke recorded his thoughts on the losses: 'After the rapid transfer of the 8th Destroyer Flotilla from the south, enemy counter-measures had to be expected. The employment of four cruisers and six destroyers demonstrated the enemy's respect and his tactic of only attacking in overwhelming strength. The 8th Flotilla has fought courageously and the loss of two destroyers, whilst very painful, has been alleviated by the relatively high number of survivors rescued. The high risk was clear to me beforehand.' The over-estimation of the Allied forces was the result of identification errors aboard the destroyers.

The British, whilst pleased with the sinking of two enemy destroyers, considered the results unsatisfactory in view of the large expenditure of ammunition – in particular torpedoes, of which fourteen were fired for one hit. Torpedo drill was considered to be inadequate and on many an occasion British destroyers expended torpedoes as if they were two a penny for little return. The Canadian destroyers' performance had not improved since their action in April, when, with the cruiser *Black Prince*, sixteen

torpedoes were fired at German torpedo boats at ranges of between 450 and 2,700m without any hits, and similar results were evident with destroyers of the Eastern Fleet.

It was intended to salvage as much equipment as possible from *Z32* as she lay on the rocks, listing to starboard but outwardly intact, but the RAF arrived first. Twelve Beaufighters of No. 144 Squadron, each armed with two 250lb and two 500lb bombs, and twelve more aircraft from No. 404 Squadron RCAF armed with 60lb rocket projectiles, attacked the stranded ship on 9 June. It was No. 144 Squadron's first attempt at formation bombing, and from about 1,000m they landed the majority of their cargo on the midships section. No. 404 Squadron, in the absence of any opposition, split up into individual attacks and landed 65 known hits out of a possible 96, converting the destroyer to a shattered wreck while a Boston from Coastal Command HQ circled around taking photographs.

There now remained only *Z32* and *Z24* of the 8th Flotilla, whose effectiveness was further reduced by the destruction of the destroyers' ammunition dump at Jonzac by the French Resistance on 2 July. The former was in dock at La Pallice, while *Z24* required repairs following the action on 9 June. After completing repairs she again fell victim to air attack on 14 August whilst in the roads at Royan. Five rockets and some ninety 20mm hits damaged the turret traverse mechanism, both rangefinders, the radio equipment, one torpedo tube and a number of cabins, and the turret armour was shot through by a rocket. Further repairs were necessary in Bordeaux, using parts from *Z23* and *Z37*. Finally, on the 24th of the same month, whilst off Le Verdon with *T24*, she suffered yet another attack at the hands of Nos. 404 Squadron RCAF and 236 Squadron RAF. The aircraft, armed with rocket projectiles, had flown

inland south of the Gironde and then climbed up to the north where they surprised the ships. Despite putting up very heavy flak, *T24* was sunk. *Z24* received numerous hits but was able to crawl over to the quay, where the crew abandoned her; shortly afterwards she rolled over and sank.

On 12 August *Z23* was damaged in an air attack on La Pallice by fourteen Lancasters. A bomb fell just aft of the foremast, passed through the forward boiler room and exploded on the bed of the harbour; almost at the same moment another bomb fell to port alongside the bridge, hitting a workshop boat. No. 3 boiler room flooded, and No. 2 as well as a generator room began to flood also, cable and various other compartments being destroyed or damaged. The ship listed to port, unable to use her pumps until a supply was connected from shore. She was towed to a U-boat bunker four days later but, repair plainly being impossible, she was formally paid off on the 20th, when all equipment was destroyed. The following day she was handed over to the naval yard at La Pallice, where she remained until the surrender. With all its destroyers in western France lost, the 8th Flotilla now ceased to exist, and the unit was formerly dissolved on 25 August 1944.

Before returning north to discuss destroyer operations there during the final months of the war, the career of the one Mediterranean-based German destroyer must be mentioned. The vessel concerned was the former Greek *Vasilefs Georgios I*, a British-built 'H' class ship captured in damaged condition when the German armies took Greece and, after repairs, put into service by the Kriegsmarine as *ZG3*.

Under the command of Kapitän zur See Johannesson and later Fregattenkapitän Rechel, *ZG3* performed

admirable service, at first in the Aegean from June 1942 until the beginning of April 1943. Her main duty was convoy escort to and from Piraeus, Crete and the Dardenelles, with the occasional longer voyage to the North African coast. On 22 August 1942 she was named *Hermes* – the only German destroyer to receive a name during the war. In the course of a convoy escort between Piraeus and the Dardenelles on 16 November 1942, she detected a submarine which the escort vessel *Uj2102* subsequently sank; this proved to be the Greek *Triton*.

Hermes was transferred to the western Mediterranean in April 1943, arriving in Salerno on the 4th. Now under the command of Rechel, she operated with Italian destroyers, running troops and supplies to North Africa, minelaying, and escorting convoys. She became involved in another submarine hunt off Capri on 21 April when she detected and sank the British *Splendid*. Finally, as the Axis forces were being driven out of Tunisia, all available ships were being despatched with last-ditch reinforcements for the retreating army. *Hermes* embarked 350 troops and sailed from Salerno accompanied by the Italian *Pigafetta* and *Pancaldo* on the evening of 25 April, bound for Tunis.

The following day heavy air attacks developed, damaging *Pigafetta* and forcing the destroyers to return to Naples. A second attempt was made by *Hermes* on the 29th, this time accompanied by *Pancaldo* and *Lampo*. Once again, the massive Allied air superiority manifested itself, for on the 30th both Italian ships were sunk. *Hermes* was seriously damaged and lost all propulsion but was successfully towed into Tunis. Repairs proved impossible to complete, however, and in the face of the British advance the ship was towed to La Goulette where she was scuttled as a blockship on 7 May 1943.

12. NORWEGIAN SWANSONG: JANUARY 1943 TO MARCH 1945

The loss of *Eckoldt* reduced the number of Type 34 and 36 destroyers to six of the former and one of the latter, but in the event these would all survive hostilities; of the later classes, ten (*Z23–25*, *Z27–32* and *Z37*) remained afloat though not all were serviceable. The political repercussions of the 'Regenbogen' fiasco were finally to spell the end of the heavy surface forces of the Kriegsmarine, despite Grossadmiral Dönitz's success in obtaining the repeal of Hitler's 'scrap them' order, for the acute shortage of oil fuel and the dread of losing another ship dictated the policy of a 'fleet in being'. In practice, this meant months of inactivity, swinging to buoys or moored to piers in remote, inaccessible fjords far in the north of Norway, and the destroyers, required as they were to escort such heavy units as remained in the Arctic should any movements take place, suffered this enforced idleness along with the capital ships. As a consequence, the last two and a half years of the war produced little or no opportunity for real action.

Of the units left in Altafjord in early 1943, *Beitzen*, together with *Z29* and *Z30*, sailed south at the end of January, escorting the damaged *Hipper* and the light cruiser *Köln* back home to Germany, *Riedel* and *Z31* remaining in the far north for the time being, with *Galster*, *Z23* and *Z25* farther south of Tronheim. In the meantime, however, *Jacobi* and *Ihn* had now completed refits and were operational again at Gotenhafen in the eastern Baltic, where *Z32* and *Z37* were also working up, *Ihn* acting as flotilla leader with D6 (Kapitän zur See Schulze-Hinrichs) aboard.

Their next operation, another attempt to reinforce the heavy units in Norway, was code-named 'Fronttheater' and involved the return to the north of *Scharnhorst* and *Prinz Eugen*. *Jacobi*, *Ihn* and *Z24* sailed from Gotenhafen on 9 January, joining the two heavy units off the Hela minefields, and set course westwards with speed reduced to 18 knots in order to conserve fuel. On passage the destroyers formed two groups consisting of *Jacobi* and *Z24*, which oiled at sea from *Scharnhorst*, and *Ihn*, which was served by the heavy cruiser. This was not a wholly successful operation and resulted in some damage being sustained. Later, on the 11th, the squadron was sighted off the Skaw, by an aircraft of 18 Group RAF Coastal

Command at 1345 hours. The element of surprise being lost, Naval Group North ordered the breakthrough to be abandoned and the ships to return to Gotenhafen. The three destroyers, however, were ordered into the occupied Danish port of Aarhus to oil.

For some time the Germans had been aware of, and concerned over, the presence in Swedish ports of various vessels which were obviously awaiting an opportunity to break out to England with valuable cargoes of scarce alloys and ball bearings; now information had been received that two ships, *Lionel* and *Dicto*, then in Gothenburg, were about to sail. Schulze-Hinrichs was ordered to make for Kristiansand with his three ships, and he anchored off Marviken to await further instructions; the 9th VP Flotilla, meanwhile, watched the inshore waters on the Swedish coast. Between 15 and 18 January a line of five destroyers was strung across the entrance to the Skaggerak, with *Galster* under the Norwegian coast and *Z25* off the Danish shore, but no success was achieved and the only two merchant ships sighted were the German vessels *Kremhild* bound for Kristiansand from Stettin and *Pernambuco* for Standort. On 3 February *Jacobi*, *Steinbrinck*, *Z24* and *Z25* sailed from Kristiansand bound for Trondheim, being attacked en route by torpedo-carrying Hampden bombers of No. 455 Squadron RAF from Wick. Despite a skilfully executed attack, no torpedoes found their target and the destroyers reached Bergen safely during the afternoon. *Jacobi* continued northwards alone and by March was stationed in Bogen Bay, Narvik, with *Tirpitz*. *Steinbrinck*, whilst exercising at sea off Marstein with *U703* (Brünner), was hit by a practice torpedo, necessitating three days' repairs in dock at Bergen.

In southern Norway, *Beitzen* had arrived in Kristiansand for anti-blockade-runner duties early in February, having been detached from *Hipper*'s escort, but since no blockade-breakers were to be found, she was sent on convoy escort duty between that port and Aarhus. In the Baltic, meanwhile, a second attempt was being made to pass *Scharnhorst* to Norway, this time without *Prinz Eugen* (Operation 'Paderborn'). Steaming through the Skaggerak, the battlecruiser, escorted only by *Z28*, was joined by *Beitzen* off Aarhus on 6 March and by *Ihn* and *Steinbrinck*

Right: *Ihn* in Norwegian waters, with *Z28* in the background. (W. Z. Bilddienst)

off Kristiansand the following day, the torpedo boats *T16*, *T20*, *T21*, *Greif* and *Jaguar* also forming part of the escort. During the passage north the weather was atrocious and visibility poor, and the destroyers sustained a good deal of sea damage, *Beitzen* losing boats, rafts, dinghies, depth-charges and artificial smoke canisters overboard as well as sustaining machinery damage; *Steinbrinck* suffered short circuits and communication failures, and lost two men. The ships pressed on as far as Trondheim, though *Ihn* and the torpedo boats were forced to put into Bergen.

Z31 and *Riedel*, far to the north in Kaafjord, remained inactive during January, but on 4 February both sailed to escort the minelayer *Brummer* on Operation 'Bayern'. This was to be a mining sortie into the Kildin Roads, a focal point for shipping bound for Murmansk. On the morning of the following day, whilst off Nordkinn to the east of the North Cape, *Riedel* sighted three torpedo tracks approaching from port, but, ordering full ahead on the port engine and full astern on the starboard, she managed to avoid them. The torpedoes had been fired by the Soviet submarine *L20*. A little later, hydrophone noises were heard to port, and the destroyer turned, ran down their bearing and dropped two patterns of depth-charges but without obvious effect; returning to her escort duties, she turned over the hunt to a patrol vessel. In the course of the afternoon another contact was obtained, thought to be a diving submarine. *Z31* confirmed the target but no attack was made. By 2050 hours the Russian coast was in sight and an hour later the lay commenced. All the mines were dropped without incident, and shortly before midnight the squadron was on the way home again.

On the return journey, *Riedel* once again obtained a submarine contact whilst off Tanafjord and, warning *Z31* and *Brummer*, she turned on to its bearing, picking up an echo at 3,400m by S-Gerät; depth-charges were dropped, keeping the submarine down but not sinking her. Her CO, Fregattenkapitän Riede, appreciating the danger to

Brummer (which was only capable of 20 knots), was concerned that she and *Z31* were clearing the area too slowly and sent a signal hurrying them along, but after fifteen minutes' hunt contact was lost and the destroyer returned to course. Hardly had she been steadied on the new course than contact was regained; further depth-charges were dropped, which resulted in an oil slick coming to the surface. Seven minutes later, another torpedo was sighted to port, forcing the destroyer to alter course hard to starboard to avoid it.

To the destroyer's crew it must have appeared that the sea was full of submarines, for no sooner had the first torpedo been avoided than another, set too deep, passed under her bridge. She rejoined her group and continued towards Altafjord, obtaining three more contacts and dropping more depth-charges on the way. Off Oksafjord an underwater explosion was observed, the cause of which was unknown. During the afternoon of the 6th the weather deteriorated, driving snowstorms hindering navigation but effectively hiding the ships as well, so that Altafjord was reached without further incident in the evening.

Riede considered that the attacks during the homeward passage involved two submarines, and in fact the Soviet *K22* and *L20* were the boats in question. *K22* was lost at about this time, but her last signal was timed at 1900 hours on 7 February, so the likely cause of loss was mining.

STORM-TOSSED WATERS

Towards the middle of March *Tirpitz*, *Scharnhorst* and *Lützow* were escorted up from Narvik to Altafjord, which was to be the base of operations in northern waters, and with the heavy ships were *Jacobi*, *Riedel*, *Galster*, *Steinbrinck*, *Beitzen*, *Z28* and *Z31*. *Jacobi* was serving as leader for the 6th Flotilla, whilst aboard *Steinbrinck* was the new Captain (D5), Kapitän zur See Max-Eckart Wolff, who had been captain of *Thiele* at Narvik in 1940.

Lying in Langfjord, a branch of Altafjord, the destroyers were inactive during most of the month, but on the last day of March *Jacobi*, *Riedel* and *Galster* were required for an important task at sea. Germany was desperate for certain new materials to sustain her war effort, many of which could only be obtained from the Far East; with the Royal Navy's tight blockade it was possible to run only occasional German or Italian merchantmen into occupied Europe, and even this was becoming more and more difficult. Most of these blockade-runners made for western France, as was natural, but during March *Regensburg*,* which had sailed from Japan on 6 February 1943, was routed to Norway via the Denmark Strait. This ship had already made one round trip successfully between the Far East and Europe and was now on the first leg of her second. This northern route had not been used by the blockade-runners since 1939.

The three destroyers weighed from Kaafjord at 0800 hours on 31 March and proceeded via Stjernsund into the Lopphavet and the open sea. For their crews, many of whom were young, with little sea-going experience other than in the fjords and offshore waters, the sortie was to be a nightmare. At first all went well, and by midnight on the 31st the flotilla was some 300 miles north-west of the Lofoten Islands. Early the next morning the three destroyers formed line abreast and altered course to 219° at 18 knots in order to locate the blockade-runner. The weather was poor, and a Force 6 to 7 northerly wind was blowing, whipping the crests of the waves into white foam. It had soon veered north-north-east and increased 8 to 9 with the seas rising, compelling course to be reversed in order to stem the seas. Speed had to be reduced to 7 knots. By the forenoon, conditions were terrible, with very bad visibility and thick cloud. All the ships were rolling badly, awash, and the upper deck could be traversed only across the torpedo tubes. Except perhaps for the Vierlings it was impossible to fight any weapons.

Worse was to come, for by midnight the wind, now north-north-westerly, had risen to a tremendous storm, covering the mountainous seas in foam. There was ice on the decks and all the ships had suffered damage to superstructure and fittings as well as in the machinery spaces. The gun tubs were full of water from the violent rolling, and *Galster*'s stabilizer gear had become defective. It was impossible for the watchkeepers to maintain their footing, and in all the ships men were hanging on for grim death.

Throughout the morning and afternoon of the 2nd, the destroyers struggled through the storm-tossed waters, endeavouring to find an acceptable course. Below decks, stores, equipment and smashed crockery slid about in confusion. *Riedel* was further handicapped since the radio codes for April had not been brought aboard, an omission which resulted in a reprimand for her radio officer, and as a result she was unable to communicate effectively with the other ships. The continuing poor weather forced the abandonment of the search in the evening, and by 2015 hours all three ships were anchored in Narvik, having suffered serious damage from the heavy seas and lost boats, rafts and other topside gear. Cracks had appeared in the upper deck, and bulwarks and rails had stove in. It was all for nothing. *Regensburg* had been intercepted and sunk in the Denmark Strait on 30 March by the cruiser *Glasgow* (as a result of ULTRA Intelligence) without being able to get off a signal.

At the end of April *Beitzen* returned to Germany, but *Lody* and *Ihn* sailed north to replace her, joining *Jacobi*, *Riedel*, *Steinbrinck* and *Galster* up in the Arctic. Little activity took place. *Riedel* was nearly lost on 6 April when on passage from Narvik to Trondheim: first one boiler then another went out, and five hours later there was no steam on the turbines. The cause was water in the fuel, and she drifted helplessly towards the shore until a tug arrived to tow her into Trondheim.

On 10 October 1942 the 4th Destroyer Flotilla had been re-formed with *Z31*, *Z32* and *Z37*. The ships were under the command of von Berger since, of his seniors, Korvettenkapitän Langheld was sick ashore at Swinemünde and Korvettenkapitän Alberts in Norway with *Z31*. The flotilla, such as it was, worked-up in the Baltic until April 1943, during which time it was commanded successively by von Berger until 9 January, then Langheld until 6 February, and finally Fregattenkapitän Holtorf of *Z33* for a further two months until the proper Captain (D4), Kapitän zur See Johannesson, took up his post on 10 April. This switching of senior officers was cited by FdZ as an example of the personnel problems being experienced by the destroyer force in the fourth year of the war.

A SUITABLE 'SOFT' TARGET

On 10 April seven ships were allocated to the 4th Flotilla, but of these *Z32* and *Z37* had been detached to the 8th for service in France, *Z31* was with the 5th in Norway and *Z34* and *Z39* had not yet commissioned, leaving only *Z33* and *Z38*, both engaged in working-up in the Baltic. The flotilla had been ordered for duty in northern waters, but it was not until 22 July 1943 that the leader, *Z33*, sailed from Swinemünde accompanied by *Z29* bound for Norway, where they were joined by *Z31* in Altafjord.

The fuel shortage was becoming increasingly acute, forcing ships to lie idle in the cold, remote and inhospitable fjords. Morale suffered through boredom and the level of junior officers' and ratings' training deteriorated badly. Time at sea averaged only two days per month. The Naval High Command was not unaware of the problems, but the question was what to do about them. To restore morale with an operational success by half-trained crews required careful thought as to the target, but eventually a suitable 'soft' target was found and Operation 'Sizilian' scheduled.

*Disguised as MV *Cambridge* and armed with one 10.5cm; two 4cm and two MG.

This operation, which involved the largest Kriegsmarine sortie since the 'Channel Dash' of February 1942, was in reality using a sledgehammer to crack a walnut, for the target was Spitzbergen.

Spitzbergen, a small group of islands of which Vest Spitzbergen is the largest, lies some 400 miles north-north-west of the North Cape, at 79° N, 20° E. The islands belonged to Norway but their coal mines were worked by both Norwegian and Russian concerns. Until the entry of Russia into the war the islands had little strategic value, but after June 1941 the possibility of basing part of the Home Fleet there was considered, although after a visit by Rear-Admiral Vian in July 1941 the idea was adjudged not feasible. In August of that year the Norwegian and Russian miners were evacuated and the coal mines destroyed, leaving the islands to a small Norwegian garrison. Clandestine German weather-reporting parties landed from time to time, and the opponents engaged in a bizarre game of hide and seek across the frozen wastes in the hinterland. The Norwegian army's strength was only small and the islands' total defences consisted of three 3.7cm and four 2cm guns at Longyear, with one 10cm, one 5cm and two 2cm guns at Advent, but against this the Kriegsmarine prepared to send *Tirpitz* (eight 38cm guns), *Scharnhorst* (nine 28cm guns) and nine destroyers (all armed with five 15cm or 12.7cm guns). The disparity in the strength of the forces involved and the relative unimportance of the target leads to the natural conclusion that the exercise was purely one of morale-boosting.

The destroyers involved were drawn from all three flotillas then currently stationed in Arctic Norway, the 4th, 5th and 6th. The 4th, comprising *Z29*, *Z33* and *Z31*, was given the task of inshore fire support whilst the 5th (*Z27*, *Z30* and *Steinbrinck*) and 6th *(Galster, Riedel* and *Lody)* Flotillas were to land troops. Embarked aboard these six destroyers were 600 men of No. 349 Grenadier Regiment, approximately 100 to each ship; *Steinbrinck*, for example, carried one officer and ninety-one men and their equipment, including two assault boats and two inflatables. The duties allocated to the 6th Flotilla were not to the liking of Kapitän zur See Kothe, the flotilla commander: he complained, with some justification, that the 6th Flotilla had been longest in Arctic waters and he felt that, with opportunity for action so infrequent, his flotilla should have been given 'first option' to fire its guns in anger.

Under the command of Admiral Kummetz with his flag in *Tirpitz*, the squadron sailed from Altafjord on 6 September 1943. It was the last German squadron of any size to put to sea in the Second World War and it did so on the outward passage under the white ensign as a ruse. *Tirpitz* led *Scharnhorst*, with the 4th Flotilla to port, the 5th to starboard and the 6th stationed ahead. The outward passage was uneventful, except for a sudden 60° alteration of course (as a result of a report from *Tirpitz*'s hydrophones) and machinery breakdowns in *Lody*, and Spitzbergen's southern tip, Sörkapp, was sighted just after

midnight on the 8th. Steaming along the ice-shrouded coast of Jarlsberg Land, the squadron passed the mouth of Bellsund and, rounding Kap Linne, entered Isfjord at 0300 hours. Visibility was good in the pale twilight as the ships split up to head for their objectives. Both the towns, Barentsberg and Advent, lay on small fjords to the south of the main inlet, with Advent farthest east. Leaving *Scharnhorst* and the 5th and 6th Flotillas to land their troops at Gronsfjord and Advent, *Tirpitz* took the 4th Flotilla to shell Barentsberg.

Having landed their troops, *Galster* and *Riedel* were detached as A/S screen for *Tirpitz*, and *Lody* for *Scharnhorst*. *Lody*'s fuel consumption had been high, 50 per cent greater than her consorts, which necessitated her refuelling from the battlecruiser. *Galster* and *Riedel*, although not detached for bombardment duties, nevertheless opened fire to relieve their frustration. By 0955 it was all over, and Kummetz gave orders for the ships to reassemble. Coal mines and installations had been shelled as well as the shore batteries, but the latter had managed to hit *Z29*, *Z30* and *Z31* quite hard, inflicting a number of casualties. *Z29* received two 10.5cm hits in compartment IV, puncturing feedwater tanks and oil bunkers, and the destroyer had also been hit by automatic fire about the flak deck, killing a cadet officer and two men and wounding four others. *Z31* had received ten hits of various calibres in the hull, superstructure and funnels, damaging her bunkers, whilst *Z30* had been hit some thirty-six times and lost three men killed with twenty-five wounded. *Steinbrinck* had suffered flooding in compartment XIII as the result of a fractured fire main caused by her shooting.

The homeward passage was uneventful, save for a false submarine contact by *Steinbrinck*. Bear Island was passed in the early hours of the 9th, and by late afternoon the squadron was back in Altafjord. Five weeks later, the Norwegian bases were re-established by the Allies.

'SCATTERED TO THE FOUR WINDS'

At the end of September the British midget submarine attack on *Tirpitz* took place (Operation 'Source'). The destroyers played no real part, although those near the battleship kept both 3.7cm mountings and a searchlight manned; hydrophone watch was also maintained. The following day the 5th Flotilla was withdrawn from Arctic waters and sailed for home, escorting the heavy cruiser *Lützow*. *Steinbrinck*, *Jacobi* and *Z27* accompanied her into the Baltic, where they arrived in Kiel on 29 September. *Ihn* was detached to Kristiansand but later returned to Narvik.

In the Baltic, *Beitzen*, which had been undergoing major refit at Swinemünde since May, was at last ready for sea again and ordered to Norway, but whilst on passage to Bergen in company with *Z28* she ran heavily aground in Karmsund, north of Kopervik, in the early hours of 27 October. Nos. 2 and 3 boiler rooms were put out of service and the main feed pumps damaged. It was adjudged an error on the part of her CO, Korvettenkapitän Dominik, and the navigator, but her flotilla commander nevertheless recorded that he was saddened by the incident since *Beitzen* had been with the flotilla for a long time.

By the beginning of November 1943 the 5th Flotilla had effectively ceased to exist: of its members, *Steinbrinck* was attached to the 6th Flotilla, *Ihn* had been ordered home to refit, *Beitzen* was aground and *ZH1* was 1,600 miles away, serving with the 8th Flotilla in western France. Captain (D5), Max-Eckart Wolff, plaintively recorded in his war diary that his flotilla was scattered to the four winds and that he no longer had any ships. *Ihn* actually sailed south from Narvik on 6 November in company with *Galster* (6th Flotilla), which was also going home to refit. Steaming via Ålesund and Kristiansand, the two ships made Kiel shortly before midnight a week later, *Ihn* landing her ammunition and passing through the Kiel Canal to Hamburg, arriving at the Blohm und Voss yard on 15 November. The refit was scheduled to last five months, the planned completion date being 15 April 1944. *Galster* followed, but proceeded down the Elbe, around to the Weser and up to the Deschimag yard for her refit.

Meanwhile *Beitzen* was finally refloated during the evening of 5 November and towed to Hagesund Wharf to effect the necessary temporary repairs. By the 23rd she was sufficiently seaworthy to proceed to Bergen, where there were more extensive dockyard facilities to patch her up for the passage back to Germany. The weather turned, however, and it was not until the 26th, after anchoring at Larvik, that she was eventually docked in Bergen. The repairs required were considerable, and it was only on 18 December that she was able to leave for home. Steaming slowly down the Norwegian coast and around the Skaw, she passed through the Skaggerak and Kattegat and then proceeded eastwards to Swinemünde, arriving there on Christmas Eve 1943. Here she lay until 10 January, when she was moved over to the Stettiner Oderwerke yards. Her entry into dock was delayed by its being occupied by the minelayer *Ostmark*, which would not be clear until the 15th. It was fortunate, too, that an air raid on the port of Stettin on the night of the 6th had not seriously damaged the yards, so that the destroyer was eventually able to dock on the 17th. The repairs were estimated to cost RM500,000.

Beitzen was out of action until June 1944, but further machinery defects then delayed her return to service and it was not until 5 August that she was eventually operational once more. On completion she sailed from Gotenhafen bound for Norway, but trouble continued to dog her for a fire broke out in No. 1 boiler room and turbine on the way. This having been dealt with, the unlucky ship finally managed to rejoin her flotilla on the 8th after an absence of nine months.

Returning once more to the torpedo boats, *T14* arrived in Cuxhaven on 5 November 1943, the last Type 35/37 ship

to be based in France; *T20* and *T21* having been withdrawn from Norway at the beginning of September, none of this class were now outside the Baltic. The reason for this was the pressing need to train large numbers of torpedo officers for U-boat duties, for which task these fast offensive craft were, surprisingly, to be used. By the end of November 1943 nine were directly attached to the Torpedo School in Travemünde (*T4, T5, T7, T9–11, T14, T20* and *T21*) and four more to the 23rd and 24th U-boat Training Flotillas (*T16* and *T18, T15* and *T17* respectively); *T13* was attached to the torpedo experimental establishment and five more (*T1, T2, T8, T12* and *T19*) were in dockyard hands. The use of these ships for this purpose was extravagant and wasteful, for in three weeks of torpedo firings 8,100 tonnes of precious oil would be used. The selection of these boats for the task may have been made because of their weak gun armament, which was a drawback in Channel sorties, and it is probably significant that the older but better-armed Type 24 ships were left operational.

In fairness, it must be said that plans had been made to use the ubiquitous coal-fired M40 class minesweepers for this task, equipped with two single torpedo tubes on the forecastle, but the first, *M371*, was not due in service until 15 November 1943; even then delays to the programme were occurring, with the result that the boat did not finally commission until a month later. Fifteen such conversions were planned: twelve were delivered by the end of 1944 but the final three were never completed.

December proved to be a fateful month for the torpedo boats although it was one which began well. On the 1st, the 6th Flotilla was re-formed under the command of Korvettenkapitän Koppenhagen with the new ships *T28, T29* and *T30*, and then on 12 December *T3* was recommissioned at Danzig for the 2nd Flotilla after her salvage in 1941. The following day, during an air raid on Kiel (by 171 B17s of the USAAF's 1st Bomb Division), *T15*, lying in the Deutscher Werke yard, was hit amidships

Below: *Z39* in Norway in 1944. Note that this class carried seaboats at davits on the forecastle and dispensed with the heavy boat boom. (Archiv Gröner)

and sank. Efforts were put in hand to salvage her, and to avoid losing a trained crew the seaman division was sent to the new *T32* and the technical division to *T33*. A further, greater disaster occurred on the 28th, when *T25* and *T26* were lost in the Bay of Biscay during the action with *Glasgow* and *Enterprise* (see Chapter 11).

In November 1943 the Naval Command in Norway decided to send the surviving Types 34 and 34A destroyers home because they lacked the radius of action of the larger Type 36A and also on account of the poor condition of *Steinbrinck*'s machinery (see Chapter 2). Accordingly, the 6th Flotilla was withdrawn from Arctic Norway, and Kothe sailed from Narvik on 25 November with *Lody* and *Steinbrinck*. Later that night a small Norwegian steamer, *Samev*, was sighted on a collision course with *Steinbrinck*. Emergency full speed astern was quickly rung down and all watertight doors closed, but two minutes later the destroyer, which had way on for 12 knots, collided with the steamer near the Blaabackfua Light, badly damaging her bows around compartments XV and XIV, flooding the anti-gas defence store and causing leaking at frame station 103, to reduce the effects of which the ship was trimmed down at the stern by flooding some of the after tank spaces. After the damaged area had been shored up the crippled destroyer managed to crawl off shortly before midnight, making for Trondheim, but speed had very quickly to be reduced because of the danger of bulkhead XIV collapsing.

During passage the weather worsened, with poor visibility, rain and snow showers forcing the ship to anchor in Rorvik until conditions improved. It was estimated that repairs would take about three weeks but that they could be carried out locally by the repair ship *Kamerun* which was based at Narvik. It was expected that *Steinbrinck* would be serviceable again by Christmas Eve, and after being temporarily patched up she sailed for Oslo where full repairs were carried out in the Nylandswerf yard. These repairs were completed sooner than expected, for by 18 December the destroyer was able to leave for Germany, although she did not return to full operational status until 12 January 1944.

Jacobi, under refit at Germaniawerft in Kiel, was badly damaged by the US Eighth Air Force during a daylight raid on the port early in the afternoon of 13 December. Between 1215 and 1400 hours seven bombs fell close to the ship, then in dry dock, one striking the forecastle on the starboard side and four others landing in the dock itself, exploding close to the port bow, on the port and starboard quarters and abreast the starboard side; two bombs exploded just outside the dock, whilst two further bombs fell nearby but failed to detonate. All sections of the ship received shock and splinter damage, but it was the direct hit which naturally caused the most extensive damage. Lighting, heating, steam and fire mains were destroyed and a serious fire raged in the forward compartments. Below decks, the fires in compartment XII filled the fore-ends with dense black smoke. The heat was intense, preventing

fire-fighting crews from entering compartments XI and XIII and making the upper deck red hot. Of the two gangways to the docked destroyer, one had been destroyed and the second completely wrecked, thus preventing rescue and fire parties getting aboard. One of the POs, however, managed to repair one gangway at great danger to life and limb. Fire-fighting crews and equipment from the dockyard and the nearby *Riedel* were rushed aboard, but the flames were finally brought under control only after a nine-hour battle. The damage sustained during this air raid was serious, considerably delaying the ship's completion, and she was not refloated until April 1944. It was November before she returned to service.

Lody, having now also moved south, was based at Horten in Oslofjord for duties in the Skaggerak. Joined by *Riedel* and *Z31*, she carried out escort, minelaying and anti-blockade-breaker duties during November and early December 1943. It was known to the Germans that fast converted torpedo boats were being used to run valuable cargoes of ball bearings from neutral Sweden through the Skaggerak to Britain, and in fact one of these craft, *Master Standfast*, had been captured by the patrol vessel *V1606* in the area on 2 November. One of her sisters, *Gay Corsair*, as well as the merchant vessels *Dicto*, *Lionel* and *Pacific Empress*, was known to be in the Swedish port of Lysekil in January 1944 and expected to be ready for sailing. During this month *Steinbrinck* returned to her flotilla, bringing its strength back up to four units.

Early in December 1943 *Riedel* had sailed home to Germany to refit, so that when *Steinbrinck* had returned to service she and *Lody* were the only operational destroyers out of the seven survivors of the two pre-war classes. During the first five months of 1944 the two ships laid minefields to defend the entrance to the Skaggerak, escorted *Ostmark*, *Elass* and *Kaiser* as well as the cruiser *Leipzig* on minelaying duties, and also escorted convoys to and from Norway. Working-up was continued during this time, including exercises with the 1st S-boat Training Flotilla, whose six craft had moved to Norway to perfect attack and defence tactics against MTBs. By the end of April both ships were recalled home to refit, *Lody* at the Germania yard in Kiel and *Steinbrinck* at Blohm und Voss in Hamburg.

The bombing by the RAF at night and by the USAAF by day had, by this time, seriously disrupted factories and communications all over Germany, with the result that firm completion dates for refits could no longer be given – indeed, a ship was lucky if she were not destroyed or at the very least damaged whilst in her yard. *Steinbrinck* passed through the Kiel Canal on 3 May 1944 en route to Hamburg, and on the same day *Lody* began her refit at Bremen. This was virtually the end of active service for both destroyers, since refit completion dates slipped back so much that *Lody* finally managed to become serviceable once more only on 18 February 1945. Thereafter, despite the desperate situation in East Prussia, she was engaged in

working-up and post-refit trials in the Baltic until early April. Battleworthy once more, she proceeded through the Kattegat and was employed on convoy escort duties in the Skaggerak for the remaining days before the final German collapse.

Steinbrinck was rather more unfortunate. Shortly after she had begun her dockyard time Hamburg suffered a heavy air attack by the USAAF during the morning of 18 June 1944 in which the destroyer received a bomb hit in the diesel generator room and suffered other damage affecting diesel engines, electric motors, circulating, condenser, fuel oil feed and bilge pumps, boiler room fans and telegraphs and communication facilities. However, despite all difficulties, it was reported to Captain (D5) during October that the scheduled completion date of 20 November should be met, and towards the end of that month all three destroyers undergoing major refits (*Lody*, *Jacobi* and *Steinbrinck*) were re-allocated to the 8th Destroyer Flotilla for administrative purposes. Unfortunately for *Steinbrinck*, fate took a hand in matters again.

The morning of 4 November was calm and clear with good visibility. At 1120 hours an air raid alert sounded in the port, and the ship's company, with the exception of gun crews and essential watchkeepers, went ashore into the Blohm und Voss shelters. Bombs from US aircraft fell all over the port, 1,030 tons in all, causing much devastation and sinking many ships. One landed 6–10m away from the starboard side of the destroyer abreast compartment IV, throwing mud and filthy water all over the ship. A barge alongside quickly sank and No. 1 turbine room was flooded. Shore power had been cut, stopping all the pumps, with the result that a list of 5° soon developed, although the ship's engineers did manage to start a diesel generator and get the pumps working again. Nevertheless, the water damaged many electrical fittings and equipment; furthermore, a good deal of damage had been caused by the shock of the explosion itself. No casualties had been incurred by the ship's company, but a survey made it quite evident that *Steinbrinck*'s completion would now be long delayed, possibly until March 1945. Temporary repairs were made and the leaks patched up until she was watertight enough to be towed down river and around the coast to the Norddeutsche Lloyd yard at Wesermünde for further work, but it was not until 1 April 1945 that she was anything like seaworthy again, and even then she had only one engine serviceable.

By the middle of April, *Steinbrinck* having moved down-river to Cuxhaven, the situation in Germany was obviously desperate and the supplies of fuel oil almost non-existent, what little there was available being allocated to those units which were still battleworthy and employed in supporting the retreating German armies in the Baltic coastlands or rescuing the millions of refugees fleeing west from the advancing Russians. Consequently *Steinbrinck* was immobilized and many of her officers and men drafted ashore to fight last-ditch battles on land. The surrender found her still there, her new flak outfit untried and with D8, Kapitän zur See Gerlach, and his staff aboard.

A NIGHTLY OCCURRENCE

In southern Norway *Beitzen*, *Galster*, *Riedel*, *Ihn* and *Z30* continued to be based at Horten for the remainder of 1944, employed on convoy escort and minelaying duties, *Ihn* and *Riedel* having only returned to operational service in June following refits. Before leaving the Baltic, *Riedel*, for some unaccountable reason, had been involved in trials with the Fa 339 'Bachstelze' (Wagtail). This was an observation gyrokite which had been issued in limited numbers to U-boats employed in remote areas to improve their range of surface vision. The kites, towed by the U-boats, were unpopular and could only be employed where air attack was unlikely. What *Riedel* was doing at this time is not clear. During August *Ihn* and *Beitzen* ferried personnel of the UAS (Anti-Submarine Training School) and escorted the U-boat of FdU (Mitte) when U-boat training was transferred to Norway from the Eastern Baltic. Misfortune continued to dog the destroyers, for, again in August, *Riedel* suffered a serious fire in No. 1 boiler room, caused by oil-soaked insulation material being left in the bilges during her last refit and necessitating a long repair period at the Akerswerk yard in Oslo.

Continual guard had to be maintained against sabotage. Oil tanks and airfield installations ashore were frequently being set on fire by resistance groups, and on 26 September the partially completed ex-Norwegian torpedo boat *TA7* was damaged.[*] To ensure that his destroyers were on their toes in this respect Captain (D5), Kapitän zur See Langheld, made surprise visits to each, but was satisfied by the results.

The general state of training was poor, owing mainly to oil fuel shortages. Scientists in Germany were attempting to synthesize fuels but with no real degree of success. *Jacobi*, having completed her refit, was running trials between Stettin and Swinemünde at the end of October using fuel produced from pitch, but combustion problems were encountered. The other major worry was air attack. RAF Mosquitoes and Beaufighters were present in ever-increasing numbers and it was surprising that so few positive results were obtained. Scores of attacking aircraft would appear over Oslofjord even before the alert had sounded, much to the disgust of the ships' companies. Repairs to damaged ships in Norway posed considerable problems in obtaining spares and replacements from Germany, where industrial output had been hard hit, and this naturally affected the length of repair periods, in particular that of *Riedel*.

The month of October saw intensive minelaying and convoy operations in the Skaggerak by the 5th Flotilla, and in the course of one of the latter *Z30* was seriously

*The construction party standing by *TA7* at KMW Horten was finally disbanded on 6 November 1944.

damaged. She had been escorting a convoy when, on 20 October, at the entrance to Oslofjord in a driving snowstorm, she struck a mine. The explosion, which occurred at her stern, destroyed the after compartment, put the port engine out of action, jammed the starboard shaft, caused shock damage to the starboard turbine and knocked out many other pieces of equipment. *Ihn* and *Uj1702* stood by the crippled destroyer as *Beitzen* was sent out as a flak escort and two tugs were ordered out from Horten. *Ihn* took *Z30* in tow but the task proved very difficult as the mined ship's rudder had jammed hard to port. Langheld took *Galster* out to supervise the tow back into Horten, and by early afternoon he was aboard *Z30* inspecting the damage whilst *Beitzen* took off her wounded and transferred them to Horten. Of *Z30*'s company, eight had been killed, sixteen were badly wounded and three were missing. For the destroyer, it was the end of her active service: despite being docked in Oslo on the 26th, she remained there, her repairs unfinished, until May 1945.

Both *Beitzen* and *Riedel* were damaged by grounding again in November, whilst *Ihn* moved to Swinemünde for a brief refit, returning in December with an augmented flak armament. All the Type 34 and 36 survivors were now nominally in the 5th Flotilla. At the close of 1944 *Beitzen*, *Riedel*, *Ihn* and *Galster* were based at Horten for duties in the Skaggerak, whilst *Jacobi* was working-up in the Baltic; *Lody* and *Steinbrinck* were under refit. Also operating in this area was the 3rd Torpedo Boat Flotilla which nominally consisted of *T13*, *T14*, *T16*, *T17*, *T19*, *T20* and *T21*, but of these *T14* was on post-refit work-up at Pillau and *T21* under major overhaul at Schichau's Elbing yard.

At the beginning of 1945 only *Galster* and *Ihn* of the four destroyers stationed in southern Norway were operational. The chaotic situation in Germany at this period extended even the simplest refit. *Galster* had had to be sent to Frederikshavn at the beginning of December 1944 to obtain a new shaft for *Beitzen*, but, as a result of difficulties in installing it, it was not until 14 February 1945 that the destroyer was fit for operations again. *Riedel*'s problems, too, had received much attention from the flotilla's technical staff and from Kapitän zur See Langheld himself; she was finally operational again on 7 January.

The ships continued their convoy escort duties in the Skaggerak until the end of the war, but the scale of air attacks escalated greatly and only *Galster* and *Ihn* had received augmented flak armament. During the last four months of the war anti-shipping strikes were being flown across the Skaggerak and Kattegat by the 2nd Tactical Air Force (RAF), Coastal Command, the USAAF and the Fleet Air Arm in both day and night sorties. On 13 January *Ihn* and *Riedel*, in company with *T19* and *T20* and escorting *Nürnberg* and *Linz* on a minelaying operation, were caught by Halifax 'F' of No. 58 Squadron RAF in the Skaggerak and bombed. The six 500lb (227kg) bombs fell a little astern of *Ihn* and caused no damage; the aircraft escaped unharmed. On 2 March the 9,026-ton freighter *Isar*,

escorted by *Beitzen* on passage from Oslofjord to the Kattegat, was attacked by Halifax 'K' of No. 502 Squadron RAF. The merchant ship, with a damaged rudder, was stopped and *Beitzen* approaching her when the attack was made, and two bomb hits set *Isar* on fire. She later sank.

These attacks had become a nightly occurrence as the convoys ran the gauntlet across the Skaggerak, but it was not until April that one of the escorts was seriously hit.

On the night of the 2/3 April 1945, *T13*, *T16* and *T17*, together with the armed trawler *VS902* were escorting the transport *Hansa I* between the Danish port of Aarhus and Moss in Norway when, in the early hours of the 3rd, they were attacked by six or seven Halifax bombers of 52 and 502 Squadrons RAF. At this time the convoy was close to the Swedish coast, west of Gothenburg. At 0145/3 Halifax R/502 (Flight Lieutenant Davenport) aimed a stick of seven 500lb MC bombs at *T16*, the first of which landed about 10 metres off her port quarter, whilst the remainder overshot. The near-miss detonated underwater, some 6 to 7 metres from the ship abreast the port turbine room, blowing a large hole in the plating. The hull whipped and a 50mm-wide crack formed across the deck and extended 2m down the ship's side. All radar equipment was destroyed, the top mast broken off and the shafts distorted. *T17* stood by the cripple whilst the remainder of the escort shepherded *Hansa I* into Frederikshavn. The port turbine room had flooded immediately and other spaces began to take water. The starboard turbine room flooded slowly but the pumps held it under control as she proceeded on one engine into Frederikshavn at 10 knots, where she was eventually secured in a shallow water berth. Temporary repairs were made by the expedient of welding stringers of railway lines and flat strips in the way of the crack aft, but the ship was never again seaworthy and was paid off on 13 April.

Hansa I herself survived only a short while longer. On the night of 9/10 April, she was proceeding northwards in the Kattegat loaded with U-boat stores and escorted by *T13* and *F7*. In an attack by Halifax bombers of 58 Squadron RAF south-east of Laeso Island, both the merchantman and *T13* were sunk in the early hours of the 10th.

There was further misfortune for the 3rd Flotilla a few days later when the merchantman *Preussen* reported torpedo tracks whilst off the entrance to the Kattegat about midway between Lysekil and Skaggen. Her escort, *T17*, immediately obtained a contact and counter-attacked with depth-charges, producing unmistakeable evidence of a kill. Unluckily this was *U235* on passage to Norway. All A/S attacks were in fact prohibited in this area, unless ships were clearly attacked first. The 'tracks' were probably foam strips on the water caused by the snorkel. There were no survivors from the U-boat, which was an unlucky one, having been sunk once before by bombs in Kiel only to be raised and recommissioned.

On the night of the 23rd/24th, *Beitzen* and *T19* were escorting a north-bound convoy from Frederikshavn to

Oslo when, at 0335 hours, one of the seven radar-equipped bombers roaming the Kattegat that night located the ships. Which aircraft carried out the attack cannot be precisely determined from RAF records, and the German paperwork system had by this time broken down, but four aircraft, 'F', 'J', 'U' and 'X', of No. 58 Squadron and three from 502 Squadron ('H', 'S' and 'T') were on sorties in the Kattegat on the night in question: two, J/58 and X/58, were shot down while preparing to attack, while U/58 and T/502 made no run, and it thus appears likely that it was F/58, H/502 or S/502 that was responsible. *Beitzen* bore the brunt of the onslaught, her No. 1 boiler room and diesel generator room being put out of action. The hull was holed in compartment VII, causing flooding, the starboard side suffered shock and splinter damage, and the double bottom was ruptured in several places. She was still able to make 15 knots, however, and managed to remain with the convoy to Oslo, where she was docked for repairs. The end was not far off for the Third Reich, and not surprisingly it proved impossible either to obtain spares from the home dockyards (British forces were already at the gates of Bremen) or to get the Norwegians in the yard to expedite the repairs, and in consequence *Beitzen* remained non-operational at the surrender and in fact never again became seaworthy.

DUMMY MESSAGES

Following the withdrawal of the 5th and 6th Flotillas only the 4th, with *Tirpitz* and *Scharnhorst*, remained in Arctic waters by December 1943. Then, when *Scharnhorst* sailed on what was to be her last sortie, on 25 December, the flotilla (Z29, Z30, Z33, Z34 and Z38) accompanied her but, having been detached to search for the target convoy, never again regained contact with the battlecruiser. *Scharnhorst* was sunk by *Duke of York*, cruisers and destroyers on the evening of the 26th in an action in which the German destroyers took no part.

Throughout 1944 the flotilla remained with the crippled *Tirpitz*, largely inactive. *Z31* returned to Arctic waters early in May, but Z30 left a few days later to serve with the 5th Flotilla in the Skaggerak. During the summer and into the autumn the destroyers were stationed close to the battleship and took part, sometimes sustaining damage, in her flak defence in the course of the numerous air attacks which were launched during this period. By October the Soviet armies had begun to push against the Arctic front, causing withdrawals by the German forces. The destroyers covered these operations and the evacuations of the few Arctic strongholds until Christmas 1944, when Z29 returned home to refit. Her four consorts remained in Tromsö until January 1945, when the flotilla was ordered home for service in the Baltic. Z31, Z34 and Z38 sailed from Tromsö for the last time on 25 January 1945 and steamed southwards for Narvik, thus ending the destroyers' three and a half years' association with the Arctic.

The move south by the flotilla became known to British Naval Intelligence through 'Ultra' intercepts when *Z33*, then lying in Bogen Bay, Narvik, with defects, was ordered on 24 January to transmit dummy messages on 317kc/s for the next few days, the object being to cover the 4th Flotilla's absence. Two possibilities were envisaged by the British, a passage down the sheltered inner leads or a high-speed run south outside the leads. Against that latter course the Admiralty ordered Admiral Dalrymple-Hamilton, in command of the 10th Cruiser Squadron in Scapa Flow, to sail with *Diadem* and *Mauritius* to a point near Bergen and then sweep northwards. Both cruisers cleared the boom at Scapa early in the afternoon of the 27th and steamed north-eastwards, then, in the evening, eastwards, towards their designated position.

In the meantime the 4th Flotilla continued its passage south, having been unsuccessfully bombed whilst west of Sognefjord on the evening of the 27th. At 0048 hours the following morning, when the flotilla was some fifteen miles southwest of Utvar Light, north of Bergen, both sides sighted each other almost simultaneously. Firing starshell for illumination, the cruisers opened fire on the destroyers at a range of about 20,000m (12½ miles). A brief parallel fight now developed, during which Z31 was heavily hit by between five and seven shells which destroyed her forward turret, damaged her steering motor compartment and wrecked the hydrophone compartment and torpedo transmitting station. The upper decks and superstructure were riddled with splinters and shell holes and the degaussing equipment was destroyed, whilst fires caused serious casualties to her crew. Z34 took over leadership, making three torpedo attacks on the cruisers in an effort to disengage. Z38 turned to attack also, but with a funnel fire and tube bursts in her boilers she was forced to break off.

Laying smoke, the three destroyers reversed course and ran northwards for the shelter of the Norwegian coast, pursued by the cruisers, which had successfully avoided their torpedoes. During the run north the destroyers' after guns continued to engage, hitting first *Mauritius* on the port side forward, the shell exploding in a mess deck without casualties, and six minutes later *Diadem*, hit on the boat deck amidships, causing some slight damage, killing one man and wounding three others. By 0200 hours the destroyers' superior speed had allowed them to pull ahead and gain the shelter of Aspofjord, where shore batteries opened fire on the cruisers at 0214. Seeing that the enemy had escaped, the two cruisers turned away, ceased fire and retired to Scapa Flow. The three destroyers steamed south again to Bergen, where Z31 was docked; Z34 and Z38 continued to Germany, reaching Kiel on 1 February.

Z33 left Narvik on 5 February to join Z31 but was bombed off Stadlandet four days later and towed into Trondheim. *Z31*, after temporary repairs in Oslo, finally reached Gotenhafen on 20 March 1945. Z33 did not reach Germany again until 2 March 1945, when she arrived in Swinemünde from Aarhus. There were now no longer any destroyers based in Norway outside the Skaggerak.

13. ECLIPSE: JANUARY 1944 TO MAY 1945

From 1939 until 1943 the Baltic Sea had become virtually a German lake, used extensively for training as well as the supply of stores and equipment for the armies fighting on the Leningrad front. Large mine barrages across the Gulf of Finland and the entrance to Kronstadt Bay prevented all Soviet surface ships and all but a very few submarines from breaking out into the open sea (and then not until late in 1944). In consequence there was no call for destroyers in this theatre and minesweepers and torpedo boats sufficed. The smaller torpedo boats continued to be employed on subsidiary duties, and even as late as the end of March 1944 twelve were still attached to the Torpedo School (*T2, T3, T7, T8, T9, T11* and *T12* of the 2nd Flotilla and *T13, T17, T19, T20* and *T21* of the 3rd); one other boat was

engaged on torpedo trials, whilst five more were in dockyard hands. Of the larger units, *T30* was operational with Naval Command East and *T31* working-up, but those vessels attached to the Torpedo School were occasionally released for duties in the Skaggerak or eastern Baltic when torpedo firing was not taking place.

By 1944, however, things were changing, for in January the Soviets had pushed back the German Army to Narva and Lake Peipus, making the maintenance of the mine barrages even more important. To assist in this task the 6th Destroyer Flotilla, under Kapitän zur See Kothe and now consisting of *Z28, Z39, Z25* and *Z35*, with *T30* attached, was ordered to Reval for duties with Flag Officer (Minelayers) East. They were ordered to proceed from the

Below: *Z28* at Gotenhafen in February 1945. (Archiv Gröner)

Skaggerak at low speed to conserve fuel and arrived in Gotenhafen on 16 February; *Z28* arrived in Reval on 21 February.

Until mid-March convoy duties were undertaken between Reval and Libau, and then the first offensive operation was planned. This was a two-part sortie, comprising first a bombardment of Vaikula and Saarkula on the eastern shore of Narva Bay, north of Hungerburg, on 12 March, and secondly a mine lay there during that night. Minelaying continued to be the major task throughout the spring and summer of 1944, as the flotilla was based variously at Reval and Baltischport.

June found the flotilla at full strength, with *Z28*, *T30*, *Z39*, *Z35* and *Z25* at Baltischport. *T31* was scheduled to join, but she was sunk by Soviet MTBs in the course of repelling Russian attacks in Viborg Bay and Kovisto Sound on 20 June. In a fiercely fought, close-quarters engagement, *T30* and *T31* claimed three to five MTBs sunk before losing *T31* to a torpedo from *TKA37*. *Z39* was bombed by Soviet aircraft on 23 June whilst at anchor in Baltischport, suffering two hits in the region of the after funnel which destroyed most of the flak deck and wrecked pipe work and fans in the forward turbine room and after boiler room. The damage was such that the destroyer was forced to return to Germany for repairs. Further bombing losses occurred when *T2* and *T7*, in the Deschimag yard at Bremen, were sunk during a heavy air raid on the 29th. Salvage operations were put in hand and *T2* raised; she was towed to Elbing early in November for repair but was towed back west again, untouched, before that port was captured in 1945.

In the Gulf of Finland efforts to contain the Soviet fleet continued, mainly by using that well-tried Baltic weapon, the mine. The minefields in the southern sector of the inner barrage (i.e., those in Narva Bay) were known by the code-name 'Seeigel' and had originally been laid by the minelayers *Kaiser* and *Roland* together with the minesweepers of the 3rd Flotilla in May 1942, having been reinforced at various times in 1943 and 1944 by destroyers, torpedo boats, minesweepers and landing craft. However, at the present time there were no destroyers available to the officer commanding 9th Security Division, who was responsible for its maintenance, and therefore when it became suspected that Soviet minesweepers had forced a passage through the 'Seeigel' field in August 1944 his forces available consisted of the 6th Torpedo Boat Flotilla (*T30*, *T32* and *T22*) and *T23* of the 5th, with, in addition, the boats of the 1st R-boat Flotilla. In the event, the R-boats were withdrawn from the operation owing to weather conditions.

The field was to comprise four rows totalling 216 mines laid at a depth of 1m. Two types were to be sown, UMB (anti-submarine mine Type 'B') and EMR(K), a minefield protection buoy, each torpedo boat carrying 23 EMR(K)s and 31 UMBs. It was originally intended that the R-boats would lay another four rows with twelve EMR(K)s in each. In each torpedo boat row the mine dropping interval was to be 175m, and the intended position of the field was from 59° 31.3' N, 27° 34.6' E to 59° 35.5' N, 27° 29.5' E, on a line of 329°. Laying speed was to be 15 knots and radio silence was to be maintained with minimum use of the short-wave R/T. Details were also given of friendly forces at sea in the area, these including two U-boats, *U479* (Oberleutnant zur See Sons) and *U679* (Oberleutnant zur See Breckwoldt). No Finnish boats were at sea. For navigational purposes a searchlight on the island of Gross Tutters would flash four times every twenty minutes between 2330 and 0230 hours; in addition, a searchlight at Valaste would also burn up to 0130 hours, between 290° and 0°.

DOUBLE DETONATIONS

During 16 August and the early part of the following day the forces concerned assembled for Operation 'Seeigel Xb' in the south bay at Helsinki and loaded mines from the tender *Kondor*. At 1837 hours on the evening of the 17th the four torpedo boats weighed anchor and steamed eastwards through the islands under the Finnish coast to lay their mines. Increasing speed to 27 knots at 2030 hours, the flotilla forged on and by 2159 was abreast the island of Digshar (Tiiskeri). After turning south-east, all ships closed up to action stations, maintaining the 27 knots through the calm seas. A few clouds scudded across the night sky and visibility was good. At 2230 hours *T32* signalled to the flotilla leader, 'Four small shadows on starboard beam, possibility of interception', and a minute later *T23* also logged the shadows, but the flotilla leader did not reply to *T32*. Kapitänleutnant Weinlig of *T23* believed that, because these shadows sometimes moved ahead and sometimes fell back but generally kept pace with the torpedo boats, they must have been MTBs. His forward radar reported contacts broad abeam at 4,400m, but no alarms occurred and it is difficult not to conjecture that this was a false report, since it is unlikely, under the prevailing conditions,

The Gulf of Finland

that if Soviet MTBs had been present they would not have detected the presence of the torpedo boats. At this time the German ships, steaming approximately 144°, would have been somewhere to the west of the rocky islet known as Ostrov Rodsher.

By 2336 hours the flotilla was in the south-western part of Narva Bay, where it was detected by the submerged *U679* shortly before midnight. The torpedo boats, however, do not appear to have noticed her due to their high speed. At midnight all the boats were ready to lay. The weather remained good, with a light south-south-west breeze, calm sea and good visibility. The mine-deck crews on all the ships were busy aft, preparing for the imminent lay, and at 0000 hours the officers of the watch reported to their various commanders 'Mines clear to lay'. At 0013 hours course was altered to 059°, during which time the navigator of *T23* succeeded in obtaining a fix on Konju and Valaste Lights. What navigational data were obtained by the rest of the flotilla is, of course, not known.*

*The vast majority of the information in this section is derived from the KTB of *T23*, all the others having been lost in the débâcle which was to follow.

Ten minutes after steadying on to 059° *T23* was ordered to change positions with *T30* (as laid down in the flotilla commander's orders), so as to be in the correct position for the lay when course was altered on to the mining line (329°) moments later. *T23* was now the westernmost ship as the flotilla formed up abreast. Almost before the turn had been completed, *T30* flashed her anchor light, the signal for '30 seconds to go before lay commences'. Kapitänleutnant Weinlig took this to be a signal made too early and did not order his mines to drop, but unfortunately the mining officer on his quarterdeck assumed no such error and started to lay. Despite frantic orders to the quarterdeck from the bridge to stop, communications broke down and before the order could be countermanded, eleven UMBs and seven EMRKs had been dropped.

At 0025 hours, whilst the turn was still incomplete, two heavy detonations erupted amidships on *T30*'s port side, throwing water columns 50m in the air. The explosions were heard and logged by both *U679* (0028 hours) standing to off the port beam of the torpedo boats and *U479* (0026 hours); both were surfaced at the time and saw the fires

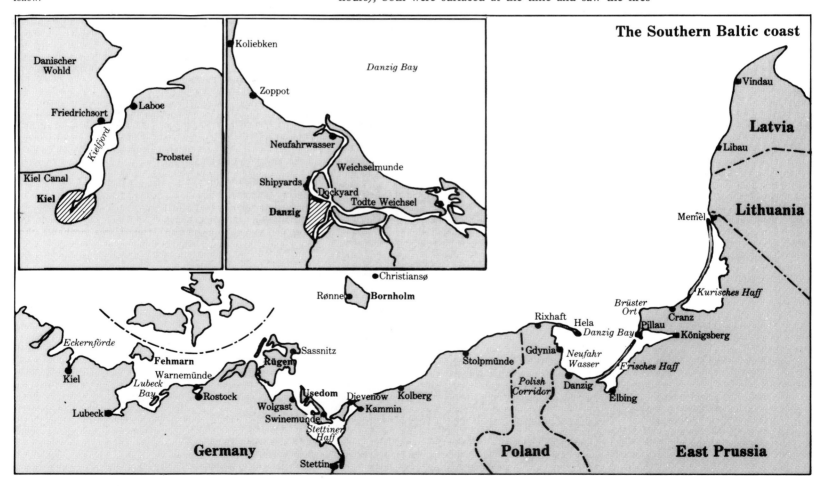

The Southern Baltic coast

aboard the unlucky ship. *T23*, nearest *T30*, stopped engines and called up the others over the short-wave radio, but she could not raise a reply from either. Weinlig assumed at this stage that the explosions were the results of floating mines, broken loose from the adjacent 'Seeigel IXb' field. Aboard *T23*, according to Fock,★ however, no mines had been detected and the explosion on *T30* was a first assumed to be due to a torpedo.

T30 lay drifting, on fire and smoking heavily and with a list to port. Then at 0026, no sooner had *T23* radioed a signal informing of the mining of *T30* than *T32*, the flotilla leader, reeled under the impact of a double detonation, which curiously enough produced no flash or fires. Aboard *T23* and presumably also *T22*, the crews aft were frantically working to set their unlaid mines to 'safe' and clear away the quarterdecks for towing. All available men were set to the task, leaving only two guns and the flak weapons closed up. No. 1 gun's crew was ordered to keep a sharp look-out for floating mines as *T23* ran on at 5 knots.

By this time, the S-Gerät operators aboard *T23*, who were searching ahead from port to starboard, began to

detect mines bearing between 30° and 65°, i.e., off the starboard bow, at a distance of about 1,200m. Weinlig took these to be from the 'Seigel IXb' field but he was not absolutely certain of the situation since the Soviets were known to have been sweeping in the old field (hence the reason for the new operation) and it was probable that there were drifting mines present as a result. At 0033 hours the damaged and disabled *T30* exploded and broke in two, probably on striking yet another mine. The stern sank quickly, leaving the fore-ends floating vertically for a few minutes as another mine on the afterdeck blew up. Once more *T23* radioed depressing news: '*T32* also mined, sinks; *T30* sunk'. Since *T23* had heard nothing so far from *T22*, she flashed 'Was ist los?'† and received the reassuring reply 'OK, nothing'. Close to the two ships, 500m to port, lay *T32* with her bows blown off. On being signalled by *T23*, *T32* replied that she had struck two mines and that her CO, Kapitänleutnant Dehnert, was seriously wounded.

By about 0040 hours the crews on the quarterdeck of *T23*, who had been working feverishly to clear away the remaining mines set to safe, finally reported that all had

★One of *T22*'s officers who survived the night's events.

†'What is the matter?'

been jettisoned. Now that his ship was at least ready to tow, Weinlig asked *T32* if she could in fact be taken. In reply, the damaged torpedo boat made 'Ship is floating, please wait on towing'. Weinlig, still uncertain, again flashed the question to the stricken ship and received the reply 'Ship not towable forward'. *T23* now stopped engines and hove to. The time was 0048.

After a few moments *T22*, which was also as yet undamaged and had been hove-to near *T23*, got under way again at 5–9 knots and made to close *T32*. This move plainly puzzled *T23*'s CO, since it was quite clear by now that they were in a minefield. Concerned, Weinlig signalled his consort, 'Caution: behind me are live mines'. *T22* acknowledged but nevertheless closed the wreck in an apparent attempt to go alongside her. After a second attempt, *T22* turned north and made a third try, but at 0105 hours two more explosions occurred close to the two ships, throwing columns of water 30–50m in the air. Shortly before these explosions the hydrophone office had reported noises, classified as torpedoes, bearing 220°. Further reports of noises were made at 0112 (at 142°) and the engineer officer, too, reported hearing noises out to starboard. All look-outs strained their ears to catch any sound, and several, including the captain, reported hearing engines. The darkness and the deadly dangers of the minefield were now causing an intolerable strain on the surviving crews.

At about 0113 hours *T23* asked *T22* if she considered a tow feasible and, if not, ordered *T32* to be scuttled. No sooner had *T22* acknowledged than, before *T23* could warn her of the detection of torpedo noises, she exploded and broke in two. Two distinct detonations were observed, literally blowing *T22* to pieces. Weinlig was of the opinion that an explosion of this magnitude must have been caused by torpedoes, an impression upheld by Kapitänleutnant Peter-Pirkham (also aboard), whose *T31* had previously been sunk by Soviet MTBs. Fock says that the mine explosion touched off the midships magazine and probably three torpedo warheads, hence the swift sinking of *T22*.

T23 remained stopped whilst Weinlig desperately tried to decide on the best course of action. The wrecks of three of his flotilla-mates lay sunk or sinking around him whilst survivors, both aboard and in the water, cried out for his help. They appeared also to be surrounded by mines and, furthermore, MTBs were thought to be in the vicinity.

A difficult decision awaited Weinlig. Whilst he pondered, the hydrophone office suddenly reported, at 0118 hours, 'Engine noises at 172°'. This was confirmed by the S-Gerät, and at the same time No. 3 gun reported a small boat moving fast aft, an observation also reported by the Vierling's crew and bridge personnel. All agreed it to be an MTB, for it appeared to have a superstructure on the forecastle. These reports made the CO's mind up for him: if he were not to lose the fourth ship, he must withdraw at once. Ordering steam for 27 knots and turning westwards, Weinlig sent off a radio message to the 9th Security

Division at 0120 hours: 'Qu 118 D67, *T22* out of sight astern after explosion, *T32* afloat in half. Request shallow-draught boats to rescue survivors. Commencing homeward journey. *T23*.' Ten minutes later, he picked up radio signals from 9th Security ordering the leader of the 25th Minesweeper Flotilla to go to the assistance of the 6th Torpedo Boat Flotilla. This signal, timed at 0108 hours, also ordered AF Group 'Cordes' to assist, and in addition the air-sea rescue unit at Reval was alerted and scrambled.* In all, four fleet minesweepers, three artillery ferries and a 'Flakjäger', as well as four Flnnish and two German S-boats, were ordered into the rescue operation.

OF ACADEMIC INTEREST

T23 continued her solitary journey home, her radar officer reporting a stream of contacts classified as MTBs between 0127 and 0150 hours. At 0150, *T23* picked up a contact by radar bearing 350° and turned towards it. This was in fact *U679*, which, having sighted the torpedo boat only some 1½ miles away and being in danger of collision, crash-dived. *T23* fired starshell before recognizing a German boat, being also observed by *U479* which herself was only 800m south-west of the torpedo boat. The detection of the submarine gave Weinlig confidence that his radar was operating correctly. Throughout the homeward journey, from 0150 until 0234 hours, numerous other contacts were obtained but no attacks developed.

By about 0300 hours *T23* lay under the Finnish coast, and at 0308 she received a signal from the 9th Defence Division (timed at 0254) requesting information as to where the field had been started and ordering her to take part in the rescue operation. From this signal, Weinlig realized that his reasons for withdrawal were not clear enough to 9th Defence, whereupon he signalled further: '*T23* 18 mines laid. *T22* blown up in rescue attempts. Enemy mine situation not clear. Numerous floating mines. Own draught certain to cause loss if take part in rescue operations. Rescue only possible with small boats. S-boats present on return journey. Lying immediate readiness Bergholm.' Following this signal, *T23* was ordered to return to Helsinki, where she secured at 1241 hours.

Meanwhile, out in the bay, rescue operations got under way. Breckwoldt in *U679* surfaced and endeavoured to piece together the night's events before joining in, whilst overhead flew a Dornier and a Focke-Wulf from the rescue squadron. To the south three AFs came into sight, and in the east the four minesweepers closed the disaster area. Sons in *U479*, also on the surface, sighted a pinnace at about 0400 and called up a minesweeper to rescue the survivors before diving again and resuming patrol.

Rescue operations continued for as long as possible, but by late morning on the 18th Soviet MTBs were preventing the aircraft from carrying out any further sorties and the surface ships had begun to withdraw. In total, only 51 men

*AF=Artilleriefährprahm, or artillery barge.

Right: *Z28* now fitted with a Vierling on the deckhouse aft and Plexiglass shields to the tube control positions. (Archiv Gröner)

were rescued by the German minesweeper effort, whilst a further 90 were picked up by the aircraft. The crippled *T32* remained afloat throughout the night until, during the following morning, she was attacked by Soviet aircraft and finally sank. A further 106 men were reported as being rescued as POWs by the Russians.

Because of the disaster the gap in the 'Seeigel IXb' field remained until 7 September when, in an operation by the 1st R-boat Flotilla and the 24th Landing Flotilla, 300 UMBs, 84 EMR(K)s and 80 'Reissbojen' were laid.

The loss of three large, modern fleet torpedo boats was, not unnaturally, a serious blow to the Kriegsmarine. However, no detailed investigation appears to have been conducted into its causes for no court of enquiry record has been found, although Kapitänleutnant Weinlig was ordered to report personally to Admiral (Eastern Baltic) a day or two after arriving back in Helsinki. It is likely that because of the withdrawal of Finland from the war on 2 September the resultant exodus of the German forces from that country meant that any detailed investigation would be of academic interest only and there were far more pressing problems for the local German commands. After the sinkings, the commanding officer of the 1st R-boat Flotilla signalled that when his vessels laid the adjacent 'IXB' field his position, in the fine weather prevailing, was accurate to 0.2 miles and was in any case being controlled by the torpedo boats acting as escort. As to the reported presence of numerous MTBs, this MOK (Ost) disbelieved: in their view Peter-Pirkham, who was aboard *T23* at the time and whose *T31* had been lost to an MTB torpedo, was probably

inclined to see or imagine MTBs where none existed. What did happen on that fateful night?

The exact courses steered by the flotilla can unfortunately no longer be ascertained for no track charts appear to have survived; furthermore, the navigational data contained in the only surviving KTB are extremely sparse. However, given the relatively mild sea and weather conditions, together with the availability of the searchlights as beacons, there should have been no great error in navigation; nevertheless, it is a factor to be considered. Floating mines, resulting from the Soviet sweeping operations, are another possibility, but the number of explosions which occurred tends to reinforce the belief that it was the 'Seeigel IXb' field which was responsible.

The possibility of Soviet MTBs being present or causing any losses through torpedo attacks can almost certainly be discounted. Had they achieved any torpedo hits, then unquestionably the Soviets would have immediately broadcast their success. Moreover, any attack would hardly have been made by a lone MTB, and despite all the radar reports only one visual sighting was made – that by *T23* at 0118 hours. This was very probably the pinnace which may have been launched by *T30* before she sank, and reported later by *U479*. This small boat's engine noises would have carried clearly over the water on a calm night as she picked up survivors and attempted to locate the remnants of the flotilla. What the boat's crew thought as they saw *T23* get under way just as they had succeeded in finding their comrades is not recorded!

On balance, it is likely that the 'Seeigel IXb' mines were

the cause of the losses, either because the earlier field was laid slightly out of position or because of a small error in navigation by the 6th Flotilla, or a combination of both. The intriguing question is what happened to the eleven mines laid by the leading ship, *T23*, before the correct executive signal.

On the other hand, Fock puts forward the theory that navigation error was unlikely given the experience of the officers in question and the prevailing conditions. He suggests that the Soviets might have laid flank minefields to protect one of their secret swept channels through the Seeigel barrage from just this type of operation.

INACCURATE POSITION

The situation in the east was by now deteriorating rapidly. The torpedo boats of the 3rd Flotilla covered the evacuation of German troops and then, in a show of strength, made a sortie into the Åland Sea. Whilst returning in the morning of 17 September, Soviet bombers attacked them north of Reval. *T18*, the leader, was hit by two rockets which exploded in her boiler rooms, and she sank with the loss of thirty men.

By November most of the smaller torpedo boats had returned to active duty and were engaged in flak protection with Naval Command East in the support operations by Task Force 2 along the Baltic littoral. In home waters, the larger boats continued to sustain losses. On 20 November 1944 *T34* was engaged on a work-up programme of day and night gunnery shoots with the target ship *Hessen*, when, in the morning, she struck a mine whilst to the northeast of Cape Arkona. The severe shock of the explosion blew off the stern, leaving it attached only loosely by the starboard plating. The boat rolled over to port and sank quickly by the stern, probably the victim of an RAF air-laid weapon.

T10, which had finished repairs only on 28 November, was damaged a second time at Libau on 15 December, when a near-miss exploded underwater alongside her. She was ordered to Elbing for repairs and her refit brought forward to coincide, but in a fatal change of plans, was docked instead in No. 4 floating dock at Deutscher Werke, Gotenhafen. Here, on the 18th, during the course of an RAF raid, the boat was sunk. The air raid warning was given at 2105 hours, the attack beginning at 2130. At 2200 the dock itself was hit and sank down at the bows and to port. *T10*, on blocks, slipped sideways ending up leaning to port with her superstructure against the dockside wall. A number of bombs are then believed to have landed between the ship's side and the dock wall followed by a number of near-misses which severely shook the ship. Connections with the shore were severed and power lost. *T10* was now listing to port 20° and down by the bows 10°. Both boiler rooms were making water as was No. 2 turbine and compartment IX. The forward ends were dry and the after part was still supported on the part of the dock still afloat. Kapitänleutnant Brunk, her CO, suggested flooding the after compartments of the dock to free his ship but suddenly the dock broke in two. *T10* was now afloat at the bows with the stern still on the after end of the dock. The salvage pump vessel *R* came alongside to pump out the slowly flooding torpedo boat but by early the following morning, the 19th, the torpedo boat's list had increased to 30° with water lapping the torpedo tube coamings. At 0313, Brunk gave orders to abandon ship and at 0320 she sank. For a while, the stern remained out of water but eventually only the bridge, funnel and superstructure remained visible. Although her raising was considered, lack of resources and other pressing matters prevented any work being done. Thus, by the turn of the year there were only twelve operational torpedo boats left: in the Baltic, the 2nd Flotilla had *T1*, *T3*, *T4* and *T8*, the 3rd *T13*, *T16* and *T17*, and the re-formed 5th *T33*, *T23* and *T28*; *T19* and *T20* of the 3rd Flotilla were based in the Skaggerak. A further eight boats were in dockyard hands or working-up, the last to be completed during the war, *T36*, having commissioned on 9 December.

The destroyers of the 6th Flotilla, *Z28*, *Z25*, *Z35* and *Z36*, operated in the Gulf of Finland, based occasionally at Turku, whither they returned in September when the Russo-Finnish armistice was imminent. Then the flotilla covered the German evacuation from Finland until the 13th, when *Z28* finally sailed for Gotenhafen, and by the end of September all four destroyers of the flotilla were once again based in Gotenhafen. The flotilla was engaged at various times until November on shore bombardment duties with *Lützow*, *Scheer* and *Prinz Eugen* against Russian positions from the Sworbe peninsula down to Memel.

Towards the end of October the Naval High Command returned once more to the question of mining the Gulf of Finland, possibly to prevent interference by Soviet heavy units in the shore bombardment work in which the majority of the Kriegsmarine's forces were employed. The strategic picture had changed considerably since the last disastrous attempt the previous August, however, because the naval forces were now home-based, thus involving a passage of some 450 miles to the laying point. Accordingly, the Skl planned the operation using destroyers, whose high speed and good mine load would make them the ideal vehicles. The operational orders (No. 5505) were issued on 14 November and detailed the 6th Destroyer Flotilla for the task. This was the only unit currently available in the Baltic, for the 4th was still in Arctic Norway whilst the 5th was operating in the Skaggerak. The 6th Flotilla, under Kapitän zur See Kothe as D6, consisted at this time of *Z25*, *Z23*, *Z35*, *Z36* and *Z43*.

It was not until December, however, that the operation could be mounted, by which time *Z25* was undergoing an overhaul and *Z28*, which had been bombed and seriously damaged off the Sworbe Peninsula on 24 October, was still under repair. As the orders called for four destroyers to lay mines, it was then necessary to detail the large Type 39 torpedo boats *T23* and *T28* (normally of the 5th Torpedo

Boat Flotilla) to the operation as replacements.

At about midday on 9 December the flotilla arrived in the Bay of Danzig, whence the two torpedo boats proceeded into Pillau whilst the destroyers secured in Peyse. At 1800 hours, as mines were being embarked, all the captains reported aboard the leader, *Z35*, for a conference on the forthcoming operation. It was revealed that the object of the sortie was to lay a field which would block the western entrance to Reval, south of the island of Nargo (Naissar), the northern exit being already closed off by the 'Nashorn' barrage. The new field would be known by the code-name 'Nil'.

The 'Nil' field was to consist of four rows of mines, for which purpose the destroyers were being loaded with 68 EMF/UES mines with 12-hour delays and *T28* with 46 EMR to be laid as a protective row. The three main rows, 15m deep and 7.96 nautical miles long, were 500m apart, with the mines in each row 220m apart. It was calculated that the field would take 27.2 minutes to lay at 17.5 knots, giving a mean spacing of 70m. *Z36* would start laying 8 seconds and *Z43* 16 seconds after *Z35*, the lay to commence on *Z35*'s showing a long blue light flash. In its final form, it would start at 59° 33.7' N, 24° 20.5' E through to 59° 28.7' N, 24° 12.6' E on 219°, thence 190° to 59° 27' N, 24° 12' E, and no gap was to be left through the field.

During the conference Kapitän zur See Kothe detailed his precise orders, some of which were not to the liking of the other commanding officers. The one which caused most concern was the ban on the use of the short-wave R/T communication link which had been ordered in addition to the expected W/T silence; it was felt that light signals passed down a chain of five ships would result in too long a delay and possible mistakes. Furthermore, radar operation was also forbidden to all except *Z35*, which would act as navigation leader. Details of own and enemy force dispositions were given, and action to be taken in the event of detection by the enemy was laid down, which meant, broadly, that if the force were detected south of Libau a feint course was to be steered and the operation continued if possible; if not, the sortie was to be abandoned. If the ships were detected during the lay, the operation was, again, to continue if possible, and all ships were free to attack after finishing. *T23*, not mine-laden, would act as escort and was to have towing wires rigged aft in case they were needed. Kothe also gave details of lights expected in the Gulf area, of which the light at Pakerort near Baltischport (Paldiski) was given as Occulting Group 1. The conference broke up with the sailing time being set for 0730 hours on 10 December.

The weather worsened during the night and, it having been established that good weather was a prerequisite, the sortie was postponed for twenty-four hours at 0700 on the 10th. In view of this, Kapitänleutnant Weinlig (*T23*) took the opportunity of moving his ship outboard of *T28* as a camouflage measure, *T28* being mine-laden. All day the flotilla remained alongside, until, early the next morning, the operation was confirmed as 'on'.

At 0700 hours on 11 December the destroyers were ready for sea. The wind blew from east-north-east, Force 3 freshening and veering and with a swell on the sea, as the three destroyers slipped anchor. The two torpedo boats joined from Pillau at 0827 hours and the flotilla formed line astern, *Z43* leading to transit the Hela minefields since *Z35*'s starboard otter was unserviceable.

By midday the flotilla was steaming northwards at 25 knots towards the northern tip of Gotland. The passage formation during the day comprised *Z35* leading with *T23* and *T28* 60° on her quarters; *Z43* and *Z36*, steaming abreast, brought up the rear of the formation. As the flotilla forged on the weather deteriorated, with low clouds and driving rain, although the seas remained slight, and the

combination of high speed and pouring rain caused considerable discomfort to look-outs, bridge personnel and other exposed men who were quickly soaked. From *Z43*, *T23* could be made out only by the glow from her funnel. Whilst on passage Kothe passed several operational signals to his flotilla, mainly concerned with the mining mission but also detailing his post-lay intentions. It would appear that these consisted of sorties against convoy traffic between Reval and Baltischport, as well as against that between Hangö and Baltischport. For the immediate operation, action stations were ordered for 2030 hours and it was emphasized that faultless darken-ship routine was necessary.

Between 1625 and 1800 hours Fårö Lighthouse, at the northern tip of Gotland, was in sight, allowing all ships to obtain running fixes but not, with the possible exception of

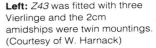

Right: A sketch of a Type 37 torpedo boat made secretly by Mhr. van der Weele whilst a young draughtsman at the Rotterdam Dry Dock company, showing the radar (although he had no idea of its purpose) and the aperture of the *Bugschutzgeräte*. (C.v.d. Weele)

Left: *Z43* was fitted with three Vierlinge and the 2cm amidships were twin mountings. (Courtesy of W. Harnack)

Z35, range and bearing fixes. By 1802 the last good fix had been obtained as course was altered from 011° to 040° for the run-up to the entrance to the Gulf of Finland. During the forenoon, weather reports had indicated that there would be a steady deterioration in conditions and this gradually became apparent. The generally east-north-east wind had increased to Force 3–4, and all ships were taking it green over bows and bridges. It was cloudy and raining, and visibility was poor: the 500m distance between ships was held as ordered, but that was the limit of visual range.

Already some doubts as to position were being raised, at least aboard T23, whose navigating officer believed that the flotilla must be running above the ordered 25 knots, for his ship had revolutions for 26 and the log showed over 26. Weinlig did not believe this however, because, in his opinion, the heavily laden destroyers would not be capable of such a speed, given the conditions. By 2210, when course was altered to 80° (at 59° 20.5' N, 21° 44' E according to the orders), T23 considered herself by dead reckoning to be some 3.5 nautical miles north of the ordered position.

The weather had by now further deteriorated, with the wind rising to Force 5 and rain still falling, but pressing on into the Gulf, the flotilla continued the sortie. At midnight it was some four hours since the last reliable fix, and possibly because of this Kothe, on reaching navigation Point 'A' (59° 30' N, 26° 26.5' E), altered course to 090° instead of the planned 076.5°. The light on Odensholm (Osmussar) had not been sighted either because of the bad weather or, more probably, because it was not lit. The new course would therefore bring the flotilla closer to the light at Pakerort, on which, it was presumed, a reliable fix could be obtained. At 0050 hours the light was in fact raised, but as the south-south-west wind had by this time risen to Force 5-6, with heavy seas, getting an accurate fix was far from easy, and it was further complicated by the 21-knot speed, which threw spray over the rangefinders, the ban (except for the leader) on the use of radar and the fact that the light was Flashing Group 1 and not occulting as expected according to the flotilla's orders. The shortness of the flashes combined with all the other conditions meant that it was almost impossible to get an accurate position. Certainly Z43, T23 and T28 did not, and it must be presumed that Z36 did not either. It remains a matter of conjecture how accurate a fix Z35 obtained, although Kapitänleutnant Rohwer, former IWO of Z35, maintains that a good fix was obtained.

At 0055 hours course was altered to 060° to run up to Point 'B' (59° 35.8' N, 24° 13.2' E) at 17 knots. The light was still visible as the various navigators desperately attempted to get a fix but without success. Again the flotilla orders actively hindered their efforts and, with hindsight, were almost certainly a major factor in the calamity which followed, for at 0115 hours speed was reduced to 12 knots as the flotilla was ordered to change steaming order, the object being to put the line of ships in the correct order for

Left: *T9* in the later years of the war, with two Vierlinge, FuMB 4 Sumatra aerials and 2cm bow-chaser but no radar. (Archiv Gröner)

laying when the flotilla was turned on to the lay course. Up to this point the steaming order was *Z35* leading, followed by *T23*, *Z43*, *T28* and *Z36*; now, on the executive signal, the order was to be changed to *T23* leading, followed by *T28*, *Z43*, *Z35* and *Z36*. This, as the various COs had envisaged at the pre-sortie conference, caused considerable problems. On a dark, rough night with poor visibility, the exercise demanded the full attention of the bridge watches in order that a collision did not occur but, more importantly, it also meant that at a time when a position fix was absolutely vital all the ships with the exception of *Z35* were manoeuvring and altering speed, and in consequence none was able to obtain even a running fix on the light. *Z35*, steaming at a constant 12 knots, retained the navigational leadership but did not signal her flotilla despite the fact that it had been agreed during the conference that a position comparison be obtained from all ships.

At this time *T28* had concluded that her position was some 3.5 nautical miles north of the intended course but, because *Z35* was able to utilize her radar, assumed that her own position was not accurate. *T23*, in the course of her position alteration manoeuvre, switched on her radar and manned the S-Gerät because Kapitänleutnant Weinlig was determined not to miss this last opportunity of a decent fix. Very shortly his navigators reported that, according to his estimates (admittedly based on running fixes), their

position was considerably further north than intended and that they should soon alter course. Weinlig, however, did not immediately accept this as accurate, and he too assumed that *Z35* knew what she was doing.

A MAJOR DISASTER

The scene was now set for a major disaster, and it is incredible that an experienced officer like Kothe was prepared to press on under such unsafe and uncertain conditions. His confidence in the flotilla navigating officer must have been considerable to take five large, valuable destroyers (out of a total of only 22 torpedo craft remaining to the Kriegsmarine) so close to a known existing minefield which, even if it had been laid accurately, was still only 2½ miles from his intended new field. He did not double-check with his flotilla as to position, and at least two of the ships were by now having considerable doubts as to their exact position. They were only too well aware of the nearness of the 'Nashorn' barrage.

T23, now in the lead, pitched on under low clouds and darkness. At 0130 hours her navigator reported that they had reached the point where, according to the orders, *T23* was to turn off to starboard to run south of the flotilla as cover during the lay. Weinlig by this time could not see the rest of his boats astern of him and, assuming that he had missed the turn signal, altered course to 119° and reduced speed to 9 knots, signalling his actions by Aldis lamp. *Z43*, next in line, could see *T23*, however, and noted her turn off to starboard as being premature. *T23*, meanwhile, assuming that her consorts were somewhere off to starboard, made a further alteration to 130° and searched to starboard with her radar; not finding a contact, she broke R/T silence at 0139 and reported 'Lost contact. *T23*.'

Kapitän zur See Kothe himself broke R/T silence a few moments later when he ordered '9 Otto 2 mit Ausführung'* at 0140 hours, and *T28* complied with the order, as did *Z28* astern of her. Temming in *T28* was still having serious anxieties about his position, his navigator once more putting the boat further north than intended and dangerously close to the 'Nashorn' barrage. Then, at 0144, *T28* signalled 'Lay start point 130°, 8.5 nautical miles'. In view of the circumstances it is difficult to judge how this information was deduced, but it undoubtedly saved two of the flotilla for Temming saw it as confirmation of his worst fears - they were too far north. Aboard *Z43*, Wenninger received a signal at 0147 from his hydrophone office, where the S-Gerät was operating an active sweep: 'Contacts bearing 340° (ships), 1,500m'. He disbelieved this at first, but seconds later the office amplified the report: 'Further contacts between 340° and 270° (ships bearing), 1,200-1,500m'.

Both captains, by now thoroughly alarmed, took matters into their own hands and at 0151 altered course to starboard, *Z43* by 90° and *T28* on to 180°. *T28* signalled her action by R/T, a signal which clearly puzzled D6 as a repeat was requested. Before a repeat could be made, however, both *T28* and *Z43* felt and observed a weak explosion astern which was thought likely to be an explosive float or detonator. At 0153 D6 signalled 'Stop', obviously by now aware that the flotilla was standing into danger. What damage *Z35* had sustained cannot now be ascertained, but shortly after ordering 'Stop' D6 signalled *T23* to close *Z35*.

Hardly had this order been made when *Z35* sheered off to port in an explosion, covered in smoke.

A mine had exploded on the port side, abreast No. 4 gun, flooding one compartment and immobilizing the port machinery. Many of her own mines were thrown off their rails, but there seemed no immediate danger to the ship. Damage control parties sprang into action and the damage to the ship was investigated. Meanwhile *Z43* asked *Z36* if he could hear D6 on the R/T and at 0200 came the reply '*Z36* to *Z43* I hear D6 . . .' The rest was lost as *Z36* herself exploded in flame and smoke, sinking quickly. Rohwer in *Z35* hurried forward to report to the bridge but he had only reached the forward tubes when his ship reeled under a second and more serious explosion in the midships area when it would appear that a boiler and ammunition exploded. Abandon ship was ordered, and one boat and many floats were launched as the ship went down. During that night, the groups of survivors drifted apart, many freezing to death before the Finnish coast and captivity was reached the following morning. According to Soviet reports there remained only about 70 survivors.

Wenninger, by now senior officer, took stock of the situation. The night was pitch black with variable visibility and a south-south-east wind Force 5–6, and a high sea was running. Of *Z35* and *Z36* there was no sight, nor could any

Below: Few photographs of *Z35* exist and they are of poor quality. (W. Z. Bilddienst)

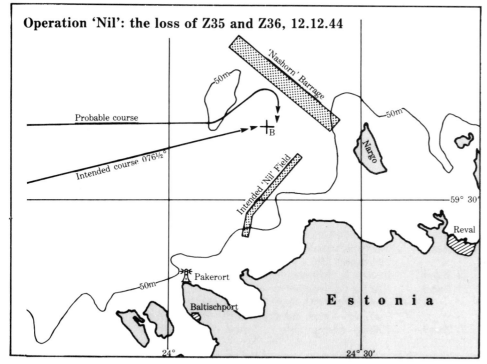

Operation 'Nil': the loss of Z35 and Z36, 12.12.44

*'119° with executive'.

response be obtained to repeated R/T signals. Both his ship and *T28* were still loaded with armed mines and they were obviously very close to the field. The position of *T23* was uncertain, although radar transmissions could be detected to the south, probably emanating from her. The water was bitterly cold, and this, together with the fire and explosions, would almost certainly mean that there would be few, if any, survivors. Finally, there was the question of enemy reaction – had the explosions been heard?

The strong winds were driving the stopped ships back into the danger area, forcing both to get under way once more to get clear of the minefields, but before any rescue attempt could be made the mines had to be defuzed. Taking *T28* under his command, Wenninger moved both ships westwards, defuzing mines as he did so, then jettisoning them. Nothing could be seen at the sinking position. The seas were difficult for launching boats, which were in any case half full of water from the rough seas on the outward passage. As the two ships steamed a reciprocal course to the approach whilst clearing for action and getting rid of the mines, *Z43* once again detected mines, 400–1,200m on the port bow, and this time there was no hesitation in accepting the hydrophone room's report! Course was quickly altered to 0° until the contacts had faded astern before both ships returned to a south-south-westerly course. All rescue thoughts had now been discarded, a correct decision in the circumstances, and, joined later by the wayward *T23*, the sorry remnant of the 6th Flotilla set course back to Gotenhafen where they arrived at 2349 hours on the 12th.

In retrospect, from a distance of nearly forty years, it seems to have been a faulty decision to continue the operation under such an adverse set of circumstances as pertained on the night of 11/12 December 1944. The pressures on Kapitän zur See Kothe to complete the

Z34 IN THE BALTIC, 1945

The tasks of the Kriegsmarine during the last four months of the war in the Baltic were shore bombardment and the escorting of refugee convoys. The nature of this work makes it extremely difficult to give a coherent narrative account of the scale and importance of the operations in question. However, in order to convey to the reader the intensity and pace of the Kriegsmarine's involvement, the war diary of *Z34*, a destroyer engaged on these operations, is summarized below.

1 February	Arrive Kiel from Norway
3 February	Sail for Gotenhafen attached 2nd Kampf Gruppe
5 February	Escort to *Admiral Scheer*; shore bombardment Tolkemit area
16 February	Convoy escort duties to Kurland
17 February	Return convoy of troops and vehicles aboard steamers *Volta* and *Bukarest* to Gotenhafen
20 February	Escort for *Hamburg* with 12,000 wounded and refugees to Sassnitz
21 February	Return escort duty: *Deutschland* to Gotenhafen
25 February	To Pillau with *T33*; embark 800 wounded for transfer to Gotenhafen
28 February	With *T3*; escort *Cometa* and *Stinnes* to Libau
4 March	Return convoy from Libau to Danzig with wounded
9 March	Shore bombardment off Kammin (190 rounds)
10 March	Shore bombardment off Dievenow, Fritzow and Kammin (74 rounds)
11 March	Shore bombardment off Kolberg
12 March	Shore bombardment off Sellnow; take on wounded over disengaged side
15 March	Shore bombardment Kolberg (95 rounds on three different targets)
16 March	Shore bombardment Kolberg; take on about 1,400 soldiers and wounded; No. 4 gun bursts
18 March	Return to Swinemünde
21 March	Sail for Gotenhafen as screen for *Lützow* with *T33* and *Z43*; attack submarine with depth charges; air raid at Gotenhafen; Russian artillery forces numerous shifts of berth in port
23 March	Engage enemy tanks in Zoppot; fired on by 12cm battery

operation are not known, but unless large movements of enemy vessels were expected out of Reval at that time it would appear that it would not have been imperative to lay that night, especially as the previous delay had not been remarked upon. It is almost certain that both destroyers were lost on the 'Nashorn' field as a result of inaccurate navigation. Even supposing the older field to have been precisely laid, the flotilla had obtained nowhere nearly enough accurate fixes to perform the operation in safety. Contributory factors here were certainly the ban on R/T and that on radar, the failure of Captain (D6) to ask his flotilla for their estimates of position and, not least, the continuation of the sortie in the severe weather conditions that were prevailing.

Z35 and *Z36* went down very close to one another at about 59° 38' N, 24° 20' E, a position about as accurate as can be determined in view of the foregoing discussion.* No survivors were rescued by the Germans, although long after the war it was reported that one or two had been picked up by a Soviet vessel.

24 March	Flak escort to *Prinz Eugen*; numerous air attacks
25 March	Bombard several targets south-west and west of Gotenhafen; more air attacks
26 March	Flak escort to *Lützow*; running air attacks by Soviet Pe-2 and I1-2 aircraft
27 March	Shore bombardment off Oliva-Pelauken; no. 2 gun bursts
28 March	Shore bombardment Neufahrwasser and Langfuhr (130 rounds); flak escort to *Lützow*; No. 3 gun bursts (last single mounting); air attack by two I1-2 and five fighters; shore bombardment Arlen and Lenienthal
30 March	Flak escort to *Franken* with *Z31*
31 March	Flak escort to *Prinz Eugen*; air attacks; RAG used for first time
1 April	Convoy from Hela escorting *Deutschland* (5,000 wounded and 5,000 refugees) and *Pretoria* (6,000 wounded and refugees)
3 April	Arrive Copenhagen with convoy and re-sail for Swinemünde
5 April	Gun changes from *Z33*
6 April	Dock at Swinemünde
10 April	Gun changes cancelled
11 April	With *T36*; escort to *Sperrbrecher 17, Goya, Marburg, Lappland* and *Mars*
12 April	Hela; shore bombardments off Oxhoft and Schwarzau (103 rounds)
13 April	With *T36*, flak duties Hela; submarine attack (37 depth charges dropped)
15 April	Bombardment off Oxhoft; defend loaded refugee ships; No. 4 gun bursts again; fire-fighting party sent to *Pretoria* hit in air raid; return to Hela
	Two small shadows sighted at 2310 hours in 345°; torpedo hit port side, compartments IV and V; starboard engine still operative
16 April	Anchored; attacked by sixteen Pe-2 aircraft and fighter escort (serious flak damage)
15 April	Towed west to Swinemünde

The 8th Destroyer Flotilla, having been disbanded in France, was re-formed in Swinemünde under Kapitän zur See Gerlach on 1 November 1944, but not for operational duties: its purpose was to look after all destroyers and torpedo boats under refit or not otherwise operational and with their flotillas – a somewhat unenviable task for Captain (D8) at this late stage of the war. Also under the control of the flotilla was the training group of FdZ. Gerlach and his staff lodged ashore at Swinemünde with Captain (T5). The problems for the destroyer crews were acute, one of the major ones being, as usual, training: with the critical shortage of fuel oil and even the smallest refit being extended by many months, the state of readiness was lamentable. To improve matters, the flotilla was allocated the use of units of the 4th KFK Flotilla for sea experience. The KFKs, small wooden motor fishing vessels normally employed on patrol and anti-submarine tasks, were sent off from Swinemünde on three- to four-week voyages into the Skaggerak to teach seamanship, navigation and signalling. *Lody*'s crew sailed on the first trip on 11 January, returning to Swinemünde on 7 February, and further cruises were made for *Steinbrinck*, *Z39* and *T34*.

The remaining units of the Kriegsmarine were now mainly employed in supporting the withdrawal westwards of the Army in the face of the Russian advance from the east. The German forces in Kurland had been cut off from the rest of the front since October 1944, when the Russians had reached the coast between Libau and Memel. This bridgehead could only be supplied and supported by sea, with the destroyers and torpedo boats playing a vital role in its defence. From as early as August 1944 the Kriegsmarine had been intervening repeatedly in the land fighting whenever it could support its hard-pressed comrades ashore, and in the last nine months of the war many more naval shells were to be fired against land targets than ever were sent against ships in the previous five years. It was not the work for which the crews had been trained, but many of them had families in the east and the importance of the task did not go unrecognized. Even so, loitering along the coast firing at unseen targets selected by forward observers was a frustrating business for the fast destroyers.

The first operation had taken place in August 1944 when *Prinz Eugen* took *Z28*, *Z25*, *Z35*, *Z36*, *T23* and *T28* into the Gulf of Riga to bombard Soviet positions at Tukums, a road and rail junction about 15 miles inland. Then, until the end of the year, the cruiser was in action with *Lützow* and at various times the destroyers *Z25*, *Z28*, *Z35*, *Z36* and *Z43*, together with *T3*, *T5*, *T9*, *T12*, *T16*, *T19*, *T20*, *T21*, *T23* and *T28*, against Soviet forces in the Memel, Libau and Sworbe areas, particularly Sworbe, where the larger units bombarded from the west while the lighter units often engaged from the east. The fighting for this peninsula reached a peak in October and November as the German land forces were compressed into the narrow, wooded

*The positions given by Gröner should be treated with some reserve. These put the losses to the east of Wulf Island and partly ashore to the east of the Vumise peninsula in Musiga Bay.

tongue at the southern end of the island of Osel. Finally, as *Admiral Scheer* with *Z25*, *Z35*, *T3*, *T12*, *T5*, *T9*, *T13* and *T16* opened fire to keep the attackers' heads down on the night of 23/24 November, barges of the 24th Landing Flotilla evacuated the army remnants, leaving the Russians to find a deserted peninsula the following morning.

The destroyers and torpedo boats continued to work tirelessly, escorting the heavy units and engaging in shore bombardment themselves when required. On 29 January *Z23*, *Z25*, *Jacobi*, *T33* and *T35* escorted *Prinz Eugen* off Cranz in Samland as, in bitterly cold, snowy weather, the 20.3cm guns of the cruiser supported the breakout of XXVIII Corps and the evacuation of refugees. Strong, icy winds drove snow squalls across the sky, and the sea was littered with ice-floes, interspersed with small rescue craft of all descriptions ferrying the refugees out to larger ships and relative safety. Continual Russian air attacks forced all the ships' flak weapons to remain at immediate readiness, but despite all the Soviet attempts the destroyers and torpedo boats escaped relatively lightly. Furious fighting continued in the Pillau/Gross-Heidekrug/Königsberg areas well into March 1945, with most of the operational ships being involved at one time or another; at times, even the lighter forces bombarded from the Königsberg Sea Canal.

The Soviet thrust which had severed communications between Pillau and Königsberg was followed by the attack from the Soviet 1st White Russian Front on East Prussia, towards Kolberg and the Stettiner Haff, beginning on 26 February. Once again, all the available forces of the Kriegsmarine were thrown into the battle. On the first day, *Admiral Scheer*, escorted by *Jacobi*, *Z31*, *Z38* and *T36*, was in action off Wollin; then for the next three weeks the destroyers were continually engaged in supporting the defenders of Kolberg by bombarding Russian positions in Dievenow, Fritzow and Kammin.

February drifted into March as the desperate actions continued along the low, sandy Pomeranian shore. *Z28*, having completed escorting an evacuation convoy, anchored in Sassnitz Bay on 5 March to await further orders, but the following night the destroyer was bombed by Soviet aircraft, and, hit at least twice, broke in two and sank.

Kolberg remained surrounded, though continually supported by the guns of the fleet. *Z34* particularly distinguished herself on 10 March when her gunfire assisted the 1st Naval Division in fighting off fierce attacks, and she was credited with the destruction of twelve tanks and four anti-tank guns. The destroyers, in common with all other surface ships employed in shore bombardment and evacuation duties, were extremely vulnerable to air attack as the Luftwaffe had by now disappeared and the Soviet Air Force had unquestioned air superiority. Losses and damage rapidly escalated, *Z31* being hit by bombs in Danzig Bay on 8 April and *Z43* struck the following day, in No. 1 boiler room. She later detonated a ground mine which blew a hole in her port side about 15m long by 4m deep, breaching both Numbers 2 and 3 boiler rooms, the whip of the explosion breaking her back and snapping off the upper part of the mast. As it was the change of watch, (1607 hours) a large part of the engineering department was lost. *T33* took the casualty in tow but *Z43* later made Warnemünde and then Rostock under her own power. Her makeshift repairs were carried out with one or two beams being welded to the hull to strengthen it. All of her light flak and many of her crew were landed to join the desperate fighting ashore.

Z34, whilst off Hela, was attacked by two Soviet MTBs shortly before midnight: she managed to avoid one torpedo but the second hit on the port side, flooding the after turbine room and knocking out both engines. All power and command elements were lost as the ship took on a heavy list. The MTBs were driven off and *Z34* managed to

Right: *Z38* at Swinemünde in May 1945. Her light flak has been augmented by two single 3.7cm amidships in lieu of the 2cm. (Archiv Gröner)

Right: *Z38* at Swinemünde in May 1945. Her light flak has been augmented by two single 3.7cm amidships in lieu of the 2cm. (Archiv Gröner)

remain afloat, being later towed in to Swinemünde for repairs.

The torpedo boat force, too, now began to suffer further casualties. On 14 March *T3* and *T5* were engaged on convoy duties from Hela when *T5* struck a mine just as she was recovering her sweeps. She sank within a few minutes; shortly afterwards *T3* was also mined, but she remained afloat for about two hours before finally going down. Both boats are believed to have been victims of a barrage laid earlier by the Soviet submarine *L21*.

In parallel with the work of shore bombardment, the main task which fell to the destroyers and torpedo boats was the escorting of refugee ships from the east to the comparative safety of the west. From the ports of Libau, Memel, Gotenhafen, Hela and Swinemünde, convoys sailed daily as the large liners which had been laid up as accommodation ships in those ports were reactivated, packed with refugees and sailed westwards. FdZ's ships played a major part in escorting these convoys and, indeed, carried many thousands of civilians and wounded soldiers themselves. This undertaking was a mammoth effort, and by the end of the war about two million individuals had been shipped to the west, although there were three occasions when overcrowded liners were torpedoed with very heavy loss of life, a major factor in these incidents being the intense cold of the Baltic winter, when the freezing sea and very low air temperatures resulted in many deaths due to exposure amongst survivors in the water. These operations had begun about the turn of the year, and continued until some days after the armistice. Memel had been evacuated on 27 January, Gotenhafen and Danzig at the end of March, Königsberg and Pillau on 25 April and Kolberg during mid-April. Often referred to as 'Germany's Dunkirk', the operation reflects the greatest credit upon the Kriegsmarine which forced it through successfully despite heavy opposition from the Soviet Air Force and the

collapse of Germany's internal organization. The destroyers and torpedo boats escaped serious loss, but there were numerous casualties amongst the very exposed flak crews.

The last days of April saw *Z31* and *Z33* withdrawn west to Brunsbüttel, and on 2 May *Jacobi* and *Z43* (the latter, with no flak guns, no main armament ammunition, a reduced crew and damaged, was hardly an effective unit any longer) sailed from Warnemünde for Kiel, leaving *Z34*, *Z38* and *Z39*, together with *T33* and *T36*, in the Swinemünde area for final operations. On the 4th all five were loaded with evacuees and sailed for Copenhagen. However *T36*, already damaged by a mine the previous day, was bombed and sunk just outside the harbour, making her the last loss to be suffered by the destroyer and torpedo boat force during the war.

On 4 May German forces in north-west Germany surrendered, but before the total capitulation on the 8th the opportunity was taken to run further rescue convoys to the surrounded areas in East Prussia. The port of Hela was still in German hands and many thousands of soldiers and refugees had crossed the Gulf of Danzig to await possible rescue. On the 5th *Lody*, *Ihn*, *Riedel* and *Z25*, with *T17*, *T19*, *T23*, *T28* and *T35*, sailed from Denmark to Hela where, with transport, some 45,000 refugees were picked up and brought to Copenhagen the following day. Immediately after unloading, the fastest vesels, *Galster*, *Ihn*, *Lody*, *Riedel*, *Z25*, *T17*, *T19*, *T23* and *T28*, returned to Hela again, where they were joined by *Z38*, *Z39* and *Z33* from Swinemünde. In Hela they embarked a further 22,000 soldiers and refugees before sailing early on the 8th. Reaching the west safely, the refugees were disembarked in Glücksberg after the surrender had come into force.

This was the Kriegsmarine's final operation, and, a war lost for the second time, ships' companies lowered their ensigns, struck the commissioning pennants and placed the ships out of service to await the arrival of the victors.

14. PEACE

Left: A detail view of the after shelter deck of *Steinbrinck*, with the 'Barbara' flak rearmament after the surrender in May 1945. Behind can be seen the bridge and 'Tormast' of *Jacobi*. (IWM)

At the close of the war in Europe, on 8 May 1945, the Kriegsmarine's surface fleet was practically non-existent. The largest ship afloat and operational was the heavy cruiser *Prinz Eugen*, and only two other cruisers had survived, *Nürnberg* and *Leipzig*, although the latter, seriously damaged in a collision in 1944, was without main engines and unseaworthy. Apart from these there remained only fifteen destroyers in various conditions and eleven torpedo boats: *Beitzen, Steinbrinck, Lody, Galster, Jacobi, Riedel, Ihn, Z25, Z29, Z30, Z31, Z33, Z34, Z38* and *Z39*, and *T4, T11, T12, T14, T17, T19, T20, T23, T28, T33* and *T35*.

At the surrender *Beitzen, Z30* and *T20* were still lying in a damaged condition in Oslofjord, while *Steinbrinck* and *Z33* were immobilized in Cuxhaven. The remainder had been involved in the final evacuation convoys from East Prussia and by the 9th had surrendered at Flensburg. During the next few months all the seaworthy survivors, i.e., all except *Beitzen, T20* and *Z30* (which were handed over to the Royal Norwegian Navy for care and maintenance on 15 July 1945), were moved to Wilhelmshaven under British control where they were to remain until the three Allied powers had decided upon their allocations to the victors. By the summer of 1945 a large proportion of their crews had been landed into POW camps, leaving only a nucleus of mainly technical staff consisting of about five officers and sixty-eight men aboard. This reduced complement was retained for upkeep and maintenance, to ensure that the ships remained in good condition for handing over. In Wilhelmshaven Konteradmiral Kurt Weyher and Konteradmiral (Ing) Zieb, under the command of the British NOIC, supervised the overhaul of most of the destroyers, partly to keep the workforce employed and also to make use of such spare gear and replacement parts as remained in the yard, which would not be available once the ships were turned over to the victors. Willy Zieb had formerly been superintendent of dockyards in the Black Sea and had fought his way back up the Danube in 1944 after the Roumanian collapse.

The British naval command in Wilhelmshaven, mindful of the events of 1919 in Scapa Flow, were extremely edgy about the security of the surrendered vessels and, having heard rumours that acts of sabotage were being planned aboard the cruiser *Nürnberg*, took steps to prevent any such incidents. An elaborate plan code-named Operation 'Silver' was devised, to secure all the ships at Wilhelmshaven. This was put into effect on Sunday 16 December 1946, when 163 officers and men of the Royal Marines went on board and seized the ships. Surprise was complete and no bloodshed occurred, some of the German crews not even having turned-to when the boarding parties arrived at 0916 hours. The operation had been timed to coincide with the arrival of the Russian steaming crews for the Soviet quota, and when the German crews were allowed back on board again they were dismayed to find the Russians in possession of their ships. In retrospect, there is no real evidence that such a large-scale scuttling as happened at Scapa was ever intended.

By the close of 1946 the Allied Tripartite Commission had finally agreed on the division of the surrendered tonnage. As far as the destroyers were concerned, Great Britain was to receive *Beitzen, Lody, Jacobi, Riedel, Z25, Z30, Z31* and *Z38*, whilst Russia was to have *Steinbrinck, Ihn, Galster* and *Z33*; the United States claimed *Z29, Z34* and *Z39*. Under the terms of the Commission the Russian contingent was to be handed over by 16 February 1946. *Galster* was ready for sea on 24 December 1946 and *Steinbrinck* on 5 January. *Ihn*, however, developed defects in her boilers which, on examination, required a good deal of corroded steam piping and several boiler tubes to be replaced. It was estimated that repairs would take until at least the end of January to complete, and in view of this the British Command proposed that *Riedel* embark the Russian steaming crew from *Ihn* and that she be transferred in her place. Admiral Levchenko turned down this idea, probably because of *Riedel*'s past history but also possibly owing to a Russian fear that there might be other motives for the swap. In the event, *Ihn* was re-examined and it was found possible to effect the necessary repairs in much less than the six weeks originally estimated. Nevertheless, it was agreed that a large quantity of spare boiler tubes, fittings and other parts be loaded aboard before sailing so that further repairs could be undertaken on arrival in Russia.

Z33 and *Steinbrinck*, with mixed Russian/German passage

crews embarked, sailed from Wilhelmshaven on 2 January 1946 in company with the light cruiser *Nürnberg*, which wore the flag of Vice-Admiral Rall of the Soviet Navy. There had been, understandably, some reluctance on the part of the German crews to sail to Russia with the Soviet contingent, fearing, probably with some justification, that they would never be allowed to return home. However, the Western Allies offered guarantees that they would be repatriated and sent the former depot ship *Otto Wunsche* with the first and second groups of ships to bring their crews back to Germany; furthermore, HMS *Hambledon* was supplied as escort for the first stage of the voyage. *Z33*, *Steinbrinck* and the cruiser were delivered to Libau in Latvia, where they were joined by *Galster* and *Ihn* in March of the same year.

Of Great Britain's allocation, *Z25*, *Z31*, *Z38* and *Lody* were seaworthy, but *Beitzen* needed about five months' repairs if she was ever to be operational again whilst *Jacobi* needed repairs to her diesels and had leaks in some of her fuel tanks. *Riedel*, having suffered two collisions, had underwater defects and circulatory problems. *Lody* had minor defects only, and it was expected that she would be able to sail for the UK by 5 January and the other two by the 16th. *Lody*, in company with *Z25*, *T23*, and *T108*, departed on 6 January, escorted by the destroyers *Myngs*, *Zodiac* and *Obedient*, and arrived in Portsmouth the following day. *Riedel*, having developed engine room defects, was unable to sail with her group (*Jacobi*, *F4 Walter Holtzapfel* and *Freda Peters*), which left under escort of *Myngs*, *Zealous* and *Zodiac* on the 16th bound for Rosyth. A few days later *Zambesi* shepherded the now repaired *Riedel* across to Rosyth. The damaged *Beitzen* arrived in tow by the fleet tug *Enchanter* from Horten on 7 February, as had *Z30* the previous day under tow by *Enforcer* and *Chaser*.

None of the Type 34 or 36 destroyers was to be commissioned into the Royal Navy: they were instead to be used for trials and experiments by the various constructional and engineering establishments, for training of personnel in high-pressure boiler operation and on other subsidiary tasks. *Lody* and *Beitzen* were allocated the pennant numbers R38 and H97 for signalling purposes, but *Lody* later received H40 since her original number was required for the new 'C' class destroyer *Crystal* which was due to commission as the Norwegian *Stavanger* in February 1946.

Lody was employed initially as an instructional hulk for acquainting engineering staff with the high-pressure boiler concept, and for this purpose a small German contingent was retained until the last member, Kapitänleutnant (Ing) Eubel returned to Germany in October. Following this the destroyer was brought round to Thornycroft's yard in Southampton, where she was used as an accommodation ship. She remained in reserve until January 1949 when, having been sold to the British Iron and Steel Corporation (BISCO), she was towed to Sunderland for breaking up by Thomas Young, at whose yard she arrived on 17 July 1949.

Beitzen, owing to her poor condition resulting from wartime air attacks, had a rather shorter life. After the war's end a large number of surplus warships had been disposed of for various duties, one being target service. Special Military Branch Aquaint No. 2932, dated 8 March 1946, listed various ships to be expended as targets, amongst them the damaged *Beitzen*. She was actually allocated to target use in September that year, but in December she developed a dangerous leak as a result of extensive corrosion in the main circulating inlet pipe. Action was taken to beach her, following which temporary repairs were made.

The programme of ship target trials envisaged by the Royal Navy's constructors was considerably cut-back by demand of the Treasury with the effect that certain ships

Left: HMS *Nonsuch* enters Portsmouth in 1947. (WSS)

embarked for use were not in fact used. One of these was *Beitzen* which was instead taken into reserve and subsequently approved for disposal in January 1947. In 1948 she was handed over to BISCO and allocated to C. W. Dorkin for breaking up, arriving at their yard in Gateshead on 10 January 1949.

Of the other two large destroyers taken over by the Royal Navy, *Z30* was damaged and in such poor state of repair that she could only be used for ship construction experiments after her arrival in Rosyth in February 1946. She was towed to Loch Striven to be used as a target for underwater explosion tests, when between May and September 1948, three 500kg (1,090lb) charges of torpex (equivalent to a Mark IXa mine) were detonated at various distances beneath her. Despite plating damage the welded

hull withstood the stresses and remained intact. After the second test, *Z30* was docked at Govan for examination, but after the third, handed over to the shipbreakers on 9 September 1948 and towed direct to the breaker's yard at Dalmuir.

Z38, however, was unique in that she was the only ex-German destroyer to be commissioned into the Service, being used for trials purposes under the name *Nonsuch*. This seemingly unusual name in fact had a long lineage, *Z38* being the eleventh ship to receive it since its first use in 1603. Initially she was allocated the pennant number R40 but this was later changed to D107. Shortly after her arrival in UK waters she was employed on various trial and evaluation duties in the Clyde area before going to lay up in Porchester Creek. In October 1946 it was decided to commission the ship for extended machinery trials concurrent with service as an Air Target Ship in the Rosyth Local Command, replacing one of the current flotilla. Her poor condition delayed her entry into service, but in January 1947 it was reported that she had completed to full complement and by June she was expected to commission the following month, relieving *Fernie* as an aircraft target. In September 1948 *Nonsuch* was scheduled to pay off into care and maintenance on completion of the current trials, in about mid-October. Then in December that year approval was given to scrap the ship following demonstration of her auxiliary machinery to British manufacturers and the removal of certain equipment. In March 1949, however, it was decided instead to allocate her for ship target trials in place of *Kimberley*, whereupon she was disarmed and towed to Loch Striven. In October 1949, a 500kg charge was detonated under the ship, thowing a plume of water 250ft high, breaking her back 1.6 seconds after the explosion. No. 2 boiler room flooded immediately and the others gradually filled, necessitating her beaching. On inspection she was found too badly damaged to refloat and in consequence handed directly over to the shipbreakers on the beach. By August 1950 the breakers had cut off the damaged section at frame 71.5 and refloated the after part. This was examined at the breaker's yard for further information but the fore-end was broken up 'as lies' on the beach. Both Z30 and Z38 had withstood shock well, failure only arising as a result of poor weld design detail.

The USA received three destroyers, Z29, Z34 and Z39, but of these the first was lying in Bremerhaven in a damaged state only part way through a refit, while Z34, damaged by a torpedo from a Soviet MTB on 16 April 1945, had never been repaired. This left Z39 as the only seaworthy unit – and in fact the most modern German destroyer still afloat. The two damaged ships were not retained by the USN, and after examination Z34 was loaded with gas ammunition and towed out into the Skaggerak where she was scuttled on 26 March 1946. Later that year Z29, together with the torpedo boat T21, both again loaded with gas ammunition, were towed out and scuttled in deep water south-west of Farsund in the entrance to the Skaggerak on 10 June. (T156 was scuttled on this occasion as well.)

Z39 sailed from Wilhelmshaven on 6 July 1945 under British escort bound for the UK, in company with Z38, T28 and T35. By morning the next day the group stood off the Humber, and all ships oiled. Z38 and T28 then sailed immediately for Southampton, but the other two remained and did not sail until the following day. In the morning of the 8th Z39, under Lieutenant-Commander Forsberg RN and assisted by the German CO Kapitänleutnant Heinlein, sailed with T35 for Plymouth, where both ships were to be turned over to the US Navy, and by the morning of the 10th the two vessels were moored alongside the British destroyer Obedient. On passage all compartments had been painted, so that when she was inspected by the First Sea Lord on arrival she was spotless. At midday on 12 July, Z39 was officially turned over to US control when nine officers and 102 senior and junior rates of the USN came aboard. One of the first actions by the Americans was to throw all German and British rations overboard, replacing them with USN issue!

The next twelve days were taken up mainly in familiarizing the Americans with the German ship, and then on 24 July Z39 sailed for docking in Falmouth. Here, because no docking plans were available, the hydrophone cover was damaged on settling on the blocks, causing some oil leaks; furthermore, there was some unpleasantness between the Falmouth workmen and the German crew; while preparations were being made to weld the damaged bottom plates the dock was suddenly flooded – it had, apparently only been rented for the morning! After repairs, Z39 returned to Plymouth, sailing for the United States on 30 July. In company with T35, the destroyer crossed the Atlantic via the Azores, arriving in Argentia,

Below: DD935, ex-T35, at speed on trials by the US Navy. Except for the US-pattern radar on the bridge front, she is basically as she appeared in her last days with the Kriegsmarine. (USN)

Newfoundland, on 5 August, having been hampered in the last stages by fog, icebergs and low temperatures. Here, the US crew attempted unsuccessfully to raise steam, but after the German crew had managed to do so passage was made to Boston. Numerous trials in connection with the engines, boilers, turning circles, vibration and speed were conducted until the end of September, and then on the 28th of that month the remaining German crew members were disembarked and sent home in the trooper *West Point*, sailing from Norfolk, Virginia, on 25 October. Under the US designation DD939 the destroyer continued in experimental service until sale to France in November 1947.

'GROUPE MARCEAU'

The arbitrary division of the surrendered tonnage by the three major powers incensed France, who had initially received nothing. However, following strong representations from that country a number of vessels were subsequently handed over, amongst them the two seaworthy Type 34s of the UK allocation, *Jacobi* and *Riedel*, as well as *Z25* and *Z31*. The French Ministry of Marine had been pressing hard for enormous quantities of captured German war materials, from guns to bunting, for re-equipping their shattered forces, but on Britain's part these requests had been met with belated and devious replies, since, for political reasons, it had been decided that France was not to be included in the great share-out. Thus, following the tardy transfer of the four destroyers, French requests for live and practice ammunition for the 12.7cm guns sufficient for two years' service were answered to the effect that the only 12.7cm ammunition available was 573 practice projectiles, but in the end it was agreed that the Tripartite Commission scale of ammunition to be supplied with transferred vessels – two complete outfits excluding 40mm, according to the German Navy's rate book – would be adhered to and that, in addition, the two outfits from *Lody* and *Beitzen* would also be turned over.

Jacobi and *Beitzen* arrived in Cherbourg during January 1946; *Z25* arrived under her own steam with a German crew on 2 February, and *Z31* also arrived at this time. On 4 February, in the presence of the Minister of the Armed Forces, M. Michelet, Armaments Minister M. Tillon and Vice-Admiral Lemonnier, all four ships were renamed and hoisted the tricolour: *Z25* as *Hoche*, *Z31* as *Marceau*, *Jacobi* as *Desaix* and *Beitzen* as *Kléber*, all four ships commemorating units of the improved *Mogador* class vessels cancelled on the outbreak of the Second World War. All the names were, furthermore, important French historical figures. Together with some ex-German torpedo boats, these four vessels formed 'Groupe Marceau', comprised of ex-enemy vessels and commanded by Capitaine de Vaisseau Bosvieux who was, at the same time, commanding officer of the destroyer *Marceau* herself. Based in Cherbourg, most of the ships in the group received short refits before sailing on their first sorties under the French flag.

Above: *DD939*, ex-*Z39* open for visitors at Annapolis, October 1945. (USN)

Left: *T19*, under USN colours, supervises the scuttling of *T63*, which can just be made out behind her on the original print, on 2 July 1946. (USN)

Above: *Z29* at the end of the year. (USN)

Hoche was initially attached to the 1st Division of 'contre-torpilleurs' and in August 1946 took part in exercises with the newly arrived aircraft carrier *Colossus* (later named *Arromanches*), and later in the year sailed down the Biscay coast. Together with *Arromanches* and *Desaix*, she escorted *Richelieu* on the Presidential voyage to Conakry in April 1947, returning to Cherbourg in June. In 1948 she operated off the west coast of France and in the Mediterranean and in December visited Portsmouth, but by this time she had been allocated to the Cherbourg port reserve, although she did not pay off until 1 January 1949. *Hoche* remained in reserve for a year, then entered Cherbourg Arsenal for a major refit.

In the course of this refit the destroyer received an operations room, a command post, new radar, anti-submarine torpedo tubes, a new anti-aircraft outfit and new sonar sets. She ran trials between March and May 1953, then joined the 'Groupe d'Action Sous-marine' on 1 October 1953. *Hoche* sailed from Cherbourg to her new base at Toulon, where she was to be engaged in experimental anti-submarine trials. She was by this time reclassified as an 'escorteur rapide 1ère classe'. She continued to be so employed until 1956, when a major refit was necessary, but the hull was not now worth the expense. On 20 August 1956 *Hoche* was placed into 'Special B' reserve and then turned over to port control at Toulon on 1 September. She had steamed 46,000 miles under the tricolour in five years' service. *Hoche* was condemned on 2 January 1958, redesignated *Q102* and released for sale on 30 June.

Marceau, following her service in the 'Groupe Marceau', underwent a major refit at Toulon between 1 January 1948 and 3 October 1950, then on 18 October, with pennant number T01, she joined the cruiser group at Toulon. During her refit the forward 15cm gun was replaced, the bridge enlarged and the AA armament altered to eight 40mm singles. She served here for the next few years,

visiting Oran, Dakar and Bizerte regularly on exercises with the French Fleet. At the end of 1952 her voyages took her as far as Ajaccio in Corsica and Augusta in Sicily.

In May 1953 *Marceau* was ordered to Cherbourg to refit, where she remained until December. On completion of her refit, she was reclassified as an 'escorteur rapide' with the pennant number D601 and based at Cherbourg. Her remaining service life was brief, for she was now about twelve years old and, like her colleagues, becoming worn out. In February 1954 she was placed in ordinary reserve at Cherbourg then gradually through lower grades of reserve ('Special A' on 1 August 1956 and 'Special B' on 1 August 1957) until, on 2 January 1958, she was condemned and redesignated Q103. Authorized for sale as scrap, the ex-destroyer was then turned over to the dockyard for disposal.

Spare parts for the ex-German vessels presented something of a problem for they were, of course, no longer readily available. However, the former *Z39*, which had been taken over by the USA in 1945, was by August 1947 surplus to US Navy requirements following the completion of exhaustive comparative trials. France made enquiries in that direction, with the result that Naval Engineer Perrin was sent over to Annapolis, where *Z39* (now DD939) was lying. The French Navy took delivery of her at Annapolis on 10 November the same year, and arrangements were made to bring her back to Europe. After crossing the Atlantic via Fort de France (Martinique), she arrived in Casablanca on 15 December 1947 under tow by the light cruiser *Georges Leygues*. Finally, she was towed to Cherbourg, being renamed *Léopard* on arrival, although further examination showed her to be unfit for service and she lost her name and was merely numbered *Q128*. Between 1947 and 1953 she was gradually cannibalized for spares until being condemned on 15 June 1953. She was finally disposed of in 1958.

Kléber received a short refit between 31 August and 10 September 1946 and then undertook a short work-up cruise to Bordeaux between 28 October and 21 December, during which she rescued the crew of the collier *France-Hélène* (3,971 tons) which sank on 31 October 1946.

During 1947, by now attached to the 1st Division of 'contre-torpilleurs' with the pennant number T03, *Kléber* remained based at Cherbourg and visited many of the French Atlantic ports in the course of the year. Towards the end of the year she escorted the submarine *Doris* (ex-*Vineyard*) back to the UK on her reversion to Royal Navy control. The submarine was turned over in Londonderry, Northern Ireland, where the destroyer remained from 13 to 15 November, returning to Cherbourg by 25 November.

Between 1948 and 1951 she was taken in hand for a major refit at Cherbourg dockyard, when her bridge structure was considerably modified and enlarged. The forward funnel was fitted with a redesigned clinker screen, similar to but rather larger than that fitted to *Marceau*, and at the same time the German-pattern anti-aircraft weapons were removed and replaced by six single 40mm Bofors. These were positioned similarly to those of *Desaix*, i.e., abreast No. 2 gun, abreast the after funnel and on No. 3 gun deck. No. 3 12.7cm gun was removed during this refit. New radar was fitted, of American pattern, and the foremast was altered. The refit was completed by the first week in December 1951, and on 20 December she weighed anchor and sailed for Toulon where she was now to be based.

For the next twenty-two months, *Kléber* operated in the Mediterranean as part of the 3rd Destroyer Division, visiting most of the French North African ports including Bizerte (May), Oran (June), Agadir, Casablanca and Arzew (July). On her return from Arzew in July 1952, following exercises with the Fleet off Toulon, she was taken under refit once more, between 22 July and 16 October. In 1953 she continued to be based in Toulon (now part of the 3rd Division of 'escorteurs rapides') but was ordered back to Cherbourg towards the middle of the year, where she arrived at the end of October. Her active life was by now nearly over since on 20 December 1953 her status was altered to reserve, category 'Special A'. In August 1956 she was reduced to reserve category 'B'.

Various tasks were considered for the ex-German destroyer as she lay derelict in Cherbourg harbour during 1957, including that of a floating barracks and an annexe for the damage control school. However, inspection showed that the ship was by now in very poor condition, her hull, in particular, being badly corroded. A refit was considered too expensive, and on 3 April 1957 it was proposed to condemn the ship. The Secretary of State for the Navy issued the necessary agreement on 10 April, whereupon she ceased to be known as *Kléber* and received instead the number Q85. This step having been taken, the hulk was handed over to the local dockyard administration for useful equipment to be removed and then offered for sale, and the former *Beitzen* was finally broken up at Rouen.

Desaix also joined the 1st Division of 'contre-torpilleurs' at Cherbourg in 1946 and ran trials from that port in September. In October she, too, sailed on a work-up voyage down to Brest, returning to Cherbourg by the end of 1946. Between 23 March and 13 June 1947 she took part in the Presidential cruise to North Africa and Dakar, during which she formed part of the escort to the battleship *Richelieu*. In the second half of the year another cruise was made to North Africa. The year 1948 saw *Desaix* involved in fleet exercises in the spring and a naval review by the President of the Republic at Brest on 30 May, following which she was present at St-Malo for the centenary of Chateaubriand. The end of the year saw one more cruise to Bordeaux and the ship returned to Cherbourg on 4 November 1948.

Desaix had a shorter active life than her sister: her crew was reduced before the end of 1948 and in January 1949 she was placed in reserve. Between 1949 and 1954, having been reduced to category 'B' reserve, she was cannibalized for spares, and after a docking in May 1952 had shown her to be in poor condition, she was proposed for disposal on 16 February 1954. This was agreed and the ship was condemned the following day and the hulk given the number Q02. In June 1954 the ship was sold for scrap and towed to Rouen for breaking up.

EXTENSIVE REFIT

The careers of the four units allocated to the USSR are somewhat obscure. Although official Soviet sources deny the existence of these vessels, it is certain that one of the Type 34 ships was commissioned into the Soviet Navy in 1946 and renamed *Pylkii*. The second unit has usually been quoted as having been renamed *Zorkii*, but this is unlikely since there already existed a vessel of that name, the ex-NKVD patrol vessel which had been taken over by the Navy during the war. Which unit was renamed is not certain. *Ihn* was operational at the end of hostilities and therefore a likely candidate, but she had not been given the full major anti-aircraft refit as had *Steinbrinck*; the latter, whilst non-operational at the war's end, did get a subsequent refit in Wilhelmshaven whilst under British control, and on balance it is likely that this was the ship which was commissioned, *Ihn* probably being cannibalized for spares.

Galster, the sole surviving Type 36 destroyer, was eventually recommissioned in 1946 as *Prochnyi*. The operational careers of both recommissioned units were probably only short, and certainly not longer than three years. Both were originally attached to the Soviet 4th Fleet based at Rostock and operated from there at least until 1948. *Pylkii* was next observed in May 1949 whilst moored at the Petrozavod Yard in Leningrad, apparently undergoing overhaul and refit on conversion to a training ship. This yard was the former Russkii Diesel Works and Oktinski Yard. Here she was disarmed, and when seen she was painted a light green with the pennant number 31. She was seen again on 24 August 1959 in Leningrad coaling harbour as an auxiliary, in which category she remained, probably as an accommodation ship for crews joining the 'Kotlin' and 'Krupnyi' class destroyers then building, until April 1960. After this there is no further record of her, and it would appear that she was soon scrapped.

Prochnyi (ex-*Galster*) also remained with the 4th Fleet, but at the beginning of 1950 was seen under refit at the Zhadanov Yard in Leningrad, where she appeared to be in the course of conversion to a training ship. On 10 October 1950 Intelligence reported her moored in the Ekateringofskii Canal at Gutuevskii Island near the Zhadanov Yard, derelict and in a poor state of preservation. In 1954 she was reported as having the pennant number 12, and in the autumn of 1956 she was again seen in Leningrad, this time in use as an accommodation or barracks ship. She remained in this state, according to

Intelligence reports, until April 1960, but some time after this, and before January 1965, she was deleted and presumably scrapped.

Z33 sailed for Libau on 2 January 1946 in the *Nürnberg* group and was commissioned into the Soviet Navy later the same year, renamed *Provornyi*. Two years later she was attached to the 4th Fleet and based at Rostock in East Germany. Here, in the Neptunwerft yard, she received an extensive refit between 1947 and 1950, during which she had all her armament removed except the twin turret. Little is then known of her movements until in 1954 she was observed wearing the pennant number 13; in the autumn of that year she appeared in Kronstadt assigned to the Baltic Fleet Training Detachment with the pennant number 15, but by the spring of 1955 the number had been altered once more, to 37. During these years two 15cm guns were reinstated aft in Nos. 2 and 3 positions and twelve Russian pattern 3.7cm L/63 twin mountings shipped. In the spring of 1957 *Provornyi* disappeared from the list of pennant numbers for the Soviet Fleet and was apparently no longer a commissioned destroyer. Up until April 1960 she was listed as an auxiliary, being used as a barracks ship at Kronstadt, but by 1965 her name no longer appeared in the list and one can only assume that in the intervening years she had been discarded and broken up.

'SPARE PARTS RESERVE'

The surviving torpedo boats were also divided amongst the Allies but, once again, apart from trials and investigations, only the French and Russian Navies actually put any into service. Those acquired by France were, like their destroyers, very much 'third hand', having been originally allocated to the UK or USA. From Britain, France received *T28* and *T35* (Type 39 design) and *T11* and *T20* (Type 35/37), and from the USA she received in addition *T35* and *T14*. *T35* had been taken to the United States for investigation and redesignated DD935. She was towed to France in 1947 and used as a 'spare parts reserve' for *T23* (now renamed *Alsacien*) and *T28* (*Lorraine*), before being finally condemned at Cherbourg on 3 October 1952. Both *Alsacien* and *Lorraine* saw considerable service with the French Fleet, commissioning for the ex-German group on 16 May and 1 June 1946 respectively before going to the Mediterranean for several years. *Alsacien* was finally condemned on 9 June 1954 and renumbered *Q11* before being sold for scrapping. *Lorraine* lasted a little longer, not entering category 'B' reserve until 1 May 1955. At the end of October that year she was redesignated *Q69*, but it was not for another four years, on 21 July 1959, that she was condemned for scrap.

In contrast to the larger torpedo boats, the smaller Type 35/37 ships saw no service under the French flag. Both *T11* and *T20* had arrived in France in February 1946 and had been renamed *Birhakeim* and *Baccarat* respectively, but they were then sent straight into reserve where they remained until both were struck off on 8 October 1951. *T14*, which had lain at Bremerhaven since the end of the war, was brought to Cherbourg in 1947, arriving on 24 October. Her subsequent career, under the name *Dompaire*, was similar to those of *T11* and *T20*.

T12, *T17* and *T33* were renamed *Podvischny*, *Porivisty* and *Primierny* after their allocation to the Soviet Union. Little is known of their subsequent employment but they were probably used for trials and training before being discarded in the 1950s.

MISFORTUNES OF WAR

With the scrapping of the French vessels and the end of the Russian units in sight, if indeed they still existed, the last of the Kriegsmarine's destroyers and torpedo boats disappeared. What is the verdict on their performance in the exacting circumstances of war? They undoubtedly proved a disappointment in service, predominantly from the point of view of mechanical reliability – a factor of paramount importance in wartime. The primary requirements of a warship are that it should be able to float, steam and fight, but all too often these ships could not steam. As regards fighting ability, they were all well equipped to look after themselves, but the possession of a good armament is only a part of the story. Properly

handled, they achieved some successes, as the encounters with *Jersey*, *Javelin*, *Charybdis* and *Limbourne*, as well as certain phases of the Narvik battles, testified.

The Narvik campaign was certainly not the one-sided affair that it appeared on paper and, but for torpedo defects, tactical errors and shortage of fuel and ammunition, it might well have turned out very differently. However, such are the misfortunes of war, and the losses at Narvik crippled the German destroyer strength for the rest of the conflict because new construction was neither adequate in quantity nor rapid enough to give the numbers that would have allowed the High Command to treat them to a degree as expendable. As a result, the destroyers were tethered on the same leash which held the cruisers and capital ships, and in consequence were never employed with the aggressiveness of, for example, their British counterparts. The officers and crews of the destroyers, moored in remote, cold and inhospitable Norwegian fjords, chafed at the enforced inactivity and longed for aggressive action. Unfortunately, the longer the ships remained idle, the poorer became the state of training, and with the gradually increasing difficulties of obtaining fuel oil the situation became critical in the last two or three years of the war. Thus after 1942 these ships, even with their heavy armament, and given steam plants fully operational, would almost certainly have suffered severely at the hands of Allied destroyers in action. Their lack of success after 1940 can be attributed to many things, both technical and political, but it was proved once again that in war at sea numbers count, and there were never enough German destroyers.

In the technical field, the introduction of the 15cm gun was undoubtedly a mistake, for it resulted in a cruiser armament on a destroyer platform, without the gun control facilities, seakeeping ability and height of command that a cruiser hull conferred. It is not insignificant that on four missions, when confronted by British 6in-gunned cruisers, the German destroyers, although superior in numbers of ships and fire power, came off decidedly the worse and in three of these engagements lost themselves three of their number. Admittedly, on several of these occasions the seas were rough, but this merely underlines the folly of putting too heavy a gun on a small hull. In the Arctic weather the British cruiser gun crews in their enclosed turrets were at a great advantage over the enemy serving open mounts in freezing conditions.

Radar, too, played an important part in the war at sea, and German naval radar was always technically behind the Allies' systems. Again, in the cruiser engagements, the British ships in each case fired by radar under adverse weather conditions. Finally, the crippling oil shortages which hampered operational use probably contributed indirectly to the failure to develop any form of Action Information Centre or plot, with the result that on the occasions when action was joined much confusion and a lack of appreciation of the tactical position developed, leading to a failure to press home such advantages that did occur.

This, then, is the story of the Kriegsmarine's destroyer force. It started with such high hopes in 1939, only to receive shattering blows in 1940. Nevertheless, it remained active until the final desperate attempts to rescue the fleeing refugees and soldiers from the advancing Russians in 1945.

APPENDIXES

1. TECHNICAL DATA: DESTROYERS

TYPES 34, 34A (*Z1-16*)
Displacement:
Z1-4 2,232 tons (standard), 3,156 tons (full load)
Z5-8 2,171 tons (standard), 3,110 tons (full load)
Z9-13 2,270 tons (standard), 3,190 tons (full load)
Z14-16 2,239 tons (standard), 3,165 tons (full load)
Length:
Z1-8 114m (pp), 119m (oa)
Z9-16 116m (pp), 121m (oa)
Beam: 11.3m
Draught: 3.8/4.3m
Machinery:
Six Wagner 70kg/cm² boilers (*Z1-8*) or six Benson 110kg/cm² boilers (*Z9-16*)
Two sets Wagner geared turbines, 70,000 shp = 38 knots
Two turbogenerators of 200kW each
Two diesel generators of 60kW each and one of 50kW (*Z9-16* three 50kW sets)
670*/770 tonnes oil fuel = 1,530*/1,900 miles at 19 knots
Armament:
Five 12.7cm SK C/34 in single mountings, 120rpg
Four 3.7cm SK C/30 in twin mountings, 2,000rpg
Six 2cm C/30 in single mountings, 2,000rpg
Eight 53.3cm torpedo tubes in two quadruple banks
Sixty mines
*Benson ships.

TYPE 36 (*Z17-22*)
Displacement:
2,411 tons (standard), 3,415 tons (full load)
Length:
Z17-19 120m (pp), 123m (oa)
Z20-22 120m (pp), 125m (oa)
Beam: 11.8m
Draught: 3.8/4.3m

Machinery:
Six Wagner 70kg/cm² boilers
Two sets Wagner geared turbines, 70,000shp = 38 knots
Two turbogenerators of 200kW each
One diesel generator of 40kW and two of 80kW each
787 tonnes oil fuel = 2,020 miles at 19 knots
Armament:
Five 12.7cm SK C/34 in single mountings, 120rpg
Four 3.7cm SK C/30 in twin mountings, 2,000rpg
Seven 2cm C/30 in single mountings, 2,000rpg
Eight 53.3cm torpedo tubes in two quadruple banks
Sixty mines

TYPE 36A (*Z23-30*)
Displacement:
Z23-24 2,603 tons (standard), 3,605 tons (full load)
Z25-27 3,079 tons (standard), 3,543 tons (full load)
Z28 2,596 tons (standard), 3,519 tons (full load)
Z29-30 2,603 tons (standard), 3,597 tons (full load)
Length: 121.9m (pp), 127m (oa)
Beam: 12m
Draught: 3.9/4.65m
Machinery:
Six Wagner 70kg/cm² boilers, four at 54 tonnes/hr and two at 48 tonnes/hr
Two sets Wagner geared turbines, 70,000shp = 36-38.5 knots
Two turbogenerators of 200kW each
Four diesel generators of 80kW each
801 tonnes oil fuel (*Z23-27*), 769 (*Z28*), 825 (*Z29-30*)=2,174 miles (*Z23-27*), 2,087 (*Z28*), 2,239 (*Z29-30*) at 19 knots
Armament:
Five (*Z28* four) 15cm TBK C/36 (1x2, 3x1), 120rpg

Four 3.7cm SK C/30 (2x2), 2,000 rpg
Five (*Z28* six) 2cm C/30 (5x1), 2,000rpg
Eight 53.3cm torpedo tubes in two quadruple banks
Sixty mines

TYPE 36A (Mob) (*Z31-34, Z37-39*)
All details as for *Z29* and *Z30* (Type 36A); differences confined to visual appearance except only one 200kW turbogenerator fitted, in No.1 turbine room

TYPE 36B (Mob) (*Z35, Z36, Z43-47*)
Z44-47 not completed (*Z46-47* reallocated to Type 36C)
Displacement:
2,527 tons (standard), 3,507 tons (full load)
Length: 121.9m (pp), 127m (oa)
Beam: 12m
Draught: 3.54/4.32m
Machinery:
As Type 36C but boiler temperatures 426°C
Armament:
Five 12.7cm SK C/34 in single mountings, 120rpg
Four 3.7cm Sk C/30 in twin mountings, 2,000rpg
Fifteen 2cm C/30 in three Vierling and three single mounts
Eight 53.3cm, torpedo tubes in quadruple banks
Seventy-six mines
Note: A modified design with two 15cm single guns replacing the forward 12.7cm was also prepared.

TYPE 36C (*Z46-50*)
Not completed
Displacement:
2,754 tons (standard), 3,594 tons (full load)
Length: 121.5m (pp), 126.2m (oa)
Beam: 12.2m
Draught: 3.62/4.45m

Machinery:
As Type 36A
Armament:
Six 12.8cm in twin mountings, 120rpg
Six 3.7cm in twin mountings, 2,000rpg
Six 2cm in single mountings, 2,000rpg

TYPE 36D
Design Project
Alternative design for Type 36A in case of non-delivery of scheduled 15cm twin turrets

TYPE 38A (*Z40-42*)
Design project
Renamed 'Spähkreuzer 38'

TYPE 38B
Displacement:
2,000 tonnes (standard), 2,550 tonnes (full load)
Length: 111.70m
Beam: 11.3m
Draught: 3.19/4.03m
Machinery:
Four Wagner 70kg/cm² boilers
Twin-shaft geared turbines, 50,000shp = 35.4 knots, 2,660 miles at 19 knots
Armament:
Four 12.7cm in twin mountings
Two 3.7cm
Two 2cm
Eight 53.3cm torpedo tubes in quadruple banks
Four depth-charge throwers
Note: This was an attempt to design the smallest possible destroyer for North Sea operations; the Type 34 and 36 destroyers had proved oversize.

TYPE 41 (*Z48-51*)
Design projects A, B, C, D
Displacement:
(A, B) 2,995 tonnes standard; (C, D) 2,805 tonnes standard
Normal displacement:
(A) 3,410; (B) 3,555; (C) 3,220; (D) 3,395 tonnes

Loaded displacement:
(A) 3,705; (B) 3,975; (C) 3,515; (D) 3,840 tonnes
Length:
129m
Beam: 12.7m
Draught:
(A) 4.12; (B) 4.25; (C) 3.90; (D) 4.10m
Horsepower:
(A, B) 80,000; (C, D) 70,000
Speed with 40% fuel:
(A) 38.2; (B) 37.4; (C) 37.1; (D) 36.4 knots
Speed with 75% fuel:
(A) 36.5; (B) 35.3; (C) 34.9; (D) 33.7 knots
Fuel:
(A) 700; (B) 1,050; (C) 700; (D) 1,100 tonnes
Endurance at 19 knots:
(A) 2,150; (B) 3,150; (C) 2,300; (D) 3,450 miles
Armament:
Six 12.7cm in twin mountings
Four 3.7cm in twin mountings
Eight 2cm in quadruple and twin mountings
Eight 53.3cm torpedo tubes (4 spare torpedoes)
Note: Proposed following the decision to cancel 'Spähkreuzer' construction in favour of extra destroyers. Four ships planned and ordered from Deschimag at Bremen but none laid down. Later re-designated Type 36C and added to Z46 and Z47 (except Z51, see below).

TYPE 42 (Z51-58)
Design projects
Standard displacement:
(42) 2,084: (42A) 2,230; (42B) 2,860;
(42C) 2,985 tonnes
Normal displacement:
(42) 2,328; (42B) 3,170; (42C) 3,295 tonnes
Loaded displacement:
(42B) 3,650; (42C) 3,763 tonnes
Overall length:
(42) 108; (42A) 114; (42B) 124; (42C) 126m
Beam:
(42) 11; (42A) 11.5; (42B) 12.5; (42C) 12.6m
Draught
(42C) 4.10m
Engines:
(42) 6; (42A) 6; (42B) 8; (42C) 8
Shafts:
(42) 3; (42A) 3; (42B) 2; (42C) 2
Horsepower:
(42) 57-60,000; (42A) 57,300; (42B) 75,800; (42C) 75,800-80,000
Speed:
(42A) 35.9; (42B) 38.2; (42C) 38 knots
Range at 19 knots:
(42) 5,200; (42A) 5,500; (42B) 6,500; (42C) 6,500 miles
Armament:
(42) 4 x 12.7cm (single); 8 x 3.7cm (twin), 12 x 2cm (quad), 6 x 53.3cm TT; (42A) 4 x 12.8cm (single), 8 x 53.3cm TT; (42B) 4 x 12.8cm (twin), 2 x 12.8cm (single), 8 x 3.7cm, 8 x 2cm, 8 x 53.3cm TT (+4 spare); (42C) 6 x 12.8cm (twin), 3 x 5.5cm (single), 14 x 3cm (twin), 8 x 53.3cm TT (+8 spare).
Note: Type 42 referred to Z51 only, Types 42A B and C applying to other alternative designs from Z52 on. The Type 42 differed from previous and later classes in its smaller hull. It was

originally designed for six MAN Type 12 Z32/44 diesel engines but it was decided to rush completion at Deschimag (Bremen) with four engines geared on to the centre shaft and install the fifth and sixth on to the wing shafts when ready. Each motor had a rated capacity of 10,000hp and an actual output of 9,500hp at 600rpm.
Eight diesel generators in two circuits produced a total of 320kW.

TYPE 43
Design projects
Standard displacement:
(43) 2,900; (43A) 2,950; (43A(Mod)) 3,020 tonnes
Length:
(43) 124; (43A) 128; (43A(Mod)) 128m
Beam:
(43) 12.5; (43A) 12.6; (43A(Mod)) 13m
Shafts:
(43) 2; (43A) 3; (43(Mod)) 3
Horsepower:
(43) 75,000; (43A) 75,000; (43A(Mod)) 75,000
Speed with 40% fuel:
(43) 37.75; (43A) 38; (43A(Mod)) 37.25
Endurance at 19 knots:
(43) 5,500; (43A) 5,500; (43A(Mod)) 5,500-6,000 miles
Armament:
(43) 6 x 12.8cm (twin); 10 x 53.3cm TT; (43A) 4 x 12.8cm (single), 8 x 53.3cm TT; (43A(Mod)) 6 x 12.8cm, 10 x 53.3cm TT
Note: Construction of Type 43 was to

succeed Type 42C when delivery problems of 12.8cm turrets were solved. Both 2- and 3-shaft designs proposed, preference being given to former because of machinery arrangements and also because speed and endurance were almost identical.
All these variations were to be equipped with new 8-engine drive introduced in Type 42C and were expected to achieve greater speed through economy in weight and various hull simplifications.

TYPE 45
Design project
Displacement:
2,657 tonnes (standard), 3,700 tonnes (full load)
Length: 118m
Beam: 11.8m
Draught: 3.88m
Machinery:
Four Wagner 70kg/cm² boilers
Twin-shaft geared turbines, 80,000shp = 39.5 knots
800 tonnes oil fuel = 3,600 miles at 19 knots
Armament:
Eight 12.8cm in twin mountings
Four 5.5cm in single mountings
Twelve 3cm in twin mountings
Eight 53.3cm torpedo tubes
100 mines

---

2. TECHNICAL DATA: TORPEDO BOATS

TYPE 23 (*Albatros, Falke, Greif, Kondor, Möwe, Seeadler*)
Displacement:
938 tonnes (type), 1,310 tonnes (full load)
Length: 85.73m (wl), 87.7m (oa)
Beam: 8.25m
Draught: 3.65m (mean, full load)
Machinery:
Three 18.5kg/cm² boilers
Two-shaft geared turbines, 23,000shp = 32-34 knots
321 tonnes oil fuel = 1,800 miles at 17 knots
Armament:
Three 10.5cm L/45
Two 2cm added
Six 50cm (later 53.3cm) torpedo tubes in two triple mountings
Crew: 120

TYPE 24 (*Iltis, Jaguar, Leopard, Luchs, Tiger, Wolf*)
Displacement:
948 tonnes (type), 1,319 tonnes (full load)
Length: 89m (wl), 92.6m (oa)
Beam: 8.6m
Draught: 3.52m (mean, full load)
Machinery:
Three 18.5kg/cm² boilers
Two-shaft geared turbines, 23,000shp = 32-34 knots
327 tonnes oil fuel = 1,997 miles at 17 knots
Armament:
Three 10.5cm SK C/28
Two 2cm added
Six 50cm (later 53.3cm) torpedo tubes in two triple mountings
Crew: 129

TYPE 35 (*T1-12*)
Displacement:
859.2 tonnes (type), 1,108.3 tonnes (full load)
Length: 82.16m (wl), 84.3m (oa)
Beam: 8.62m
Draught: 2.83m (mean, full load)
Machinery:
Four 70kg/cm² boilers, 460°C
Two-shaft geared turbines, 31,000shp = 35 knots
190.6 tonnes oil fuel = 1,200 miles at 19 knots
Armament:
One 10.5cm SK C/32
One 3.7cm SK C/30
Two 2cm MG C/30
Six 53.3cm torpedo tubes in two triple mountings
Crew: 117

TYPE 37 (*T13-21*)
Displacement:
888.2 tonnes (type), 1,139 tonnes (full load)
Length: 81.97m (wl), 85.2m (oa)
Beam: 8.87m
Draught: 2.8m (mean, full load)
Machinery:
Four 70kg/cm² boilers, 460°C
Two-shaft geared turbines, 31,000shp = 35 knots
199.9 tonnes oil fuel = 1,600 miles at 19 knots
Armament:
One 10.5cm SK C/32
One 3.7cm SK C/30
Two 2cm MG C/30
Six 53.3cm torpedo tubes in two triple mountings
Crew: 119

TYPE 39 (*T22-36*)
Displacement:
1,318 tonnes (type), 1,780 tonnes (full load)
Length: 97m (wl), 102.5m (oa)
Beam: 10m
Draught: 3.25m (mean, full load)
Machinery:
Four 70kg/cm² boilers, 460°C
Two-shaft geared turbines, 32,000shp = 33.5 knots
375 tonnes oil fuel = 2,400 miles at 19 knots
Armament:
Four 10.5cm SK C/32
Four 3.7cm SK C/30
Six 2cm MG C/38
Six 53.3cm torpedo tubes in two triple mountings
Crew: 185

TYPE 41 (*T37-51*)
Displacement:
1,514 tonnes (type), 2,190 tonnes (full load)
Length: 102m (wl), 106m (oa)
Beam: 10.7m
Draught: 3.72m (mean, full load)
Machinery:
Four 70kg/cm² boilers, 460°C

Two-shaft geared turbines, 40,000shp = 34 knots
559 tonnes oil fuel = 2,800 miles at 19 knots
Armament:
Four 10.5cm SK C/32
Six 3.7cm SK C/30
Eight 2cm MG C/38
Six 53.3cm torpedo tubes in two triple mountings
Crew: 197

TYPE 41A
Displacement:
1,630 tonnes (type), 2,260 tonnes (full load)
Length: 102m (wl)
Beam: 10.7m
Draught: 3.31m (mean, full load)
Machinery:
Four 70kg/cm² boilers, 460°C
Two-shaft geared turbines, 52,000shp = 38 knots
520 tonnes oil fuel = 1,900 miles at 19 knots
Armament:
Four 10.5cm
Six 3cm FLK/44
Eight 2cm MG C/38
Six 53.3cm torpedo tubes in two triple

mountings
Crew: 214

TYPE 44(A)
Displacement:
1,491 tonnes (type), 1,860 tonnes (full load)
Length: 99m (wl)
Beam: 10.1m
Draught: 3.56m (mean, full load)
Machinery:
Four 70kg/cm² boilers, 460°C
Two-shaft geared turbines, 52,000shp = 37.25 knots
Endurance 1,900 miles at 19 knots
Armament:
Four 10.5cm KM/44
Ten 3cm FLK/44
Six 53.3cm torpedoes in two triple mountings
Crew: 176

TYPE 44(B)
Displacement:
1,461 tonnes (type), 1,821 tonnes (full load)
Length: 97m (wl)
Beam: 10m
Draught: 3.56m (mean, full load)
Machinery:

Four 70kg/cm² boilers, 460°C
Two-shaft geared turbines, 52,000shp = 37.5 knots
Endurance 1,900 miles at 19 knots
Armament:
Four 10.5cm KM/44
Eight 3cm FLK/44
Six 53.3cm torpedo tubes in two triple mountings
Crew: 160

TYPE 40 (*T61-72*)
Displacement:
1,957 tonnes (type), 2,587 tonnes (full load)
Length: 110m (wl)
Beam: 11.25m
Draught: 3.4m (mean, full load)
Machinery:
Three 28kg/cm² boilers, 380°C
Two-shaft geared turbines, 49,500shp = 35 knots
561 tonnes oil fuel = 2,350 miles at 19 knots
Armament:
Four 12.7cm SK C/34
Four 3.7cm SK C/30
Sixteen 2cm MG C/38
Eight 53.3cm torpedo tubes
Crew: 205

3. CONSTRUCTION AND CAREER NOTES: DESTROYERS

Z1 (*Leberecht Maass*)
Historical note:
Konteradmiral Maass was Flag Officer (Scouting Forces) aboard SMS *Köln* during the action with British battle-cruisers off Heligoland on 28 August 1914. He was killed when *Köln* was lost.
Ship details:
Type 34
Ordered 7.7.34
Builder Deutscher Werke (Kiel)
Yard No. K242
Laid down 10.10.34
Launched 18.8.35
Completed 14.1.37
Commanding officers:
K.Kpt. F.T. Schmidt 14.1.37-29.9.37
K.Kpt./F.Kpt. G. Wagner 5.10.37-4.4.39
K.Kpt. F. Bassenge 5.4.39-22.2.40
Career summary:
Up to June 1939 Leader destroyer of FdT
September 1939 Poland
Up to December 1939 Refit
February 1940 2nd Flotilla; mercantile warfare in Skaggerak
Fate:
Sunk in error 22 February 1940 NW of

Borkum by Luftwaffe He 111 1H+1M (possibly also mined on undiscovered British minefield); 283 crew lost.

Z2 (*Georg Thiele*)
Historical note:
Korvettenkapitän Thiele was aboard the torpedo boat *S119* as senior oficer of the 7th Torpedo Boat Half-Flotilla during a minelaying sortie with *S115*, *S117* and *S118* into the Downs in 1914. The four torpedo boats were intercepted on 17 October by the light cruisers *Arethusa* and *Undaunted* together with four destroyers, in 52° 48' N, 3° 49' E when all the German ships were sunk. Thiele was lost with *S119*.
Ship details:
Type 34
Ordered 7.7.34
Builder Deutscher Werke (Kiel)
Yard No. K243
Laid down 25.10.34
Launched 18.8.35
Completed 27.2.37
Commanding officers:
K.Kpt. H. Hartmann 27.2.37-7.8.38
K.Kpt. R. von Pufendorf 8.8.37-27.10.38

K.Kpt. M. E. Wolff 30.10.38-13.4.40
Career summary:
September 1939 Poland
January-April 1940 Repairs/refit; 1st Flotilla
Fate:
Scuttled 13 April 1940 in Rombaksfjord during Second Battle of Narvik.

Z3 (*Max Schultz*)
Historical note:
Korvettenkapitän Schultz, as senior officer of the 6th Torpedo Boat Flotilla, was killed aboard *V69* during an encounter with British cruisers off the mouth of the River Maas on 23 January 1917. *V69* was seriously damaged but managed to struggle into Ijmuiden.
Ship details:
Type 34
Ordered 7.7.34
Builder Deutscher Werke (Kiel)
Yard No. K244
Laid down 2.1.35
Launched 30.11.35
Completed 8.4.37
Commanding officers:
K.Kpt. M. Baltzer 8.4.37-24.10.38
K.Kpt. C. Trampedach 25.10.38-22.2.40

Career summary:
August 1939 Collision with *Tiger*
Up to October 1939 Repairs
Up to January 1940 1st Flotilla; Fleet operations/mercantile warfare
Fate:
Bombed in error 22 February 1940 by HE 111 1H+1M off Borkum during operation 'Wikinger'.

Z4 (*Richard Beitzen*)
Historical note:
Kapitänleutnant Beitzen, as senior officer of the 14th Torpedo Boat Flotilla, was killed aboard *G87* whilst endeavouring to rescue survivors from *G39* and *G94* which had been mined in the North Sea on 30 March 1918. *G87* was also mined and sunk.
Ship details:
Type 34
Ordered 7.7.34
Builder Deutscher Werke (Kiel)
Yard No. K245
Laid down 7.1.35
Launched 30.11.35
Completed 13.5.37
Commanding officers:
K.Kpt. H-J. Gadow 13.5.37-15.5.38

K.Kpt. M. Schmidt 16.5.38-24.10.39
K.Kpt. H. von Davidson 1.11.39-
    30.1.43
K.Kpt. H. Dominik 31.1.43-1.44
K.Lt. W. Ludde-Neurath 4.44-6.44
K.Kpt. R. Gade 6.44-9.44
K.Kpt. H. Neuss 9.44-5.45
Career summary:
September 1939 Poland
Minelaying 12.39-2.40
'Wikinger' 2.40
France 1940-41
Norway 1941
'Cerberus' 2.42
Norway 1942-43 ('RegenBogen')
Skaggerak 1943-45
1945 UK; target service
Fate:
Sold C. W. Dorkin for breaking up;
    arrived Gateshead 10 January 1949.

Z5 (Paul Jacobi)
Historical note:
During the First World War Korvetten-
kapitän Jacobi was senior officer of the
8th Torpedo Boat Half-Flotilla and was
killed when his ship, V25, was mined
and sunk off the Amrum Bank whilst
acting as escort to the 2nd Minesweeper
Division on 12 February 1915.
Including Jacobi, 79 men were lost from
V25.
Ship details:
Type 34A
Ordered 9.1.35
Builder Deschimag A.G. (Bremen)
Yard No. W899
Laid down 15.7.35
Launched 24.3.36
Completed 29.6.37
Commanding officers:
K.Kpt. R. Peters 29.6.37-3.11.38
K.Kpt. H. G. Zimmer 4.11.38-2.41
K.Kpt. H. Schlieper 1.4.41-9.7.44
K.Kpt. M. Bulter 10.7.44-9.5.45
Capitaine de Frégate Douguet 4.2.46
Capitaine de Frégate Béret 20.6.47
Capitaine de Frégate Delort-Laval
    10.7.48
Career summary:
Norway 1940
Western France 1940-41
'Cerberus' 2.42
Norway 1942-44
Baltic 1944-45
UK 1945
To France 1946
Fate:
Paid off for disposal by French Navy 17
    February 1954.

Z6 (Theodore Riedel)
Historical note:
Korvettenkapitän Riedel was senior
officer of the 6th Torpedo Boat Half-
Flotilla and was killed at Jutland on 31
May 1916, probably aboard S54.
Ship details:
Type 34A
Ordered 9.1.35

Builder Deschimag A.G. (Bremen)
Yard No. W900
Laid down 18.7.35
Launched 22.4.36
Completed 2.7.37
Commanding officers:
K.Kpt. M. Fechner 6.7.37-30.10.38
K.Kpt. G. Bohmig 31.10.38-25.11.40
K.Kpt. W. Riede 9.4.41-19.9.43
K.Kpt. Freiherr von Hausen 20.9.43-
    3.1.44
K.Kpt. R. Menge 4.1.44-9.6.44
K.Kpt. H. Blose 10.6.44-21.5.45
Capitaine de Frégate Bourely 2.4.46
Capitaine de Frégate Poncet 8.9.47
Capitaine de Frégate Chatereau 19.6.50
Capitaine de Frégate Schlumberger
    27.9.51
Capitaine de Frégate Cassiarino
    22.12.52
Career summary:
Minelaying 1939-40
Weserübung 1940
France 1940
Refit and non-operational, Baltic 1941-
    42
Norway 1942-43
Spitzbergen 1943
Skaggerak 1943-45
Fate:
Condemned as French Kléber 3 April
    1957.

Z7 (Hermann Schoemann)
Historical note:
Kapitänleutnant Schoemann was senior
officer of the Flanders Torpedo Boat
Flotilla. He was killed on 1 May 1915
when his ship, A2, was sunk by HMS
Laforey after accounting for a trawler of
the Dover Patrol.
Ship details:
Type 34A
Ordered 9.1.35
Builder Deschimag A.G. (Bremen)
Yard No. W901
Laid down 7.9.35
Launched 16.7.36
Completed 9.9.37
Commanding officers:
K.Kpt. E. S. Monting 9.9.37-25.10.38
K.Kpt. T. Detmers 26.10.38-15.7.40
K.Kpt. Wittig 20.10.40-2.5.42
Career summary:
Minelaying/mercantile warfare 1939-
    1940
Fleet operations 1940
Arctic 1941
'Cerberus' 1942
Norway 1942
Fate:
Scuttled after being immobilized in
    action with HMS Edinburgh and
    destroyers in the Barents Sea at 72°
    20' N, 35° 05' E, 2 May 1942. Eight of
    her crew were lost.

Z8 (Bruno Heinemann)
Historical note:
Kapitänleutnant Heinemann was first

lieutenant of the battleship König. He
was killed during the German naval
mutiny on 5 November 1918.
Ship details:
Type 34A
Ordered 9.1.35
Builder Deschimag A.G. (Bremen)
Yard No. W902
Laid down 14.1.36
Launched 15.9.36
Completed 8.1.38
Commanding officers:
F.Kpt. Berger 8.1.38-3.12.39
K.Kpt. Langheld 4.12.39-14.5.40
K.Kpt. Alberts 15.5.40-25.1.42
Career summary:
Poland 1939
Minelaying/mercantile warfare 1939-40
Weserübung 1940
France 1941
Fate:
Mined and sunk 25 January 1942 off
    the eastern entrance to the English
    Channel whilst on passage to Brest for
    Operation 'Cerberus'.

Z9 (Wolfgang Zenker)
Historical note:
Leutnant zur See Zenker was one of the
officers killed aboard SMS König during
the mutiny on 5 November 1918.
Ship details:
Type 34A
Ordered 4.8.34
Builder Germaniawerft (Kiel)
Yard No. G535
Laid down 22.3.35
Launched 27.3.36
Completed 2.7.38
Commanding officers:
K.Kpt. G. Pönitz 2.7.38-13.4.40
Career summary:
Poland 1939
Mercantile warfare/minelaying 1939-40
Norway 1940
Fate:
Scuttled 13 April 1940 in Rombaksfjord
    during Second Battle of Narvik;
    undamaged but no fuel or
    ammunition remaining.

Z10 (Hans Lody)
Historical note:
Oberleutnant zur See Lody, a reserve
officer unable to serve at sea due to poor
eyesight, was arrested in 1914 in Ireland
and charged by the British with
espionage on behalf of Germany. He
was executed by firing squad in the
Tower of London on 6 November
1914.
Ship details:
Type 34A
Ordered 4.8.34
Builder Germaniawerft (Kiel)
Yard No. G536
Laid down 1.4.35
Launched 14.5.36
Completed 13.9.38
Commanding officers:

K.Kpt. von Puttkamer 13.9.38-22.8.39
K.Kpt. Freiherr von Wangenheim
    23.8.39-31.10.40
K.Kpt. Pfeiffer 1.11.40-10.8.42
K.Kpt. Zenker 11.8.42-10.3.43
KS Marks 4.43-15.11.43
FK Haun 15.11.43-5.45
Career summary:
1939-40 Mercantile warfare/minelaying
1940 Norway
1940 Western France
1942 'Cerberus'
1941-44 Norway
1945 Baltic
Fate:
To UK 1945 (pennant no. R38, then
    H40); sold BISCO and arrived T.
    Young (Sunderland) 17 July 1949 for
    breaking up.

Z11 (Bernd von Arnim)
Historical note:
Kapitänleutnant von Arnim was captain
of the torpedo boat G42, a member of
the 3rd Torpedo Boat Half-Flotilla
based in Flanders. During a sortie into
the Dover Straights to bombard Calais
and Dover, six boats of the flotilla were
intercepted by the destroyers Broke and
Swift, and G42 was rammed and sunk
by the former with heavy loss of life,
including von Arnim; G85 was also sunk
on this occasion, 21 April 1917.
Ship details:
Type 34A
Ordered 4.8.34
Builder Germaniawerft (Kiel)
Yard No. G537
Laid down 26.4.35
Launched 8.7.36
Completed 6.12.38
Commanding officers:
K.Kpt. K. Rechel 6.12.38-13.4.40
Career summary:
1939 Poland
1939-40 North Sea minelaying
1940 Norway
Fate:
Scuttled in Rombaksfjord 13 April 1940
    following the Second Battle of Narvik.

Z12 (Erich Giese)
Historical note:
Kapitänleutnant Giese, as captain of the
torpedo boat S20, was killed when his
ship was sunk in action with HMS
Centaur of the Harwich Force in the
Channel on 5 June 1917.
Ship details:
Type 34A
Ordered 4.8.34
Builder Germaniawerft (Kiel)
Yard No. G538
Laid down 3.5.35
Launched 12.3.36
Completed 4.3.39
Commanding officers:
K.Kpt. K. Schmidt 4.3.39-13.4.40
Career summary:
1939-40 Mercantile warfare/minelaying

1940 Norway
Fate: Sunk in action with British surface forces off Narvik harbour during the Second Battle of Narvik, 13 April 1940.

Z13 (*Erich Koellner*)
Historical note:
Kapitänleutnant Koellner was senior officer of the 8th Minesweeper Flotilla in the First World War. During an operation on 20 April 1918, whilst north of Terschelling, *M95* was mined; whilst attempting to rescue her crew, Koellner's *M64* was mined and sunk. Koellner was lost with his ship.
Ship details:
Type 34A
Ordered 10.11.34
Builder Germaniawerft (Kiel)
Yard No. G539
Laid down 12.10.35
Launched 18.3.37
Completed 28.8.39
Commanding officers:
K.Kpt. Schulze-Hinrichs 28.8.39-13.4.40
Career summary:
1939-40 Mercantile warfare/minelaying
1940 Norway
Fate:
Destroyed by British surface forces off Djupvik on 13 April 1940 whilst in a damaged condition and acting as a floating battery.

Z14 (*Friedrich Ihn*)
Historical note:
Kapitänleutnant Ihn was captain of the torpedo boat *S35*, a unit of the 9th Flotilla, and lost his life when she was sunk in action at Jutland on 31 May 1916.
Ship details:
Type 34A
Ordered 19.1.35
Builder Blohm und Voss (Hamburg)
Yard No. B503
Laid down 30.5.35
Launched 5.11.36
Completed 6.4.38
Commanding officers:
K.Kpt. C. Trampedach 9.4.38-25.10.38
F.Kpt. E. Bey 26.10.38-3.4.39
K.Kpt. von Pufendorf 9.4.39-10.39
K.Kpt. G. Wachsmuth 10.39-10.11.42
K.Kpt. G. Fromme 11.11.42-31.1.44
K.Kpt. C-A. Richter-Oldekop 1.44-10.5.45
Career summary:
1939 Poland
1939-40 Mercantile warfare/minelaying
1941 Western France
1942-44 Norway
1942 'Cerberus'
1944-45 Skaggerak
Fate:
Allocated to the USSR at the end of the war and disposed of in the 1960s.

Z15 (*Erich Steinbrinck*)
Historical note:
Kapitänleutnant Steinbrinck was captain of the torpedo boat *V29* of the 9th Flotilla. During the Battle of Jutland she was torpedoed and sunk by HMS *Petard* on 31 May 1916, losing 43 dead, including her captain.
Ship details:
Type 34A
Ordered 19.1.35
Builder Blohm und Voss (Hamburg)
Yard No. B504
Laid down 30.5.35
Launched 24.9.36
Completed 31.5.38
Commanding officers:
K.Kpt. R. Johannesson 31.5.38-19.1.42
K.Kpt. Freiherr von Loringhoven 20.1.42-29.12.42
K.Kpt. O. Teichmann 28.12.42-30.11.44
K.Kpt. W. Röver 15.11.44-23.9.45
Career summary:
Poland 1939
North Sea minelaying 1939-40
Norway 1940
Western France 1940-41
1942 Repairs, refit trials, training
1943-44 Norway/Arctic
1944 Skaggerak
1944-45 Refit
Fate:
To USSR 1946; discarded in the 1960s.

Z16 (*Friedrich Eckoldt*)
Historical note:
Kapitänleutnant Eckoldt lost his life as captain of the torpedo boat *V48* when she was sunk during the Battle of Jutland on 31 May 1916.
Ship details:
Type 34A
Ordered 19.1.35
Builder Blohm und Voss (Hamburg)
Yard No. B505
Laid down 4.11.35
Launched 21.3.37
Completed 28.7.38
Commanding officers:
K.Kpt. Schemmel 28.7.38-20.7.42
K.Kpt. R. Menge (temp) 9.41-10.41
K.Kpt. L. Gerstung 19.8.42-23.12.42
K.Kpt. Schemmel (temp) 23.12.42-31.12.42
Career summary:
Poland 1939
North Sea 1939-40
Norway 1940
Western France 1940-41
Norway 1941-42
Fate:
Sunk by gunfire of HMS *Sheffield* during Battle of Barents Sea, 31 December 1942.

Z17 (*Diether von Roeder*)
Historical note:
Kapitänleutnant Freiherr Diether von Roeder was senior officer of the 13th

Torpedo Boat Half-Flotilla. He was killed along with 76 crewmen when his ship *S66* was mined and sunk on 11 July 1918 in 57° 47′ N, 4° 52′ E whilst attempting to rescue the survivors of *S62* which had been mined earlier.
Ship details:
Type 36
Ordered 6.1.36
Builder Deschimag A.G. (Bremen)
Yard No. W919
Laid down 9.9.36
Launched 19.8.37
Completed 29.8.38
Commanding officers:
K.Kpt. E. Holtorf 29.8.38-13.4.40
Career summary:
1940 5th Division then 3rd Flotilla; North Sea mercantile warfare/minelaying
Operation 'Weserübung' 1940
Fate:
Scuttled 13 April 1940 following Second Battle of Narvik; she had been irreparably damaged on 10 April.

Z18 (*Hans Lüdemann*)
Historical note:
Hans Lüdemann, a junior engineer officer, distinguished himself by his bravery during an accident in the engine room of the torpedo boat *S148* before the First World War on 14 May 1913. Because of his action many of the engine room staff were able to escape.
Ship details:
Type 36
Ordered 6.1.36
Builder Deschimag A.G. (Bremen)
Yard No. W920
Laid down 9.9.36
Launched 1.12.37
Completed 8.10.38
Commanding officers:
K.Kpt. H. Friedrichs 8.10.38-13.4.40
Career summary:
Minelaying in North Sea/mercantile warfare 1939/40
Norway 1940
Fate:
Scuttled in Rombaksfjord on 13 April 1940 during the Second Battle of Narvik.

Z19 (*Hermann Künne*)
Historical note:
Torpedomatrose Künne was a member of the crew of the torpedo boat *S53* which lay in Zeebrugge harbour alongside the mole when the famous attack took place on 23 April 1918. Künne and a British officer killed one another during fierce hand-to-hand fighting.
Ship details:
Type 36
Ordered 6.1.36
Builder Deschimag A.G. (Bremen)
Yard No. W921
Laid down 5.10.36

Launched 22.12.37
Completed 12.1.39
Commanding officers:
K.Kpt. F. Kothe 12.1.39-13.4.40
Career summary:
Mercantile warfare/North Sea minelaying 1939-40
Norway 1940
Fate:
Beached and scuttled in Herjangsfjord during the Second Battle of Narvik, 13 April 1940.

Z20 (*Karl Galster*)
Historical note:
Kapitänleutnant Galster was commanding officer of the torpedo boat *S22* when she was mined and sunk at 53° 46′ N, 5° 04′ E, about 35 miles west of the Borkum Riff Lightship. Galster and seventy-five of his crew perished.
Ship details:
Type 36
Ordered 6.1.36
Builder Deschimag A.G. (Bremen)
Yard No. W922
Laid down 14.9.37
Launched 15.6.38
Completed 21.3.39
Commanding officers:
K.Kpt. von Bechtolsheim 21.3.39-3.8.42
K.Kpt. F. Harmsen 4.8.42-5.1.45
F.Kpt. K. Schmidt 5.1.45-10.5.45
Career summary:
North Sea mercantile warfare and minelaying 1939/40
Western France 1940-41
Norway 1941-44
Skaggerak 1944-45
Baltic 1945
Fate:
Allocated to USSR in 1946 and renamed *Prochnyi*; discarded in the mid-1960s.

Z21 (*Wilhelm Heidkamp*)
Historical note:
Obermaat Heidkamp was serving aboard the battlecruiser *Seydlitz* during the First World War when she was in action at the Dogger Bank with Admiral Beatty's battlecruisers. When one of her 28cm turrets was hit Heidkamp was instrumental in saving his ship by flooding the magazines despite suffering from badly burned hands and gas poisoning. He was promoted for his bravery.
Ship details:
Type 36
Ordered 6.1.36
Builder Deschimag A.G. (Bremen)
Yard No. W923
Laid down 15.12.37
Launched 20.8.38
Completed 20.6.39
Commanding officers:
K.Kpt. H. Erdmenger 20.6.39-11.4.40
Career summary:

North Sea minelaying/mercantile warfare 1939-40
1940 Norway; leader destroyer of FdZ
Fate:
Torpedoed and sunk by HMS *Hardy* whilst at anchor in Narvik harbour on 11 April 1940.

Z22 (*Anton Schmitt*)
Historical note:
Bootsmannsmaat Schmitt was serving as gun captain of No. 4 gun aboard the light cruiser *Frauenlob* when she was sunk at Jutland during the night of 31 May/1 June 1916. His gun's crew continued to engage as the cruiser sank until they were waist deep in water.
Ship details:
Type 36
Ordered 6.1.36
Builder Deschimag A.G. (Bremen)
Yard No. W924
Laid down 3.1.38
Launched 20.9.38
Completed 24.9.39
Commanding officers:
K.Kpt. Böhme 24.9.39-11.4.40
Career summary:
North Sea minelaying 1940
Norway 1940
Fate:
Hit by two torpedoes and broken in half whilst at anchor in Narvik harbour, 11 April 1940.

Z23
Ship details:
Type 36A
Ordered 23.4.38
Builder Deschimag A.G. (Bremen)
Yard No. W957
Laid down 15.11.38
Launched 15.12.39
Completed 14.9.40
Commanding officers:
K Kpt. Böhme 14.9.40-12.5.42
K Kpt. Wittig 13.5.42-11.3.44
K Kpt. von Manthey 12.3.44-21.8.44
Career summary:
Baltic and Norway 1940-41
Western France 1941
Norway and Arctic 1941-42
Western France 1943-44
Fate:
Damaged by air attack at La Pallice on 12 August 1944; paid off 20 August and handed over to La Pallice Navy Yard the next day. Towed to Cherbourg 1947 and cannibalized for spares. Stricken 7 October 1951.

Z24
Ship details:
Type 36A
Ordered 23.4.38
Builder Deschimag A.G. (Bremen)
Yard No. W958
Laid down 2.1.39
Launched 7.3.40
Completed 23.10.40

Commanding officers:
K Kpt. Saltzwedel 23.10.40-9.10.43
K Kpt. Birnbacher 12.43-25.8.44
Career summary:
Baltic and Norway 1940-41
France 1941
Norway and Arctic 1941-42
Western France 1943-44
Fate:
Sunk by RAF air attack off Le Verdon on 25 August 1944.

Z25
Ship details:
Type 36A
Ordered 23.4.38
Builder Deschimag A.G. (Bremen)
Yard No. W959
Laid down 15.2.39
Launched 16.3.40
Completed 30.11.40
Commanding officers:
K. Kpt. Gerlach 30.11.40-7.41
K. Kpt. Peters 24.9.41-20.8.43
K. Kpt. Birnbacher 21.8.43-30.11.43
K. Kpt. Gohrbandt 1.12.43-12.5.45
Capitaine de Corvette Vigneau 4.2.46
Capitaine de Frégate Aman 11.5.46
Capitaine de Frégate Caroff 1950-51
Capitaine de Frégate Chapuis 2.52
Capitaine de Frégate Lehle 1953-54
Capitaine de Frégate Bordemes 11.7.55
Capitaine de Frégate Claeyssen 10.7.57
Career summary:
Baltic and Norway 1941
Artic 1942
Norway 1943
Baltic 1944-45
Fate:
To France 1946; renamed *Hoche*. Sold for breaking up 1958.

Z26
Ship details:
Type 36A
Ordered 23.4.38
Builder Deschimag A.G. (Bremen)
Yard No. W960
Laid down 1.4.39
Launched 2.4.40
Completed 11.1.41
Commanding officers:
K. Kpt. von Berger 11.1.41-29.3.42
Career summary:
Home waters and Arctic 1941-42
Fate:
Sunk in action with HMSS *Trinidad* and *Eclipse* in Barents Sea, 29 March 1942.

Z27
Ship details:
Type 36A
Ordered 23.4.38
Builder Deschimag A.G. (Bremen)
Yard No. W961
Laid down 27.12.39
Launched 1.8.40
Completed 26.2.41
Commanding officers:

K. Kpt. Smidt 26.2.41-31.8.42
K. Kpt. Shultz 1.9.42-28.12.43
Career summary:
Baltic 1941
Arctic 1941-42
Norway 1942
Baltic 1943
Western France 1943-44
Fate:
Sunk in action with HMSS *Glasgow* and *Enterprise* in the Bay of Biscay, 28 December 1943.

Z28
Ship details:
Type 36A
Ordered 23.4.38
Builder Deschimag A.G. (Bremen)
Yard No. W962
Laid down 30.11.39
Launched 20.8.40
Completed 9.8.41
Commanding Officers:
K. Kpt. Erdmenger 9.8.41-11.2.43
K. Kpt. Reinicke 15.2.43-17.3.43
K. Kpt. Zenker 3.43-31.10.44
K. Kpt. Lampe 11.1.45-6.3.45
Career summary:
Norway 1942-43
Baltic 1944-45
Fate:
Sunk by air attack in Sassnitz Bay, 6 March 1945.

Z29
Ship details:
Type 36A
Ordered 23.4.38
Builder A.G. (Bremen)
Yard No. W963
Laid down 21.3.40
Launched 15.10.40
Completed 9.7.41
Commanding officers:
K. Kpt. Rechel 9.7.41-31.3.43
K. Kpt. von Mutius 1.4.43-8.5.45
Career summary:
Norway 1941-42
1942 'Cerberus'
Norway 1942-44
Fate:
Loaded with gas ammunition and scuttled in the Skaggerak, 16 December 1946.

Z30
Ship details:
Type 36A
Ordered 23.4.38
Builder Deschimag A.G. (Bremen)
Yard No. W964
Laid down 15.4.40
Launched 8.12.40
Completed 15.11.41
Commanding officers:
K. Kpt. Kaiser 15.11.41-10.3.43
K. Kpt. Lampe 3.43-12.44
Career summary:
Norway 1942-44
Skaggerak 1944

Baltic 1944-45
Fate:
To Britain 1946. Sold 1948; arrived Arnott Young & Co (Dalmuir) September 1948 and broken up.

Z31
Ship details:
Type 36A (Mob)
Ordered 19.9.39
Builder Deschimag A.G. (Bremen)
Yard No. W1001
Laid down 1.9.40
Launched 15.5.41
Completed 11.4.42
Commanding officers:
K. Kpt. Alberts 11.4.42-12.43
K. Kpt. Paul 12.43-8.5.45
Capitaine de Vaisseau Bosvieux 4.2.46-24.7.47
Capitaine de Vaisseau Antoine 24.7.47
Capitaine de Corvette Guillauton
Career summary:
Baltic 1942
Norway 1943-45
Fate:
To Britain 1945; transferred to France and renamed *Marceau*. Sold for breaking up 1958.

Z32
Ship details:
Type 36A (Mob)
Ordered 19.9.39
Builder Deschimag A.G. (Bremen)
Yard No. W1002
Laid down 1.11.40
Launched 15.8.41
Completed 15.9.42
Commanding officers:
K.Kpt. von Berger 15.9.42-9.6.44
Career summary:
Baltic 1942
Western France 1943-44
Fate:
Driven ashore on Ile de Batz during action with HMCSS *Haida* and *Huron* on 9 June 1944; wreck destroyed by air attack.

Z33
Ship details:
Type 36A (Mob)
Ordered 19.9.39
Builder Deschimag A.G. (Bremen)
Yard No. W1003
Laid down 22.12.40
Launched 15.9.41
Completed 6.2.43
Commanding officers:
K. Kpt. Holtorf 6.2.43-6.44
F. Kpt. Menge 6.44-3.45
K. Lt. Peter-Pirkam 19.3.45-8.5.45
Career summary:
Baltic 1943
Norway 1943-45
Baltic 1945
Fate:
To USSR; renamed *Provornyi*. Discarded in the early 1960s.

Z34
Ship details:
Type 36A (Mob)
Ordered 19.9.39
Builder Deschimag A.G. (Bremen)
Yard No. W1004
Laid down 15.1.41
Launched 5.5.42
Completed 5.6.43
Commanding officers:
K. Kpt. Hetz 5.6.43-8.5.45
Career summary:
Norway 1943-45
Baltic 1945
Fate:
To USA 1946. Loaded with gas
ammunition and scuttled in Skaggerak
26 March 1946.

Z35
Ship details:
Type 36B
Ordered 17.2.41
Builder Deschimag A.G. (Bremen)
Yard No. W1005
Laid down 6.6.41
Launched 2.10.42
Completed 22.9.43
Commanding officers:
K. Kpt. Batge 22.9.43-12.12.44
Career summary:
Baltic 1943-44
Fate:
Lost in German minefield in Gulf of
Finland, 12 December 1944.

Z36
Ship details:
Type 36B
Ordered 17.2.41
Builder Deschimag A.G. (Bremen)
Yard No. W1006
Laid down 15.9.41
Launched 15.5.43
Completed 19.2.44
Commanding officers:
K. Kpt. von Hausen 19.2.44-12.12.44
Career summary:
Baltic 1943-44

Fate:
Mined with *Z35* in Gulf of Finland, 12
December 1944.

Z37
Ship details:
Type 36A (Mob)
Ordered 19.9.39
Builder Germaniawerft (Kiel)
Yard No. G627
Laid down 2.1.40
Launched 24.2.41
Completed 16.7.42
Commanding officers:
K. Kpt. Langheld 16.7.42-25.2.44
Career summary:
Baltic 1942-43
Western France 1943-44
Fate:
Damaged in collision with *Z32* on 30
January 1944; repairs not completed,
ship disarmed and paid off.
Abandoned in dry dock at Forges et
Chantiers de la Gironde (Bordeaux)
24 August 1944.

Z38
Ship details:
Type 36A (Mob)
Ordered 19.9.39
Builder Germaniawerft (Kiel)
Yard No. G628
Laid down 15.4.40
Launched 5.8.41
Completed 20.3.43
Commanding officers:
K. Kpt. Brutzer 20.3.43-17.9.44
K. Kpt. von Lyncker 18.9.44-8.5.45
Lt Butler RN 3.3.47-13.10.47
Lt-Cdr Hennessy RN 14.10.47
Career summary:
Baltic 1943
Norway 1943-45
Baltic 1945
Fate:
To Britain 1946; renamed *Nonsuch*.
Sold 8 November 1949 to Arnott
Young & Co Ltd for scrapping;
arrived at Dalmuir May 1950.

Z39
Ship details:
Type 36A (Mob)
Ordered 19.9.39
Builder Germaniawerft (Kiel)
Yard No. G629
Laid down 15.8.40
Launched 2.12.41
Completed 21.8.43
Commanding officers:
K. Kpt. Loerke 21.8.43-8.5.45
Lt-Cdr Forsberg RN 6.7.45-11.7.45
Cdr Dawes Jr USN 17.7.45
Career summary:
Skaggerak 1943
Baltic 1944-45
Fate:
To USA 1946; redesignated DD939.
To France 10 November 1947 and
renamed *Léopard*, then *Q128*. Not
commissioned; cannibalized for
spares. Sold for scrap 1958.

Z43
Ship details:
Type 36B (Mob)
Ordered 17.2.41
Builder Deschimag A.G. (Bremen)
Yard No. W1029
Laid down 1.5.42
Launched September 1943
Completed 24.3.44
Commanding officers:
Kpt.z.S. Wenniger 24.3.44-30.3.45
F.Kpt. Lampe 5.4.45-3.5.45
Career summary:
Baltic 1944-45
Fate:
Damaged by mines and bombs, then
scuttled in Geltinger Bay 3 May 1945.

Z44 (not completed)
Ship details:
Type 36B (Mob)
Ordered 17.2.41
Builder Deschimag A.G. (Bremen)
Yard No. 1030
Laid down 1.8.42
Launched 20.1.44

Fate:
Sunk by bombs whilst fitting-out in
Industriehaven 29 July 1944. Broken
up 1946-7.

Z45 (not launched)
Ship details:
Type 36B (Mob)
Ordered 17.2.41
Builder Deschimag A.G. (Bremen)
Yard No. 1031
Laid down 1.9.43
(Previously quoted launch date of
15.4.44 appears to have been the
scheduled launch date.)

Z46 (not launched)
Ship details:
Type 36C
Ordered 8.10.41
Builder Deschimag A.G. (Bremen)
Yard No. 1071
Laid down 1.8.43
Fate:
Damaged on slip by air attack 1944;
broken up.

Z47 (not launched)
Ship details:
Type 36C
Ordered 8.10.41
Builder Deschimag A.G. (Bremen)
Yard No. 1072
Laid down 1.5.44
Fate:
Damaged on slip by air attack; broken
up.

Z51
Ship details:
Type 42
Ordered 25.11.42
Builder Deschimag A.G. (Bremen)
Yard No. 1109
Laid down 1943
Launched 2.10.44
Fate:
Sunk by bomb during an air raid on
Bremen 21 March 1945. Broken up
1946-7.

4. CONSTRUCTION AND CAREER NOTES: TORPEDO BOATS

Albatros
Ship details:
Type 23
Builder Wilhelmshaven Navy Yard
Laid down 5.10.25
Launched 15.7.26
Completed 15.5.28
Commanding officers:
Kpt.Lt. H. M. Schultz 11.38-11.39

Kpt.Lt. Strelow 12.39-4.40
Career summary:
August 1939 to November 1939
Skaggerak & Home waters
December 1939 to March 1940
Dockyard refit Germaniawerft (Kiel)
April 1940 'Weserübung'
Fate:
Wrecked in Oslofjord April 1940.

Falke
Ship details:
Type 23
Builder Wilhelmshaven Navy Yard
Laid down 17.11.25
Launched 29.9.26
Completed 15.7.28
Commanding officers:
Kpt.Lt. Hessler 3.39-3.40

Kpt.Lt. Hansen-Nootbaar 3.40-12.41
Kpt.Lt. H. Hoffman 12.41-10.42
Kpt.Lt. Loerke 10.42-3.43
Kpt.Lt. Buch 3.43-9.43
Kpt.Lt. Krüger 9.43-6.44
Career summary:
August 1939 to August 1940 Home
waters & Skaggerak
September 1940 to December 1940

France

January 1941 to February 1941 Norway
March 1941 to May 1941 Refit at
    Rotterdam
June 1941 to December 1941 Baltic &
    Skaggerak
January 1942 to February 1942 Holland
    & France
March 1942 to April 1942 France
June 1942 to August 1942 Dockyard,
    Wilhelmshaven
October 1942 to June 1944 France
Fate:
Sunk by air raid on Le Havre 14.6.44.

Greif

Ship details:
Type 23
Builder Wilhelmshaven Navy Yard
Laid down 5.10.25
Launched 15.7.26
Completed 15.3.27
Commanding officers:
Kpt.Lt. Verlohr 11.38-11.39
Kpt.Lt.Frhr.v. Lyncker 11.39-10.40
Kpt.Lt. H. Hoffman 10.40-12.41
Ob.Lt.z.S. Schramm 12.41-1.42
Ob.Lt.z.S. Kolbe 1.42-8.42
Kpt.Lt. R. Fuchs 10.42-7.43
Kpt.Lt. Lüdde-Neurath 9.43-10.43
Kpt.Lt. R. Fuchs 10.43-3.44
Kpt.Lt.Frhr.v. Lüttitz 3.44-5.44
Career summary:
August 1939 to February 1940 Home
    waters & Skaggerak
March 1940 Dockyard, Stettin
April 1940 to August 1940 Home
    waters & Skaggerak
September 1940 to March 1941
    Western France
April 1941 to May 1941 Dockyard,
    Rotterdam
June 1941 to November 1941
    Skaggerak & Home waters
December 1941 to December 1942
    Dockyard hands
January 1943 to February 1943
    Working-up
March 1943 to April 1943 Norway
May 1943 to May 1944 France
Fate:
Sunk by No. 415 Squadron Albacore,
    NE of Port-en-Bessin, Seine Bay,
    24.5.44.

Kondor

Ship details:
Type 23
Builder Wilhelmshaven Navy Yard
Laid down 17.11.25
Launched 22.9.26
Completed 15.7.28
Commanding officers:
Kpt.Lt. Wilcke 4.39-10.40
Kpt.Lt.Frhr.v. Lyncker 10.40-6.41
Kpt.Lt. Burkart 6.41-7.42
Ob.Lt.z.S. Holzapfel 4.42-5.42
Kpt.Lt. Peter-Pirkham 9.42-12.43
Ob.Lt.z.S. P. Hermann 12.43-4.44
Ob.Lt.z.S. Rönnau 4.44-6.44

Career summary:
August 1939 to November 1939 Home
    waters
December 1939 to March 1940
    Dockyard Kiel
April 1940 to August 1940 Home
    waters, North Sea
September 1940 to February 1941
    Western France
March 1941 to May 1941 Dockyard,
    Rotterdam
June 1941 to October 1941 Skaggerak
    & Home waters
November 1941 to December 1941
    Overhaul, Rotterdam
February 1942 to April 1942 Holland &
    France
June 1942 to August 1942 Dockyard,
    Wilhelmshaven
September 1942 to November 1942
    Baltic, training
November 1942 to May 1944 western
    France
Fate:
Mined and damaged 23 May 1944;
    canibalized and paid off 28 June 1944;
    either destroyed by air raids after
    paying off or scuttled before capture of
    Le Havre. Hit in foreship by bombs
    1944. Not worth repair.

Möwe

Ship details:
Type 23
Builder Wilhelmshaven Navy Yard
Laid down 2.3.25
Launched 24.3.26
Completed 1.10.26
Commanding officers:
Kpt.Lt. Edler von Rennenkampf 11.38-
    3.40
Kpt.Lt. Neuss 3.40-4.40
Kpt.Lt. P. Koch 4.42-6.42
Kpt.Lt. Loerke 6.42-9.42
Kpt.Lt. Lüdde-Neurath 12.42-1.43
Kpt.Lt. H. Bastian 1.43-6.44
Career summary:
September 1939 North Sea & Skaggerak
December 1939 to March 1940 Refit
March 1940 to May 1940 North Sea &
    Skaggerak
May 1940 to April 1941 Repairing
    torpedo damage, Wilhelmshaven
April 1941 to March 1943 Non-
    operational or in dockyard hands,
    Baltic area
April 1943 to May 1943 Norway
May 1943 to June 1944 France
Fate:
Sunk by air raid on Le Havre 14.6.44

Seeadler

Ship details:
Type 23
Builder Wilhelmshaven Navy Yard
Laid down 5.10.25
Launched 15.7.26
Completed 15.3.27
Commanding officers:
Kpt.Lt. Hartenstein 11.38-10.39

Kpt.Lt. Kohlauf 11.39-1.42
Ob.Lt.z.S. Holzapfel 1.42-2.42
Kpt.Lt. Strecker 3.42-5.42
Career summary:
September 1939 to May 1940 North
    Sea & Home waters
May 1940 to August 1940 Dockyard,
    Seebeck (Wesermünde)
September 1940 to February 1941 France
March 1941 to May 1941 Dockyard,
    Rotterdam
June 1941 to November 1941 Skaggerak
December 1941 to February 1942
    Dockyard, Rotterdam
March 1942 to April 1942 France
Fate:
Torpedoed and sunk by British MTBs off
    Boulogne, 14.5.42

Iltis

Ship details:
Type 24
Builder Wilhelmshaven Navy Yard
Laid down 8.3.27
Launched 12.10.27
Completed 1.10.28
Commanding officers:
Kpt.Lt. Schuur 2.38-11.40
Kpt.Lt. Jacobsen 11.40-5.42
Career summary:
September 1939 to December 1939
    North Sea & Skaggerak
January 1940 to May 1940 Dockyard,
    Seebeck (Wesermünde)
June 1940 to September 1940 Group(N)
September 1940 to March 1941 France
April 1941 to June 1941 Dockyard,
    Wilton-Schiedam
July 1941 to October 1941 Skaggerak
January 1942 to May 1942 France
Fate:
Torpedoed and sunk by British MTBs off
    Boulogne, 14.5.42

Jaguar

Ship details:
Type 24
Builder Wilhelmshaven Navy Yard
Laid down 4.5.27
Launched 15.3.28
Completed 15.8.29
Commanding officers:
Kpt.Lt. Kohlauf 4.39-10.39
Kpt.Lt. Hartenstein 10.39-3.41
Kpt.Lt. F-K. Paul 3.41-5.42
Kpt.Lt. Strecker 5.42-10.42
Kpt.Lt. Loerke 10.42-10.43
ObLt.z.S. Sonnenburg 11.43-6.44
Career summary:
September 1939 to December 1939
    North Sea & Skaggerak
December 1939 to March 1940
    Dockyard, Seebeck (Wesermünde)
April 1940 to August 1940 Skaggerak &
    Home waters
September 1940 to March 1941 France
April 1941 to May 1941 Norway &
    repairs at Rotterdam
June 1941 to October 1941 Skaggerak
November 1941 to May 1943 Mainly

non-operational in Baltic or in
    Dockyard hands
May 1943 to June 1944 western France
Fate:
Destroyed in air raid on Le Havre
    14.6.44

Leopard

Ship details:
Type 24
Builder Wilhelmshaven Navy Yard
Laid down 4.5.27
Launched 15.3.28
Completed 1.6.29
Commanding officers:
Kpt.Lt. Kassbaum 10.38-10.39
Kpt.Lt. Trummer 10.39-10.40
Career summary:
September 1939 to March 1940 North
    Sea
Fate:
Sunk in collision with minelayer
    Preussen in Skaggerak 30.4.40.

Luchs

Ship details:
Type 24
Builder Wilhelmshaven Navy Yard
Laid down 2.4.27
Launched 15.3.28
Completed 15.4.29
Commanding officers:
Kpt.Lt. Prölss 3.38-10.39
Kpt.Lt. Kassbaum 10.39-7.40
Career summary:
September 1939 North Sea
April 1940 Norway ('Weserübung')
May 1940 to June 1940 Dockyard, Kiel
Fate:
Torpedoed and sunk by HM submarine
    Thames or possibly struck by drifting
    mine, off Karmöy 26.7.40.

Tiger

Ship details:
Type 24
Builder Wilhelmshaven Navy Yard
Laid down 2.4.27
Launched 15.3.28
Completed 15.1.29
Commanding officers:
Kpt.Lt. Neuss 2.38-8.39
Fate:
Lost in collision with Max Schultz off
    Christiansö east of Bornholm, 25.9.39.

Wolf

Ship details:
Type 24
Builder Wilhelmshaven Navy Yard
Laid down 8.3.27
Launched 12.10.27
Completed 15.11.28
Commanding officers:
Kpt.Lt. Gerstung 2.38-1.40
Ob.Lt.z.S. B. Peters 1.40-1.41
Career summary:
September 1939 to December 1939
    North Sea & Skaggerak
January 194 to February 1940

Dockyard, Wilhelmshaven
March 1940 to April 1940 Group (West)
May 1940 to August 1940 Dockyard, Oderwerke (Stettin)
September 1940 to January 1941 France
Fate:
Mined and sunk off Dunkirk 8.1.41.

T1
Ship details:
Type 35
Ordered 16.11.35
Builder Schichau (Elbing)
Yard No. S1380
Laid down 14.11.36
Launched 17.2.38
Completed 1.12.39
Commanding officers:
Kpt.Lt. H. Rost 1.12.39-9.40
Kpt.Lt. Richter-Oldekop 9.40-15.8.41
Kpt.Lt. P. Koch 6.42-10.43
Kpt.Lt. Kopka 10.43-4.44
Kpt.Lt. Schurdt 4.44-4.45
Career summary:
Until October 1940 Home waters (in dockyard hands for most of the time; deployment to France in September 1940 aborted)
November 1940 to March 1941 Norwegian waters
April 1941 to August 1941 Baltic (non-operational)
15 August 1941 to June 1942 Paid off
June 1942 to October 1943 Attached to Torpedo School
November 1943 to March 1944 Refit
April 1944 to April 1945 Eastern Baltic
Fate:
Sunk by RAF air attack at Deutscher Werke (Kiel) Hit by 2-3 bombs 2227 hours and 2248 hours 9.4.45. Wreck blown up 20.5.46.

T2
Ship details:
Type 35
Ordered 16.11.35
Builder Schichau (Elbing)
Yard No. S1381
Laid down 14.11.36
Launched 7.4.38
Completed 2.12.39
Commanding officers:
Kpt.Lt. Bätge 2.12.39-9.40
Kpt.Lt. Gödecke 9.40-2.42
Kpt.Lt. Quaet-Faslem 12.42-9.43
Kpt.Lt. W. Lange 9.43-5.44
Kpt.Lt. T. Lampe 5.44-7.44
Career summary:
Until June 1940 Dockyard hands & Home waters
June 1940 to September 1940 Home waters
September 1940 Abortive deployment to France. Damaged on return
November 1940 to January 1941 Home waters
February 1941 to June 1941 Schichau dockyard. Trials & training
July 1941 to October 1941 Skaggerak,

Eastern Baltic (occupation of Ösel and Dagö)
November 1941 to mid-December 1941 Dockyard hands
End December 1941 to February 1942 Group (West)
March 1942 to February 1943 Reserve, Dockyard Seebeck (Wesermünde) & Blohm & Voss (Hamburg)
March 1943 to June 1943 Western France
10 July 1943 to September 1943 Flag Officer (U-Boats), 25th U-Boat Flotilla, Libau
October 1943 to Mid-1944 Torpedo School
Fate:
Sunk by USAAF air raid at Deschimag (Bremen) 29.7.44. Raised 4 September 1944. Departed 9.12.44 in tow to Swinemünde. Arrived Elbing 31.1.45. Towed west again unrepaired February 1945. Broken up at Cuxhaven 1946. (Reported as a wreck at Brunsbüttel May 1945.)

T3
Ship details:
Type 35
Ordered 16.11.35
Builder Schichau (Elbing)
Yard No. S1382
Laid down 14.11.36
Launched 23.6.38
Completed 3.2.40
Commanding officers:
Kpt.Lt. H. Bruns 3.2.40-9.40
Kpt.Lt. H. von Diest 12.12.43-14.3.45
Career summary:
Until July 1940 Dockyard hands in Home waters
August/September 1940 Group (North)
September 1940 Deployed to western France
18 September 1940 Bombed and sunk by RAF in Le Havre; raised, towed to Germany and repaired
Recommissioned 12.12.43 at Danzig
January 1944 to November 1944 Torpedo School
December 1944 to March 1945 Operational, Eastern Baltic
Fate:
Lost on mine barrage (laid by Soviet submarine *L21*) off Hela in Gulf of Danzig 14.3.45.

T4
Ship details:
Type 35
Ordered 16.11.35
Builder Schichau (Elbing)
Yard No. S1383
Laid down 29.12.36
Launched 15.9.38
Completed 27.5.40
Commanding officers:
Kpt.Lt. E. Hesse 27.5.40-10.41
Ob.Lt.z.S. Sommerlatt 10.41-12.41
Kpt.Lt. Bieling 12.41-8.42
Kpt.Lt. Weinlig 10.42-1.43

Kpt.Lt. T-L. von Trotha 20.4.43-7.43
Kpt.Lt. Waldenburger 19.7.43-4.44
Ob.Lt.z.S. S. Adolph 4.44-1.45
Kpt.Lt. Brunk 1.45-5.45
Career summary:
Until October 1940 Dockyard hands & Home waters
October 1940 to January 1941 Norwegian waters
February 1941 to August 1941 Dockyard Oderwerke (Stettin)
September 1941 to February 1942 North Sea and French Channel coast
March 1942 to May 1942 North Sea and Norway
June 1942 to December 1942 France
January 1943 to April 1943 Paid off in dockyard hands, Wesermünde. Recommissioned 11 May 1943
May 1943 to February 1944 Normally attached Torpedo School
March 1944 to June 1944 Machinery overhaul
July 1944 to March 1945 Gulf of Finland & Eastern Baltic
Fate:
To USA 1946. Sold to Denmark 18.6.48 for use as MTB leader but not commissioned. Broken up 1950/51.

T5
Ship details:
Type 35
Ordered 15.1.36
Builder Deschimag (Bremen)
Yard No. 934
Laid down 30.12.36
Launched 22.11.37
Completed 23.1.40
Commanding officers:
Kpt.Lt. Koppenhagen 23.1.40-3.40
Kpt.Lt. H. Hoffmann 3.40-5.40
Kpt.Lt. Koppenhagen 5.40-12.42
Kpt.Lt. Denhert 12.42-9.43
Ob.Lt.z.S. Freiherr von Lüttitz 9.43-2.44
Kpt.Lt. Güttner 2.44-1.45
Ob.Lt.z.S. Wätjen 2.45-3.45
Career summary:
Until June 1940 Dockyard hands
June 1940 to October 1940 Skaggerak, North Sea & Home waters
November 1940 to February 1941 Norway
March 1941 to September 1941 Refit, Deschimag (Bremen)
October 1941 to December 1941 Baltic & Home waters
January/February 1942 France
March 1942 to May 1942 Norway
August 1942 to November 1942 Dockyard (Schichau-Elbing)
December 1942 to February 1943 Baltic
March 1943 to June 1943 Western France
July 1943 Engine overhaul
October 1943 to February 1944 Torpedo School
March 1944 to August 1944 Dockyard hands

September 1944 to March 1945 Baltic
Fate:
Sunk on mine barrage (laid by Soviet submarine *L21*) off Hela with *T3*, 14.3.45.

T6
Ship details:
Type 35
Ordered 15.1.36
Builder Deschimag (Bremen)
Yard No. 935
Laid down 3.1.37
Launched 16.12.37
Commissioned 30.4.40
Commanding officers:
Kpt.Lt. R.R. Wolfram 30.4.40-7.11.40
Career summary:
Until July 1940 Dockyard & Home waters
July 1940 to October 1940 Skaggerak, S. North Sea & Channel
October to November 1940 Norway
Fate:
Mined and sunk east of Aberdeen 7.11.40

T7
Ship details:
Type 35
Ordered 15.1.36
Builder Deschimag (Bremen)
Yard No. 936
Laid down 20.8.37
Launched 18.6.38
Completed 20.12.39
Commanding officers:
Kpt.Lt. W. Erhardt 20.12.39-4.41
Kpt.Lt. Quaet-Faslem 4.41-12.42
Kpt.Lt. Weinlig 1.43-19.5.43
Kpt.Lt. G. Schmidt 20.5.43-9.43
Kpt.Lt. O. Müller 9.43-7.44
Career summary:
Until July 1940 Dockyard hands & Home waters
August 1940 to October 1940 North Sea & Channel
November 1940 to December 1940 Norway
January 1941 to August 1941 Dockyard, Lloyd (Wesermünde)
September 1941 to January 1942 Baltic, Skaggerak & Channel
February 1942 to March 1942 Home waters
April 1942 to July 1942 Norway
August 1942 to September 1942 Dockyard, Schichau (Elbing)
October 1942 to December 1942 Reserve
January 1943 to April 1944 Torpedo School
May 1944 to July 1944 Dockyard hands
Fate:
Sunk by USAAF air raid at Deschimag, Bremen, 29.7.44. Raised 25 October 1944 but abandoned. Possibly sunk by bombing again 30.4.45. Broken up post-war.

T8
Ship details:
Type 35
Ordered 15.1.36
Builder Deschimag (Bremen)
Yard No. 937
Laid down 28.8.37
Launched 10.8.38
Completed 8.10.39
Commanding officers:
Kpt.Lt. H. Erdmann 8.10.39-4.41
Kpt.Lt. T-L. von Trotha 4.41-12.41
Kpt.Lt. W. Wenzel 6.42-4.44
Kpt.Lt. Strömer 4.44-5.45
Career summary:
Until June 1940 Dockyard hands &
Home waters
July 1940 to December 1940 North
Sea, Channel & S. Norway
January 1941 to June 1941 Dockyard,
Stettiner-Oderwerke
July 1941 to December 1941 Work-up
& Eastern Baltic
December 1941 to June 1942 Paid off
into reserve (1.1.42)
July 1942 to October 1943 Believed
attached to Torpedo School
October 1943 to January 1944
Dockyard, Schichau (Elbing)
February 1944 to April 1945 Eastern
Baltic, Gulf of Finland
Fate:
Scuttled in Strander Bay, Kiel, 3.5.45.
Wreck destroyed with depth-charges
10.12.45.

T9
Ship details:
Type 35
Ordered 29.6.36
Builder Schichau (Elbing)
Yard No. S1393
Laid down 24.11.36
Launched 3.11.38
Completed 4.7.40
Commanding officers:
Kpt.Lt. Blöse 4.7.40-8.41
Kpt.Lt. Gründ 6.42-8.43
Lt.z.S. E. Noodt 5.43-10.43 (temp)
Ob.Lt.z.S. Sonnenburg 10.43-11.43
(temp)
Kpt.Lt. Rolle 2.44-8.44
Kpt.Lt. O. Müller 8.44-5.45
Career summary:
Until August 1940 Baltic, working up
September 1940 to February 1941
Home waters, then Norway
March 1941 to July 1941 Dockyard,
Deutscher Werke (Kiel)
Paid off 15.8.41, reserve until June 1942
August 1942 to October 1942 Norway
November 1942 to April 1943 France
9 May 1943 to August 1943 Dockyard,
Schichau (Elbing)
September 1943 to mid-1944 Torpedo
School
Mid-1944 to May 1945 Eastern Baltic
Fate:
Damaged by bombs at Danzig 8 March
1945; scuttled in Strander Bay, Kiel

3.5.45. Wreck destroyed by depth-
charges 10.12.45.

T10
Ship details:
Type 35
Ordered 29.6.36
Builder Schichau (Elbing)
Yard No. S1394
Laid down 24.11.36
Launched 19.1.39
Completed 5.8.40
Commanding officers:
Kpt.Lt. Hoepner 5.8.40-4.41
Kpt.Lt. Sommerlatt 3.42-12.42
Kpt.Lt. Meentzen 5.43-11.43
Kpt.Lt. Brunk 11.43-12.44
Career summary:
September 1940 to October 1940 Baltic
& Home waters
November 1940 to December 1940
Norway
January 1941 to February 1941 Group
(North)
March 1941 to July 1941 Dockyard,
Deutscher Werke (Kiel)
15 August 1941 to 13 May 1942 Paid
off in reserve
August 1942 to December 1942
Western France
December 1942 to 20 April 1943 Paid
off in reserve
May 1943 to June 1943 Torpedo
School
10 July 1943 to August 1943 25th U-
Boat Flotilla, Libau
September 1943 to February 1944
Torpedo School
February 1944 to April 1944 Dockyard
May 1944 to 28 November 1944
Eastern Baltic, Gulf of Finland
Fate:
Bombed and sunk at Deutscher Werke
yard, Gotenhafen, by RAF 18.12.44
whilst in No.4 floating dock.

T11
Ship details:
Type 35
Ordered 29.6.36
Builder Deschimag (Bremen)
Yard No. 938
Laid down 1.7.38
Launched 1.3.39
Completed 24.5.40
Commanding officers:
Kpt.Lt. H. Hoffman 5.40-31.10.40
Kpt.Lt. G. Grund 6.6.41-1.6.42
Kpt.Lt. Sommerlatt 12.42-2.43
Kpt. Lt. F.-K. Paul 2.43-22.10.43
Kpt.Lt. E. Walser 23.10.43-21.2.45
Kpt.Lt. G Heilig 22.2.45-8.5.45
Capitaine de Corvette Cevaer 1946
Career summary:
July 1940 to November 1940 Skaggerak
& Channel (damaged at Cherbourg by
Blenheims of No. 56 Squadron
18.9.40)
December 1940 to June 1941 Paid off
at Wesermünde Dockyard

July 1941 to November 1941 Baltic &
Skaggerak
December 1941 to February 1942
Home waters & Channel
March 1942 to May 1942 Norway
June 1942 to December 1942
Dockyard, Stettiner-Oderwerke. Paid
off into reserve
January 1943 to March 1943 Training,
trials & work up, Baltic
April 1943 to mid-1944 Torpedo
School
Mid-1944 to December 1944 Refit and
work up
January 1945 to May 1945 Baltic
Fate:
To UK February 1946. Transferred to
France and renamed *Birhakeim*
4.2.46. Never commissioned.
Condemned 8.10.51, broken up.

T12
Ship details:
Type 35
Ordered 29.6.36
Builder Deschimag (Bremen)
Yard No. 939
Laid down 20.8.38
Launched 12.4.39
Completed 3.7.40
Commanding officers:
Kpt.Lt. Mellin 7.40-1.42
Kpt.Lt. T-L. von Trotha 1.42-11.43
Kpt.Lt. W. Gross 11.43-5.45
Career summary:
September 1940 to February 1941
Norway
March 1941 to September 1941
Dockyard, Lloyd (Wessermünde)
October 1941 to December 1941
Group (North)
December 1941 to February 1942
France
March 1942 to May 1942 Norway
May 1942 to August 1942 Dockyard,
Germany
August 1942 to October 1942 Norway
October 1942 to April 1943 Western
France
May 1943 to October 1943 Dockyard,
Kiel
December 1943 to mid-1944 Torpedo
School
Fate:
Transferred to USSR in 1946 at Libau.
Renamed *Podvischny*. Scrapped in the
1960s.

T13
Ship details:
Type 37
Ordered 18.9.37
Builder Schichau (Elbing)
Yard No. S1401
Laid down 26.9.38
Launched 15.6.39
Completed 31.5.41
Commanding officers
Kpt.Lt. Gotzmann 5.41-11.43
Kpt.Lt. Seyfried 11.43-10.44
Ob.Lt.z.S. Rönnau 10.44-4.45

Career summary:
July 1941 to August 1941 Trials, New
Construction Command (EKK)
October 1941 to January 1942 Baltic
February 1942 to June 1942 Dockyard,
Rotterdam
July 1942 to February 1943 Western
France
March 1943 to July 1943 Dockyard,
Hamburg
August 1943 to March 1944 Baltic,
Torpedo School & Experimental
Establishment
Mid-1944 to December 1944 Group
(East) & 2nd Task Force
January 1945 to April 1945 Skaggerak
Fate:
Bombed and sunk by Halifax of No. 58
Squadron, RAF Coastal Command, in
the Kattegat, 10.4.45.

T14
Ship details:
Type 37
Ordered 18.9.37
Builder Schichau (Elbing)
Yard No. S1402
Laid down 5.11.38
Launched 20.7.39
Completed 14.6.41
Commanding officers:
Kpt.Lt. H. Jüttner 14.6.41-5.5.43
Kpt.Lt. Düvelius 6.5.43-12.8.43
Kpt.Lt. H. Bartels 13.8.43-14.8.44
Kpt.Lt. P. Wegner 15.8.44-8.5.45
Capitaine de Corvette Cevaer 1946
Career summary:
Until November 1941 Trials, New
Construction Command
December 1941 to March 1942 Home
waters, Baltic
April 1942 to May 1942 Dockyard
August to October 1943 Western
France
November 1943 to January 1944
Torpedo School, 23rd U-Boat Flotilla
February 1944 to 2 November 1944
Dockyard refit
November 1944 to May 1944 Group
(East), Baltic
Fate:
Allocated to USA 1946 but transferred
to France in September 1947. Arrived
Cherbourg 24.10.47 and renamed
Dompaire. Never commissioned.
Stricken 8.10.51 & broken up.

T15
Ship details:
Type 37
Ordered 18.9.37
Builder Schichau (Elbing)
Yard No. S1403
Laid down 3.1.39
Launched 16.9.39
Completed 26.6.41
Commanding officers:
Kpt.Lt. Düvelius 6.41-7.41
Kpt.Lt. Quedenfeldt 7.41-3.43
Kpt.Lt. Haberkorn 3.43-12.43

Career summary:
Until November 1941 Trials and
  training, Baltic
December 1941 to March 1942 North
  Sea & Holland
March 1942 to June 1942 Norway
August 1942 to September 1942
  Torpedo School
October 1942 to February 1943 Refit,
  Oderwerke (Stettin)
April 1943 to June 1943 Torpedo
  School
July 1943 to August 1943 Dockyard,
  Rostock
September 1943 to November 1943
  Attached 25th U-Boat Flotilla (Libau)
  and 24th U-Boat Flotilla (Memel)
Fate:
Bombed and sunk at Kiel during air
  raid by USAAF on 13.12.43.

T16
Ship details:
Type 37
Ordered 18.9.37
Builder Schichau (Elbing)
Yard No. S1404
Completed 24.7.41
Commanding officers:
Kpt.Lt. Düvelius 7.41-3.43
Kpt.Lt. Fimmen 4.43-10.43
Kpt.Lt. K. Paul 10.43-11.43
Ob.Lt.z.S. Strömer 11.43-4.44
Kpt.Lt. Balser 25.6.44-4.45
Career summary:
Until January 1942 Work up & training,
  Baltic
February 1942 to April 1942
  'Cerberus', then Norway
May 1942 to September 1942 Dockyard
  Kiel
October 1942 to February 1943
  Training , Baltic
February 1943 to March 1943 Aborted
  deployment to France
March 1943 to April 1943 Machinery
  overhaul, Kiel
April 1943 to August 1943 Training,
  then further dockyard time at Kiel
September 1943 to December 1943
  Attached 23rd U-Boat Flotilla
  (Memel & Danzig)
21 February 1944 Mined off Memel
  (repairs at Oderwerke, Stettin until
  August 1944)
September 1944 to April 1945 Baltic,
  then Skaggerak
Fate:
Seriously damaged by Halifaxes of No.
  58 Squadron on 3.4.45. Limped into
  Frederikshavn. Paid off 22.4.45.
  Transferred to Aarhus and broken up
  sometime between September 1946
  and March 1947.

T17
Ship details:
Type 37
Ordered 18.9.37
Builder Schichau (Elbing)

Yard No. S1405
Completed 28.8.41
Commanding officers:
Kpt.Lt. Blöse 8.41-6.43
Kpt.Lt. Liermann 9.43-5.45
Career summary:
Until December 1941 Trials and
  training
January 1941 to March 1942 Home
  waters
March 1942 to September 1942
  Dockyard refit
October 1942 to February 1943
  Western France
March 1943 to July 1943 Dockyard,
  Kiel
September 1943 to December 1943
  24th U-Boat Flotilla (Memel) and
  23rd U-Boat Flotilla
February 1944 to June 1944 Torpedo
  School
June 1944 to July 1944 Machinery
  overhaul, Oderwerke (Stettin)
August 1944 to October 1944 2nd
  Battle Group, Baltic
November 1944 to May 1945
  Skaggerak
Fate:
Allocated to USSR. Transferred at
  Libau February 1946; renamed
  Poryvisyti. Scrapped in the 1960s.

T18
Ship details:
Type 37
Ordered 18.9.37
Builder Schichau (Elbing)
Yard No. S1406
Laid down 27.7.39
Launched 1.6.40
Completed 22.11.41
Commanding officers:
Kpt.Lt. Hoepner 11.41-4.43
Kpt.Lt. Vorsteher 4.43-9.43
Kpt.Lt. G. Albers 9.43-5.44
Ob.Lt.z.S. Meyer-Abich 5.44-9.44
Career summary:
Until April 1942 Baltic, trials & training
May 1942 to September 1942 Torpedo
  School
September 1942 to June 1943 Western
  France
July 1943 Torpedo School
September 1943 to November 1943
  23rd U-Boat Flotilla (Memel and
  Danzig)
December 1943 to May 1944 Refit,
  Schichau (Elbing)
June 1944 to September 1944 Eastern
  Baltic and Gulf of Finland
Fate:
Sunk by rocket attack from Soviet
  aircraft north of Moon Sound, Gulf of
  Finland, 13.9.44.

T19
Ship details:
Type 37
Ordered 5.10.38
Builder Schichau (Elbing)

Yard No. S1446
Laid down 23.9.39
Launched 20.7.40
Completed 18.12.41
Commanding officers:
Kpt.Lt. Richter-Oldekop 12.41-5.43
Kpt.Lt. Weinlig 5.43-9.43
Kpt.Lt. Uhde 9.43-11.43
Kpt.Lt. W. Westphal 11.43-12.44
Kpt.Lt. Freiherr von Luttitz 12.44-5.45
Career summary:
Until April 1942 Trials & training
May 1942 to September 1942 Torpedo
  School
September 1942 to September 1943
  Western France
October 1943 to January 1944
  Dockyard refit, Bremen
February 1944 to May 1944 Torpedo
  School
June 1944 to October 1944 Eastern
  Baltic & 2nd Battle Group
November 1944 to May 1945
  Skaggerak
Fate:
Allocated to USA 1946. Sold to
  Denmark for $5.000, 1947. Use as
  leader for MTBs abandoned. Broken
  up 1950/51.

T20
Ship details:
Type 37
Ordered 5.10.38
Builder Schichau (Elbing)
Yard No. S1447
Laid down 28.11.39
Launched 12.9.40
Completed 5.6.42
Commanding officers:
Kpt.Lt. K-A. Richter-Oldekop 5.6.42-
  6.6.42
Kpt.Lt. K. Reitsch 7.6.42-25.6.43
Kpt.Lt. N. Bätge 26.6.43-27.9.43
Kpt.Lt. H. Eichel 28.9.43-27.9.44
Kpt.Lt. T. Lampe 28.9.44-8.5.45
(Norwegian C.O. unknown – if any)
Capitaine de Corvette Cevaer 1946
Career summary:
Until February 1943 Trials & training
February 1943 to April 1943 France &
  Norway
May 1943 to September 1943 Norway
October 1943 to March 1944 Torpedo
  School
March 1944 to August 1944 Dockyard
  refit
September 1944 to October 1944
  Baltic, 2nd Battle Group
November 1944 to May 1945
  Skaggerak
Fate:
To UK 1946. Transferred to France
  4.2.46 and renamed *Baccarat*. Never
  commissioned. Stricken 8.10.51.

T21
Ship details:
Type 37
Ordered 5.10 38
Builder Schichau (Elbing)

Yard No. S1448
Laid down 27.3.39
Launched 2.11.40
Completed 11.7.42
Commanding officers:
Kpt.Lt. Temming 7.42-4.44
Kpt.Lt. Kultzen 4.44-5.45
Career summary:
Until January 1943 Work up & training,
  Baltic
February 1943 to April 1943 France &
  Norway
May 1943 to September 1943 Norway
October 1943 to April 1944 Torpedo
  School
May 1944 to August 1944 E. Baltic &
  Skaggerak
August 1944 to September 1944 Refit,
  Stettiner-Oderwerke
October 1944 to November 1944 Baltic
  & Skaggerak
December 1944 to February 1945
  Dockyard, Elbing (towed to
  Deschimag (Bremen) 4.2.45). Paid off
  22 April 1945.
Fate:
To USA 1946. Cannibalized at Bremen.
  Scuttled in Skaggerak, 10.6.46.

T22
Ship details:
Type 39
Ordered 10.11.39 (Originally as Type
  37 on 5.10.38)
Builder Schichau (Elbing)
Yard No. S1481
Launched 1941
Completed 28.2.42
Commanding officers:
Kpt.Lt. Hansen-Nootbaar 2.42-5.43
Kpt.Lt. Jüttner 5.43-22.6.43
Kpt.Lt. Blöse 23.6.43-4.44
Kpt.Lt. Waldenburger 4.44-8.44
Career summary:
Until September 1942 Trials & training
October 1942 to February 1944
  Western France
March 1944 to June 1944 Refit,
  Schichau (Elbing)
July 1944 to August 1944 Gulf of
  Finland
Fate:
Mined and sunk in 'Seeigel IXb'
  barrage, Narva Bay, Gulf of Finland
  18.8.44.

T23
Ship details:
Type 39
Ordered 10.11.39 (originally as Type 37
  on 5.10.38)
Builder Schichau (Elbing)
Yard No. S1482
Laid down 1.8.40
Launched 14.6.41
Completed 14.6.42
Commanding officers:
Kpt.Lt. F.K. Paul 14.6.42-2.11.43
Kpt.Lt. W. Weinlig 3.11.43-8.5.45
Capitaine de Corvette Millot 2.46-
  11.46 (FN)

Capitaine de Corvette Roumeas 11.46-1947 (FN)
Capitaine de Corvette Guillanton 1948-49 (FN)
Capitaine de Corvette Rebut 24.6.49-26.11.50
Capitaine de Corvette Lanes 10.10.50-1.10.51 (FN)
Capitaine de Frégate Coat 22.10.51-6.6.52 (FN)
Career summary:
Until October 1942 Trials & training, Baltic
November 1942 to January 1944 Western France
February 1944 to June 1944 Refit, Bremen
July 1944 to September 1944 Gulf of Finland
October 1944 to November Dockyard at Danzig & Gotenhafen for repairs & re-arming
December 1944 to May 1945 Baltic
Fate:
UK 1945. Transferred to France 4.2.46 and renamed *Alsace*, then *Alsacien*. Condemned 9.6.54 and renamed *Q11*. Sold out February 1955 for scrapping.

T24
Ship details:
Type 39
Ordered 10.11.39 (originally as Type 37 on 5.10.38)
Builder Schichau (Elbing)
Yard No. S1483
Laid down 21.9.40
Launched 13.9.41
Completed 17.10.42
Commanding officers:
K.Kpt. H. Hoffman 17.10.42-17.11.43
Kpt.Lt. Meentzen 18.11.43-24.8.44
Career summary:
Until March 1943 Trials & training, Baltic
April 1943 to May 1943 Norway, then repairs at Kiel
June 1943 to August 1944 Western France
Fate:
Sunk by rocket and cannon fire from Beaufighters of Nos. 236 and 404 Squadrons whilst lying in the Gironde, 24.8.44.

T25
Ship details:
Type 39
Ordered 10.11.39 (originally as Type 37 on 30.3.39)
Builder Schichau (Elbing)
Yard No. S1484
Laid down 30.11.40
Launched 1.12.41
Completed 12.11.42
Commanding officers:
Kpt.Lt. Koppenhagen 12.11.42-19.4.43
K. Kpt. von Gartzen 20.4.43-28.12.43
Career summary:
Until May 1943 Trials & training, Baltic

June 1943 to December 1943 Western France
Fate:
Sunk in action with British cruisers *Glasgow* and *Enterprise*, Bay of Biscay, 28.12.43.

T26
Ship details:
Type 39
Ordered 10.11.39 (originally as Type 37 on 30.3.39)
Builder Schichau (Elbing)
Yard No. S1485
Laid down 10.5.41
Launched 26.3.42
Completed 28.2.43
Commanding officers:
Kpt.Lt. Frieherr von Lyncker 28.2.43-22.9.43
Kpt.Lt. Quedenfeldt 23.9.43-28.12.43
Career summary:
Until August 1943 Trials & training, Baltic
August 1943 to December 1943 Western France
Fate:
as *T25*.

T27
Ship details:
Type 39
Ordered 10.11.39 (originally as Type 37 on 30.3.39)
Builder Schichau (Elbing)
Yard No. S1486
Laid down 2.7.41
Launched 20.6.42
Completed 17.4.43
Commanding officers:
K.Kpt. Verlohr 17.4.43-7.11.43
Kpt.Lt. Gotzmann 8.11.43-29.4.44
Career summary:
Until August 1943 Trials & training, Baltic
August 1943 to April 1944 Western France
Fate:
Beached 29.4.44 near St. Brieux after action with HMCS *Haida*. Capsized 4.5.44 and total loss.

T28
Ship details:
Type 39
Ordered 10.11.39 (originally as Type 37 on 30.3.39)
Builder Schichau (Elbing)
Yard No. S1487
Laid down 24.9.41
Launched 8.10.42
Completed 19.6.43
Commanding officers:
K.Kpt. Richter-Oldekop 19.6.43-25.1.44
Kpt.Lt. Temming 1.5.44-8.5.45
Capitaine de Corvette Millot 2.46-11.46
Capitaine de Corvette Roumeas 11.46-1947
Capitaine de Corvette Hello 1948-1949
Capitaine de Corvette Lorenzi 1949-1950

Capitaine de Corvette Sicard 1950-1952
Capitaine de Corvette Graignic 1952-1953
Capitaine de Corvette Lapistolle 1953-1955
Career summary:
Until December 1943 Trials & training, Baltic
December 1943 to January 1944 Norway and Home waters
January 1944 to July 1944 Western France
August 1944 to September 1944 Gulf of Finland
October 1944 to December 1944 Dockyard (Gotenhafen)
January 1945 to May 1945 Baltic
Fate:
UK 1946. Transferred to France February 1946 and renamed *Lorraine*, then *Lorrain*, 4.2.46. Placed in reserve May 1945 and renamed *Q59*, 31.10.55. Condemned 21.7.59 sold out for scrap.

T29
Ship detail:
Type 39
Ordered 10.11.39 (originally as Type 37 on 30.3.39)
Builder Schichau (Elbing)
Yard No. S1488
Completed 21.8.43
Commanding officers:
Kpt.Lt. Grund 21.8.43-26.4.44
Career summary:
Until January 1944 Trials & training, Baltic
January 1944 to April 1944 Western France
Fate:
Sunk in action with HMCSS *Athabaskan* and *Haida* in English Channel 26.4.44.

T30
Ship details:
Type 39
Ordered 10.11.39 (originally as Type 37 on 30.3.39)
Builder Schichau (Elbing)
Yard No. S1489
Laid down 10.4.42
Launched 13.3.43
Completed 24 10.43
Commanding officers:
Kpt.Lt. Buch 24.10.43-18.8.44
Career summary:
Until January 1944 Trials & training, Baltic
January 1944 to March 1944 Baltic
April 1944 to August 1944 Gulf of Finland
Fate:
As *T22*.

T31
Ship details:
Type 39

Ordered 20.1.41
Builder Schichau (Elbing)
Yard No. S1513
Launched 1943
Completed 5.2.44
Commanding officer:
Kpt.Lt. Peter-Pirkham 5.2.44-20.6.44
Career summary:
Until May 1944 Work up, trials & training, Baltic
June 1944 Gulf of Finland
Fate:
Torpedoed and sunk by Soviet MTB *TKA37* in inner Gulf of Finland 20.6.44.

T32
Ship details:
Type 39
Ordered 20.1.41
Builder Schichau (Elbing)
Yard No. S1514
Laid down 27.10.42
Launched 17.4.43
Completed 8.5.44
Commanding officer:
Kpt.Lt. Dehnert 8.5.44-18.8.44
Career summary:
Until July 1944 Trials & training, Baltic
July 1944 to August 1944 Gulf of Finland
Fate:
As *T22*.

T33
Ship details:
Type 39
Ordered 20.1.41
Builder Schichau (Elbing)
Yard No. S1515
Completed 16.6.44
Commanding officer:
Kpt.Lt. Priebe 16.6.44-8.5.45
Career summary:
Until September 1944 Trials & training, Baltic
October 1944 Danzig Dockyard
October 1944 to May 1945 Baltic
Fate:
USSR 1946. Renamed *Primernyi*.

T34
Ship details:
Type 39
Ordered 20.1.41
Builder Schichau (Elbing)
Yard No. S1516
Laid down 5.3.43
Launched 23.10.43
Completed 12.8.44
Commanding officers:
Kpt.Lt. Freiherr von Lüttitz 12.8.44-20.11.44
Career summary:
Never completed work-up training.
Fate:
Mined and sunk off Cape Arkona 20.11.44

T35
Ship details:
Type 39
Ordered 20.1.41
Builder Schichau (Elbing)
Yard No. S1517
Laid down 20.4.43
Launched 12.12.43
Completed 7.10.44
Commanding officers:
Kpt.Lt. Buch 7.10.44-8.5.45
Career summary:
Until March 1945 Training & Work up, Baltic
March 1945 to May 1945 Baltic
Fate:
To USA 1946 as *DD935*. Transferred to France as spares reserve 1947 and towed back to France from Annapolis. Condemned at Cherbourg 3.10.52.

T36
Ship details:
Type 39
Ordered 20.1.41
Builder Schichau (Elbing)
Yard No. S1518
Laid down 10.6.43
Launched 5.2.44
Completed 9.12.44
Commanding officers:
Kpt.Lt. Hering 9.12.44-4.5.45
Career summary:
Until February 1945 Trials & training
February 1945 to May 1945 2nd Battle Group and E. Prussia
Fate:
Mined and damaged off Swinemünde 4.5.45. Bombed and sunk by Soviet aircraft 5.5.45.

Type 41 Torpedo Boat
In June 1944 PR sorties first revealed the existence of the Type 41 design by its extra length.
T37 laid down between 26 July 1943 and 10 October 1943
T38 actually laid down 11 October 1943
T39 to *T42* all laid down between 10 October 1943 and 19 February 1944
T43 to *T45* all laid down between 19 February 1944 and 19 June 1944
No further units were laid down as all six slipways were occupied although one was wide enough to take three hulls.
T37 launched between 19 February 1944 and 19 April 1944
T38 & T39 launched between 19 April 1944 and 19 June 1944
T40 launched between 7 August 1944 and 25 October 1944
No others were put afloat but *T41* was almost ready for launch
There is some evidence to suggest that one hull, probably that of *T45*, was being dismantled by January 1945 possibly in anticipation of the switch to the Type 44 design and the laying down of *T52*

T37
Left Elbing about 23 January 1945 in tow to west to complete at Deschimag, Bremen. Awaiting escort from Brunsbüttel to Wesermünde p.m. 21 February 1945. Captured at Bremerhaven having had no further work done. Scuttled by US forces 1946.

T38 and **T39**
As *T37* but proceeded only to Kiel although *T38* was scheduled to complee at Deschimag. Both scuttled at sea 10 May 1946 in 58.07° 48' N, 10.46° 30' E and 58.08° 12' N, 10.47° 48' E respectively.

T40
As *T37*. Left Gotenhafen in tow 1600, 9 March 1945, bound for Eckenförde with twelve 'Linsen' aboard. Scuttled shortly after off Brossen north of Danzig as it was unlikely that the tow would get through.

Type 44 Torpedo Boat
T52 to *T56* (Yard Nos. S1721 to 1725) ordered 28.3.44
T57 to *T60* Projected
Very doubtful whether any were laid down.

T61
Ship details:
Type 40
Ordered 19.11.40
Builder Wilton-Fijenoord (Schiedam)
Laid down 1942
Launched 15.8.44
Fate:
Left Hook of Holland 12 September 1944 under tow with *Neubau 88* as Convoy 1275, escorted by seven units of the 20th Vp Flotilla. Attacked by Beaufighters of 143 Squadron RAF off the West Fresian islands the same day. Sank after bomb or rocket damage off Den Helder before the ship could be beached.

T62
Ship details:
Type 40
Ordered 19.11.40
Builder Wilton-Fijenoord (Schiedam)
Yard No. 692
Laid down 1.4.42
Fate:
Never launched, broken up on slipway.

T63
Ship details:
Type 40
Ordered 19.11.40
Builder Rotterdam D.D. (Rotterdam)
Yard No. 243
Laid down 1.7.42
Launched 28.10.44
Fate:
Towed to Germany, In Emden

29.11.44, arrived Schillig roads 21.12.44, passed Kiel 23.12.44, arrived Schichau? Towed west to Kiel once more. Scuttled by Allied forces 31.12.46 in the Skaggerak. Her retention beyond the date required by the Tripartite Commission for the destruction of Category C ships was necessitated by her conversion to dispose of chemical warfare munitions.

T64
Ship details:
Type 40
Ordered 19.11.40
Builder Rotterdam D.D (Rotterdam)
Yard No. 244
Laid down 1.4.42 (No. 5 slipway)
Fate:
Never launched, broken up.

T65
Ship details:
Type 40
Ordered 19.11.40 (provisional); 6.1.41 (definitive)
Builder De Schelde (Vlissingen)
Yard No. 224
Laid down 1.12.42
Launched 8.7.44
Fate:
8.9.44 towed to Germany for completion in Convoy 1277, arriving at Den Helder 15.9.44. Arrived Borkum 16.9.44. At Bremen 10.44. Ordered to Elbing for completion, Tow delayed in Western Baltic, (Mines) 29-30. 12.44. At Schichau 1.45. 22.1.45 towed to Danzig for completion, then to Bremen again. Scuttled incomplete by US Forces, loaded with gas ammunition 2.7.46.

T66
Ship details:
Type 40
Ordered 19.11.40 (provisional); 6.1.41 (definitive)
Bulder De Schelde (Vlissingen)
Yard No. 225
Laid down 1.12.42
Launched 29.7.44
Fate:
Uncertain, possibly destroyed in air raid on yard 1944. Alternative Dutch sources state work never even started on this ship.

T67
Ship details:
Type 40
Ordered 19.11.40
Builder Nederlandsche Scheepsbouw (Amsterdam)
Yard No. 305, but transferred due to the *Hansa* programme: Re-ordered 6.5.43
Builder De Schelte (Vlissingen)
Yard No. 257

Laid down 23.11.43
Fate:
Damaged by bombing on the slip October 19.44. Broken up November-December 1945.

T68
Ship details:
Type 40
Ordered 19.11.40
Builder Nederlandsche Scheepsbouw (Amsterdam)
Yard No. 306
Order transferred to Wilton as Yard No. 699, September 1943 because of the *Hansa* programme. Probably never laid down.

T69
Ship details:
Type 40
Ordered 3.5.41
Builder Wilton Fijenoord (Schiedam)
Yard No. 693
Laid down 1.4.42. (?)
Fate:
Never launched if actually begun.

T70
Ship details:
Type 40
Ordered 3.5.41
Builder Rotterdam D.D. (Rotterdam)
Yard No. 245
Laid down 1.4.42
Fate:
Laid down on same slip as *T64*, side by side. Suspended by April 1943. Never launched, broken up post-war. Was originally Nederlandsche Sheepsbouw Yard No. 307.

T71
Ship details:
Type 40
Ordered 16.12.40 (provisional); 6.1.41 (definitive)
Builder De Schelde (Vlissingen)
Fate:
Never laid down. Suspended by April 1943.

T72
Ship details:
Type 40
Ordered 3.5.41
Builder Nederlandsche Scheepsbouw (Amsterdam)
Yard No. 309
Transferred to Rotterdam D.D. because of the *Hansa* programme in 1943. Never laid down.
On 27.8.41 a further twelve units were ordered, *T73* to *T84*, with yard allocations as follows:
T73-75, Wilton; *T76-78*, Rotterdam DD; *T79-81*, De Schelde; *T82-84*, Nederlandsche Scheepsbouw. Only *T73* and *T74* received yard nos (704 and 705).

5. DESTROYER AND TORPEDO BOAT ARMAMENT

15cm Torpedoboots Kanone C/36

Gun:

Calibre	149.1mm
Muzzle velocity	835m/sec
Barrel length	48cal (7,165mm)
Liner length	45.7cal (6,815mm)
Construction gas pressure	3,000kg/cm²
Barrel life	1,100 rounds
Recoil force (0° elev)	58,000kg
Length of rifling	5,587mm
Type of rifling	Cubic parabola, 45/30cal
No. of grooves	44
Weight of breech and barrel	8,564kg
Max range	21,950m

Construction: Jacket with loose inner tube; cross wedge breech

Ammunition:

	HE	HE mh
Weight of shell	45.3kg	45.3kg
Weight of charge	6kg	3.89kg
HE charge	Fp02	Fp02
Length of shell	700mm	678.9mm
Weight of cartridge	23.5kg	24kg
Length of cartridge	865mm	865mm
Fuzes	Time S/30	Inst. nose C/27

Mounting LC/36 (single):

Elevation/depression	+30°/–10°
Training limits	±360° = 720°
Elevation change per handwheel rev	1° 52'
Training change per handwheel rev	3°
Weight of gun cradle	1,730kg
Weight of base	2,400kg
Weight of pedestal	3,885kg
Weight of sighting gear	650kg
Electric power	450kg
Weight of shield	3,185kg
Total weight of mounting	16,100kg
Armour	10mm fwd; 6mm side and deck

Mounting LDrh LC/38 (twin turret):

Elevation/depression	+65°/–10°
Training limits	290°
Elevation change per handwheel rev	1° 30'
Training change per handwheel rev	45', 4° 30', 3°
Weight of gun cradle	4,300kg
Weight of pedestal	22,250kg
Weight of sighting gear	650kg
Electric power	2,400kg
Weight of shield	13,750kg
Total weight of mounting	60,400kg
Armour	30mm fwd; 20mm side and deck; 15mm rear
Armour type	Whn/A

12.7cm C/34 on Centre Pivot Mounting C/34

Gun:

Calibre	128mm
Muzzle velocity	830m/sec
Barrel length	45cal (5,760mm)
Liner length	42.5cal (5,430mm)
Barrel life	1,650 rounds
Recoil force (0° elev)	38,000kg
Length of rifling	4,536mm
Type of rifling	Cubic parabola, 35/30cal
No. of grooves	40
Weight of breech and barrel	3,645kg
Max range	17,400m

Construction: Jacket vertical sliding wedge breech; hydraulic brake and two spring recuperators

Ammunition:

Weight of shell	28kg
Weight of charge	8.5kg
HE charge	Fp02
Length of shell	564.7mm
Weight of cartridge	16kg
Length of cartridge	732mm
Propellant	RCP/32
Fuzes	Nose inst. nf C/27; nose time f S/60

Mounting:

Elevation/depression	+30°/–10°
Training limits	±360° = 720°
Elevation change per handwheel rev	2.95°
Training change per handwheel rev	3.08°
Weight of gun cradle	1,320kg
Weight of base	1,290kg
Weight of pedestal	2,605kg
Weight of sighting gear	530kg
Electric power	260kg
Weight of shield	1,870kg
Total weight of mounting	10,220kg
Armour	8mm front, top and sides
Armour type	Wsh

10.5cm SK C/32ns on 10.5cm MPL C/32ge Mounting

Gun:

Calibre	105mm
Muzzle velocity	780m/sec
Barrel length	45cal (4,740mm)
Liner length	42cal (4,400mm)
Constructional gas pressure	2,850kg/cm²
Barrel life	4,100 rounds
Recoil force (0° elev)	22,600kg
Weight of breech and barrel	1,765kg
Max range	15,175m

Ammunition:

Weight of shell	15.1kg
Weight of charge	3.8kg
Length of shell	459mm
Weight of cartridge	24kg
Length of cartridge	1,050mm

Mounting:

Elevation/depression	+70°/–10°
Elevation change per handwheel rev	3°
Training change per handwheel rev	3°
Weight of cast gun cradle	655kg
Weight of pedestal	2,100kg
Weight of sighting gear	350kg
Electric power	210kg
Weight of shield	1,670kg
Total weight of mounting	6,750kg
Armour	12mm front; 4mm side and deck
Armour type	Wsh

3.7cm SK C/30 on Twin Mounting C/30

Gun:

Calibre	37mm
Muzzle velocity	1,000m/sec
Muzzle energy	38mt
Barrel length	83cal (3,074mm)
Bore length	80cal (2,960mm)
Constructional gas pressure	3,450kg/cm²
Barrel life	7,500 rounds
Recoil force (0° elev)	1,000kg
Length of rifling	2,554mm
Type of rifling	Cubic parabola 50/35 cal
No. of grooves	16
Weight of breech and barrel	243kg
Max horizontal range	8,500m
Max vertical range	6,800m (tracer 4,800m)

Construction: Monoblock barrel with drawn on breech ring; vertical sliding block breech; hydraulic brake and spring recuperator

Ammunition:

Weight of shell	0.742kg
Weight of charge	0.365kg
HE charge	Fp02
Length of shell	162mm
Weight of cartridge	0.97kg
Length of cartridge	381mm
Propellant	RPC/32
Weight of complete round	2.1kg
Length of complete round	516.5mm
Fuzes	E nose C/30; nose C/34; ERs St C/34 (tracer)
Duration of tracer	12 sec
Rate of fire	160 rounds/min cyclic; 80 rounds/min practical

Mounting:

Elevation/depression	+85°/–10°
Training limits	±360° = 720°
Elevation change per handwheel rev	3°
Training change per handwheel rev	4°
Weight of cradle, brake, etc. (swinging mass)	243kg
Weight of cast gun cradle	152.5kg
Weight of base	71kg
Weight of pedestal	2,162kg
Weight of sighting gear	87kg

Weight of electric
power 630kg
Total weight of
mounting 3,670kg

3.7cm MK/42 on 3.7cm Flak Mounting LM/42

Gun:
Calibre 37mm
Muzzle velocity 850m/sec (HE)
Muzzle energy 24.4mt
Barrel length 69cal (2,568mm)
Barrel life 7,000 rounds
Recoil force
(0° elevation) 1,240kg
Length of rifling 2,289mm
Type of rifling Constant r,
7° = 25.6 cal
No. of grooves 16
Weight of breech
and barrel 109kg
Construction:
Monoblock barrel
with breech ring
connected by
bayonet joint;
vertical sliding
block breech;
hydraulic brake
and spring
recuperator
Ammunition:
Weight of shell
(HE) 0.61kg
Weight of cartridge 0.51kg
Weight of complete
round 1.3kg
Length of complete
round 355mm
Type of fuze Nose 40
Fuze filling Duplex detonator
Supply 8-round linked clips

3.7cm Flak 43

Gun:
Calibre 37mm
Muzzle velocity 870m/sec (HE);
770m/sec (AP);
1,150m/sec
(AP40)
Muzzle energy 21.8mt
Barrel length 57cal
Constructional gas
pressure 2,900kg/cm2
Barrel life 8,000 rounds
Recoil force
(0° elevation) 1,500kg
Length of rifling 1,838mm
Type of rifling Kupa 3°/5°
No of grooves 20
Weight of breech
and barrel 127kg
Max horizontal
range 6,400m (Mgr 18)
Max vertical range 4,800m
Construction:
Modified Rhein-
metall 108 MK

103 aircraft
cannon with gas-
operated breech
Ammunition:
Weight of shell 0.625kg (HE);
0.685kg (AP)
Weight of complete
round 1.5kg
Length of complete
round 368mm
Fuze Nose
Fuze fitting Duplex detonator
Supply 8-round linked
clips
Mounting:
Elevation/
depression +90°/–10°
Training limits 360°
Weight of
mounting 1,900kg approx

2cm C/30 2cm Pedestal L/30

Gun:
Calibre 20mm
Muzzle velocity 835m/sec
Barrel length 65cal (1,300mm)
Bore length 65cal (1,300mm)
Constructional gas
pressure 2,800kg/cm2
Barrel life 22,000 rounds
Recoil force
(0° elevation) 250kg
Length of rifling 720mm
Weight of breech
and barrel 64kg
Max horizontal
range 4,900m
Max vertical range 3,700m
Ammunition:
Weight of shell 0.134kg
Weight of charge 0.0395kg
Length of shell 78.5mm
Weight of complete
round 0.32kg
Length of complete
round 203mm
Rate of fire 280 rounds/min
cyclic; 120 rounds/
min practical
Supply 20-round magazine
Mounting:
Elevation/
depression +85°/–11°
Training limits None
Weight of cradle,
brake, etc.
(swinging mass) 43kg
Weight of mounting
(without sights) 282kg
Weight of complete
gun 420kg

2cm C/38 on 2cm Pedestal L/30

Gun:
As 2cm C/30 but recoil force at 0° =
290kg and weight of barrel and breech
= 57.5kg
Ammunition:
As 2cm C/30 but rate of fire improved

to 480 rounds/min cyclic, 220
rounds/min practical
Mounting:
As 2cm C/30 but weight of complete
gun including spent cartridge net =
416kg

2cm Flak 35 on Vierling L/38

Gun:
Four 2cm C/38 barrels
Ammunition:
As 2cm C/38 but rate of fire 1,800
rounds/min cyclic, 880 rounds/min
practical
Mounting:
Weight of cradle
and brake 410kg
Weight of mounting
less sights 828kg
Weight of sights 96.6kg
Weight of power
training 31.5kg
Weight of armour 500kg
Weight of complete
gun 2,150kg

Type G7a Torpedo

Calibre 53.3cm
Propulsion Compressed air
Warhead 430kg TNT
Range at 30 knots 15,000m
Range at 40 knots 5,000m
Range at 45 knots 4,500m
Gyro angling Up to 90° left/right
in 1° steps
Depth setting Up to 52m in 1m
steps

Anti-Submarine Armament

Note: Destroyers were basically
equipped with what was classified as a
'Medium A/S Outfit' comprising four
depth-charge throwers, two sided port
and starboard, with reload racks,
together with six single depth-charges in
individual racks. Sufficient depth-
charges for two to four attacks (each of
16 charges) were carried. Depth-charge
type was WBF or WBG ('Wasserbombe
F' or 'G').

	WBF	WBG
Weight of explosive	60kg	60kg
Total weight of depth-charge	139kg	180kg
Depth-setting options	15, 25, 35, 45, 60, 75m	20, 35, 50, 70, 90, 120m
Minimum depth setting	6m	6m
Sink speed	2.23m/sec	3.5m/sec
Effective area		
Destruction zone	0-5.6m	
Danger zone	5.6-17m	
Damage zone	17-28m	
Safety zone	Over 28m	
Minimum dropping interval	30m	30m

8.6cm Raketen, Abschussgerät M42/M43

Launching equipment for 8.6cm
rockets:
Calibre 86mm
Launcher length 1,270mm approx
Weight of
launcher 27kg approx
Weight of
mounting 36kg approx
Arc of training 360°
Elevation limit 90°
Note: fairly crude equipment with early
versions not being fitted even with
sights.
Ammunition:
(a) 8.6cm Rkt. Speinggranate L/4.8
(high-explosive rocket)
Weight 8.4kg approx
Length 417mm
Propellant Black powder
Range 400, 600 or 800m
Warhead Equivalent to 8.8cm
HE shell

Identification
colour Yellow
(b) 8.6cm Rkt. Drahtseilgerät
(parachute and cable rocket)
Weight 5kg (R.Dg. 400);
5.3kg (R.Dg.
1000)
Length 392mm (R.Dg.
400); 426mm
(R.Dg. 1000)
Propellant Black powder
Range 400m or 1,000m
Opening height 300-400m (R.Dg.
400); 800-1,000m
(R.Dg. 1000)
Wire length 100m
(c) 8.6cm Rkt. Leuchtgeschoss
(starshell)
Weight 4.3kg (R. Lg.)
Length 392mm
Propellant Black powder
Horizontal range 1,100m @ 40°
elevation
Vertical range 350m @ 40°
elevation
Burn time 30 sec
Other types of rocket, for smoke-
making, signalling, etc., were
originally proposed or manufactured,
but representation from the Fleet over
the variety caused a reduction in types
issued. The rockets described above
were the main variants.

Mines

EMC (Einheitsminen 'C'):
Type Contact, moored
Explosive charge 300kg
Diameter 1.1m (approx)
Height 2.1m (inc. damper
spring)
Case wall thickness 3.5mm (steel)
Weight of mine
and sinker
carriage 1,100-1,300kg

Standard wire
lengths   100m 12.5mm dia
    200m 11.5mm dia
    300m 9.5mm dia
    500m 8.0mm dia
Detonators   7 (5 upper hemi-
    sphere, 2 lower)
    lead sleeved horns
Normal depth
setting   3-6m

Note: The 'standard' contact mine. Modifications included a wide variety of auxiliary detonating devices, including floating snag lines, secondary floats and submarine contact detonators; a subscript to the mine designation denoted which, if any, of these devices were incorporated. Anti-sweeping devices were also fitted on occasion, usually by replacing the first 6m of wire directly below the mine with 16mm chain. This added weight, and consequently the wire length was reduced and the mine could not be employed in as deep water as the simple EMC type.

EMF (Einheitsminen 'Fernzundung')
Type   Influence, moored
Firing mode   Magnetic
Explosive charge   350kg
Diameter   1.1m (approx)
Case wall thickness   7mm (aluminium composite)

Standard wire
lengths   200m 11mm dia
    300m 9.5m dia
    500m 8mm dia
Normal depth
setting   12-15m
Firing mechanism   Bipolar, activated by vertical component of magnetism; operated at 5-10mg.

Note: There were a number of varieties of magnetic mine, of which some were ground mines, i.e., they remained on the sea-bed when laid. These were used in shallower waters than the EMF type and were laid mainly by submarines, aircraft and S-boats where their lighter weight was an advantage (there was no heavy carriage or cable). The mines detailed above were the ones most commonly laid by destroyers and torpedo boats. *Moored* influence mines LMA and TMB and C were laid by aircraft and submarines or coastal forces craft respectively.

Anti-sweeping devices and decoys
The object of laying mines is to close waters to the enemy, and the longer this can be achieved the greater is the disruption to the enemy's shipping. It is not always necessary to sink enemy vessels, since the mere knowledge of a field will inhibit attempts to cross it. However, once a field is detected, operations will begin to clear it and, once again, the more difficult it is made for the field to be swept, the longer will be its effective life. To this end, various measures were adopted by both sides in order to make minesweepers' tasks more difficult. These measures included dummy mines (thus wasting the sweepers' time), wire cutters (to break the sweep wires), mines specially laid to catch the minesweepers themselves, and mixtures of mine types (thus requiring the field to be swept for contact, magnetic and perhaps acoustic mines). To complicate matters further, the firing mechanism of influence mines might also incorporate a delay device which could be set to prevent the mine arming itself for up to 200 days and alternatively (or additionally) a ship counter which prevented the mine arming until, say, ten ships had passed over it. All these measures added to the minesweepers' tasks, and if one considers all the possible permutations and the vast numbers of mines laid during the Second World War, it will be clear why there are still former mined areas closed to shipping even today. Time has a marked effect on influence mines, which contain batteries, but contact mines, provided the casing does not corrode, can remain dangerous for a very much longer period of time.

RB (Reissboje)
This was literally a 'cutterbuoy' and consisted of a pear-shaped, steel-cased buoy moored to the bottom and on the mooring wires of which were fixed one or two cutter jaws (depending upon whether the area was affected by currents or not). No explosive charge was carried, its sole purpose being to sever the sweep wires. It was equipped for laying in up to 100m depths of water.

EMR (Einheitsminen 'Reisen')
As its name suggests, this was an empty EM 'standard' mine case which could be fitted with five dummy detonator horns to simulate a lethal EMC mine. It was normally fitted with a 50m anti-sweep chain incorporated into the mooring and could also be equipped with cutters. A further modification had a double chain mooring, but this could not be laid in such deep water as the normal EMR. Like the RB, no explosive charge was incorporated. Its purpose was to disguise the channels through a minefield, preventing their detection by ASDIC or S-Geräte. An enemy would not be able to distinguish live from inert mines.

6. BOILER SYSTEMS

	Wagner Large	Small	Benson	Admiralty 3-drum*
Normal evaporation (lb/hr)	120,500	105,000	132,000	125,000
Pressure at drum (psi)	995	995	1,635	300
Temperature at superheater outlet (F°)	850	850	842	640
Feed temperature (F°)	347	347	212	–
Designed efficiency (%)	78	78	77	76
Boiler heating surface (ft²)	4,240	3,720	5,350	7,770
Superheater surface (ft²)	1,076	925	667	1,300
Air pre-heater (ft²)	6,650	5,720	–	–
Radiant heating surface (ft²)	336	308	–	–
Furnace volume (ft³)	594	501	660	991
Forcing rate (lb/ft²)	32.2	30.8	–	44.5
Weight of boiler (dry) (tons)	41.3	38.6	40	46.25
Overall length (ft)	21	21	23	14.1
Overall height (ft)	18.5	17.75	23	16.75
Overall width (ft)	12	11.5	14	20.5
Burners	2	2	2	–
Type	double-ended Saake	double-ended Saake	double-ended Blohm und Voss	9
Fuel quantity (lb/hr)	10,700	9,360	8,750	8,900 approx

*As fitted, HMS *Faulknor*, 1934

7. MINELAYING OPERATIONS

North Sea Minelaying Successes 1939-40

Date	Ship	Tonnage	Nation	Type	Position	Op.*
22.10.39	*Whitemantle*	1,692	Bri	SC	6m E Withernsea L	1
23.10.39	*Albania*	1,214	Swe	SC	3m N Humber LS	1
29.10.39	*Varangmalm*	3,551	Nor	SC	53.50N 00.17E	1
30.10.39	*Juno*	1,241	Fin	SC	53.45N 00.17E	1
3.11.39	*Canada*	11,108	Den	MC	53.40N 00.17E	1
4.11.39	*Sig*	1,342	Nor	SC	53.43N 00.17E	1
13.11.39	*Blanche*	1,360t	Bri	Des	Tongue LS	2
13.11.39	*Ponzano*	1,346	Bri	SC	51.29N 01.25E	2
13.11.39	*Matra*	8,003	Bri	SC	1m E Tongue LS	2
15.11.39	*Woodtown*	794	Bri	SC	¾m NE Spit Buoy	2
18.11.39	*Simon Bolivar*	8,309	Neth	SC	51.49N 01.41E	3
18.11.39	*Blackhill*	2,492	Bri	SC	145° 7½C Longsand Buoy	3
19.11.39	*Grazia*	5,857	It	SC	5m N Foreland	2
19.11.39	*B. O. Borjesson*	1,585	Swe	SC	53.36N 00.21E	4
19.11.39	*Rhuys*	2,921	Fre	SC	2m Humber LS	4
19.11.39	*Torchbearer*	1,267	Bri	SC	025 2m Shipwash LS	3
20.11.39	*Mastiff*	520t	Bri	Tr	Thames Estuary	3
21.11.39	*Tereukuni Maru*	11,930	Jap	MC	51.50N 01.30E	3
21.11.39	*Gipsy*	1,335t	Bri	Des	Off Harwich	3
21.11.39	*Geraldus*	2,495	Bri	SC	3m WNW Sunk LS	3
22.11.39	*Lowland*	974	Bri	SC	2m ENE Gunfleet Buoy	3
23.11.39	*Hookwood*	1,537	Bri	SC	3½m ENE Tongue LS	2
24.11.39	*Mangelore*	8,886	Bri	SC	288° 1½m Spurn LS	4
26.11.39	*Pilsudski*	14,294	Pol	PL	314° 26m Outer Dowsing	4
27.11.39	*Spaarndam*	8,857	Neth	SC	2m NE Tongue LS	2
28.11.39	*Rubislaw*	1,014	Bri	SC	1½m ENE Tongue LS	2
30.11.39	*Sheafcrest*	2,730	Bri	SC	51.32N 01.26E	2
30.11.39	*Realf*	8,083	Nor	MT	53.55N 00.20E	4
1.12.39	*Dalryan*	4,558	Bri	SC	2½m SW Tongue LS	2
2.12.39	*San Calisto*	8,010	Bri	MT	2½m NNE Tongue LS	2
4.12.39	*Horstead*	1,670	Bri	SC	53.48N 00.16E	4
4.12.39	*Gimle*	1,271	Nor	SC	53.48N 00.16E	4
6.12.39	*Paralos*	3,435	Grk	SC	2m ENE Tongue LS	2
8.12.39	*Merel*	1,088	Bri	SC	Gull LS, Ramsgate	2
8.12.39	*Corea*	751	Bri	SC	2½m NE ½N Cromer L	5
10.12.39	*Ray of Hope*	98t	Bri	Dr	Thames Estuary	3
15.12.39	*Ursus*	1,499	Swe	SC	51.35N 01.36E	2
31.12.39	*Box Hill*	5,677	Bri	SC	53.32N 00.24E	1

Date	Ship	Tonnage	Nation	Type	Position	Op.*
12.12.39	*King Egbert*	4,535	Bri	MC	4m SW Haisboro' LS	5
13.12.39	*Rosa*	1,146	Bel	SC	Off River Tyne	6
13.12.39	*William Hallett*	202t	Bri	Tr	Off River Tyne	6
14.12.39	*Inverlane*	9,141	Bri	MT	55.05N 01.07W	6
14.12.39	*James Ludford*	506t	Bri	Tr	Off River Tyne	6
15.12.39	*Strindheim*	321	Nor	SC	Off River Tyne	6
15.12.39	*Ragni*	1,264	Nor	SC	55.02N 01.12W	6
15.12.39	*H. C. Flood*	1,907	Nor	SC	55.02N 01.12W	6
16.12.39	*Evalina*	202t	Bri	Tr	Off River Tyne	6
16.12.39	*Sedgefly*	520t	Bri	Tr	Off River Tyne	6
16.12.39	*Amble*	1,162	Bri	SC	54.55N 01.03W	6
19.12.39	*Jytte*	1,877	Den	SC	Off River Tyne	6
20.12.39	*Mars*	1,877	Swe	SC	1m St Mary's LS	6
6.1.40	*Eta*	81	Bri	FV	6m N½W Outer Gabbard LS	7

Date	Ship	Tonnage	Nation	Type	Position	Op.*
7.1.40	*Cedrington Court*	5,160	Bri	SC	2m NE North Goodwin LS	7
7.1.40	*Towneley*	2,888	Bri	SC	1m ENE NE Spit Buoy, Margate	7
9.1.40	*Dunbar Castle*	10,002	Bri	SC	51.23N 01.34E	7
9.1.40	*Truida*	176	Neth	MC	51.27N 01.50E	7
16.1.40	*Josephine Charlotte*	3,310	Bel	SC	51.32N 01.33E	7
19.1.40	*Grenville*	1,485t	Bri	Des	51.39N 02.17E	7
11.1.40	*Lucida*	251	Bri	FV	55.00N 00.53W	8
11.1.40	*Traviata*	5,123	It	SC	8m SE Cromer Knoll	9
12.1.40	*Granata*	2,719	Bri	SC	53.13N 01.21E	9
17.1.40	*Asteria*	3,313	Grk	SC	NE Haisboro' LS	9
13.2.40	*British Triumph*	8,501	Bri	MT	53.06N 01.25E	10
14.2.40	*Giorgio Ohlsen*	5,694	It	SC	53.18N 01.08E	10
17.2.40	*Baron Ailsa*	3,656	Bri	SC	53.17N 01.12E	10
24.2.40	*Clan Morrison*	5,936	Bri	SC	53.07N 01.22E	10
24.2.40	*Jevington Court*	4,544	Bri	SC	53.08N 01.22E	10
11.3.40	*Armor*	2,325	Neth	SC	51.24N 02.09E	10
11.3.40	*Halifax*	165	Bri	FV	3m SE Aldeburgh LS	10
15.3.40	*Melrose*	1,589	Bri	SC	51.21N 02.13E	10
17.3.40	*Capitaine Augustin*	3,137	Fre	SC	51.31N 01.27E	10
17.3.40	*Sint Annaland*	2,248	Neth	SC	51.23N 02.10E	10
18.3.40	*Tina Primo*	4,853	It	SC	51.20N 01.42E	10
27.2.40	*PLM 25*	5,391	Fre	SC	53.19N 01.12E	11
9.3.40	*Chevychase*	2,719	Bri	SC	53.18N 01.13E	11
12.3.40	*Gardenia*	3,745	Bri	SC	53.04N 01.33E	11

Other British ships damaged but not lost were:

Date	Ship	Tonnage	Nation	Type	Position	Op.*
18.11.39	*James J. McGuire*	10,525	Bri	MT	51.46N 01.40E	3
14.12.39	*Atheltemplar*	8,239	Bri	MT	55.05N 01.07W	6
21.12.39	*Dosina*	8,053	Bri	MT	½m SW Haisboro' LS	5
22.12.39	*Gryfevale*	4,434	Bri	SC	3m E River Tyne	6?
26.12.39	*Adellen*	7,984	Bri	MT	51.30N 01.43E	2?

*Destroyers taking part were:
Operation 1 (Humber) *Heidkamp*; *Eckoldt, Roeder, Galster, Lüdermann*
Operation 2 (Thames) *Heidkamp*; *Künne, Lüdermann, Galster*
Operation 3 (Thames) *Arnim*; *Heidkamp, Künne*
Operation 4 (Humber) *Lody*; *Eckoldt, Künne*
Operation 5 (Cromer) *Lody*; *Giese*
Operation 6 (Newcastle) *Künne*; *Ihn, Steinbrinck, Beitzen, Heinemann*
Operation 7 (Thames) *Eckoldt*; *Steinbrinck, Ihn*
Operation 8 (Newcastle) *Heidkamp*; *Galster, Schmitt, Ecxkoldt, Beitzen, Ihn*
Operation 9 (Cromer) *Heinemann*; *Zenker, Koellner*
Operation 10 (Shipwash) *Eckoldt*; *Beitzen, Schultz*
Operation 11 (Cromer) *Heinemann*; *Zenker, Koellner*

Mining operations off Falmouth 28/29.9.40

Date	Ship	Tonnage	Type
30.9.40	*Sappho*	387	Yacht (RN)
3.10.40	*Lady of the Isles*	166	Mercantile
6.10.40	*Jersey Queen*	910	Mercantile
6.11.40	*Sevra*	253	Trawler (RN)
8.11.40	*Anz*	221	Trawler (RN)

Note: Tonnages are given in gross registered tons unless followed by the letter 't', which indicates tons displacement

8. WEIGHT STATEMENTS: DESTROYERS

Ship	Z14	Z17	Z25	Z32	Z35	Ship	Z46	Z51
Type	34	36	36A	36A	36B	Type	36C	42
Date	4.41	9.41	26.5.43	30.3.43	1.7.44	Date	1.7.44	1.7.44
Hull	869.1	951.3	1014.7	1028.3	1044.4	Hull	1031.3	769.0
Main machinery	790.0	814.9	827.9	838.8	859.5	Main machinery	874.1	833.3
Aux. machinery	169.3	167.6	149.3	156.0	144.8	Auxiliary machinery	141.6	90.2
Gun armament	88.3	93.9	116.4(a)	165.5(c)	108.2	Gun armament	171.3	86.8
Torpedo	34.7	35.5	29.1	30.9	29.4	Torpedo	35.4	27.1
Mine equipment	7.9		13.0	14.6	6.2	Mine equipment	8.0	8.0
EMPTY SHIP (i)	1959.3	2062.9	2164.8(b)	2248.8(d)	2224.1(e)	EMPTY SHIP (i)	2276.7(a)	1839.4(c)
General equipment	49.9	52.1	55.9	55.9	54.7	General equipment	51.0	36.5
Nautical equipment	5.4	5.4	3.2	3.2	2.2	Nautical equipment	2.2	1.9
Rigging		2.9				Rigging		
Radio equipment	13.4	11.2	10.4	10.4		Radio equipment		15.9
Machinery equipment	111.9	89.5	146.0	146.0	136.7	Machinery equipment	136.2	
Gunnery equipment	12.8	14.3	11.6	10.4	17.6	Gunnery equipment	12.2	12.5
Torpedo equipment	4.1	8.6	13.6	13.6	17.9	Torpedo equipment	20.1	11.9
Mining equipment	11.1	24.2	11.0	8.6	7.7	Mining equipment	1.7	8.8
Water in pipes	3.5	2.7	5.4	5.4	4.5	Water in pipes	2.0	2.6
EMPTY SHIP (ii)	2171.4	2273.8	2421.9	2502.3	2466.5(f)	EMPTY SHIP (ii)	2503.2(b)	1930.5(b)
Ammunition	49.2	57.9	79.2	78.1	73.3	Ammunition	83.5	68.7
Torpedoes	19.6	12.9	3.7	3.7	5.6	Torpedoes	3.4	3.0
Mining	7.8	1.0	7.8	7.8	6.8	Mining	6.8	7.3
Consumables	14.0	12.4	13.2	13.2	10.8	Consumables	10.8	6.1
Crew	24.0	23.5	24.0	24.0	22.5	Crew	23.5	17.7
Effects	15.8	18.0	16.8	16.8	15.6	Effects	16.4	12.3
Provisions	10.0	32.4	9.8	9.8	10.2	Provisions	10.2	10.6
Potable water	21.8	9.2	9.0	8.8	8.3	Potable water ⎫	22.9	17.6
Washing water	32.4	3.6	13.8	13.8	14.3	Washing water ⎭		
TYPE DISPLACEMENT	2366.0	2443.8	2599.2	2678.3	2633.9	TYPE DISPLACEMENT	2680.7	2073.8
Feed water	90.6	39.4	55.6	32.9	31.2	Feed water	36.1	1.8
Fuel oil	282.0	277.3	295.3	309.0	318.7	Fuel oil	330.9	0.7
Diesel oil	5.1	7.2	8.1	8.0	8.0	Diesel oil	8.6	200.4
Lube oil	9.4	8.4	9.2	10.2	10.2	Lube oil	11.2	19.2
CONSTRUCTION DISPLACEMENT	2753.1	2776.1	2967.4	3038.4	3002.0	CONSTRUCTION DISPLACEMENT	3067.5	2295.9
Feed water	33.5	59.1	17.4	29.2	29.9	Feed water	29.2	2.6
Fuel oil	320.6	416.0	506.5	483.2	474.0	Fuel oil	491.9	1.1
Diesel oil	10.2	10.9	12.1	12.0	12.0	Diesel oil	12.9	310.6
Lube oil	32.0	12.5	16.4	15.3	15.3	Lube oil	16.8	28.9
Fresh water res.	32.6	19.2	34.1	33.8	34.0	Fresh water res.	34.4	26.4
FULL LOAD	3182.0	3293.8	3553.9	3611.9	3567.2	FULL LOAD	3652.7	2656.5

(a) Without turret.
(b) Includes 14.4 tonnes ballast.
(c) With turret.
(d) Includes 14.8 tonnes ballast
(e) Includes unaccounted growth of 31.6 tonnes
(f) Includes gas defence equipment of 1.1 tonnes

(a) Includes reserve of 15.00 tonnes
(b) Includes anti-gas equipment of 1.1 tonnes
(c) Includes reserve of 25.00 tonnes

9. WEIGHT STATEMENTS: TORPEDO BOATS

Ship	T5	–	T26	T31	–
Type	35	37	39	39	40
Date	9.9.40	20.8.40	26.1.43	29.4.44	15.4.43
Hull	310.6	287.74	571.52	559.56	825.89
Main machinery	315.9	310.92	345.95	343.72	597.01
Aux. machinery	59.0	54.87	60.41	58.08	97.28
Gun armament	8.5	9.05	65.89	62.84	86.88
Torpedo	21.1	19.60	24.40	24.75	28.33
Mine equipment	4.3	9.38	16.39	11.84	17.30
EMPTY SHIP (i)	719.4	691.56	1095.11(a)	1078.27(c)	1687.69(d)
General equipment	15.0	22.85	28.30	29.08	43.88
Nautical equipment	4.0	4.62	2.46	1.67	0.75
Rigging		0.91			
Radio equipment	2.6		7.49	9.19	10.00
Machinery equipment	45.3	44.23	57.82	59.10	88.60
Gunnery equipment	1.4	2.39	8.20	7.75	11.00
Torpedo equipment	5.4	5.45	2.55	2.55	4.01
Mining equipment	7.7	9.20	8.24	7.40	9.77
Water in pipes	0.9	0.55	0.58	58	2.32
EMPTY SHIP (ii)	801.7	781.76	1227.47(b)	1195.54	1858.02
Ammunition	6.4	7.07	41.34	42.91	67.50
Torpedoes	12.3	12.33	10.53	10.58	16.77
Mining	3.4	3.52	7.76	7.76	6.30
Consumables	2.0	3.00	4.30	4.30	8.20
Crew	9.0	8.85	13.88	14.25	16.72

Ship	T5	–	T26	T31	–
Type	35	37	39	39	40
Date	9.9.40	20.8.40	26.1.43	29.4.44	15.4.43
Effects	6.2	6.23	9.70	9.93	11.65
Provisions	2.4	2.13	3.26	3.32	10.15
Potable water	8.0	16.05	15.13	15.13	16.80
Washing water	7.8				
TYPE DISPLACEMENT	859.2	840.94	1333.37	1303.72	2012.11
Feed water	22.4	21.07	15.43	15.43	10.00
Fuel oil	97.8	99.72	153.03	155.29	224.06
Diesel oil	3.0	2.14	5.84	5.84	3.20
Lube oil	3.4	4.94	5.27	5.27	3.20
CONSTRUCTION DISPLACEMENT	985.8	968.81	1512.94	1485.55	2252.57
Feed water	23.7	15.58	25.45	25.45	15.00
Fuel oil	92.4	100.13	221.42	220.68	329.96
Diesel oil	3.0	2.14	6.90	6.96	4.80
Lube oil	3.4	4.94	7.90	7.90	4.80
Fresh water res.			22.78	24.74	25.20
FULL LOAD	1108.3	1091.60	1780.73	1771.28	2632.33

(a) Includes 10.55 tonnes growth after inclination test
(b) Includes 16.72 tonnes ballast.
(c) Includes 17.40 tonnes growth after inclination test.
(d) Includes reserve of 35.00 tonnes

BIBLIOGRAPHY

War Diaries
Naval Command Group West
Naval Command Group North
Führer der Zerstörer
4th, 5th, 6th and 8th Destroyer Flotillas
Führer der Torpedoboote
1st, 2nd, 3rd, 4th, 5th and 6th Torpedo
  Boat Flotillas
*Hans Lody, Erich Giese, Paul Jacobi,
  Bruno Heinemann, Max Schultz,
  Friedrich Ihn, Karl Galster, Leberecht
  Maass, Erich Steinbrinck, Richard
  Beitzen, Theodore Riedel, Hermann
  Schoemann, Z23, Z24, Z27, Z29, Z31,
  Z32, Z35, Z36, Z38, Z39, Z43, ZH1,
  ZG3*
T22, T23, T25, T26, T27, T28, T34

Official Logs
HM Ships *Newcastle, Jersey, Sheffield,
  Jamaica, Mauritius, Enterprise,
  Emerald, Diadem, Glasgow, Trident*

Reports of Proceedings
HM Ships *Edinburgh* (1.5.42), *Trinidad*
  (29.3.42), *Glasgow* (28.12.43)
10th Flotilla (9.6.44)

RAF Operational Record Books
Nos. 144, 236, 404 and 502 Squadrons

RAF Stornaway
RAF Davidstowe Moor

Official Handbooks
Konstruktion Rheinmetall-Borsig:
  Angaben über Marine-Geschütze
Handbuch für Deutscherkriegschiffstypen
  (Heft 1, M. Dv. Nr. 401, 1944)
Handbuch der U-Bootsjagd (M. Dv. Nr.
  93, OKM 1/1944)

Other Official Documents
Ballistics of Naval Instruments, F. H.
  Pub., BIOS Gp. 2, Hec 723
KI EP Nr. 1260/40
KI ZB 1460
Skl IIIa 4261 (10.2.44)
Skl IIIa 9464
Skl QuAI SF25 661/43 (16.12.43)
Skl QuAI St 833/44
Y.A.R.D. Report YE47A (1948)

Books
Barker, R.: *The Ship Busters* (Chatto &
  Windus, 1957)
Bekker, C.: *Hitler's Naval War*
  (Macdonald, 1974)
Busch, F. O.: *Prinz Eugen* (Futura,
  1975)

Dickens, Capt. P.: *Narvik* (Ian Allan,
  1974)
Gröner, E.: *Die deutschen Kriegschiffe
  1815-1936* (Lehmanns Verlag, 1937)
— *Die deutschen Kriegschiffe 1815-1945*
  (Lehmanns Verlag, 1966)
— *Die Schiffe der deutschen Kriegsmarine
  und Luftwaffe 1939-1945* (Lehmanns
  Verlag, 1954)
Güth, R.: *Zerstörer Z34* (Koehler, 1980)
Harnack, W.: *Zerstörer unter deutscher
  Flagge* (Kohlers Verlag, 1977)
Jung, D. et al: *Anstriche und
  Tarnanstriche der deutschen
  Kriegsmarine* (Bernard & Graefe
  Verlag, 1977)
Lenton, H. T.: *German Surface Vessels*
  Vol. I (Macdonald, 1966)
Lohmann, W. and Hildebrand, H. H.:
  Die deutschen Kriegsmarine 1939-45
  (Pozdun Verlag, 1956)
Macintyre, D.: *Fighting Ships and
  Seamen* (Evans, 1963)
— *The Naval War against Hitler*
  (Kimber)
March, E.: *British Destroyers* (Seeley
  Service, 1966)
Mars, A.: *British Submarines at War
  1939-45* (Kimber, 1971)
Potter, J. D.: *Fiasco* (Heinemann, 1970)
Rohwer, J. and Hümmelchen, G.:
  Chronology of the War at Sea Vols. I
  and II (Ian Allan, 1974)
Roskill, S. W.: *The War at Sea* Vols. I-
  III (HMSO, 1957)
Ruge, F.: *Der Seekrieg* (USNI, 1957)
Thomas, E.: *Torpedoboot und Zerstörer*
  (Stalling Verlag, 1964)
Wagge, J.: *The Narvik Campaign*
  (Harrap, 1964)
Whitley, M.J.: *The Type 35 Torpedoboats*,
  World Ship Society, 1988
British Vessels Lost at Sea (PSL, 1977)
Jane's Fighting Ships (Sampson Low,
  1942)

Articles
Hümmelchen, G.: 'Minenerfolge
  deutscher Zerstörer an der englischen
  Ostküste 1939-1940' *Marine-
  Rundschau* (1960/1)
Whitley, M. J.: 'Kriegsschauplatz
  Finnenbusen 1944: Der Verlust der
  Zerstörer Z35 und Z36' *Marine-
  Rundschau* (1981/5)
— 'Das Desaster in Der Bucht von
  Narva' Marine-Rundschau (1983/10).

INDEX

ADDENDA to page 213

Additional information for fates of the following ships:

T63
Left Emden 1703hrs 10.12.44, Convoy 112, escort: *K4*, *V1104–V1107*, *Flkjr 22*, *M327*, *M348*, tugs *Rixhoft* and *Wangerooge*, M/S *Demokrat* and *K4* to Jade only. 11.12.44 forced into Jade by bad weather; *T63* stranded for 12 hrs then towed into Wilhelmshaven undamaged. Anchored in Schilling roads 21.12.44 with *M348*. *M305* and *V1105* left Cuxhaven to join escort, 22.12.44. 2040 hrs delivered to Brunsbuttel.

T65
8.9.44 towed to Germany for completion in convoy 1277, arriving at Den Helder 15.9.44. Arrived Borkum 16.9.44. At Bremen 10.44. Ordered to Elbing for completion. 28.12.44 left Wesermünde in tow *Abeille* and *Nesserland*; excort *M305*, *M342*, *V1103*, *Flkjr 21* and *23*, for Elbe. 29.12.44 arrived Cuxhaven. Tow delayed in western Baltic (mines) 29/30.12.44. 14/15.1.45 arrived in tow *Neufahrwasser*, tugs *Nemmert* and *Memel*, Escort *M445*. Ordered to Pillau but delayed by weather. 21.3.45 delivered to Pillau. Never reached Schichau?